OECD Insurance Statistics 2020

OECD

BETTER POLICIES FOR BETTER LIVES

Please cite this publication as:
OECD (2021), *OECD Insurance Statistics 2020*, OECD Publishing, Paris,
https://doi.org/10.1787/adfe5566-en.

ISBN 978-92-64-76339-5 (print)
ISBN 978-92-64-81043-3 (pdf)

OECD Insurance Statistics
ISSN 2307-8421 (print)
ISSN 2307-843X (online)

Corrigenda to publications may be found on line at: *www.oecd.org/about/publishing/corrigenda.htm.*

Table of contents

Conventional signs and abbreviations 5
Common definitions and notes 7

Part I. **International comparisons** 9

1. Balance sheet and income, direct insurance (All insurance companies) 10
2. Balance sheet and income, direct insurance (Life insurance companies) 11
3. Balance sheet and income, direct insurance (Non-life insurance companies) 12
4. Portfolio allocation, direct insurance (All insurance companies) 13
5. Portfolio allocation, direct insurance (Life insurance companies) 14
6. Portfolio allocation, direct insurance (Non-life insurance companies) 15
7. Total gross premiums (Life and Non-life) 16
8. Total gross premiums (Life) 17
9. Total gross premiums (Non-life) 18
10. Market share in OECD (Life and Non-life) 19
11. Market share in OECD (Life) 20
12. Market share in OECD (Non-life) 21
13. Density (Life and Non-life) 22
14. Density (Life) 23
15. Density (Non-life) 24
16. Penetration (Life and Non-life) 25
17. Penetration (Life) 26
18. Penetration (Non-life) 27
19. Life insurance share 28
20. Direct total gross premiums per insurance company employee 29
21. Retention ratio (Life and Non-life) 30
22. Retention ratio (Life) 31
23. Retention ratio (Non-life) 32
24. Ratio of reinsurance accepted (Life and Non-life) 33
25. Ratio of reinsurance accepted (Life) 34
26. Ratio of reinsurance accepted (Non-life) 35
27. Market share of foreign companies in the domestic market (Life) 36
28. Market share of foreign undertakings in total domestic business (Life) 37
29. Market share of foreign companies in the domestic market (Non-life) 38
30. Market share of foreign undertakings in total domestic business (Non-life) 39

Part II. **Country tables** 41

Australia 42
Austria 45
Belgium 49
Canada 53
Chile 57

Colombia........ 60
Czech Republic........ 64
Denmark........ 68
Estonia........ 71
Finland........ 75
France........ 78
Germany........ 82
Greece........ 85
Hungary........ 89
Iceland........ 93
Ireland........ 96
Israel........ 100
Italy........ 104
Japan........ 108
Korea........ 111
Latvia........ 114
Lithuania........ 118
Luxembourg........ 122
Mexico........ 126
Netherlands........ 130
New Zealand........ 133
Norway........ 137
Poland........ 140
Portugal........ 143
Slovak Republic........ 147
Slovenia........ 151
Spain........ 155
Sweden........ 159
Switzerland........ 162
Turkey........ 165
United Kingdom........ 169
United States........ 173

Conventional signs and abbreviations

Signs and abbreviations

c	Confidential data
..	Not available
.	Decimal point
|	Break in series

ISO country codes and abbreviations for currency

	ISO code	Currency	Abbreviation
Australia	AUS	dollar	AUD
Austria	AUT	euro	EUR
Belgium	BEL	euro	EUR
Canada	CAN	dollar	CAD
Chile	CHL	peso	CLP
Colombia	COL	peso	COP
Czech Republic	CZE	koruna	CZK
Denmark	DNK	krone	DKK
Estonia	EST	euro	EUR
Finland	FIN	euro	EUR
France	FRA	euro	EUR
Germany	DEU	euro	EUR
Greece	GRC	euro	EUR
Hungary	HUN	forint	HUF
Iceland	ISL	króna	ISK
Ireland	IRL	euro	EUR
Israel	ISR	sheqel	ILS
Italy	ITA	euro	EUR
Japan	JPN	yen	JPY
Korea	KOR	won	KRW
Latvia	LVA	euro	EUR
Lithuania	LTU	euro	EUR
Luxembourg	LUX	euro	EUR
Mexico	MEX	peso	MXN
Netherlands	NLD	euro	EUR
New Zealand	NZL	dollar	NZD
Norway	NOR	krone	NOK
Poland	POL	zloty	PLN
Portugal	PRT	euro	EUR
Slovak Republic	SVK	euro	EUR
Slovenia	SVN	euro	EUR
Spain	ESP	euro	EUR
Sweden	SWE	krona	SEK
Switzerland	CHE	franc	CHF
Turkey	TUR	lira	TRY
United Kingdom	GBR	pound	GBP
United States	USA	dollar	USD

Common definitions and notes

Notes on data sources

All the data in the statistical tables of each country have been reported by the relevant national insurance authorities. Regarding comparative tables of indicators, the data are mainly drawn from the tables by country. Data on exchange rates are taken from the IMF International Financial Statistics database. Data on population are taken from the IMF publication *World Economic Outlook*. Data on GDP come from the OECD Annual National Accounts database for OECD countries and from the IMF publication *World Economic Outlook* for all the other countries.

To achieve greater clarity, the number of variables selected and displayed in this publication has been limited. Data have been extracted from the Global Insurance Statistics database. The complete database can be accessed online at the following link:

OECD Insurance Statistics, *http://dx.doi.org/10.1787/ins-data-en.*

A significant effort has been made to achieve comparability among countries. Definitions, classifications, calculation methods, and units have been standardised as far as possible.

General notes

a) Life and non-life categories follow the definitions used in national law. However, the premiums for accident and sickness insurance underwritten by life companies should be included in non-life figures.

b) Up until 2008, the insurance business is broken down between life and non-life business. As of 2009, the insurance business is broken down between the business of pure life, pure non-life and composite undertakings. The insurance business of composite undertakings is further broken down between life and non-life components. Some countries do not allow for insurance undertakings to be active in both life and non-life insurance business and therefore composite insurance undertakings do not exist in these countries. In other countries (e.g., Austria, Hungary, Mexico, Spain) however, composite insurance undertakings account for more than 25% of all insurance undertakings operating in these countries. Therefore, to have comparable data across years for life business data (respectively non-life), one has to sum up the life (respectively non-life) business of pure life (respectively non-life) undertakings and the life (respectively non-life) business of composite undertakings as of 2009.

c) Figures provided for the number of companies and for insurance premiums should include all insurance companies licensed or authorised in the reporting country, *including* professional reinsurers, whether or not these are controlled, but *excluding* any statutory system of social security administered by the State.

d) *Domestic companies* means those companies incorporated under national law, together with those companies in the reporting country which are unincorporated, but excluding the branches and agencies of foreign companies.

e) *Foreign-controlled companies* means those domestic companies controlled by foreign interests, such "control" being defined according to national law (see the definition of foreign controlled companies in notes by country). The data of *foreign-controlled companies* are part of those of *Domestic companies*.

f) *Foreign companies* means companies incorporated outside the reporting country.

In 2016, a new supervisory framework for insurance and reinsurance companies was implemented in the European Union (EU) and the European Economic Area (EEA). This framework includes harmonised reporting requirements across EU/EEA countries. These requirements led to changes in national data collection, which may hamper the data comparability with the ones collected before 2016 for some countries which only collect data with the Solvency II framework.

International Comparisons:

Detailed metadata at: *http://metalinks.oecd.org/ins/20190221/0f8b*.

Country tables

In this part, the main insurance statistics are presented through separate tables for each OECD member country. Figures refer to the calendar year. The premiums and other amounts are described in millions of the national currency unit.

International comparisons

Table 1. Balance sheet and income, direct insurance (All insurance companies)

2019

Million US dollars

	Gross claims payments	Gross operating expenses	Commissions	Outstanding claims provision (changes)	Total assets	Gross technical provisions	Gross technical provisions unit-linked	Shareholders' equity	Net income
Argentina	6 862	2 625	1 595	1 784	20 205	5 524	..	4 709	1 350
Australia	52 005	9 993	2 740	..	206 314	157 767	..	28 862	1 985
Austria	17 319	1 057	3 711	343	148 615	104 344	20 658	12 003	..
Belgium	27 893	3 185	3 744	1 999	348 142	293 394	50 075	18 713	2 809
Bolivia	303	226	56	..	1 120	500	..	1 700	38
Brazil	12 253	12 686	6 331	124	306 646	269 599	226 089	23 376	5 906
Canada	..	..	..	..	..	..	..	..	..
Chile	8 340	2 066	1 021	2 741	71 495	61 428	5 814	6 910	572
Colombia	4 869	3 316	762	-536	26 130	19 047	..	4 670	686
Costa Rica	686	318	238	74	4 456	1 637	0	2 031	126
Cuba	..	..	..	..	..	..	..	..	..
Czech Republic	4 312	2 066	391	70	20 751	14 797	4 345	3 520	759
Denmark	26 267	2 498	287	46 783	559 802	448 062	196 784	28 992	2 841
Dominican Republic	..	..	..	..	..	..	..	..	..
Ecuador	736	300	133	435	2 156	364	0	647	103
Egypt	1 024	176	361	..	7 097	..	..	2 098	317
El Salvador	362	224	93	101	932	222	..	400	37
Estonia	524	214	..	..	2 240	1 301	616	468	83
Finland	11 042	1 362	259	-210	84 959	75 172	..	7 118	1 214
France	273 111	54 646	..	79 891	3 309 617	2 602 374	437 243	211 457	14 481
Germany	188 540	17 286	23 183	8 130	1 914 031	1 741 282	142 569	70 364	2 852
Greece	2 604	1 205	..	..	21 204	15 751	3 111	4 137	..
Guatemala	504	297	159	..	1 435	660	..	520	122
Honduras	383	66	114	..	718	233	..	284	877
Hong Kong, China	..	..	..	..	..	..	..	..	..
Hungary	2 344	985	600	81	9 934	8 443	4 330	1 040	241
India	62 747	..	..	..	..	..	..	..	..
Indonesia	13 234	2 716	2 572	29	46 277	34 031	17 955	8 453	1 599
Iceland	451	114	..	..	1 270	767	59	522	110
Ireland	32 815	1 333	3 482	..	449 114	392 602	285 309	33 548	..
Israel[1]	11 991	1 909	2 238	670	177 442	156 740	109 929	7 725	531
Italy	113 770	16 057	12 714	-1 222	1 041 008	900 144	180 325	78 533	9 661
Japan	331 122	74 834	13 275	17 581	3 888 899	3 042 998	..	142 062	15 465
Korea	..	..	..	..	..	..	..	..	..
Latvia	615	151	73	-9	1 589	1 186	444	297	38
Lithuania	390	193	11	-30	1 576	1 081	314	352	54
Luxembourg	15 060	5 372	3 651	11 159	284 656	258 729	163 400	11 529	492
Malaysia	10 083	2 732	1 420	125	82 821	65 543	13 486	8 459	1 297
Mexico	15 994	1 838	4 082	5 111	88 782	68 266	..	12 412	3 012
Morocco	..	..	..	..	..	..	..	..	..
Netherlands	84 279	..	..	..	..	..	..	..	..
New Zealand	4 657	1 240	920	-63	14 723	8 614	891	5 319	790
Nicaragua	..	..	..	..	..	..	..	..	..
Norway	13 801	2 470	517	-34	221 950	188 619	..	22 032	2 602
Panama	..	..	..	..	..	..	..	..	..
Paraguay	193	197	59	4	626	414	..	257	43
Peru	2 294	1 241	738	93	16 199	11 972	..	2 630	455
Poland	10 391	5 262	2 754	436	50 810	28 878	10 955	17 123	1 882
Portugal	10 111	1 899	910	76	63 072	34 230	14 310	6 258	324
Puerto Rico	..	..	..	..	..	..	..	..	..
Russia	9 921	6 188	5 042	3 078	53 914	33 566	..	13 089	3 235
Singapore	17 176	2 050	2 471	..	222 745	181 751	29 973	21 235	2 883
Slovak Republic	1 748	975	..	..	9 658	6 097	1 727	585	..
Slovenia	1 752	559	129	16	8 668	6 249	1 424	1 725	181
South Africa	..	..	..	..	..	..	..	..	..
Spain	52 105	10 780	6 500	353	381 476	260 658	20 553	49 774	5 280
Sri Lanka	..	..	..	..	..	..	..	..	..
Sweden	16 470	3 505	1 034	30 064	558 283	208 105	..	135 484	28 657
Switzerland	78 928	4 875	5 323	-19 546	531 113	391 046	24 551	62 447	11 625
Thailand	..	..	..	..	..	..	..	..	..
Tunisia	..	..	..	..	..	..	..	..	..
Turkey	5 678	2 192	1 745	869	38 991	14 594	..	4 783	1 321
United Kingdom	388 434	45 619	..	-6 247	3 326 986	2 796 445	1 750 288	220 992	..
United States	1 507 074	411 355	144 318	90 642	6 979 973	1 234 737	..	1 545 954	141 310
Uruguay	600	297	183	478	5 270	4 360	..	627	97

.. Not available

Note: Detailed metadata at: *http://metalinks.oecd.org/ins/20210324/016e.*

1. Information on data for Israel: *http://oe.cd/israel-disclaimer.*

Source: *Balance sheet and income, OECD Insurance Statistics (database)*

INTERNATIONAL COMPARISONS

Table 2. Balance sheet and income, direct insurance (Life insurance companies)

2019

Million US dollars

	Gross claims payments	Gross operating expenses	Commissions	Outstanding claims provision (changes)	Total assets	Gross technical provisions	Gross technical provisions unit-linked	Shareholders' equity	Net income
Argentina	223	99	17	-1	3 169	2 559	..	363	167
Australia	27 522	4 389	1 427	..	125 305	102 201	..	12 458	52
Austria	1 070	38	81	7	12 514	10 280	3 877	305	..
Belgium	777	67	75	-11	13 266	11 273	1 433	988	67
Bolivia	134	105	28	..	693	415	..	676	18
Brazil	574	1 555	214	-37	158 597	153 176	144 799	3 468	656
Canada	..	..	..	..	..	..	..	..	..
Chile	6 241	1 256	497	2 570	63 544	55 388	5 814	5 541	467
Colombia	2 377	1 576	281	-410	16 182	12 352	..	2 990	529
Costa Rica	..	..	..	..	..	..	..	..	..
Cuba	..	..	..	..	..	..	..	..	..
Czech Republic	269	108	3	3	2 175	1 971	1 004	113	31
Denmark	19 199	814	52	46 404	533 649	433 672	196 784	20 901	1 476
Dominican Republic	..	..	..	..	..	..	..	..	..
Ecuador	95	45	1	14	266	135	0	62	11
Egypt	470	73	140	..	3 909	..	..	759	132
El Salvador	65	94	38	61	319	104	..	104	12
Estonia	.. c	.. c	..	..	.. c	.. c	.. c	..	..
Finland	8 104	431	125	91	68 934	64 255	..	2 967	610
France	152 479	19 104	..	78 721	520 001	444 531	81 286	..	..
Germany	85 053	4 219	6 373	386	1 284 779	1 205 942	142 507	20 489	961
Greece	280	51	..	..	4 080	3 483	201	505	..
Guatemala	..	..	..	..	..	..	..	..	..
Honduras	48	0	27	..	0	0	..	0	0
Hong Kong, China	..	..	..	..	..	..	..	..	..
Hungary	639	118	57	24	2 964	2 904	1 188	203	18
India	46 216	..	..	..	..	..	..	..	..
Indonesia	10 698	1 746	1 403	9	41 335	31 609	17 955	3 900	1 008
Iceland	19	12	..	..	153	72	59	52	22
Ireland	24 397	704	1 683	..	372 497	344 577	285 309	16 436	..
Israel[1]	..	..	..	..	..	..	..	..	..
Italy	25 593	1 129	749	19	288 535	272 303	98 695	10 070	1 366
Japan	274 909	43 862	..	18 100	3 613 018	3 042 998	..	105 793	11 407
Korea	..	..	..	..	..	..	..	..	..
Latvia	..	..	..	..	..	..	..	..	..
Lithuania	39	19	0	0	367	327	278	34	12
Luxembourg	13 606	1 439	733	46	240 575	229 805	163 400	4 081	420
Malaysia	7 364	1 616	1 094	..	71 971	60 416	13 486	3 670	742
Mexico	1 067	88	98	92	19 762	17 903	..	1 585	296
Morocco	..	..	..	..	..	..	..	..	..
Netherlands	22 238	..	..	..	..	..	..	..	..
New Zealand	600	237	134	242	4 667	2 603	422	1 907	199
Nicaragua	..	..	..	..	..	..	..	..	..
Norway	6 918	954	104	..	194 164	175 459	..	12 748	933
Panama	..	..	..	..	..	..	..	..	..
Paraguay	0	0	0	..	..	19	..	..	..
Peru	270	163	87	2	1 236	1 588	..	316	50
Poland	4 504	1 362	708	439	24 841	16 045	10 955	7 029	673
Portugal	3 516	323	147	1	34 385	16 972	14 026	1 609	36
Puerto Rico	..	..	..	..	..	..	..	..	..
Russia	2 226	461	1 375	26	21 188	18 151	..	2 078	869
Singapore	7 722	582	1 219	..	120 297	103 077	20 046	6 430	1 376
Slovak Republic	197	185	..	..	2 066	1 104	719	167	..
Slovenia	..	..	..	..	..	..	..	..	..
South Africa	..	..	..	..	..	..	..	..	..
Spain	2 786	458	252	-22	28 530	21 262	3 171	2 646	271
Sri Lanka	..	..	..	..	..	..	..	..	..
Sweden	7 729	1 443	388	3 213	485 626	172 484	..	117 546	24 512
Switzerland	52 819	1 105	856	-17 025	339 641	296 029	24 539	14 896	1 522
Thailand	..	..	..	..	..	..	..	..	..
Tunisia	..	..	..	..	..	..	..	..	..
Turkey	842	723	538	26	25 982	2 407	..	1 620	641
United Kingdom	286 093	10 533	..	-9 701	2 466 502	2 156 448	1 607 862	98 574	..
United States	401 890	75 232	52 348	44 760	4 496 210	20 314	..	475 257	51 474
Uruguay	0	0	0	0	0	0	..	0	0

.. Not available; c Confidential data

Note: Detailed metadata at: *http://metalinks.oecd.org/ins/20210324/016e*.

1. Information on data for Israel: *http://oe.cd/israel-disclaimer*.

Source: *Balance sheet and income, OECD Insurance Statistics (database)*

Table 3. Balance sheet and income, direct insurance (Non-life insurance companies)

2019

Million US dollars

	Gross claims payments	Gross operating expenses	Commissions	Outstanding claims provision (changes)	Total assets	Gross technical provisions	Gross technical provisions unit-linked	Shareholders' equity	Net income
Argentina	3 134	685	332	858	5 839	523	..	1 132	147
Australia	24 484	5 604	1 314	..	81 009	55 566	..	16 403	1 933
Austria	2 194	149	861	30	16 562	4 638	0	5 220	..
Belgium	1 723	403	825	1 313	20 474	12 239	..	3 334	98
Bolivia	169	121	29	..	427	84	..	1 024	20
Brazil	1 476	1 387	778	-124	7 139	4 320	0	1 483	261
Canada	..	..	..	..	..	..	..	..	..
Chile	2 099	810	524	171	7 952	6 040	0	1 369	105
Colombia	2 492	1 740	481	-126	9 947	6 696	..	1 680	157
Costa Rica	25	14	12	0	98	52	0	32	2
Cuba	..	..	..	..	..	..	..	..	..
Czech Republic	215	204	32	10	691	324	0	217	24
Denmark	7 068	1 684	236	379	26 153	14 391	0	8 091	1 365
Dominican Republic	..	..	..	..	..	..	..	..	..
Ecuador	51	30	21	32	192	14	0	70	2
Egypt	554	103	220	..	3 188	..	..	1 339	185
El Salvador	176	54	22	14	232	38	..	125	2
Estonia	384	176	..	..	1 053	459	0	468	83
Finland	2 939	931	133	-301	16 025	10 917	..	4 151	603
France	120 633	35 542	..	1 169	345 718	154 154	..	..	..
Germany	103 487	13 067	16 811	7 744	629 252	535 340	62	49 875	1 891
Greece	293	287	..	..	2 055	1 033	0	791	..
Guatemala	19	18	7	..	149	33	..	82	13
Honduras	144	0	30	..	0	0	..	0	0
Hong Kong, China	..	..	..	..	..	..	..	..	..
Hungary	111	86	55	23	437	213	0	153	17
India	16 530	..	..	..	..	..	..	..	..
Indonesia	2 536	970	1 169	19	4 942	2 422	..	4 553	591
Iceland	432	103	..	..	1 117	695	0	469	88
Ireland	7 328	629	1 662	..	76 617	48 025	..	17 112	..
Israel[1]	664	9	97	190	4 901	3 542	0	649	130
Italy	6 714	3 432	2 683	-163	28 023	17 061	..	7 597	696
Japan	56 213	30 972	13 275	-519	275 880	..	..	36 268	4 059
Korea	..	..	..	..	..	..	..	..	..
Latvia	452	132	67	-9	769	492	..	178	29
Lithuania	292	156	11	-28	822	462	0	233	35
Luxembourg	1 455	3 933	2 918	11 113	44 081	28 925	0	7 448	72
Malaysia	2 719	1 116	326	125	10 850	5 127	0	4 789	555
Mexico	1 693	469	583	1 293	8 731	4 792	..	2 160	448
Morocco	..	..	..	..	..	..	..	..	..
Netherlands	62 040	..	..	..	..	..	..	..	..
New Zealand	3 504	753	559	-341	8 784	5 557	0	2 619	512
Nicaragua	..	..	..	..	..	..	..	..	..
Norway	6 883	1 515	413	-34	27 786	13 161	..	9 284	1 670
Panama	..	..	..	..	..	..	..	..	..
Paraguay	0	0	0	..	..	188	..	..	..
Peru	410	245	126	-4	2 067	558	..	344	40
Poland	5 888	3 900	2 046	-3	25 968	12 833	0	10 094	1 209
Portugal	1 735	614	319	21	4 317	2 465	0	1 131	113
Puerto Rico	..	..	..	..	..	..	..	..	..
Russia	6 929	5 289	3 370	2 881	29 846	14 272	..	9 645	2 169
Singapore	3 061	757	164	..	19 973	10 039	0	7 503	445
Slovak Republic	20	43	..	..	142	77	..	8	..
Slovenia	485	64	1	8	340	117	..	177	15
South Africa	..	..	..	..	..	..	..	..	..
Spain	11 127	3 461	1 821	137	30 022	15 540	0	9 258	1 132
Sri Lanka	..	..	..	..	..	..	..	..	..
Sweden	8 741	2 062	646	26 851	72 656	35 621	..	17 938	4 146
Switzerland	26 110	3 770	4 467	-2 521	191 473	95 018	11	47 551	10 103
Thailand	..	..	..	..	..	..	..	..	..
Tunisia	..	..	..	..	..	..	..	..	..
Turkey	4 836	1 469	1 207	842	13 009	12 187	..	3 163	680
United Kingdom	26 006	13 078	..	-238	116 596	63 681	..	32 554	..
United States	1 105 184	336 123	91 970	45 882	2 483 763	1 214 423	..	1 070 697	89 836
Uruguay	19	13	6	4	56	23	..	25	1

.. Not available

Note: Detailed metadata at: *http://metalinks.oecd.org/ins/20210324/016e*.

1. Information on data for Israel: *http://oe.cd/israel-disclaimer*.

Source: *Balance sheet and income, OECD Insurance Statistics (database)*

Table 4. Portfolio allocation, direct insurance (All insurance companies)

2019

Million US dollars

	Cash and deposits	Land and buildings	Equity	Bills and bonds	Loans	Collective investment schemes	Private equity funds	Hedge funds	Structured products	Assets for unit-linked contracts	Total investments
Argentina	327	358	965	7 267	54	4 603	0	0	0	0	15 791
Australia	5 904	3 248	7 601	50 436	2 358	7 721	..	..	..	70 988	148 785
Austria	3 966	10 684	16 236	56 665	4 735	26 281	148	0	1 269	21 395	141 466
Belgium	8 723	10 423	19 321	225 757	41 038	17 154	1 012	..	1 391	49 763	376 102
Bolivia	32	118	8	409	43	0	51	0	0	0	661
Brazil	464	313	424	23 797	130	19 665	6 945	456	0	224 098	276 337
Canada	..	..	..	..	..	..	..	..	..	..	..
Chile	1 794	9 223	614	32 435	8 060	5 499	0	0	0	5 344	62 946
Colombia	767	10	1 638	14 934	46	691	469	0	58	0	18 952
Costa Rica	245	0	130	2 819	438	41	0	0	0	0	3 673
Cuba	..	..	..	..	..	..	..	..	..	..	..
Czech Republic	..	..	..	..	..	..	..	..	..	..	..
Denmark	12 215	1 643	149 180	120 153	5 654	18 641	..	..	..	207 732	559 802
Dominican Republic	..	..	..	..	..	..	..	..	..	..	..
Ecuador	37	155	29	631	0	0	221	0	0	0	1 073
Egypt	..	..	..	..	..	..	..	..	..	..	..
El Salvador	269	7	0	248	34	12	..	..	..	..	574
Estonia	..	..	..	..	..	..	..	..	..	..	..
Finland	5 151	1 491	3 565	15 761	1 550	6 616	..	..	..	45 928	82 443
France	..	..	..	..	..	..	..	..	..	..	..
Germany	15 986	35 732	162 106	912 979	119 093	699 193	7 267	..	20 244	141 432	2 116 673
Greece	953	775	224	12 701	124	1 377	0	0	6	3 068	19 673
Guatemala	235	49	17	553	5	..	..	..	..	..	972
Honduras	32	5	284	0	20	0	0	0	0	0	661
Hong Kong, China	..	..	..	..	..	..	..	..	..	..	..
Hungary	256	140	87	4 511	19	363	..	..	..	4 359	9 920
India	..	..	..	..	..	..	..	..	..	..	..
Indonesia	3 739	1 162	3 968	9 417	15	7 122	..	..	..	17 732	43 186
Iceland	89	22	299	506	20	213	..	..	..	59	1 209
Ireland	..	..	..	..	..	..	..	..	..	..	..
Israel[1]	3 940	2 590	1 641	31 756	5 997	1 967	2 020	130	66	109 987	161 988
Italy	8 604	6 429	69 022	565 366	5 138	..	..	..	..	180 536	970 295
Japan	..	..	..	..	..	..	..	..	..	..	..
Korea	..	..	..	..	..	..	..	..	..	..	..
Latvia	117	21	10	664	28	142	1	0	0	450	1 439
Lithuania	59	8	16	765	12	86	0	0	1	337	1 317
Luxembourg	3 125	270	2 393	41 139	91	7 047	..	..	..	164 359	273 519
Malaysia	5 604	1 226	7 660	38 094	2 986	..	..	..	..	14 513	79 537
Mexico	554	921	817	52 550	1 484	10 733	0	..	..	..	71 319
Morocco	..	..	..	..	..	..	..	..	..	..	..
Netherlands	..	..	..	..	..	..	..	..	..	..	..
New Zealand	1 743	46	446	5 681	..	3 306	..	..	..	..	11 428
Nicaragua	..	..	..	..	..	..	..	..	..	..	..
Norway	1 559	16 779	11 233	76 202	17 085	38 801	..	..	..	45 448	211 431
Panama	..	..	..	..	..	..	..	..	..	..	..
Paraguay	57	16	6	231	1	0	0	0	0	0	311
Peru	850	1 008	676	9 777	7	663	5	0	0	0	13 775
Poland	1 137	736	6 714	22 042	865	4 200	40	9	4	11 950	47 615
Portugal	2 405	441	3 529	33 946	98	2 577	92	1	227	14 382	57 622
Puerto Rico	..	..	..	..	..	..	..	..	..	..	..
Russia	12 005	1 046	3 269	23 895	380	110	..	..	..	..	40 858
Singapore	..	..	..	..	..	..	..	..	..	..	..
Slovak Republic	..	..	..	..	..	..	0	0	0	437	..
Slovenia	210	295	693	4 541	26	423	..	..	7	1 907	8 112
South Africa	..	..	..	..	..	..	..	..	..	..	..
Spain	20 020	13 003	18 252	257 081	2 833	15 040	710	957	6 287	25 379	352 281
Sri Lanka	..	..	..	..	..	..	..	..	..	..	..
Sweden	10 511	12 774	152 763	145 404	10 619	69 183	..	..	..	155 087	576 231
Switzerland	19 884	47 866	21 560	197 350	55 508	21 442	3 940	2 444	168	21 089	450 143
Thailand	..	..	..	..	..	..	..	..	..	..	..
Tunisia	..	..	..	..	..	..	..	..	..	..	..
Turkey	7 612	89	424	3 508	39	356	..	..	..	980	13 007
United Kingdom	94 573	4 911	19 324	368 602	71 764	56 472	573	1 697	126	1 521 955	2 141 128
United States	..	..	..	..	..	..	..	..	..	..	..
Uruguay	526	12	7	4 194	7	0	0	0	0	0	4 747

.. Not available

Note: Detailed metadata at: *http://metalinks.oecd.org/ins/20210324/7c21*.

1. Information on data for Israel: *http://oe.cd/israel-disclaimer*.

Source: *Outstanding investment by direct insurance companies, OECD Insurance Statistics (database)*

Table 5. Portfolio allocation, direct insurance (Life insurance companies)

2019

Million US dollars

	Cash and deposits	Land and buildings	Equity	Bills and bonds	Loans	Collective investment schemes	Private equity funds	Hedge funds	Structured products	Assets for unit-linked contracts	Total investments
Argentina	9	36	12	1 836	2	834	0	0	0	0	3 081
Australia	3 002	3 164	6 674	21 500	636	..	..	..	..	70 988	106 188
Austria	89	9	98	3 193	194	4 836	5	..	50	3 906	12 384
Belgium	618	329	582	6 327	2 415	1 731	19	..	295	1 436	14 006
Bolivia	24	92	4	288	43	0	42	0	0	0	493
Brazil	136	36	8	5 759	130	5 670	128	171	0	144 020	156 080
Canada	..	..	..	..	..	..	..	..	..	..	..
Chile	1 334	9 163	599	30 970	8 046	5 350	0	0	0	5 344	60 714
Colombia	499	4	1 085	11 586	41	511	405	..	45	..	14 471
Costa Rica	..	..	..	..	..	..	..	..	..	..	..
Cuba	..	..	..	..	..	..	..	..	..	..	..
Czech Republic	..	..	..	..	..	..	..	..	..	..	..
Denmark	9 132	1 282	144 698	105 564	5 141	17 070	..	..	..	207 732	533 649
Dominican Republic	..	..	..	..	..	..	..	..	..	..	..
Ecuador	0	8	3	159	0	0	41	0	0	0	210
Egypt	..	..	..	..	..	..	..	..	..	..	..
El Salvador	108	6	0	117	6	2	..	..	..	..	240
Estonia	..	..	..	..	..	..	..	..	..	..	..
Finland	3 344	783	1 818	11 708	875	3 197	..	..	..	45 928	68 322
France	..	..	..	..	..	..	..	..	..	..	..
Germany	6 893	22 485	69 592	584 772	97 350	484 082	3 865	..	15 343	141 370	1 427 913
Greece	171	5	102	3 389	0	33	0	0	0	214	3 998
Guatemala	..	..	..	..	..	..	..	..	..	..	..
Honduras	..	..	..	..	..	..	..	..	..	..	..
Hong Kong, China	..	..	..	..	..	..	..	..	..	..	..
Hungary	65	7	11	1 647	4	114	..	..	..	1 202	3 060
India	..	..	..	..	..	..	..	..	..	..	..
Indonesia	1 741	1 090	3 043	7 894	12	5 787	..	..	..	17 732	37 299
Iceland	4	0	3	64	0	10	..	..	..	59	140
Ireland	..	..	..	..	..	..	..	..	..	..	..
Israel[1]	..	..	..	..	..	..	..	..	..	..	..
Italy	2 349	299	5 449	149 655	82	..	..	..	..	98 810	278 158
Japan	96 893	55 216	172 642	1 745 352	277 816	..	..	..	..	..	3 524 556
Korea	..	..	..	..	..	..	..	..	..	..	..
Latvia	..	..	..	..	..	..	..	..	..	..	..
Lithuania	17	0	0	63	0	2	0	0	0	279	362
Luxembourg	1 493	60	1 644	23 316	91	6 221	..	..	..	164 359	237 756
Malaysia	3 431	1 096	7 480	35 394	2 976	..	..	..	..	14 513	69 917
Mexico	8	22	9	18 239	235	9	0	..	..	..	19 469
Morocco	..	..	..	..	..	..	..	..	..	..	..
Netherlands	..	..	..	..	..	..	..	..	..	..	..
New Zealand	496	20	211	2 421	..	2 328	..	..	..	..	5 634
Nicaragua	..	..	..	..	..	..	..	..	..	..	..
Norway	721	15 979	9 672	66 050	16 734	34 786	..	..	..	45 448	193 237
Panama	..	..	..	..	..	..	..	..	..	..	..
Paraguay	..	..	..	..	..	..	..	..	..	..	..
Peru	167	161	79	1 327	3	45	0	0	0	0	1 802
Poland	659	168	547	9 095	380	1 751	0	0	4	11 950	24 558
Portugal	551	149	222	17 260	92	531	26	0	33	14 126	32 977
Puerto Rico	..	..	..	..	..	..	..	..	..	..	..
Russia	3 975	117	212	15 922	5	19	..	..	..	..	20 333
Singapore	..	..	..	..	..	..	..	..	..	..	..
Slovak Republic	77	3	..	802	4	36	0	0	0	711	1 757
Slovenia	..	..	..	..	..	..	..	..	..	..	..
South Africa	..	..	..	..	..	..	..	..	..	..	..
Spain	1 443	314	446	21 935	260	721	134	24	1 173	4 542	30 857
Sri Lanka	..	..	..	..	..	..	..	..	..	..	..
Sweden	8 544	10 038	134 933	123 723	8 592	58 423	..	..	..	152 301	513 852
Switzerland	9 165	39 883	15 049	152 816	43 144	10 961	2 618	1 404	102	21 076	309 808
Thailand	..	..	..	..	..	..	..	..	..	..	..
Tunisia	..	..	..	..	..	..	..	..	..	..	..
Turkey	1 858	43	46	697	39	106	..	..	..	980	3 768
United Kingdom	5 759	2 971	7 322	194 187	63 237	32 907	174	940	118	1 506 746	1 811 763
United States	109 889	23 118	162 316	3 075 418	685 147	..	..	28 910	1 960	..	4 317 979
Uruguay	0	0	0	0	0	0	0	0	0	0	0

.. Not available

Note: Detailed metadata at: *http://metalinks.oecd.org/ins/20210324/7c21*.

1. Information on data for Israel: *http://oe.cd/israel-disclaimer*.

Source: *Outstanding investment by direct insurance companies, OECD Insurance Statistics (database)*

Table 6. Portfolio allocation, direct insurance (Non-life insurance companies)

2019

Million US dollars

	Cash and deposits	Land and buildings	Equity	Bills and bonds	Loans	Collective investment schemes	Private equity funds	Hedge funds	Structured products	Assets for unit-linked contracts	Total investments
Argentina	73	83	96	1 957	2	1 712	0	0	0	0	4 806
Australia	2 903	83	927	28 936	1 722	7 721	..	..	..	..	42 596
Austria	1 751	824	8 326	1 598	205	2 265	0	..	4	0	14 974
Belgium	854	526	1 601	6 831	288	2 503	1	..	75	..	12 701
Bolivia	8	27	4	121	0	0	9	0	0	0	169
Brazil	47	6	13	2 019	0	1 148	1	22	0	0	3 256
Canada	..	..	..	..	..	..	..	..	..	..	..
Chile	460	60	15	1 464	14	149	0	0	0	0	2 232
Colombia	268	6	553	3 348	5	180	63	..	13	..	4 481
Costa Rica	11	0	0	47	16	0	0	0	0	0	73
Cuba	..	..	..	..	..	..	..	..	..	..	..
Czech Republic	..	..	..	..	..	..	..	..	..	..	..
Denmark	3 083	360	4 482	14 590	513	1 571	..	..	..	0	26 153
Dominican Republic	..	..	..	..	..	..	..	..	..	..	..
Ecuador	4	11	3	43	0	0	29	0	0	0	91
Egypt	..	..	..	..	..	..	..	..	..	..	..
El Salvador	53	0	0	37	2	2	..	..	..	..	94
Estonia	175	0	1	721	3	28	0	0	0	0	931
Finland	1 806	708	1 747	4 053	675	3 419	..	..	..	..	14 121
France	..	..	..	..	..	..	..	..	..	..	..
Germany	9 093	13 247	92 514	328 207	21 743	215 111	3 403	..	4 901	62	688 760
Greece	238	181	36	1 087	2	223	0	0	1	0	1 814
Guatemala	38	3	0	71	2	..	..	..	..	..	131
Honduras	..	..	..	..	..	..	..	..	..	..	..
Hong Kong, China	..	..	..	..	..	..	..	..	..	..	..
Hungary	39	6	0	313	0	6	..	..	..	0	375
India	..	..	..	..	..	..	..	..	..	..	..
Indonesia	1 998	73	925	1 523	3	1 335	..	..	..	..	5 887
Iceland	85	22	296	442	20	203	..	..	..	0	1 069
Ireland	..	..	..	..	..	..	..	..	..	..	..
Israel[1]	318	63	107	1 746	233	969	77	13	5	0	3 560
Italy	713	489	2 193	14 199	28	..	..	..	..	0	20 499
Japan	18 718	7 806	49 441	64 805	13 842	..	..	..	..	..	242 586
Korea	..	..	..	..	..	..	..	..	..	..	..
Latvia	85	21	10	441	28	28	0	0	0	0	616
Lithuania	33	8	6	446	5	54	0	0	0	0	582
Luxembourg	1 632	210	749	17 823	0	826	..	..	..	0	35 763
Malaysia	2 172	130	179	2 700	10	..	..	..	..	..	9 620
Mexico	172	213	97	3 362	38	120	0	..	..	..	4 329
Morocco	..	..	..	..	..	..	..	..	..	..	..
Netherlands	..	..	..	..	..	..	..	..	..	..	..
New Zealand	894	2	45	2 168	..	671	..	..	..	..	3 814
Nicaragua	..	..	..	..	..	..	..	..	..	..	..
Norway	838	800	1 560	10 152	351	4 015	..	..	..	..	18 194
Panama	..	..	..	..	..	..	..	..	..	..	..
Paraguay	..	..	..	..	..	..	..	..	..	..	..
Peru	77	66	110	184	0	32	0	0	0	0	625
Poland	478	568	6 167	12 946	485	2 448	40	9	0	0	23 057
Portugal	210	110	46	2 458	4	148	5	0	17	0	2 998
Puerto Rico	..	..	..	..	..	..	..	..	..	..	..
Russia	7 473	876	2 664	6 815	335	45	..	..	..	..	18 217
Singapore	..	..	..	..	..	..	..	..	..	..	..
Slovak Republic	26	..	..	..	..	..	0	0	0	..	33
Slovenia	31	20	1	215	..	9	..	..	..	..	276
South Africa	..	..	..	..	..	..	..	..	..	..	..
Spain	2 717	2 278	2 688	9 550	484	4 534	172	201	117	0	22 827
Sri Lanka	..	..	..	..	..	..	..	..	..	..	..
Sweden	1 967	2 736	17 829	21 681	2 027	10 760	..	..	..	2 786	62 379
Switzerland	10 719	7 983	6 511	44 534	12 364	10 481	1 322	1 040	66	12	140 335
Thailand	..	..	..	..	..	..	..	..	..	..	..
Tunisia	..	..	..	..	..	..	..	..	..	..	..
Turkey	5 754	45	378	2 811	..	251	..	..	..	0	9 239
United Kingdom	2 610	197	1 833	17 604	580	3 260	3	0	0	0	26 230
United States	157 630	19 705	556 334	1 300 170	23 350	..	..	0	15	..	2 230 969
Uruguay	9	0	0	24	0	0	0	0	0	0	32

.. Not available

Note: Detailed metadata at: *http://metalinks.oecd.org/ins/20210324/7c21*.

1. Information on data for Israel: *http://oe.cd/israel-disclaimer*.

Source: *Outstanding investment by direct insurance companies, OECD Insurance Statistics (database)*

INTERNATIONAL COMPARISONS

Table 7. Total gross premiums (Life and Non-life)

Million US dollars

	2012	2013	2014	2015	2016	2017	2018	2019
Argentina	13 983	16 643	18 622	19 376	19 749	18 519	20 137	12 574
Australia	85 880	87 591	97 011	78 796	74 145	72 339	69 991	61 277
Austria	..	25 084	25 102	21 091	20 647	20 485	21 880	21 090
Belgium	41 936	37 521	38 345	30 746	30 432	30 839	33 703	35 152
Bolivia	316	..	..	..	468	499	549	610
Brazil	..	..	69 867	55 519	58 914	66 431	61 462	62 990
Canada	97 020	98 512	93 189	83 612	81 909	87 408	87 012	..
Chile	11 298	11 776	10 976	11 413	12 401	12 860	14 006	12 893
Colombia	9 144	10 207	9 690	8 003	8 050	8 978	9 409	9 392
Costa Rica	927	1 036	1 157	1 049	1 211	1 319	1 333	1 416
Cuba	..	..	..	..	..	..	..	..
Czech Republic	7 846	7 998	7 608	6 173	6 002	6 402	7 052	7 214
Denmark	32 745	225 775	37 098	31 997	33 498	37 549	40 976	38 589
Dominican Republic	..	..	..	..	..	..	1 222	..
Ecuador	..	..	..	2 316	2 135	..	..	1 797
Egypt	..	..	..	..	..	..	..	1 968
El Salvador	503	546	572	609	619	..	658	702
Estonia	617	774	839	764	815	924	1 092	1 102
Finland	9 352	13 061	14 125	11 917	10 012	10 084	5 156	6 744
France	258 641	275 750	294 033	250 873	314 251	314 319	338 708	332 471
Germany	302 739	333 713	338 764	293 086	294 660	311 208	335 669	344 268
Greece	5 781	5 407	5 056	3 964	3 908	4 213	4 485	4 538
Guatemala	611	683	749	804	856	953	964	1 006
Honduras	..	368	379	398	..	..	631	624
Hong Kong, China	33 191	37 856	43 121	47 901	59 301	64 310	69 089	..
Hungary	3 377	3 582	3 584	2 991	3 146	3 484	3 767	3 955
India	..	..	..	70 878	..	100 841	..	..
Indonesia	16 249	15 782	14 325	14 629	17 290	19 483	18 967	19 763
Iceland	404	419	444	420	487	611	652	612
Ireland	45 586	45 314	52 557	48 802	54 182	49 821	48 129	49 889
Israel[1]	12 471	13 941	14 366	14 117	15 142	17 427	18 560	19 324
Italy	138 232	161 161	193 455	165 854	151 423	150 732	163 781	158 241
Japan	475 139	349 905	347 080	313 822	434 737	390 096	402 773	399 088
Korea	163 016	169 166	187 090	183 675	185 593	189 491	192 869	..
Latvia	574	626	687	589	589	730	893	960
Lithuania	665	753	798	716	786	895	1 037	1 059
Luxembourg	25 168	24 705	28 945	21 278	20 289	24 314	24 539	28 130
Malaysia	16 338	16 974	17 588	15 346	15 100	15 156	16 716	17 667
Mexico	23 596	27 184	27 349	24 929	24 150	26 569	28 250	31 346
Morocco	..	..	..	..	..	..	..	..
Netherlands	51 267	51 142	48 603	37 399	77 358	80 465	86 997	..
New Zealand	4 590	5 139	5 359	4 657	4 753	5 144	..	7 258
Nicaragua	138	157	178	191	204	..	224	..
Norway	25 748	25 536	26 461	20 647	20 210	20 407	21 993	22 064
Panama	1 159	1 316	..	..	..	..	..	1 707
Paraguay	226	363	..	428	368	390	..	438
Peru	3 041	3 392	3 602	3 709	3 354	3 500	3 938	4 263
Poland	19 231	18 307	17 412	14 539	14 213	16 495	17 211	16 627
Portugal	13 559	17 003	18 667	13 945	12 079	12 941	14 868	13 338
Puerto Rico	..	9 610	9 108	11 145	13 470	..	..	..
Russia	..	..	26 658	17 299	18 218	22 517	24 301	23 675
Singapore	24 947	27 186	30 379	30 331	33 160	36 830	..	44 929
Slovak Republic	2 772	2 959	2 986	2 400	..	5 047	..	2 823
Slovenia	2 816	2 808	2 783	2 386	2 416	2 596	2 863	2 963
South Africa	51 452	54 268	51 527	47 054	42 473	..	..	..
Spain	72 880	77 177	76 604	65 514	73 655	74 242	78 578	74 106
Sri Lanka	..	..	746	931	..	1 128	1 147	..
Sweden	24 669	27 203	49 890	40 254	39 107	44 382	49 044	48 704
Switzerland	70 214	74 264	74 480	70 367	67 483	67 772	69 456	69 982
Thailand	..	..	..	..	..	..	..	..
Tunisia	..	..	..	..	864	909	..	..
Turkey	11 399	13 212	12 314	11 775	13 718	13 074	11 333	12 126
United Kingdom	368 525	340 385	365 688	336 743	403 794	394 114	469 120	418 667
United States	2 279 817	2 289 921	2 431 323	2 621 083	2 703 793	2 836 293	2 632 284	2 773 916
Uruguay	1 062	1 208	1 303	1 277	..	1 576	..	1 554
OECD Total	4 698 713	4 874 977	4 960 762	4 851 339	5 213 834	5 344 749	5 308 135	5 029 906

.. Not available

Note: Detailed metadata at: *http://metalinks.oecd.org/ins/20210324/7de6*.

1. Information on data for Israel: *http://oe.cd/israel-disclaimer*.

Source: *Insurance activity indicators, OECD Insurance Statistics (database)*

Table 8. Total gross premiums (Life)

Million US dollars

	2012	2013	2014	2015	2016	2017	2018	2019
Argentina	2 891	2 969	3 076	2 966	3 158	2 724	2 886	1 716
Australia	46 069	48 122	59 315	46 633	41 066	37 668	34 664	26 477
Austria	..	8 556	8 901	7 440	6 701	6 493	6 543	6 065
Belgium	27 140	21 651	21 664	17 045	16 560	16 547	18 437	18 181
Bolivia	69	..	..	..	157	202	238	274
Brazil	..	..	42 061	34 819	38 935	44 172	40 919	43 685
Canada	31 143	32 379	26 712	24 001	23 795	25 754	26 213	..
Chile	7 400	7 830	7 224	7 795	8 726	8 930	9 633	8 641
Colombia	4 285	5 214	4 602	3 727	3 879	4 567	4 710	4 751
Costa Rica	110	139	142	133	186	194	215	226
Cuba	..	..	..	..	..	..	..	..
Czech Republic	3 680	3 657	3 429	2 537	2 435	2 451	2 583	2 314
Denmark	22 489	215 331	25 124	22 055	23 001	25 945	28 664	27 518
Dominican Republic	..	..	..	..	..	..	196	..
Ecuador	..	..	..	453	471	..	..	524
Egypt	..	..	..	..	..	..	..	860
El Salvador	114	146	147	156	153	..	165	180
Estonia	209	227	254	238	245	252	275	283
Finland	4 786	7 423	8 108	6 943	5 063	5 115	5 156	6 744
France	160 618	172 187	188 634	160 946	182 414	173 606	186 967	185 390
Germany	107 425	120 293	121 746	99 628	97 651	99 769	106 802	112 711
Greece	2 497	2 238	2 500	2 000	1 846	2 125	2 220	2 310
Guatemala	124	136	156	156	170	196	197	213
Honduras	..	114	134	145	..	..	210	201
Hong Kong, China	28 123	32 425	37 459	41 972	53 421	58 134	62 257	..
Hungary	1 790	1 951	1 965	1 529	1 559	1 679	1 742	1 751
India	..	..	..	55 415	..	71 312	..	..
Indonesia	11 465	10 720	9 490	10 093	12 560	14 530	13 832	13 941
Iceland	29	33	36	35	43	54	54	51
Ireland	36 584	36 525	43 221	38 853	37 127	39 617	36 272	35 902
Israel[1]	6 602	7 374	7 426	7 568	7 986	9 368	10 016	10 615
Italy	91 858	115 147	148 645	129 077	114 779	112 984	122 310	118 872
Japan	475 139	349 905	347 080	313 822	328 210	293 005	302 966	292 247
Korea	96 166	100 249	106 200	104 820	104 530	102 221	102 538	..
Latvia	101	118	142	128	137	164	171	255
Lithuania	213	241	286	262	273	261	293	303
Luxembourg	23 497	22 711	27 166	19 641	18 568	22 318	22 523	25 512
Malaysia	9 907	10 200	10 594	9 306	9 317	9 603	10 709	11 628
Mexico	10 900	12 523	12 812	11 530	11 266	11 421	12 672	14 118
Morocco	..	..	..	..	..	..	..	..
Netherlands	24 392	24 263	23 202	16 307	15 198	14 654	14 136	..
New Zealand	..	..	..	..	..	..	..	1 714
Nicaragua	22	27	32	33	38	..	46	..
Norway	14 051	13 838	14 629	11 383	11 202	11 313	12 291	12 351
Panama	447	523	..	..	..	..	..	428
Paraguay	..	44	..	57	1	54	..	58
Peru	1 435	1 587	1 768	1 794	1 519	1 644	1 909	2 082
Poland	11 170	9 892	9 087	7 302	6 051	6 499	6 009	5 372
Portugal	8 582	11 984	13 617	9 411	7 200	7 581	9 188	7 567
Puerto Rico	..	411	570	542	1 279	..	..	..
Russia	..	..	3 353	2 408	3 721	6 171	7 784	6 842
Singapore	16 402	18 449	20 808	21 033	23 739	27 593	..	30 926
Slovak Republic	1 493	1 642	1 621	1 229	..	3 712	..	1 372
Slovenia	623	629	637	552	545	582	621	617
South Africa	40 746	42 679	41 476	37 576	33 870	..	..	..
Spain	33 821	34 397	33 612	28 532	34 695	33 262	34 263	30 780
Sri Lanka	..	..	265	395	..	467	474	..
Sweden	13 311	14 190	34 734	29 507	29 302	33 761	37 087	36 812
Switzerland	33 598	35 791	36 140	34 407	31 672	30 486	30 835	30 560
Thailand	..	..	..	..	..	..	..	..
Tunisia	..	..	..	..	175	179	..	..
Turkey	1 758	2 072	1 510	1 390	2 048	2 268	1 801	2 433
United Kingdom	277 966	246 475	268 267	246 702	277 703	269 267	336 122	301 117
United States	919 547	881 541	880 040	973 634	970 503	1 009 291	1 139 513	1 180 619
Uruguay	280	347	384	427	..	665	..	686
OECD Total	2 500 932	2 568 599	2 490 291	2 388 610	2 423 975	2 424 992	2 666 291	2 512 327

.. Not available

Note: Detailed metadata at: *http://metalinks.oecd.org/ins/20210324/7de6*.

1. Information on data for Israel: *http://oe.cd/israel-disclaimer*.

Source: *Insurance activity indicators, OECD Insurance Statistics (database)*

INTERNATIONAL COMPARISONS

Table 9. Total gross premiums (Non-life)

Million US dollars

	2012	2013	2014	2015	2016	2017	2018	2019
Argentina	11 092	13 673	15 546	16 410	16 591	15 795	17 251	10 859
Australia	39 812	39 469	37 695	32 163	33 079	34 671	35 328	34 800
Austria	..	16 527	16 201	13 651	13 946	13 992	15 337	15 025
Belgium	14 796	15 870	16 681	13 701	13 871	14 292	15 266	16 971
Bolivia	248	..	..	..	312	297	311	336
Brazil	..	..	27 806	20 699	19 979	22 258	20 543	19 305
Canada	65 877	66 133	66 477	59 610	58 115	61 654	60 799	..
Chile	3 898	3 946	3 751	3 619	3 676	3 930	4 373	4 252
Colombia	4 860	4 993	5 088	4 276	4 171	4 411	4 699	4 640
Costa Rica	816	897	1 014	916	1 024	1 125	1 118	1 190
Cuba	..	..	..	..	..	..	..	..
Czech Republic	4 165	4 341	4 179	3 636	3 566	3 951	4 469	4 901
Denmark	10 256	10 445	11 974	9 943	10 497	11 604	12 312	11 071
Dominican Republic	..	..	..	..	..	..	1 026	..
Ecuador	..	..	..	1 864	1 665	..	..	1 274
Egypt	..	..	..	..	..	..	..	1 108
El Salvador	389	400	412	437	446	..	493	522
Estonia	408	547	584	526	570	672	817	818
Finland	4 566	5 638	6 017	4 974	4 949	4 968	..	..
France	98 023	103 563	105 399	89 928	131 837	140 713	151 741	147 082
Germany	195 315	213 420	217 018	193 459	197 010	211 439	228 866	231 557
Greece	3 284	3 169	2 556	1 964	2 063	2 088	2 265	2 227
Guatemala	487	547	593	648	685	757	767	792
Honduras	..	254	246	253	..	..	421	424
Hong Kong, China	5 068	5 431	5 661	5 929	5 880	6 177	6 832	..
Hungary	1 587	1 631	1 619	1 462	1 588	1 804	2 025	2 204
India	..	..	..	15 463	..	29 529	..	..
Indonesia	4 784	5 062	4 835	4 537	4 730	4 954	5 136	5 823
Iceland	374	385	408	384	444	556	598	561
Ireland	9 002	8 789	9 335	9 949	17 055	9 625	10 006	12 517
Israel[1]	5 868	6 567	6 940	6 548	7 156	8 059	8 544	8 709
Italy	46 374	46 013	44 811	36 777	36 645	37 748	41 470	39 369
Japan	..	..	..	..	106 527	97 090	99 808	106 841
Korea	66 850	68 917	80 890	78 855	81 063	87 270	90 330	..
Latvia	473	507	546	462	452	566	721	704
Lithuania	452	512	513	454	513	634	744	756
Luxembourg	1 671	1 993	1 779	1 637	1 720	1 996	2 016	2 618
Malaysia	6 431	6 773	6 994	6 041	5 782	5 553	6 007	6 038
Mexico	12 696	14 661	14 536	13 399	12 884	15 148	15 578	17 228
Morocco	..	..	..	..	..	..	..	..
Netherlands	26 875	26 878	25 401	21 093	62 160	64 818	71 621	..
New Zealand	4 590	5 139	5 359	4 657	4 753	5 144	..	5 544
Nicaragua	116	130	146	158	166	..	178	..
Norway	11 697	11 697	11 833	9 264	9 008	9 094	9 702	9 713
Panama	713	793	..	..	..	..	..	1 279
Paraguay	161	318	..	371	367	335	..	380
Peru	1 605	1 805	1 834	1 916	1 835	1 856	2 029	2 181
Poland	8 061	8 416	8 325	7 237	8 162	9 996	11 202	11 255
Portugal	4 977	5 018	5 050	4 534	4 879	5 360	5 680	5 771
Puerto Rico	..	9 199	8 538	10 603	12 191	..	..	..
Russia	..	..	16 937	14 891	14 497	16 346	16 518	16 833
Singapore	8 544	8 737	9 571	9 298	9 421	9 238	..	14 003
Slovak Republic	1 279	1 318	1 366	1 171	..	1 335	..	1 451
Slovenia	2 192	2 179	2 146	1 833	1 871	2 014	2 242	2 346
South Africa	10 706	11 589	10 051	9 478	8 602	..	..	..
Spain	39 059	42 780	42 992	36 982	38 959	40 979	44 315	43 325
Sri Lanka	..	..	481	535	..	661	673	..
Sweden	11 357	13 013	15 156	10 746	9 805	10 621	11 957	11 892
Switzerland	36 616	38 474	38 340	35 959	35 811	37 287	38 621	39 421
Thailand	..	..	..	..	..	..	..	..
Tunisia	..	..	..	..	689	730	..	..
Turkey	9 641	11 140	10 804	10 386	11 670	10 806	9 532	9 693
United Kingdom	90 559	93 910	97 421	90 041	126 091	124 847	132 998	117 550
United States	1 360 270	1 408 380	1 551 283	1 647 449	1 733 290	1 827 002	1 492 771	1 593 297
Uruguay	782	862	918	850	..	911	..	868
OECD Total	2 197 781	2 306 378	2 470 471	2 462 728	2 789 859	2 918 185	2 638 754	2 516 108

.. Not available

Note: Detailed metadata at: *http://metalinks.oecd.org/ins/20210324/7de6.*

1. Information on data for Israel: *http://oe.cd/israel-disclaimer.*

Source: *Insurance activity indicators, OECD Insurance Statistics (database)*

Table 10. Market share in OECD (Life and Non-life)

Per cent

	2012	2013	2014	2015	2016	2017	2018	2019
Australia	1.8	1.8	2.0	1.6	1.4	1.4	1.3	1.2
Austria	..	0.5	0.5	0.4	0.4	0.4	0.4	0.4
Belgium	0.9	0.8	0.8	0.6	0.6	0.6	0.6	0.7
Canada	2.1	2.0	1.9	1.7	1.6	1.6	1.6	..
Chile	0.2	0.2	0.2	0.2	0.2	0.2	0.3	0.3
Colombia	..	..	..	..	..	..	..	..
Czech Republic	0.2	0.2	0.2	0.1	0.1	0.1	0.1	0.1
Denmark	0.7	4.6	0.7	0.7	0.6	0.7	0.8	0.8
Estonia	0.0	0.0	0.0	0.0	0.0	0.0	0.0	0.0
Finland	0.2	0.3	0.3	0.2	0.2	0.2	0.1	0.1
France	5.5	5.7	5.9	5.2	6.0	5.9	6.4	6.6
Germany	6.5	6.9	6.8	6.1	5.7	5.8	6.3	6.9
Greece	0.1	0.1	0.1	0.1	0.1	0.1	0.1	0.1
Hungary	0.1	0.1	0.1	0.1	0.1	0.1	0.1	0.1
Iceland	0.0	0.0	0.0	0.0	0.0	0.0	0.0	0.0
Ireland	1.0	0.9	1.1	1.0	1.0	0.9	0.9	1.0
Israel	0.3	0.3	0.3	0.3	0.3	0.3	0.4	0.4
Italy	2.9	3.3	3.9	3.4	2.9	2.8	3.1	3.2
Japan	10.1	7.2	7.0	6.5	8.4	7.3	7.6	7.9
Korea	3.5	3.5	3.8	3.8	3.6	3.6	3.6	..
Latvia	0.0	0.0	0.0	0.0	0.0	0.0	0.0	0.0
Lithuania	0.0	0.0	0.0	0.0	0.0	0.0	0.0	0.0
Luxembourg	0.5	0.5	0.6	0.4	0.4	0.5	0.5	0.6
Mexico	0.5	0.6	0.6	0.5	0.5	0.5	0.5	0.6
Netherlands	1.1	1.1	1.0	0.8	1.5	1.5	1.6	..
New Zealand	0.1	0.1	0.1	0.1	0.1	0.1	..	0.1
Norway	0.5	0.5	0.5	0.4	0.4	0.4	0.4	0.4
Poland	0.4	0.4	0.4	0.3	0.3	0.3	0.3	0.3
Portugal	0.3	0.4	0.4	0.3	0.2	0.2	0.3	0.3
Slovak Republic	0.1	0.1	0.1	0.1	..	0.1	..	0.1
Slovenia	0.1	0.1	0.1	0.0	0.0	0.0	0.1	0.1
Spain	1.6	1.6	1.5	1.4	1.4	1.4	1.5	1.5
Sweden	0.5	0.6	1.0	0.8	0.8	0.8	0.9	1.0
Switzerland	1.5	1.5	1.5	1.5	1.3	1.3	1.3	1.4
Turkey	0.2	0.3	0.2	0.2	0.3	0.2	0.2	0.2
United Kingdom	7.9	7.0	7.4	7.0	7.8	7.4	8.9	8.3
United States	48.6	47.1	49.1	54.1	51.9	53.2	49.7	55.3
OECD Total	100.0	100.0	100.0	100.0	100.0	100.0	100.0	100.0

.. Not available

Note: Detailed metadata at: *http://metalinks.oecd.org/ins/20210324/7de6*.

Source: *Insurance activity indicators, OECD Insurance Statistics (database)*

INTERNATIONAL COMPARISONS

Table 11. Market share in OECD (Life)

Per cent

	2012	2013	2014	2015	2016	2017	2018	2019
Australia	1.8	1.9	2.4	2.0	1.7	1.6	1.3	1.1
Austria	..	0.3	0.4	0.3	0.3	0.3	0.2	0.2
Belgium	1.1	0.8	0.9	0.7	0.7	0.7	0.7	0.7
Canada	1.2	1.3	1.1	1.0	1.0	1.1	1.0	..
Chile	0.3	0.3	0.3	0.3	0.4	0.4	0.4	0.3
Colombia	..	..	..	..	..	..	..	..
Czech Republic	0.1	0.1	0.1	0.1	0.1	0.1	0.1	0.1
Denmark	0.9	8.4	1.0	0.9	1.0	1.1	1.1	1.1
Estonia	0.0	0.0	0.0	0.0	0.0	0.0	0.0	0.0
Finland	0.2	0.3	0.3	0.3	0.2	0.2	0.2	0.3
France	6.4	6.7	7.6	6.7	7.5	7.2	7.0	7.4
Germany	4.3	4.7	4.9	4.2	4.0	4.1	4.0	4.5
Greece	0.1	0.1	0.1	0.1	0.1	0.1	0.1	0.1
Hungary	0.1	0.1	0.1	0.1	0.1	0.1	0.1	0.1
Iceland	0.0	0.0	0.0	0.0	0.0	0.0	0.0	0.0
Ireland	1.5	1.4	1.7	1.6	1.5	1.6	1.4	1.4
Israel	0.3	0.3	0.3	0.3	0.3	0.4	0.4	0.4
Italy	3.7	4.5	6.0	5.4	4.7	4.7	4.6	4.7
Japan	19.0	13.7	14.0	13.2	13.6	12.1	11.4	11.7
Korea	3.9	3.9	4.3	4.4	4.3	4.2	3.9	..
Latvia	0.0	0.0	0.0	0.0	0.0	0.0	0.0	0.0
Lithuania	0.0	0.0	0.0	0.0	0.0	0.0	0.0	0.0
Luxembourg	0.9	0.9	1.1	0.8	0.8	0.9	0.8	1.0
Mexico	0.4	0.5	0.5	0.5	0.5	0.5	0.5	0.6
Netherlands	1.0	0.9	0.9	0.7	0.6	0.6	0.5	..
New Zealand	..	..	..	..	..	..	..	0.1
Norway	0.6	0.5	0.6	0.5	0.5	0.5	0.5	0.5
Poland	0.4	0.4	0.4	0.3	0.3	0.3	0.2	0.2
Portugal	0.3	0.5	0.5	0.4	0.3	0.3	0.3	0.3
Slovak Republic	0.1	0.1	0.1	0.1	..	0.2	..	0.1
Slovenia	0.0	0.0	0.0	0.0	0.0	0.0	0.0	0.0
Spain	1.4	1.3	1.4	1.2	1.4	1.4	1.3	1.2
Sweden	0.5	0.6	1.4	1.2	1.2	1.4	1.4	1.5
Switzerland	1.3	1.4	1.5	1.4	1.3	1.3	1.2	1.2
Turkey	0.1	0.1	0.1	0.1	0.1	0.1	0.1	0.1
United Kingdom	11.1	9.6	10.8	10.3	11.5	11.1	12.6	12.0
United States	36.8	34.4	35.4	40.8	40.1	41.7	42.8	47.1
OECD Total	100.0	100.0	100.0	100.0	100.0	100.0	100.0	100.0

.. Not available

Note: Detailed metadata at: *http://metalinks.oecd.org/ins/20210324/7de6.*

Source: *Insurance activity indicators, OECD Insurance Statistics (database)*

Table 12. Market share in OECD (Non-life)

Per cent

	2012	2013	2014	2015	2016	2017	2018	2019
Australia	1.8	1.7	1.5	1.3	1.2	1.2	1.3	1.4
Austria	..	0.7	0.7	0.6	0.5	0.5	0.6	0.6
Belgium	0.7	0.7	0.7	0.6	0.5	0.5	0.6	0.7
Canada	3.0	2.9	2.7	2.4	2.1	2.1	2.3	..
Chile	0.2	0.2	0.2	0.1	0.1	0.1	0.2	0.2
Colombia	..	..	..	..	..	..	..	..
Czech Republic	0.2	0.2	0.2	0.1	0.1	0.1	0.2	0.2
Denmark	0.5	0.5	0.5	0.4	0.4	0.4	0.5	0.4
Estonia	0.0	0.0	0.0	0.0	0.0	0.0	0.0	0.0
Finland	0.2	0.2	0.2	0.2	0.2	0.2	..	..
France	4.5	4.5	4.3	3.7	4.7	4.8	5.8	5.9
Germany	8.9	9.3	8.8	7.9	7.1	7.3	8.7	9.2
Greece	0.2	0.1	0.1	0.1	0.1	0.1	0.1	0.1
Hungary	0.1	0.1	0.1	0.1	0.1	0.1	0.1	0.1
Iceland	0.0	0.0	0.0	0.0	0.0	0.0	0.0	0.0
Ireland	0.4	0.4	0.4	0.4	0.6	0.3	0.4	0.5
Israel	0.3	0.3	0.3	0.3	0.3	0.3	0.3	0.3
Italy	2.1	2.0	1.8	1.5	1.3	1.3	1.6	1.6
Japan	..	..	..	..	3.8	3.3	3.8	4.3
Korea	3.0	3.0	3.3	3.2	2.9	3.0	3.4	..
Latvia	0.0	0.0	0.0	0.0	0.0	0.0	0.0	0.0
Lithuania	0.0	0.0	0.0	0.0	0.0	0.0	0.0	0.0
Luxembourg	0.1	0.1	0.1	0.1	0.1	0.1	0.1	0.1
Mexico	0.6	0.6	0.6	0.5	0.5	0.5	0.6	0.7
Netherlands	1.2	1.2	1.0	0.9	2.2	2.2	2.7	..
New Zealand	0.2	0.2	0.2	0.2	0.2	0.2	..	0.2
Norway	0.5	0.5	0.5	0.4	0.3	0.3	0.4	0.4
Poland	0.4	0.4	0.3	0.3	0.3	0.3	0.4	0.4
Portugal	0.2	0.2	0.2	0.2	0.2	0.2	0.2	0.2
Slovak Republic	0.1	0.1	0.1	0.0	..	0.0	..	0.1
Slovenia	0.1	0.1	0.1	0.1	0.1	0.1	0.1	0.1
Spain	1.8	1.9	1.7	1.5	1.4	1.4	1.7	1.7
Sweden	0.5	0.6	0.6	0.4	0.4	0.4	0.5	0.5
Switzerland	1.7	1.7	1.6	1.5	1.3	1.3	1.5	1.6
Turkey	0.4	0.5	0.4	0.4	0.4	0.4	0.4	0.4
United Kingdom	4.1	4.1	4.0	3.7	4.5	4.3	5.0	4.7
United States	62.0	61.2	62.9	67.0	62.2	62.7	56.7	63.4
OECD Total	100.0	100.0	100.0	100.0	100.0	100.0	100.0	100.0

.. Not available

Note: Detailed metadata at: *http://metalinks.oecd.org/ins/20210324/7de6.*

Source: *Insurance activity indicators, OECD Insurance Statistics (database)*

Table 13. Density (Life and Non-life)

US dollar per inhabitant

	2012	2013	2014	2015	2016	2017	2018	2019
Argentina	333	393	405	418	422	393	427	264
Australia	3 328	3 350	3 688	2 926	2 660	2 540	2 383	2 010
Austria	2 492	2 603	2 657	2 227	2 143	2 176	2 284	2 197
Belgium	3 684	3 260	3 308	2 653	2 613	2 653	2 903	2 853
Bolivia	31	..	..	..	42	43	47	50
Brazil	334	337	346	273	287	321	295	300
Canada	2 562	2 538	2 168	1 930	1 919	2 011	2 086	..
Chile	645	665	613	630	675	692	740	668
Colombia	194	214	199	163	162	179	185	183
Costa Rica	198	218	241	216	246	265	265	278
Cuba	35	..	..	..	..	..	..	..
Czech Republic	733	747	712	574	555	590	651	663
Denmark	5 823	6 079	6 543	5 610	5 699	6 315	6 842	6 486
Dominican Republic	..	..	..	..	..	..	119	..
Ecuador	..	..	..	139	127	98	100	103
Egypt	..	..	..	..	..	14	17	19
El Salvador	..	..	..	..	..	..	94	99
Estonia	466	587	638	581	619	702	828	835
Finland	1 699	2 371	2 556	2 150	1 797	1 803	935	1 221
France	3 645	3 893	4 110	3 554	4 108	4 248	4 569	4 472
Germany	2 890	3 112	3 131	2 597	2 602	2 838	3 049	3 095
Greece	511	480	457	361	359	388	414	420
Guatemala	39	43	46	48	50	55	54	56
Honduras	42	43	43	44	..	..	67	65
Hong Kong, China	4 403	5 003	5 658	6 259	7 652	8 266	8 803	..
Hungary	336	357	360	300	317	350	381	401
India	..	..	..	55	63	72	..	..
Indonesia	63	60	55	56	66	73	71	72
Iceland	1 232	1 270	1 329	1 245	1 436	1 783	1 840	1 684
Ireland	9 702	9 606	11 052	10 154	11 107	10 205	9 554	9 492
Israel[1]	1 577	1 731	1 749	1 685	1 772	2 001	2 090	2 134
Italy	2 239	2 600	3 125	2 678	2 445	2 437	2 645	2 595
Japan	3 355	2 545	2 580	2 370	3 201	2 893	3 010	2 989
Korea	3 089	3 181	3 503	3 418	3 437	3 478	3 504	..
Latvia	277	309	343	297	299	374	461	497
Lithuania	222	254	272	246	274	317	370	380
Luxembourg	47 314	45 569	51 995	37 506	35 103	41 043	40 668	43 263
Malaysia	514	520	530	454	441	439	481	504
Mexico	198	226	224	203	194	211	223	244
Morocco	..	..	..	..	..	115	124	..
Netherlands	3 023	3 002	2 846	2 176	4 532	4 626	4 971	4 871
New Zealand	1 024	1 141	1 169	964	983	1 006	..	1 440
Nicaragua	23	26	29	30	32	34	35	..
Norway	5 111	5 011	5 132	3 967	3 972	3 858	4 131	4 120
Panama	286	321	..	..	..	..	..	372
Paraguay	46	54	..	63	53	56	61	61
Peru	99	110	116	118	106	109	122	130
Poland	500	475	453	372	361	420	436	418
Portugal	1 237	1 570	1 735	1 293	1 110	1 189	1 370	1 228
Puerto Rico	..	2 661	2 552	3 182	3 927	..	..	..
Russia	..	..	176	115	120	149	161	156
Singapore	3 728	4 047	4 489	4 400	4 631	5 411	..	5 799
Slovak Republic	508	542	544	434	..	927	..	518
Slovenia	1 202	1 209	1 198	1 012	1 028	1 105	1 223	1 257
South Africa	..	986	923	830	733	..	..	..
Spain	1 518	1 529	1 521	1 295	1 458	1 471	1 559	1 460
Sri Lanka	..	..	35	44	..	51	52	..
Sweden	2 376	2 644	4 908	3 961	3 796	4 248	4 646	4 575
Switzerland	7 634	7 898	7 892	7 456	7 025	6 904	6 962	6 878
Thailand	..	..	..	..	..	..	..	..
Tunisia	..	..	..	..	75	75	72	..
Turkey	146	168	151	145	162	152	126	131
United Kingdom	5 316	4 793	5 098	4 598	3 950	5 113	5 645	5 041
United States	5 752	5 686	5 970	6 305	6 500	6 717	7 082	7 482
Uruguay	310	351	377	368	..	451	425	442
OECD Total	3 090	3 026	3 183	3 048	3 198	3 305	3 501	3 572

.. Not available

Note: Detailed metadata at: *http://metalinks.oecd.org/ins/20210324/7de6.*

1. Information on data for Israel: *http://oe.cd/israel-disclaimer.*

Source: *Insurance activity indicators, OECD Insurance Statistics (database)*

Table 14. Density (Life)

US dollar per inhabitant

	2012	2013	2014	2015	2016	2017	2018	2019
Argentina	68	70	70	67	70	60	63	37
Australia	1 856	1 898	2 321	1 781	1 521	1 335	1 180	847
Austria	981	1 007	1 039	860	765	735	735	676
Belgium	2 445	1 937	1 930	1 512	1 458	1 454	1 613	1 580
Bolivia	7	..	..	..	14	17	20	22
Brazil	210	204	209	171	190	214	196	208
Canada	820	834	629	555	561	604	625	..
Chile	424	444	406	432	475	481	509	448
Colombia	92	111	96	77	80	93	94	94
Costa Rica	24	29	30	27	38	39	43	45
Cuba	..	..	..	..	..	..	..	..
Czech Republic	350	348	326	241	229	230	242	216
Denmark	4 005	4 236	4 443	3 878	4 006	4 495	4 939	4 719
Dominican Republic	..	..	..	..	..	..	19	..
Ecuador	..	..	..	28	28	27	30	30
Egypt	..	..	..	..	..	6	7	9
El Salvador	..	..	..	..	..	..	24	25
Estonia	158	172	193	181	186	191	209	215
Finland	885	1 366	1 485	1 268	923	929	935	1 221
France	2 305	2 486	2 684	2 344	2 391	2 450	2 641	2 587
Germany	1 326	1 445	1 456	1 180	1 148	1 197	1 282	1 352
Greece	225	203	228	184	171	197	207	216
Guatemala	8	9	10	9	10	11	11	12
Honduras	20	21	15	16	..	..	22	21
Hong Kong, China	3 882	4 446	5 082	5 644	7 041	7 642	8 149	..
Hungary	180	197	199	155	159	171	178	179
India	..	..	..	43	48	54	..	..
Indonesia	47	43	38	39	49	56	52	52
Iceland	92	103	111	107	128	161	155	142
Ireland	7 851	7 803	9 158	8 141	7 729	8 197	7 413	7 231
Israel[1]	835	915	904	903	935	1 076	1 128	1 172
Italy	1 487	1 866	2 413	2 096	1 864	1 837	1 994	1 963
Japan	3 355	2 545	2 580	2 370	2 496	2 252	2 348	2 277
Korea	1 894	1 966	2 070	2 032	2 015	1 960	1 951	..
Latvia	49	59	71	64	70	84	89	132
Lithuania	71	81	97	90	95	92	105	109
Luxembourg	44 173	41 868	48 768	34 604	32 123	37 673	37 331	39 401
Malaysia	332	333	340	294	290	295	325	351
Mexico	93	105	106	95	92	92	101	111
Morocco	..	..	..	..	..	51	55	..
Netherlands	1 457	1 446	1 378	964	895	857	823	806
New Zealand	..	..	..	..	..	..	..	340
Nicaragua	4	4	5	5	6	7	7	..
Norway	2 789	2 715	2 837	2 187	2 133	2 139	2 309	2 306
Panama	112	128	..	..	..	..	..	96
Paraguay	..	7	..	8	0	8	9	8
Peru	47	51	57	57	48	52	59	64
Poland	293	260	239	192	159	171	158	141
Portugal	816	1 146	1 309	908	697	736	894	737
Puerto Rico	..	114	161	156	373	..	..	..
Russia	..	..	23	16	25	42	53	47
Singapore	2 725	3 045	3 392	3 404	3 611	4 374	..	4 564
Slovak Republic	276	303	299	227	..	683	..	252
Slovenia	303	305	309	268	264	282	300	298
South Africa	..	794	760	678	602	..	..	..
Spain	722	729	712	606	737	706	727	649
Sri Lanka	..	..	13	19	..	22	22	..
Sweden	1 362	1 469	3 562	2 994	2 931	3 335	3 625	3 566
Switzerland	4 177	4 385	4 378	4 113	3 739	3 573	3 592	3 532
Thailand	..	..	..	..	..	..	..	..
Tunisia	..	..	..	..	15	15	16	..
Turkey	23	26	19	17	25	27	21	28
United Kingdom	4 054	3 488	3 781	3 411	2 508	3 652	4 114	3 786
United States	2 641	2 472	2 475	2 576	2 587	2 641	2 779	2 941
Uruguay	82	101	111	123	..	190	169	195
OECD Total	1 786	1 679	1 761	1 642	1 597	1 647	1 746	1 764

.. Not available

Note: Detailed metadata at: *http://metalinks.oecd.org/ins/20210324/7de6*.

1. Information on data for Israel: *http://oe.cd/israel-disclaimer*.

Source: *Insurance activity indicators, OECD Insurance Statistics (database)*

INTERNATIONAL COMPARISONS

Table 15. Density (Non-life)

US dollar per inhabitant

	2012	2013	2014	2015	2016	2017	2018	2019
Argentina	265	323	335	351	352	333	364	227
Australia	1 473	1 453	1 367	1 145	1 139	1 205	1 203	1 163
Austria	1 511	1 596	1 617	1 367	1 377	1 441	1 550	1 521
Belgium	1 239	1 323	1 378	1 142	1 156	1 200	1 290	1 273
Bolivia	24	..	..	..	28	25	27	27
Brazil	124	133	138	102	97	108	99	92
Canada	1 743	1 704	1 539	1 375	1 358	1 407	1 461	..
Chile	221	221	208	198	200	211	231	220
Colombia	102	103	103	85	83	86	91	88
Costa Rica	174	189	211	188	208	226	222	233
Cuba	35	..	..	..	..	..	..	..
Czech Republic	383	399	386	333	325	360	409	448
Denmark	1 818	1 843	2 101	1 732	1 692	1 820	1 903	1 767
Dominican Republic	..	..	..	..	..	..	100	..
Ecuador	..	..	..	112	98	71	71	73
Egypt	..	..	..	..	..	8	10	10
El Salvador	..	..	..	..	..	..	70	74
Estonia	308	415	444	400	433	510	620	620
Finland	814	1 005	1 071	882	875	873	..	..
France	1 340	1 407	1 427	1 209	1 717	1 798	1 928	1 885
Germany	1 564	1 667	1 674	1 417	1 454	1 641	1 767	1 743
Greece	286	277	229	177	188	190	207	204
Guatemala	31	34	36	39	40	43	43	44
Honduras	22	22	28	28	..	..	45	44
Hong Kong, China	521	557	577	615	611	624	654	..
Hungary	156	160	161	145	158	179	203	222
India	..	..	..	12	15	18	..	..
Indonesia	17	17	18	17	17	18	18	20
Iceland	1 140	1 166	1 217	1 138	1 308	1 621	1 685	1 542
Ireland	1 851	1 803	1 894	2 013	3 378	1 890	1 915	2 116
Israel[1]	742	815	845	782	838	925	962	962
Italy	752	735	712	582	581	600	651	632
Japan	..	..	..	..	705	641	662	712
Korea	1 196	1 215	1 433	1 386	1 421	1 519	1 553	..
Latvia	228	250	273	232	230	290	373	365
Lithuania	151	173	175	156	179	224	265	272
Luxembourg	3 141	3 700	3 227	2 902	2 980	3 370	3 337	3 862
Malaysia	182	187	190	160	150	144	156	153
Mexico	105	121	118	108	103	119	122	133
Morocco	..	..	..	..	..	64	69	..
Netherlands	1 566	1 556	1 467	1 212	3 637	3 768	4 148	4 065
New Zealand	1 024	1 141	1 169	964	983	1 006	..	1 100
Nicaragua	19	21	24	25	26	28	28	..
Norway	2 322	2 295	2 295	1 780	1 840	1 719	1 822	1 813
Panama	174	192	..	..	..	..	..	275
Paraguay	27	48	..	54	53	48	53	53
Peru	53	59	59	61	58	58	62	66
Poland	207	216	214	180	202	249	278	277
Portugal	421	424	426	385	413	454	476	491
Puerto Rico	..	2 546	2 391	3 026	3 554	..	..	..
Russia	..	..	110	98	95	107	108	109
Singapore	1 004	1 001	1 098	996	1 021	1 037	..	1 235
Slovak Republic	232	238	244	207	..	244	..	266
Slovenia	899	904	889	744	765	823	923	959
South Africa	..	192	163	152	131	..	..	..
Spain	795	800	809	690	721	765	833	812
Sri Lanka	..	..	22	25	..	30	30	..
Sweden	1 015	1 175	1 346	967	865	913	1 021	1 009
Switzerland	3 458	3 513	3 514	3 343	3 286	3 331	3 370	3 346
Thailand	..	..	..	..	..	..	..	..
Tunisia	..	..	..	..	60	59	56	..
Turkey	123	141	131	128	137	125	105	103
United Kingdom	1 262	1 306	1 317	1 188	1 441	1 461	1 531	1 255
United States	3 111	3 214	3 495	3 729	3 913	4 076	4 304	4 541
Uruguay	228	250	266	245	..	261	256	247
OECD Total	1 304	1 347	1 421	1 405	1 601	1 657	1 754	1 808

.. Not available

Note: Detailed metadata at: *http://metalinks.oecd.org/ins/20210324/7de6.*

1. Information on data for Israel: *http://oe.cd/israel-disclaimer.*

Source: *Insurance activity indicators, OECD Insurance Statistics (database)*

INTERNATIONAL COMPARISONS

Table 16. Penetration (Life and Non-life)

Per cent

	2012	2013	2014	2015	2016	2017	2018	2019
Argentina	2.3	2.4	2.4	2.6	2.6	2.6	2.3	2.1
Australia	4.8	5.1	6.0	5.6	5.0	4.4	4.1	3.7
Austria	5.1	5.1	5.1	5.0	4.7	4.6	4.5	4.4
Belgium	8.2	7.0	6.9	6.4	6.2	6.0	6.1	6.2
Bolivia	1.2	..	..	..	1.4	1.3	1.3	1.4
Brazil	2.7	2.7	2.8	3.1	3.3	3.2	3.3	3.5
Canada	4.9	4.8	4.2	4.4	4.5	4.4	4.5	..
Chile	4.2	4.2	4.2	4.6	4.9	4.6	4.7	4.5
Colombia	2.4	2.6	2.5	2.7	2.8	2.8	2.8	2.8
Costa Rica	2.0	2.1	2.3	1.9	2.1	2.3	2.2	2.3
Cuba	..	..	..	..	..	..	..	..
Czech Republic	3.7	3.7	3.6	3.2	3.0	2.9	2.8	2.8
Denmark	9.9	9.9	10.4	10.5	10.4	11.0	11.1	10.9
Dominican Republic	..	..	..	..	..	..	1.4	..
Ecuador	..	..	..	2.3	2.1	1.6	1.6	1.7
Egypt	..	..	..	..	..	0.7	0.7	0.6
El Salvador	..	..	..	..	..	..	2.4	2.5
Estonia	2.7	3.1	3.1	3.3	3.4	3.4	3.6	3.5
Finland	3.6	4.7	5.1	5.0	4.1	3.9	1.9	2.5
France	8.6	8.8	9.2	9.4	10.7	10.6	10.6	10.7
Germany	6.6	6.7	6.5	6.3	6.2	6.4	6.4	6.7
Greece	2.3	2.2	2.1	2.0	2.0	2.1	2.0	2.1
Guatemala	1.2	1.2	1.2	1.2	1.2	1.2	1.2	1.2
Honduras	1.9	2.0	1.9	1.9	..	..	2.6	2.5
Hong Kong, China	12.0	13.1	14.1	14.8	17.6	17.9	18.2	..
Hungary	2.6	2.6	2.5	2.4	2.4	2.4	2.4	2.4
India	..	..	..	3.4	3.6	3.6	..	..
Indonesia	1.7	1.6	1.6	1.7	1.8	1.9	1.8	1.7
Iceland	2.7	2.6	2.4	2.4	2.3	2.5	2.5	2.5
Ireland	19.9	18.6	19.9	16.4	17.6	14.7	12.2	12.1
Israel[1]	4.8	4.8	4.6	4.7	4.8	4.9	5.0	4.9
Italy	6.5	7.3	8.8	8.9	7.9	7.5	7.7	7.8
Japan	6.8	6.4	6.8	6.8	7.7	7.4	7.8	7.3
Korea	12.1	11.7	12.0	11.9	11.7	11.0	10.5	..
Latvia	2.0	2.1	2.2	2.2	2.1	2.4	2.6	2.8
Lithuania	1.6	1.6	1.6	1.7	1.8	1.9	1.9	2.0
Luxembourg	43.8	39.6	43.2	36.6	33.3	37.8	34.5	37.4
Malaysia	4.8	4.8	4.7	4.7	4.6	4.4	4.3	4.5
Mexico	1.9	2.1	2.0	2.1	2.2	2.3	2.3	2.4
Morocco	..	..	..	..	..	3.6	3.7	..
Netherlands	6.0	5.7	5.4	4.8	9.8	9.5	9.3	9.3
New Zealand	2.6	2.7	2.7	2.5	2.5	2.4	..	3.5
Nicaragua	1.3	1.4	1.5	1.5	1.5	1.6	1.7	..
Norway	5.1	4.9	5.3	5.4	5.7	5.1	5.1	5.5
Panama	2.7	2.7	..	..	..	..	..	2.3
Paraguay	0.9	0.9	..	1.0	1.0	1.0	1.0	1.0
Peru	1.6	1.7	1.8	1.9	1.7	1.6	1.7	1.8
Poland	3.8	3.5	3.2	3.0	2.9	3.0	2.8	2.7
Portugal	6.0	7.2	7.8	6.7	5.6	5.5	5.8	5.3
Puerto Rico	..	9.3	8.8	10.7	12.8	..	..	..
Russia	..	..	1.2	1.2	1.4	1.4	1.4	1.4
Singapore	6.7	7.1	7.8	7.9	8.2	9.0	..	9.0
Slovak Republic	2.9	3.0	2.9	2.7	..	5.3	..	2.7
Slovenia	5.3	5.1	4.9	4.8	4.8	4.7	4.7	4.8
South Africa	..	14.5	14.4	14.5	13.9	..	..	..
Spain	5.4	5.3	5.2	5.0	5.5	5.2	5.1	4.9
Sri Lanka	..	..	0.9	1.1	..	1.3	1.3	..
Sweden	4.1	4.3	8.2	7.7	7.4	7.9	8.6	8.9
Switzerland	9.1	9.2	9.1	9.0	8.7	8.5	8.4	8.4
Thailand	..	..	..	..	..	..	..	..
Tunisia	..	..	..	..	2.0	2.2	2.1	..
Turkey	1.3	1.3	1.2	1.3	1.5	1.4	1.3	1.4
United Kingdom	12.5	11.0	10.7	10.2	9.6	12.7	13.1	11.9
United States	11.2	10.7	10.9	11.1	11.2	11.2	11.2	11.5
Uruguay	2.1	2.1	2.3	2.4	..	2.6	2.5	2.7
OECD Total	8.3	8.1	8.4	8.6	8.8	8.8	8.9	9.0

.. Not available

Note: Detailed metadata at: *http://metalinks.oecd.org/ins/20210324/7de6*.

1. Information on data for Israel: *http://oe.cd/israel-disclaimer*.

Source: *Insurance activity indicators*, *OECD Insurance Statistics (database)*

INTERNATIONAL COMPARISONS

Table 17. Penetration (Life)

Per cent

	2012	2013	2014	2015	2016	2017	2018	2019
Argentina	0.5	0.4	0.4	0.4	0.4	0.4	0.3	0.3
Australia	2.7	2.9	3.7	3.4	2.8	2.3	2.0	1.6
Austria	2.0	2.0	2.0	1.9	1.7	1.5	1.4	1.4
Belgium	5.5	4.1	4.0	3.7	3.5	3.3	3.4	3.4
Bolivia	0.3	..	..	..	0.5	0.5	0.6	0.6
Brazil	1.7	1.7	1.7	1.9	2.2	2.2	2.2	2.4
Canada	1.6	1.6	1.2	1.3	1.3	1.3	1.3	..
Chile	2.8	2.8	2.8	3.2	3.4	3.2	3.2	3.0
Colombia	1.2	1.4	1.2	1.3	1.4	1.5	1.4	1.5
Costa Rica	0.2	0.3	0.3	0.2	0.3	0.3	0.4	0.4
Cuba	..	..	..	..	..	..	..	..
Czech Republic	1.8	1.7	1.6	1.3	1.2	1.1	1.0	0.9
Denmark	6.8	6.9	7.1	7.3	7.3	7.8	8.0	7.9
Dominican Republic	..	..	..	..	..	..	0.2	..
Ecuador	..	..	..	0.5	0.5	0.4	0.5	0.5
Egypt	..	..	..	..	..	0.3	0.3	0.3
El Salvador	..	..	..	..	..	..	0.6	0.6
Estonia	0.9	0.9	0.9	1.0	1.0	0.9	0.9	0.9
Finland	1.9	2.7	2.9	3.0	2.1	2.0	1.9	2.5
France	5.4	5.6	6.0	6.2	6.2	6.1	6.1	6.2
Germany	3.0	3.1	3.0	2.9	2.7	2.7	2.7	2.9
Greece	1.0	0.9	1.1	1.0	0.9	1.0	1.0	1.1
Guatemala	0.2	0.3	0.3	0.2	0.2	0.3	0.2	0.3
Honduras	0.9	1.0	0.7	0.7	..	..	0.9	0.8
Hong Kong, China	10.6	11.6	12.6	13.3	16.2	16.6	16.8	..
Hungary	1.4	1.4	1.4	1.2	1.2	1.2	1.1	1.1
India	..	..	..	2.7	2.7	2.7	..	..
Indonesia	1.2	1.2	1.1	1.2	1.3	1.4	1.3	1.2
Iceland	0.2	0.2	0.2	0.2	0.2	0.2	0.2	0.2
Ireland	16.1	15.1	16.5	13.2	12.3	11.8	9.5	9.2
Israel[1]	2.6	2.5	2.4	2.5	2.5	2.7	2.7	2.7
Italy	4.3	5.3	6.8	6.9	6.0	5.7	5.8	5.9
Japan	6.8	6.4	6.8	6.8	6.0	5.8	6.1	5.6
Korea	7.4	7.2	7.1	7.1	6.9	6.2	5.9	..
Latvia	0.4	0.4	0.5	0.5	0.5	0.5	0.5	0.7
Lithuania	0.5	0.5	0.6	0.6	0.6	0.5	0.5	0.6
Luxembourg	40.9	36.4	40.5	33.7	30.5	34.7	31.7	34.0
Malaysia	3.1	3.1	3.0	3.0	3.0	3.0	2.9	3.1
Mexico	0.9	1.0	1.0	1.0	1.0	1.0	1.0	1.1
Morocco	..	..	..	..	..	1.6	1.6	..
Netherlands	2.9	2.8	2.6	2.1	1.9	1.8	1.5	1.5
New Zealand	..	..	..	..	..	..	..	0.8
Nicaragua	0.2	0.2	0.3	0.3	0.3	0.3	0.3	..
Norway	2.8	2.6	2.9	3.0	3.0	2.8	2.8	3.1
Panama	1.0	1.1	..	..	..	..	..	0.6
Paraguay	..	0.1	..	0.1	0.0	0.1	0.1	0.1
Peru	0.7	0.8	0.9	0.9	0.8	0.8	0.8	0.9
Poland	2.2	1.9	1.7	1.5	1.3	1.2	1.0	0.9
Portugal	4.0	5.3	5.9	4.7	3.5	3.4	3.8	3.2
Puerto Rico	..	0.4	0.6	0.5	1.2	..	..	..
Russia	..	..	0.2	0.2	0.3	0.4	0.5	0.4
Singapore	4.9	5.3	5.9	6.1	6.4	7.3	..	7.1
Slovak Republic	1.6	1.7	1.6	1.4	..	3.9	..	1.3
Slovenia	1.3	1.3	1.3	1.3	1.2	1.2	1.1	1.1
South Africa	..	11.6	11.8	11.8	11.4	..	..	..
Spain	2.5	2.5	2.4	2.4	2.8	2.5	2.4	2.2
Sri Lanka	..	..	0.3	0.5	..	0.5	0.5	..
Sweden	2.4	2.4	6.0	5.8	5.7	6.2	6.7	6.9
Switzerland	5.0	5.1	5.0	5.0	4.6	4.4	4.3	4.3
Thailand	..	..	..	..	..	..	..	..
Tunisia	..	..	..	..	0.4	0.4	0.5	..
Turkey	0.2	0.2	0.2	0.2	0.2	0.3	0.2	0.3
United Kingdom	9.5	8.0	8.0	7.6	6.1	9.0	9.6	8.9
United States	5.1	4.7	4.5	4.5	4.5	4.4	4.4	4.5
Uruguay	0.5	0.6	0.7	0.8	..	1.1	1.0	1.2
OECD Total	4.8	4.5	4.7	4.6	4.4	4.4	4.4	4.4

.. Not available

Note: Detailed metadata at: *http://metalinks.oecd.org/ins/20210324/7de6*.

1. Information on data for Israel: *http://oe.cd/israel-disclaimer*.

Source: *Insurance activity indicators, OECD Insurance Statistics (database)*

INTERNATIONAL COMPARISONS

Table 18. Penetration (Non-life)

Per cent

	2012	2013	2014	2015	2016	2017	2018	2019
Argentina	1.8	2.0	2.0	2.2	2.1	2.2	2.0	1.8
Australia	2.1	2.2	2.2	2.2	2.1	2.1	2.1	2.2
Austria	3.1	3.1	3.1	3.1	3.0	3.0	3.0	3.1
Belgium	2.8	2.8	2.9	2.8	2.7	2.7	2.7	2.8
Bolivia	0.9	..	..	..	0.9	0.8	0.8	0.8
Brazil	1.0	1.1	1.1	1.1	1.1	1.1	1.1	1.1
Canada	3.3	3.2	3.0	3.2	3.2	3.1	3.1	..
Chile	1.4	1.4	1.4	1.5	1.4	1.4	1.5	1.5
Colombia	1.3	1.3	1.3	1.4	1.4	1.4	1.4	1.4
Costa Rica	1.8	1.8	2.0	1.7	1.8	1.9	1.9	1.9
Cuba	..	..	..	..	..	..	..	..
Czech Republic	1.9	2.0	1.9	1.9	1.8	1.7	1.7	1.9
Denmark	3.1	3.0	3.3	3.2	3.1	3.2	3.1	3.0
Dominican Republic	..	..	..	..	..	..	1.2	..
Ecuador	..	..	..	1.8	1.6	1.1	1.1	1.2
Egypt	..	..	..	..	..	0.4	0.4	0.3
El Salvador	..	..	..	..	..	..	1.8	1.8
Estonia	1.8	2.2	2.2	2.3	2.4	2.5	2.7	2.6
Finland	1.7	2.0	2.1	2.1	2.0	1.9	..	..
France	3.2	3.2	3.2	3.2	4.5	4.5	4.5	4.5
Germany	3.6	3.6	3.5	3.4	3.5	3.7	3.7	3.7
Greece	1.3	1.3	1.1	1.0	1.0	1.0	1.0	1.0
Guatemala	0.9	1.0	1.0	1.0	1.0	1.0	0.9	0.9
Honduras	1.0	1.0	1.2	1.2	..	..	1.8	1.7
Hong Kong, China	1.4	1.5	1.4	1.5	1.4	1.4	1.4	..
Hungary	1.2	1.2	1.1	1.2	1.2	1.2	1.3	1.3
India	..	..	..	0.7	0.9	0.9	..	..
Indonesia	0.4	0.5	0.5	0.5	0.5	0.5	0.5	0.5
Iceland	2.5	2.3	2.2	2.2	2.1	2.2	2.3	2.3
Ireland	3.8	3.5	3.4	3.3	5.4	2.7	2.4	2.7
Israel[1]	2.3	2.2	2.2	2.2	2.2	2.3	2.3	2.2
Italy	2.2	2.1	2.0	1.9	1.9	1.9	1.9	1.9
Japan	..	..	..	..	1.7	1.6	1.7	1.7
Korea	4.7	4.5	4.9	4.8	4.9	4.8	4.7	..
Latvia	1.7	1.7	1.7	1.7	1.6	1.9	2.1	2.1
Lithuania	1.1	1.1	1.1	1.1	1.2	1.3	1.4	1.4
Luxembourg	2.9	3.2	2.7	2.8	2.8	3.1	2.8	3.3
Malaysia	1.7	1.7	1.7	1.7	1.6	1.4	1.4	1.4
Mexico	1.0	1.1	1.1	1.1	1.2	1.3	1.2	1.3
Morocco	..	..	..	..	..	2.0	2.1	..
Netherlands	3.1	3.0	2.8	2.7	7.9	7.7	7.8	7.7
New Zealand	2.6	2.7	2.7	2.5	2.5	2.4	..	2.7
Nicaragua	1.1	1.2	1.2	1.2	1.3	1.3	1.4	..
Norway	2.3	2.2	2.4	2.4	2.6	2.3	2.2	2.4
Panama	1.6	1.6	..	..	..	..	..	1.7
Paraguay	0.5	0.8	..	0.9	1.0	0.9	0.9	0.9
Peru	0.8	0.9	0.9	1.0	0.9	0.9	0.9	0.9
Poland	1.6	1.6	1.5	1.4	1.6	1.8	1.8	1.8
Portugal	2.0	2.0	1.9	2.0	2.1	2.1	2.0	2.1
Puerto Rico	..	8.9	8.3	10.2	11.6	..	..	..
Russia	..	..	0.8	1.1	1.1	1.0	1.0	1.0
Singapore	1.8	1.8	1.9	1.8	1.8	1.7	..	1.9
Slovak Republic	1.3	1.3	1.3	1.3	..	1.4	..	1.4
Slovenia	4.0	3.8	3.7	3.6	3.5	3.5	3.5	3.7
South Africa	..	2.8	2.5	2.7	2.5	..	..	..
Spain	2.8	2.8	2.7	2.7	2.7	2.7	2.7	2.7
Sri Lanka	..	..	0.6	0.6	..	0.7	0.7	..
Sweden	1.8	1.9	2.3	1.9	1.7	1.7	1.9	2.0
Switzerland	4.1	4.1	4.0	4.1	4.1	4.1	4.1	4.1
Thailand	..	..	..	..	..	..	..	..
Tunisia	..	..	..	..	1.6	1.7	1.6	..
Turkey	1.1	1.1	1.1	1.2	1.3	1.2	1.1	1.1
United Kingdom	3.0	3.0	2.8	2.6	3.5	3.6	3.6	3.0
United States	6.0	6.1	6.4	6.6	6.7	6.8	6.8	7.0
Uruguay	1.5	1.5	1.6	1.6	..	1.5	1.5	1.5
OECD Total	4.0	4.0	4.1	4.4	4.4	4.4	4.5	4.6

.. Not available

Note: Detailed metadata at: *http://metalinks.oecd.org/ins/20210324/7de6*.

1. Information on data for Israel: *http://oe.cd/israel-disclaimer*.

Source: *Insurance activity indicators, OECD Insurance Statistics (database)*

Table 19. Life insurance share

Percentage of total insurance

Per cent

	2012	2013	2014	2015	2016	2017	2018	2019
Argentina	20.7	17.8	16.5	15.3	16.0	14.7	14.3	13.6
Australia	53.6	54.9	61.1	59.2	55.4	52.1	49.5	43.2
Austria	..	34.1	35.5	35.3	32.5	31.7	29.9	28.8
Belgium	64.7	57.7	56.5	55.4	54.4	53.7	54.7	51.7
Bolivia	21.8	..	..	..	33.5	40.4	43.3	44.9
Brazil	..	..	60.2	62.7	66.1	66.5	66.6	69.4
Canada	32.1	32.9	28.7	28.7	29.1	29.5	30.1	..
Chile	65.5	66.5	65.8	68.3	70.4	69.4	68.8	67.0
Colombia	46.9	51.1	47.5	46.6	48.2	50.9	50.1	50.6
Costa Rica	11.9	13.4	12.3	12.7	15.4	14.7	16.1	16.0
Cuba	..	..	..	..	..	..	..	..
Czech Republic	46.9	45.7	45.1	41.1	40.6	38.3	36.6	32.1
Denmark	68.7	95.4	67.7	68.9	68.7	69.1	70.0	71.3
Dominican Republic	..	..	..	..	..	..	16.1	..
Ecuador	..	..	..	19.5	22.0	..	..	29.1
Egypt	..	..	..	..	..	..	..	43.7
El Salvador	22.7	26.7	25.7	25.6	24.7	..	25.1	25.6
Estonia	33.9	29.3	30.3	31.2	30.0	27.3	25.2	25.7
Finland	51.2	56.8	57.4	58.3	50.6	50.7	100.0	100.0
France	62.1	62.4	64.2	64.2	58.0	55.2	55.2	55.8
Germany	35.5	36.0	35.9	34.0	33.1	32.1	31.8	32.7
Greece	43.2	41.4	49.5	50.5	47.2	50.4	49.5	50.9
Guatemala	20.3	19.9	20.8	19.4	19.9	20.5	20.5	21.2
Honduras	..	30.9	35.3	36.4	..	..	33.3	32.2
Hong Kong, China	84.7	85.7	86.9	87.6	90.1	90.4	90.1	..
Hungary	53.0	54.5	54.8	51.1	49.5	48.2	46.2	44.3
India	..	..	..	78.2	..	70.7	..	..
Indonesia	70.6	67.9	66.2	69.0	72.6	74.6	72.9	70.5
Iceland	7.3	7.9	8.2	8.4	8.8	8.9	8.3	8.3
Ireland	80.3	80.6	82.2	79.6	68.5	79.5	75.4	72.0
Israel[1]	52.9	52.9	51.7	53.6	52.7	53.8	54.0	54.9
Italy	66.5	71.4	76.8	77.8	75.8	75.0	74.7	75.1
Japan	100.0	100.0	100.0	100.0	75.5	75.1	75.2	73.2
Korea	59.0	59.3	56.8	57.1	56.3	53.9	53.2	..
Latvia	17.6	18.9	20.6	21.6	23.2	22.5	19.2	26.6
Lithuania	32.0	32.0	35.8	36.6	34.7	29.2	28.3	28.6
Luxembourg	93.4	91.9	93.9	92.3	91.5	91.8	91.8	90.7
Malaysia	60.6	60.1	60.2	60.6	61.7	63.4	64.1	65.8
Mexico	46.2	46.1	46.8	46.3	46.7	43.0	44.9	45.0
Morocco	..	..	..	..	..	..	..	..
Netherlands	47.6	47.4	47.7	43.6	19.6	18.2	16.2	..
New Zealand	..	..	..	..	..	..	..	23.6
Nicaragua	15.8	17.2	17.8	17.4	18.6	..	20.4	..
Norway	54.6	54.2	55.3	55.1	55.4	55.4	55.9	56.0
Panama	38.5	39.7	..	..	..	..	..	25.1
Paraguay	..	12.2	..	13.3	0.2	13.9	..	13.3
Peru	47.2	46.8	49.1	48.4	45.3	47.0	48.5	48.8
Poland	58.1	54.0	52.2	50.2	42.6	39.4	34.9	32.3
Portugal	63.3	70.5	72.9	67.5	59.6	58.6	61.8	56.7
Puerto Rico	..	4.3	6.3	4.9	9.5	..	..	..
Russia	..	..	12.6	13.9	20.4	27.4	32.0	28.9
Singapore	65.8	67.9	68.5	69.3	71.6	74.9	..	68.8
Slovak Republic	53.9	55.5	54.3	51.2	..	73.6	..	48.6
Slovenia	22.1	22.4	22.9	23.1	22.5	22.4	21.7	20.8
South Africa	79.2	78.6	80.5	79.9	79.7	..	..	..
Spain	46.4	44.6	43.9	43.6	47.1	44.8	43.6	41.5
Sri Lanka	..	..	35.5	42.5	..	41.4	41.3	..
Sweden	54.0	52.2	69.6	73.3	74.9	76.1	75.6	75.6
Switzerland	47.9	48.2	48.5	48.9	46.9	45.0	44.4	43.7
Thailand	..	..	..	..	..	..	..	..
Tunisia	..	..	..	..	20.3	19.7	..	..
Turkey	15.4	15.7	12.3	11.8	14.9	17.3	15.9	20.1
United Kingdom	75.4	72.4	73.4	73.3	68.8	68.3	71.7	71.9
United States	40.3	38.5	36.2	37.1	35.9	35.6	43.3	42.6
Uruguay	26.4	28.7	29.5	33.4	..	42.2	..	44.1
OECD Total	53.2	52.7	50.2	49.2	46.5	45.4	50.2	49.9

.. Not available

Note: Detailed metadata at: *http://metalinks.oecd.org/ins/20210324/7de6.*

1. Information on data for Israel: *http://oe.cd/israel-disclaimer.*

Source: *Insurance activity indicators, OECD Insurance Statistics (database)*

Table 20. Direct total gross premiums per insurance company employee

US dollars

	2012	2013	2014	2015	2016	2017	2018	2019
Argentina	..	289 071	296 157	290 581	..	264 715	291 050	165 282
Australia	..	..	..	..	..	..	..	..
Austria	765 392	795 367	816 717	688 586	660 884	676 184	729 985	704 559
Belgium	..	..	..	..	..	..	..	..
Bolivia	..	..	..	..	112 942	99 464	101 913	106 567
Brazil	..	..	..	..	..	..	..	..
Canada	..	..	..	..	..	..	..	..
Chile	486 192	493 638	454 677	495 261	510 666	519 672	558 276	512 932
Colombia	..	..	502 752	375 951	347 555	..	..	..
Costa Rica	..	..	..	..	..	..	..	..
Cuba	..	..	..	..	..	..	..	..
Czech Republic	..	..	..	..	..	..	..	..
Denmark	2 052 306	2 215 121	2 158 639	1 927 585	2 018 459	2 661 767	3 419 049	2 616 680
Dominican Republic	..	..	..	..	..	..	..	..
Ecuador	..	..	..	2 202 989	292 344	..	..	..
Egypt	..	..	..	..	..	..	..	40 536
El Salvador	..	..	..	..	..	..	195 773	..
Estonia	224 236	200 224	221 998	200 416	..	..	..	..
Finland	949 631	1 363 735	1 514 861	1 311 479	1 088 453	1 237 491	633 977	965 645
France	..	..	..	..	..	..	..	..
Germany	1 508 895	1 607 786	1 649 160	1 371 091	1 367 654	1 520 578	1 653 171	1 701 918
Greece	..	..	..	..	..	..	..	..
Guatemala	137 904	..	159 900	..	181 604	186 479	185 720	189 576
Honduras	..	267 721	183 148	217 165	..	..	1 497 747	1 768 927
Hong Kong, China	..	..	..	..	..	617 084	632 451	..
Hungary	143 598	157 425	161 509	147 122	169 626	168 073	197 023	177 672
India	..	..	..	..	..	32 479	..	..
Indonesia	23 320	..	..	..	..	..	..	..
Iceland	..	665 881	731 603	703 782	..	..	..	..
Ireland	5 145 784	5 005 661	..	..	..	..	..	..
Israel[1]	..	..	..	..	..	..	..	..
Italy	516 300	588 605	729 106	622 717	585 098	..	..	..
Japan	..	129 385	130 139	144 659	..	1 060 963	..	..
Korea	442 456	466 422	580 368	591 071	610 886	638 233	628 010	..
Latvia	144 559	198 764	237 445	301 825	..	..	..	..
Lithuania	116 317	128 847	136 520	120 842	130 040	147 705	172 038	179 804
Luxembourg	1 776 184	1 556 437	4 328 321	2 997 287	2 886 004	3 019 973	2 823 429	2 443 072
Malaysia	567 984	651 774	650 745	461 454	465 847	435 343	475 776	493 540
Mexico	457 259	436 528	403 458	330 532	410 335	423 179	..	..
Morocco	..	..	..	..	..	..	..	..
Netherlands	..	..	..	..	..	..	..	..
New Zealand	425 805	473 708	..	..	..	..	..	..
Nicaragua	..	1 704 849	119 312	2 050 664	..	..	..	..
Norway	..	..	..	..	..	..	..	..
Panama	347 935	392 524	..	..	..	..	..	243 877
Paraguay	104 274	382 149	..	124 344	..	..	..	..
Peru	251 417	285 142	301 442	290 594	..	..	295 065	306 299
Poland	198 127	169 341	183 458	167 678	..	..	..	..
Portugal	389 138	490 972	551 505	416 277	371 983	413 352	506 932	493 481
Puerto Rico	..	780 437	704 962	856 812	1 042 984	..	..	..
Russia	..	..	73 609	..	61 185	121 961	89 910	72 008 946
Singapore	..	..	..	..	..	..	..	..
Slovak Republic	378 453	..	403 610	..	..	..	..	..
Slovenia	..	..	..	..	..	..	..	..
South Africa	..	..	..	..	..	..	..	..
Spain	..	424 700	403 450	..	..	..	..	..
Sri Lanka	..	..	24 436	26 631	..	17 383	17 439	..
Sweden	1 073 328	1 210 867	2 042 276	1 771 433	..	1 686 900	1 927 908	2 031 531
Switzerland	..	..	..	..	..	..	..	..
Thailand	..	..	..	..	..	..	..	..
Tunisia	..	..	..	..	173 680	..	..	..
Turkey	322 731	379 315	335 385	298 749	233 812	204 510	261 141	201 229
United Kingdom	..	..	..	..	..	..	..	..
United States	..	..	..	..	..	..	..	..
Uruguay	..	..	..	..	..	..	..	..
OECD Total	665 094	318 545	333 913	333 824	710 683	919 678	960 372	1 188 148

.. Not available

Note: Detailed metadata at: *http://metalinks.oecd.org/ins/20210324/7de6*.

1. Information on data for Israel: *http://oe.cd/israel-disclaimer*.

Source: *Insurance activity indicators, OECD Insurance Statistics (database)*

Table 21. Retention ratio (Life and Non-life)

Per cent

	2012	2013	2014	2015	2016	2017	2018	2019
Argentina	88.9	90.6	86.5	87.5	88.4	88.7	89.3	87.3
Australia	84.1	84.5	86.0	83.8	80.4	77.1	77.9	74.1
Austria	..	81.3	83.6	84.2	81.1	82.7	87.2	86.4
Belgium	92.6	91.2	88.7	88.5	87.2	87.5	87.2	76.2
Bolivia	50.3	..	..	..	49.8	51.5	54.9	53.9
Brazil	..	..	95.2	95.4	95.8	95.7	95.6	95.5
Canada	73.3	73.1	73.5	71.4	74.0	72.4	79.1	..
Chile	83.1	84.4	84.0	84.8	84.4	83.4	84.1	82.8
Colombia	81.3	82.9	82.5	81.5	80.1	81.6	81.1	80.4
Costa Rica	80.9	78.6	80.2	77.9	78.9	79.4	77.5	78.3
Cuba	..	..	..	..	..	..	..	..
Czech Republic	81.3	80.6	80.3	79.3	78.9	78.7	79.0	79.4
Denmark	96.3	99.4	97.2	97.1	96.9	96.7	97.2	97.8
Dominican Republic	..	..	..	..	..	..	69.1	..
Ecuador	..	..	..	72.4	72.3	..	..	67.0
Egypt	..	..	..	..	..	..	..	62.0
El Salvador	62.0	66.6	66.6	66.5	64.2	..	63.7	63.0
Estonia	..	..	..	..	..	..	..	..
Finland	96.7	97.4	97.6	97.7	97.3	97.4	99.5	99.5
France	89.2	89.3	91.0	88.6	84.8	88.0	87.7	87.0
Germany	90.2	89.7	89.0	87.7	87.9	87.5	86.1	86.4
Greece	88.1	79.8	87.6	87.2	88.8	89.2	88.7	89.6
Guatemala	68.0	66.3	64.2	64.9	67.8	67.2	65.2	65.6
Honduras	..	55.7	54.4	53.0	..	..	58.7	63.1
Hong Kong, China	87.6	87.0	87.7	88.3	90.4	90.4	90.7	..
Hungary	83.3	86.1	86.1	86.1	86.7	87.4	87.6	87.9
India	..	..	..	95.2	..	91.8	..	..
Indonesia	86.2	85.5	83.8	84.8	86.0	87.3	86.8	85.6
Iceland	93.3	93.9	94.4	94.8	95.4	96.0	95.9	96.3
Ireland	88.4	87.8	89.2	88.0	79.6	..	..	..
Israel[1]	85.7	87.3	88.5	88.4	84.9	86.5	85.8	85.3
Italy	95.1	96.2	97.1	97.2	96.4	96.3	96.2	96.5
Japan	94.1	94.9	94.3	94.6	89.5	89.8	88.8	85.1
Korea	95.0	94.7	94.7	94.7	94.7	94.3	94.0	..
Latvia	94.2	96.3	96.3	95.9	95.3	93.2	89.8	90.3
Lithuania	..	..	95.2	95.1	95.0	91.5	90.4	90.9
Luxembourg	68.6	74.9	71.8	84.1	82.2	85.8	76.8	73.0
Malaysia	86.9	87.8	87.8	87.9	88.3	88.6	89.2	89.9
Mexico	83.8	82.6	83.9	83.0	84.4	81.4	83.2	81.3
Morocco	..	..	..	..	..	..	..	..
Netherlands	92.0	92.3	89.4	91.7	98.3	97.6	98.0	..
New Zealand	112.4	107.9	111.2	112.7	107.0	106.8	..	70.3
Nicaragua	62.0	63.8	63.3	65.7	66.7	..	60.9	..
Norway	93.0	92.9	93.1	92.2	92.7	93.0	93.3	93.7
Panama	57.4	55.6	..	..	..	..	..	63.4
Paraguay	102.3	79.1	..	79.6	78.0	77.4	..	74.2
Peru	76.7	76.7	75.5	74.5	73.3	75.0	76.3	77.0
Poland	92.7	92.7	92.4	90.5	87.9	88.4	88.4	87.6
Portugal	89.6	91.1	92.0	90.5	88.9	88.6	89.4	86.3
Puerto Rico	..	99.6	98.6	92.9	93.9	..	..	..
Russia	..	..	86.9	88.6	88.9	91.7	92.4	91.9
Singapore	85.5	85.9	86.8	79.2	77.6	77.0	..	74.2
Slovak Republic	85.6	85.8	85.3	84.5	..	92.2	..	85.5
Slovenia	87.1	87.8	86.9	88.1	87.7	86.5	86.8	85.8
South Africa	90.9	87.6	88.2	89.7	88.9	..	..	..
Spain	92.5	90.0	91.3	91.3	91.0	90.6	91.0	89.6
Sri Lanka	..	..	87.0	86.6	..	85.6	87.9	..
Sweden	92.2	92.7	95.6	97.0	97.3	97.2	97.4	96.9
Switzerland	92.5	92.6	92.9	93.1	93.7	92.6	92.6	92.3
Thailand	..	..	..	..	..	..	..	..
Tunisia	..	..	..	..	80.9	100.0	..	..
Turkey	77.9	75.6	75.0	74.8	76.1	72.0	70.9	71.5
United Kingdom	87.7	87.4	84.8	89.0	77.0	87.9	80.6	80.5
United States	73.6	71.3	74.9	72.8	72.5	71.4	83.7	84.4
Uruguay	91.0	91.2	90.8	91.5	..	92.9	..	91.9
OECD Total	82.1	81.5	82.5	80.7	79.4	79.6	85.6	85.0

.. Not available

Note: Detailed metadata at: *http://metalinks.oecd.org/ins/20210324/7de6*.

1. Information on data for Israel: *http://oe.cd/israel-disclaimer*.

Source: *Insurance activity indicators, OECD Insurance Statistics (database)*

INTERNATIONAL COMPARISONS

Table 22. Retention ratio (Life)

Per cent

	2012	2013	2014	2015	2016	2017	2018	2019
Argentina	92.7	96.6	97.1	97.2	96.7	96.8	96.8	95.7
Australia	92.1	92.3	92.5	91.3	89.3	82.5	84.2	76.5
Austria	..	96.7	97.4	97.6	97.4	97.8	97.8	97.8
Belgium	97.7	97.0	97.6	97.9	96.7	98.0	97.7	96.9
Bolivia	79.5	..	..	..	64.6	63.7	71.9	68.2
Brazil	..	..	99.6	99.5	99.6	99.5	99.6	99.6
Canada	73.9	75.2	69.5	67.6	72.1	72.9	75.4	..
Chile	97.4	98.0	97.7	97.5	95.0	92.6	93.3	93.1
Colombia	93.7	94.4	94.2	94.7	93.9	92.8	92.0	91.2
Costa Rica	90.8	84.7	87.4	81.4	82.8	81.4	79.0	80.5
Cuba	..	..	..	..	..	..	..	..
Czech Republic	95.0	93.9	93.0	92.4	92.3	91.7	91.4	95.3
Denmark	99.7	100.0	99.8	99.8	99.8	99.8	99.9	99.9
Dominican Republic	..	..	..	..	..	..	76.5	..
Ecuador	..	..	..	81.6	99.2	..	..	99.0
Egypt	..	..	..	..	..	..	..	64.7
El Salvador	81.1	95.0	87.3	81.6	80.8	..	78.2	76.6
Estonia	..	..	..	..	..	..	..	..
Finland	99.0	99.4	99.5	99.5	99.3	99.4	99.5	99.5
France	92.9	92.5	94.1	90.7	86.5	93.2	93.9	93.1
Germany	96.9	96.8	97.0	97.0	96.6	97.0	96.2	97.3
Greece	95.1	94.8	95.6	95.9	96.2	95.0	95.1	95.7
Guatemala	76.6	75.3	76.6	76.9	80.9	79.9	78.1	79.2
Honduras	..	61.1	45.4	56.1	..	..	56.0	60.3
Hong Kong, China	91.0	90.0	90.5	91.0	92.8	92.7	93.4	..
Hungary	93.6	95.0	96.3	96.8	97.3	98.7	99.1	99.1
India	..	..	..	99.6	..	99.5	..	..
Indonesia	97.3	97.2	96.7	96.8	97.3	97.4	97.1	96.8
Iceland	82.5	83.9	82.3	83.7	85.2	85.9	85.0	85.6
Ireland	94.4	93.7	94.0	94.1	94.9	..	..	..
Israel[1]	95.2	95.3	95.2	95.5	95.1	95.2	95.4	95.8
Italy	98.3	98.8	99.0	99.1	99.1	99.1	99.1	99.5
Japan	94.1	94.9	94.3	94.6	93.1	93.6	92.7	88.2
Korea	98.8	98.8	98.8	98.7	98.6	98.4	98.4	..
Latvia	99.7	99.8	99.8	99.8	99.8	99.8	99.8	99.2
Lithuania	..	..	98.5	98.0	98.5	98.3	97.8	98.5
Luxembourg	68.9	76.4	72.1	85.3	83.6	87.4	77.4	73.5
Malaysia	96.7	97.3	96.9	96.7	96.6	95.9	96.0	95.8
Mexico	94.8	95.3	96.6	96.4	96.2	95.4	95.4	95.5
Morocco	..	..	..	..	..	..	..	..
Netherlands	94.9	95.4	89.6	94.0	97.2	96.4	97.7	..
New Zealand	..	..	..	..	..	..	..	60.6
Nicaragua	63.7	60.3	55.3	59.2	58.2	..	62.4	..
Norway	98.6	98.8	98.9	98.7	98.9	98.9	99.1	99.3
Panama	80.4	77.7	..	..	..	..	..	49.0
Paraguay	..	80.7	..	81.7	41.0	83.0	..	80.0
Peru	88.8	89.5	84.4	84.7	82.4	83.7	85.0	86.9
Poland	97.6	98.6	98.5	98.2	98.3	99.4	98.7	98.4
Portugal	96.4	97.0	97.7	97.2	96.5	96.5	96.9	96.5
Puerto Rico	..	103.3	100.0	56.0	78.0	..	..	..
Russia	..	..	98.4	98.6	98.8	99.2	99.3	99.3
Singapore	96.6	95.1	96.1	88.4	84.3	82.3	..	79.0
Slovak Republic	98.4	98.4	98.2	97.9	..	99.0	..	95.5
Slovenia	97.5	97.2	96.9	96.7	96.3	96.4	96.4	96.3
South Africa	94.9	92.5	93.2	95.2	94.6	..	..	..
Spain	94.7	93.9	96.4	96.8	97.3	96.2	97.1	97.0
Sri Lanka	..	..	96.3	96.3	..	96.0	99.5	..
Sweden	99.1	98.7	99.6	99.8	99.9	99.7	99.8	99.7
Switzerland	99.4	99.3	99.4	99.4	99.3	99.3	98.8	99.4
Thailand	..	..	..	..	..	..	..	..
Tunisia	..	..	..	..	90.4	100.0	..	..
Turkey	95.1	95.7	94.8	95.1	95.8	96.2	95.5	96.0
United Kingdom	89.0	88.9	85.4	91.2	80.3	95.3	84.5	84.3
United States	83.5	77.4	88.3	80.4	80.0	77.8	75.2	78.6
Uruguay	97.0	97.5	97.6	97.6	..	97.4	..	97.5
OECD Total	89.8	88.7	91.6	88.6	86.7	87.6	84.9	85.1

.. Not available

Note: Detailed metadata at: *http://metalinks.oecd.org/ins/20210324/7de6.*

1. Information on data for Israel: *http://oe.cd/israel-disclaimer.*

Source: *Insurance activity indicators, OECD Insurance Statistics (database)*

INTERNATIONAL COMPARISONS

Table 23. Retention ratio (Non-life)

Per cent

	2012	2013	2014	2015	2016	2017	2018	2019
Argentina	87.9	89.3	84.4	85.7	86.8	87.3	88.0	86.0
Australia	74.9	75.0	75.7	73.0	69.3	71.3	71.8	72.3
Austria	..	73.2	76.0	77.0	73.3	75.8	82.7	81.7
Belgium	83.2	83.4	77.2	76.8	75.8	75.4	74.5	54.0
Bolivia	42.2	..	..	..	42.4	43.1	41.9	42.3
Brazil	..	..	88.5	88.5	88.4	88.3	87.7	86.4
Canada	73.0	72.1	75.2	72.9	74.7	72.2	80.6	..
Chile	55.9	57.6	57.7	57.4	59.1	62.7	63.8	61.8
Colombia	70.3	70.8	72.0	69.9	67.3	70.1	70.2	69.3
Costa Rica	79.5	77.6	79.2	77.3	78.2	79.0	77.2	77.8
Cuba	..	..	..	..	..	..	..	..
Czech Republic	69.2	69.4	69.8	70.2	69.8	70.6	71.9	72.0
Denmark	88.9	88.1	91.7	91.1	90.6	89.9	91.1	92.5
Dominican Republic	..	..	..	..	..	..	67.7	..
Ecuador	..	..	..	70.1	64.7	..	..	53.8
Egypt	..	..	..	..	..	..	..	59.8
El Salvador	56.3	56.2	58.4	60.1	57.1	..	58.8	58.4
Estonia	..	..	..	..	..	..	..	..
Finland	94.3	94.7	95.0	95.2	95.3	95.4	..	..
France	83.2	84.1	85.3	84.8	82.4	81.7	80.1	79.2
Germany	86.5	85.7	84.6	82.9	83.7	83.0	81.3	81.1
Greece	82.9	69.1	79.8	78.3	82.2	83.3	82.5	83.2
Guatemala	65.9	64.0	61.0	62.0	64.5	63.9	61.8	62.0
Honduras	..	53.3	59.3	51.3	..	..	60.1	64.4
Hong Kong, China	68.7	69.3	69.0	69.8	68.9	68.7	65.8	..
Hungary	71.6	75.3	73.6	75.0	76.2	76.9	77.7	79.0
India	..	..	..	79.5	..	73.1	..	..
Indonesia	59.4	60.8	58.4	58.3	55.7	57.6	58.9	58.8
Iceland	94.2	94.7	95.5	95.8	96.3	97.0	96.9	97.2
Ireland	64.1	63.1	67.1	64.1	46.3	..	..	..
Israel[1]	75.0	78.2	81.2	80.2	73.6	76.4	74.6	72.6
Italy	89.0	89.9	90.5	90.6	87.9	87.8	87.6	87.3
Japan	..	..	..	..	78.4	78.2	76.9	76.6
Korea	89.5	88.6	89.5	89.4	89.8	89.5	88.9	..
Latvia	93.0	95.5	95.4	94.8	93.9	91.3	87.4	87.1
Lithuania	..	..	93.3	93.4	93.0	88.6	87.5	87.9
Luxembourg	64.3	58.5	65.9	68.9	66.7	67.7	69.2	68.3
Malaysia	71.8	73.6	74.0	74.4	74.9	76.0	77.0	78.4
Mexico	74.4	71.7	72.8	71.5	74.0	70.8	73.2	69.7
Morocco	..	..	..	..	..	..	..	..
Netherlands	89.4	89.5	89.2	89.9	98.5	98.1	98.3	..
New Zealand	78.7	77.5	80.0	80.5	73.8	74.4	..	73.4
Nicaragua	61.7	64.6	65.0	67.0	68.7	..	60.5	..
Norway	86.2	85.9	85.9	84.3	85.0	85.5	86.0	86.5
Panama	43.0	41.0	..	..	..	..	..	68.2
Paraguay	71.2	78.9	..	79.3	78.0	76.5	..	73.3
Peru	65.8	65.5	67.0	65.0	65.7	67.3	68.1	67.4
Poland	85.9	85.8	85.8	82.8	80.2	81.3	82.8	82.4
Portugal	77.9	76.9	76.8	76.6	77.7	77.4	77.1	72.8
Puerto Rico	..	99.5	98.5	94.8	95.5	..	..	..
Russia	..	..	82.0	87.0	86.4	88.9	89.2	88.9
Singapore	64.2	66.5	66.5	58.4	60.9	61.0	..	63.5
Slovak Republic	70.7	70.1	69.9	70.4	..	73.3	..	76.1
Slovenia	84.2	85.1	84.0	85.5	85.2	83.6	84.2	83.0
South Africa	75.7	69.8	67.7	68.0	66.8	..	..	..
Spain	90.5	86.8	87.3	87.0	85.3	86.0	86.2	84.3
Sri Lanka	..	..	81.9	79.4	..	78.3	79.8	..
Sweden	84.0	86.1	86.5	89.3	89.5	89.1	89.9	88.2
Switzerland	86.1	86.4	86.7	87.0	88.8	87.1	87.5	86.7
Thailand	..	..	..	..	..	..	..	..
Tunisia	..	..	..	..	78.6	100.0	..	..
Turkey	74.8	71.9	72.2	72.1	72.7	66.9	66.2	65.3
United Kingdom	83.8	83.4	83.2	82.8	69.5	72.0	70.7	70.5
United States	66.9	67.4	67.3	68.2	68.3	67.9	90.1	88.8
Uruguay	88.9	88.7	87.9	88.4	..	89.7	..	87.4
OECD Total	73.3	73.5	73.4	73.0	73.0	72.9	86.3	85.0

.. Not available

Note: Detailed metadata at: *http://metalinks.oecd.org/ins/20210324/7de6*.

1. Information on data for Israel: *http://oe.cd/israel-disclaimer*.

Source: *Insurance activity indicators, OECD Insurance Statistics (database)*

Table 24. Ratio of reinsurance accepted (Life and Non-life)

Per cent

	2012	2013	2014	2015	2016	2017	2018	2019
Argentina	0.5	0.3	7.2	7.0	6.7	6.6	5.5	5.5
Australia	11.1	10.9	10.1	10.9	12.5	13.0	14.3	16.1
Austria	..	12.0	9.6	8.9	9.3	6.4	7.2	6.8
Belgium	2.7	3.2	3.5	3.0	2.9	2.3	1.8	7.0
Bolivia	0.6	..	..	..	1.0	3.9	3.3	6.1
Brazil	..	..	0.0	0.0	0.0	0.0	0.0	0.0
Canada	8.5	9.7	17.7	17.6	15.6	16.1	11.3	..
Chile	0.5	0.5	0.6	0.8	1.1	0.9	0.9	1.0
Colombia	1.1	1.3	1.9	2.0	1.8	1.9	2.0	2.0
Costa Rica	0.2	0.3	0.3	0.3	0.3	0.3	0.3	0.4
Cuba	..	..	..	..	..	..	..	..
Czech Republic	1.9	1.8	1.6	2.0	2.4	2.5	2.1	2.2
Denmark	0.8	84.9	0.8	0.8	2.9	3.3	3.5	2.4
Dominican Republic	..	..	..	..	..	..	..	..
Ecuador	..	..	..	2.0	1.7	..	..	0.6
Egypt	..	..	..	..	..	..	..	4.9
El Salvador	..	..	..	..	..	..	5.1	5.5
Estonia	..	..	..	..	..	..	0.0	0.0
Finland	1.9	1.5	1.4	1.3	1.5	1.6	0.0	0.1
France	10.7	10.1	10.5	8.9	15.7	12.7	12.7	12.8
Germany	23.2	22.4	22.4	24.6	24.5	24.6	24.7	25.4
Greece	2.0	2.3	1.2	1.1	1.0	0.9	0.9	0.9
Guatemala	2.9	2.7	2.7	3.1	2.9	2.9	3.4	2.8
Honduras	..	0.0	0.0	0.0	..	..	..	0.0
Hong Kong, China	4.9	4.7	4.8	4.5	4.8	4.7	4.6	..
Hungary	1.0	1.3	0.9	1.0	1.0	1.5	1.1	1.0
India	..	..	..	0.7	..	5.8	..	..
Indonesia	4.2	4.9	2.5	2.1	2.0	1.8	1.8	2.2
Iceland	2.3	2.3	2.5	2.4	1.7	1.4	1.7	1.7
Ireland	2.0	1.8	1.9	1.9	2.2	1.2	3.0	5.8
Israel[1]	..	..	..	..	0.0	..	..	..
Italy	2.5	2.4	1.8	1.8	2.1	2.1	2.3	1.0
Japan	9.9	7.4	5.5	4.1	6.5	6.0	5.5	5.5
Korea	4.9	5.2	5.0	5.1	5.2	5.6	6.2	..
Latvia	1.4	0.0	0.0	0.0	0.0	0.0	0.0	0.1
Lithuania	0.1	0.1	0.0	0.0	0.0	0.0	0.0	0.0
Luxembourg	1.3	0.9	1.2	0.8	0.3	0.2	0.2	5.6
Malaysia	7.1	7.4	7.5	7.7	7.7	7.2	6.7	6.5
Mexico	1.8	1.7	1.8	1.7	1.6	1.7	1.7	1.8
Morocco	..	..	..	..	..	..	..	..
Netherlands	1.4	1.5	1.5	1.7	0.5	1.8	1.8	..
New Zealand	1.3	0.6	0.6	3.8	1.8	5.3	..	0.1
Nicaragua	..	0.0	..	..	..	..	..	..
Norway	..	..	..	..	..	..	..	..
Panama	6.7	6.2	..	..	..	..	..	8.2
Paraguay	2.0	1.5	..	1.1	1.0	0.7	..	0.4
Peru	1.4	1.0	0.7	0.6	0.6	0.7	0.6	0.8
Poland	1.0	1.2	1.0	2.7	3.5	3.2	3.7	4.5
Portugal	4.1	3.5	3.3	3.9	5.1	5.3	5.3	5.5
Puerto Rico	..	0.5	0.9	0.8	0.6	..	..	..
Russia	..	..	3.5	2.8	3.0	2.7	2.9	3.4
Singapore	20.6	19.6	19.2	19.7	21.7	17.6	..	26.8
Slovak Republic	1.0	0.9	1.4	2.0	..	0.2	..	0.0
Slovenia	12.3	11.3	11.3	12.5	12.1	12.1	11.7	12.2
South Africa	..	2.3	2.3	2.2	2.9	..	..	..
Spain	2.6	7.7	7.8	8.2	8.2	8.1	7.8	8.1
Sri Lanka	..	..	2.2	1.5	..	2.4	2.2	..
Sweden	7.9	6.3	4.1	3.1	3.0	3.1	3.1	3.0
Switzerland	13.5	14.5	13.8	12.7	13.3	14.2	15.0	16.0
Thailand	..	..	..	..	..	..	..	..
Tunisia	..	..	..	..	1.2	5.3	..	..
Turkey	2.9	2.7	5.0	3.1	5.9	6.0	8.5	10.0
United Kingdom	8.1	9.7	9.9	11.1	35.8	14.3	20.4	19.5
United States	20.7	21.5	21.8	22.8	22.3	23.0	11.9	11.2
Uruguay	0.0	0.0	0.0	0.0	..	0.0	..	0.0
OECD Total	14.9	15.4	15.4	16.6	18.4	17.2	11.8	11.8

.. Not available

Note: Detailed metadata at: *http://metalinks.oecd.org/ins/20210324/7de6*.

1. Information on data for Israel: *http://oe.cd/israel-disclaimer*.

Source: *Insurance activity indicators, OECD Insurance Statistics (database)*

Table 25. Ratio of reinsurance accepted (Life)

Per cent

	2012	2013	2014	2015	2016	2017	2018	2019
Argentina	1.1	0.6	3.0	2.3	3.0	2.9	2.8	3.1
Australia	7.6	8.1	7.5	8.4	9.7	12.2	14.3	18.2
Austria	..	0.2	0.2	0.2	0.2	0.2	0.2	0.3
Belgium	0.2	0.4	0.4	0.3	0.4	0.3	0.3	0.5
Bolivia	0.4	..	..	..	0.0	3.3	4.8	6.1
Brazil	..	..	0.0	0.0	0.0	0.0	0.0	0.0
Canada	8.8	9.7	16.6	17.5	15.0	14.4	11.8	..
Chile	0.0	0.0	0.1	0.4	1.0	0.8	0.8	0.9
Colombia	0.1	0.0	0.1	0.1	0.1	0.0	0.0	0.0
Costa Rica	0.1	0.0	0.0	0.0	0.0	0.0	0.0	0.0
Cuba	..	..	..	..	..	..	..	..
Czech Republic	0.0	0.0	0.0	0.0	0.6	0.6	0.7	0.9
Denmark	0.6	89.0	0.5	0.5	0.6	0.4	0.4	0.4
Dominican Republic	..	..	..	..	..	..	..	..
Ecuador	..	..	..	0.6	0.0	..	..	0.0
Egypt	..	..	..	..	..	..	..	0.3
El Salvador	..	..	..	..	..	..	5.0	5.1
Estonia	..	..	..	..	..	..	0.0	0.0
Finland	0.1	0.1	0.2	0.0	0.0	0.0	0.0	0.1
France	9.1	8.0	8.9	6.3	15.5	8.8	8.6	9.6
Germany	0.7	0.7	0.6	0.6	0.6	0.8	0.5	0.5
Greece	0.2	0.2	0.2	0.2	0.1	0.0	0.0	0.0
Guatemala	2.1	1.0	1.6	1.7	1.9	1.4	1.5	0.9
Honduras	..	0.0	0.0	0.0	..	..	..	0.0
Hong Kong, China	1.0	1.1	1.6	1.7	2.8	2.5	2.0	..
Hungary	0.0	0.0	0.0	0.0	0.0	0.0	0.0	0.0
India	..	..	..	0.0	..	0.2	..	..
Indonesia	0.0	0.0	..	..	..	..	..	..
Iceland	0.0	0.0	0.0	0.1	..	0.0	..	..
Ireland	1.2	1.1	1.1	1.2	0.7	0.2	0.1	0.3
Israel[1]	..	..	..	..	0.0	..	..	..
Italy	2.6	1.9	1.3	1.3	1.5	1.5	1.4	0.3
Japan	9.9	7.4	5.5	4.1	3.4	2.6	2.0	1.7
Korea	1.1	1.1	1.1	1.1	1.3	1.4	1.7	..
Latvia	0.0	0.0	0.0	0.0	0.0	0.0	0.0	0.0
Lithuania	0.0	0.0	0.0	0.0	0.0	0.0	0.0	0.0
Luxembourg	1.3	1.0	1.3	0.8	0.4	0.2	0.2	5.2
Malaysia	1.2	1.3	1.4	1.4	1.4	1.6	1.7	1.1
Mexico	0.5	0.6	0.7	0.4	0.5	0.6	0.4	0.6
Morocco	..	..	..	..	..	..	..	..
Netherlands	0.1	0.0	0.0	0.0	0.0	0.1	0.0	..
New Zealand	..	..	..	..	..	..	..	0.2
Nicaragua	..	0.0	..	..	..	..	..	..
Norway	..	..	..	..	..	..	..	..
Panama	5.1	5.5	..	..	..	..	..	5.2
Paraguay	..	0.8	..	0.7	0.0	0.2	..	0.0
Peru	1.6	1.2	0.6	0.5	0.3	0.1	0.0	0.2
Poland	0.1	0.1	0.1	0.1	0.1	0.1	0.0	0.0
Portugal	0.0	0.0	0.0	0.0	0.0	0.0	0.0	0.0
Puerto Rico	..	0.0	0.0	0.0	0.5	..	..	..
Russia	..	..	0.0	0.0	0.0	0.0	0.0	0.1
Singapore	11.8	10.9	10.8	10.4	14.7	11.0	..	16.3
Slovak Republic	0.0	0.0	0.0	0.0	..	0.0	..	0.0
Slovenia	..	..	..	..	..	..	..	..
South Africa	..	0.0	0.0	0.0	0.0	..	..	..
Spain	0.2	1.3	1.6	1.5	1.5	1.4	1.5	1.7
Sri Lanka	..	..	..	0.0	..	0.6	..	..
Sweden	2.3	0.2	0.0	0.0	0.0	0.0	0.0	0.0
Switzerland	1.1	1.5	1.4	1.5	1.7	1.3	1.2	1.2
Thailand	..	..	..	..	..	..	..	..
Tunisia	..	..	..	..	1.5	1.5	..	..
Turkey	1.6	2.1	1.5	1.6	4.3	3.6	3.9	3.3
United Kingdom	7.1	9.3	9.0	10.0	40.7	10.4	18.7	15.9
United States	9.8	11.3	10.4	15.1	13.8	14.9	20.2	18.0
Uruguay	0.0	0.0	0.0	0.0	..	0.0	..	0.0
OECD Total	7.4	7.5	6.7	8.8	12.4	8.9	12.4	11.7

.. Not available

Note: Detailed metadata at: *http://metalinks.oecd.org/ins/20210324/7de6*.

1. Information on data for Israel: *http://oe.cd/israel-disclaimer*.

Source: *Insurance activity indicators, OECD Insurance Statistics (database)*

Table 26. Ratio of reinsurance accepted (Non-life)

Per cent

	2012	2013	2014	2015	2016	2017	2018	2019
Argentina	0.4	0.3	8.0	7.8	7.5	7.2	6.0	5.9
Australia	15.2	14.2	14.3	14.7	16.0	13.9	14.3	14.5
Austria	..	18.2	14.7	13.6	13.7	9.2	10.2	9.4
Belgium	7.3	7.1	7.6	6.4	5.8	4.7	3.7	14.0
Bolivia	0.6	..	..	..	1.4	4.2	2.1	6.1
Brazil	..	..	0.1	0.0	0.0	0.0	0.0	0.0
Canada	8.3	9.7	18.1	17.7	15.8	16.7	11.1	..
Chile	1.2	1.4	1.5	1.6	1.3	1.1	1.1	1.2
Colombia	1.9	2.5	3.5	3.7	3.5	3.8	3.9	4.0
Costa Rica	0.2	0.4	0.3	0.4	0.3	0.3	0.4	0.4
Cuba	..	..	..	..	..	..	..	..
Czech Republic	3.5	3.3	2.9	3.4	3.7	3.7	2.9	2.8
Denmark	1.1	1.1	1.3	1.4	8.0	9.8	10.7	7.3
Dominican Republic	..	..	..	..	..	..	..	..
Ecuador	..	..	..	2.4	2.2	..	..	0.9
Egypt	..	..	..	..	..	..	..	8.5
El Salvador	..	..	..	..	..	..	5.2	5.7
Estonia	..	..	..	..	..	..	0.0	0.0
Finland	3.7	3.3	3.0	3.0	3.0	3.3	..	..
France	13.3	13.4	13.3	13.5	16.1	17.4	17.8	16.9
Germany	35.6	34.6	34.7	37.0	36.4	35.9	36.0	37.6
Greece	3.3	3.7	2.2	1.9	1.8	1.8	1.7	1.7
Guatemala	3.1	3.2	3.0	3.4	3.2	3.3	3.9	3.3
Honduras	..	0.0	0.0	0.0	..	..	..	0.0
Hong Kong, China	26.2	26.0	26.1	24.2	23.3	25.1	28.3	..
Hungary	2.2	2.9	1.9	2.1	2.0	2.9	2.0	1.7
India	..	..	..	3.0	..	19.4	..	..
Indonesia	14.4	15.2	7.3	6.8	7.5	7.2	6.6	7.3
Iceland	2.5	2.5	2.7	2.6	1.9	1.5	1.9	1.8
Ireland	5.3	5.0	5.3	4.6	5.5	5.3	6.5	16.3
Israel[1]	..	..	..	..	0.0	..	..	..
Italy	2.4	3.4	3.4	3.8	3.9	3.7	5.1	3.1
Japan	..	..	..	..	16.0	16.3	16.1	15.9
Korea	10.2	11.1	10.1	10.3	10.2	10.5	11.2	..
Latvia	1.7	0.0	0.0	0.0	0.0	0.0	0.0	0.1
Lithuania	0.2	0.2	0.0	0.0	0.0	0.0	0.0	0.0
Luxembourg	1.3	0.3	0.2	0.2	0.2	0.2	0.4	9.4
Malaysia	16.4	16.5	16.7	17.3	17.8	16.8	15.8	16.8
Mexico	2.9	2.7	2.7	2.7	2.6	2.6	2.7	2.8
Morocco	..	..	..	..	..	..	..	..
Netherlands	2.5	2.9	2.8	2.9	0.6	0.7	0.5	..
New Zealand	1.3	0.6	0.6	3.8	1.8	5.3	..	0.0
Nicaragua	..	0.0	..	..	..	..	..	..
Norway	..	..	..	..	..	..	..	..
Panama	7.7	6.6	..	..	..	..	..	9.2
Paraguay	2.2	1.5	..	1.2	1.0	0.8	..	0.5
Peru	1.3	1.0	0.8	0.7	0.8	1.3	1.1	1.4
Poland	2.3	2.5	2.1	5.3	6.1	5.2	5.7	6.7
Portugal	11.0	11.7	12.3	12.1	12.6	12.9	13.8	12.7
Puerto Rico	..	0.5	1.0	0.9	0.6	..	..	..
Russia	..	..	5.0	3.3	3.7	3.7	4.2	4.7
Singapore	37.6	38.1	37.3	40.7	39.2	37.0	..	50.0
Slovak Republic	2.1	2.1	3.1	4.0	..	0.8	..	0.0
Slovenia	15.8	14.6	14.6	16.3	15.7	15.5	14.9	15.5
South Africa	..	10.8	11.6	11.1	14.2	..	..	..
Spain	4.8	12.9	12.6	13.5	14.1	13.4	12.7	12.6
Sri Lanka	..	..	3.5	2.6	..	3.7	3.7	..
Sweden	14.6	12.9	13.5	11.4	11.8	13.0	12.6	12.4
Switzerland	24.9	26.6	25.4	23.4	23.6	24.8	26.0	27.5
Thailand	..	..	..	..	..	..	..	..
Tunisia	..	..	..	..	1.1	6.2	..	..
Turkey	3.1	2.8	5.4	3.3	6.1	6.5	9.3	11.7
United Kingdom	11.2	10.9	12.6	14.1	25.0	22.7	24.8	28.6
United States	28.2	27.8	28.2	27.4	27.0	27.4	5.6	6.2
Uruguay	0.0	0.0	0.0	0.0	..	0.0	..	0.0
OECD Total	23.5	23.5	24.1	24.2	23.6	24.0	11.1	11.8

.. Not available

Note: Detailed metadata at: *http://metalinks.oecd.org/ins/20210324/7de6.*

1. Information on data for Israel: *http://oe.cd/israel-disclaimer.*

Source: *Insurance activity indicators, OECD Insurance Statistics (database)*

Table 27. Market share of foreign companies in the domestic market (Life)

Per cent

	2012	2013	2014	2015	2016	2017	2018	2019
Argentina	18.3	31.8	31.4	30.8	30.4	30.0	27.9	29.0
Australia	15.8	16.8	15.5	17.7	20.8	25.5	29.8	37.5
Austria	..	37.5	39.2	37.7	39.3	39.7	39.7	39.1
Belgium	..	..	..	..	..	..	..	..
Bolivia	..	..	..	..	29.9	20.8	27.8	28.0
Brazil	..	..	18.6	18.3	17.2	21.3	26.5	29.5
Canada	6.3	5.6	26.0	21.0	18.7	18.1	15.2	..
Chile	43.7	46.7	45.0	41.8	41.6	44.5	43.0	45.0
Colombia	25.6	24.2	21.6	20.9	18.1	18.6	18.8	17.2
Costa Rica	5.5	12.4	17.0	23.0	25.0	33.9	37.2	37.5
Cuba	..	..	..	..	..	..	..	..
Czech Republic	97.1	96.8	96.7	96.3	96.8	96.4	95.9	97.1
Denmark	19.3	2.5	19.5	18.6	18.8	19.9	19.8	13.8
Dominican Republic	..	..	..	..	..	..	46.5	..
Ecuador	..	..	..	..	11.7	..	..	0.0
Egypt	..	..	..	..	..	..	..	..
El Salvador	9.7	17.4	9.6	9.4	9.6	..	10.3	9.9
Estonia	100.0	100.0	100.0	100.0	100.0	100.0	100.0	100.0
Finland	38.3	42.0	43.0	38.5	..	..	..	..
France	..	..	..	..	..	..	..	..
Germany	30.1	27.4	26.0	26.7	25.3	24.6	24.9	23.4
Greece	63.3	53.8	48.0	55.7	76.9	74.0	73.2	66.8
Guatemala	..	..	..	..	..	..	..	..
Honduras	..	13.8	59.6	62.2	..	..	62.7	59.6
Hong Kong, China	..	..	..	..	..	..	..	..
Hungary	93.5	95.6	96.2	95.8	96.9	96.6	96.3	96.4
India	..	..	..	0.0	..	0.1	..	..
Indonesia	..	..	..	..	..	..	..	..
Iceland	3.9	4.3	5.0	5.8	..	..	..	..
Ireland	3.9	4.9	4.5	4.7	..	5.3	2.5	1.3
Israel[1]	0.3	0.4	0.4	0.4	0.4	0.4	0.4	17.7
Italy	27.4	28.9	31.3	30.5	33.1	32.1	37.1	37.0
Japan	22.4	20.7	20.1	20.6	21.8	22.7	22.5	22.5
Korea	16.3	16.1	13.2	12.4	14.7	16.1	14.3	..
Latvia	90.0	91.8	91.0	89.8	90.8	91.3	91.6	91.8
Lithuania	96.8	97.0	97.4	97.4	97.5	97.1	97.3	97.2
Luxembourg	94.6	96.2	96.4	92.5	77.2	90.6	92.2	93.1
Malaysia	68.1	68.6	68.8	69.6	69.7	71.8	70.4	72.5
Mexico	71.1	6.3	74.0	72.3	70.6	68.0	68.8	68.5
Morocco	..	..	..	..	..	..	..	..
Netherlands	21.1	19.2	4.6	18.5	19.2	23.3	19.9	..
New Zealand	..	..	..	..	..	..	..	77.7
Nicaragua	32.6	29.1	26.6	26.4	18.0	..	25.8	..
Norway	10.7	12.3	13.3	15.1	0.7	0.7	0.5	0.4
Panama	54.1	59.9	..	..	..	..	..	39.9
Paraguay	..	6.2	..	0.0	0.0	5.5	..	5.6
Peru	20.7	23.5	30.7	56.8	28.1	27.6	23.4	35.0
Poland	51.1	48.8	50.0	50.7	54.3	45.2	44.0	44.5
Portugal	7.9	6.8	54.0	64.2	77.5	93.8	90.8	85.2
Puerto Rico	..	10.4	7.8	0.0	38.0	..	..	..
Russia	..	..	8.5	18.1	15.5	10.2	10.4	12.1
Singapore	66.3	67.2	71.3	70.6	70.0	53.3	..	53.3
Slovak Republic	90.2	90.4	90.0	89.0	..	5.6	..	87.8
Slovenia	16.8	17.6	17.2	17.0	17.1	15.7	15.4	25.3
South Africa	33.0	31.9	35.2	33.3	34.6	..	..	..
Spain	19.1	12.4	12.8	12.3	..	..	..	..
Sri Lanka	..	..	2.4	1.7	..	..	..	..
Sweden	18.4	19.5	7.9	8.8	11.2	12.2	13.2	12.3
Switzerland	30.6	31.2	27.9	26.9	25.6	25.3	26.1	10.6
Thailand	..	..	..	..	..	..	..	..
Tunisia	..	..	..	..	..	..	..	..
Turkey	27.1	47.1	47.9	59.7	54.2	56.4	59.2	52.7
United Kingdom	26.4	23.3	16.0	16.9	..	0.0	..	0.0
United States	19.6	20.0	21.0	17.4	22.5	21.7	23.0	19.8
Uruguay	33.5	32.8	33.4	30.1	..	21.3	..	21.3

.. Not available

Note: Detailed metadata at: *http://metalinks.oecd.org/ins/20210324/7de6.*

1. Information on data for Israel: *http://oe.cd/israel-disclaimer.*

Source: *Insurance activity indicators, OECD Insurance Statistics (database)*

Table 28. Market share of foreign undertakings in total domestic business (Life)

Branches or agencies

Per cent

	2012	2013	2014	2015	2016	2017	2018	2019
Argentina	1.5	1.8	3.9	3.2	3.4	3.5	3.7	5.0
Australia	..	..	..	..	..	..	..	..
Austria	..	0.0	0.0	0.0	0.0	0.0	0.0	0.0
Belgium	..	..	..	..	..	..	..	..
Bolivia	..	..	..	..	..	..	..	..
Brazil	..	..	..	0.0	0.0	0.0	0.0	0.0
Canada	2.6	2.2	15.5	15.8	13.2	12.7	9.0	..
Chile	..	..	..	..	..	..	..	..
Colombia	..	..	0.0	..	..	..	..	..
Costa Rica	0.0	0.2	0.6	1.1	1.0	1.3	1.6	1.5
Cuba	..	..	..	..	..	..	..	..
Czech Republic	8.1	7.5	7.2	10.8	10.9	11.4	11.5	14.6
Denmark	..	..	..	..	..	..	..	..
Dominican Republic	..	..	..	..	..	..	..	..
Ecuador	..	..	..	..	..	..	..	0.0
Egypt	..	..	..	..	..	..	..	..
El Salvador	9.7	17.4	9.6	9.4	9.6	..	10.3	9.9
Estonia	2.9	2.5	2.7	2.8	2.2	3.1	5.2	8.3
Finland	..	..	..	..	..	..	..	..
France	..	..	..	..	..	..	..	..
Germany	4.0	4.0	3.9	4.0	3.9	4.0	3.8	3.7
Greece	0.4	0.0	0.0	0.0	0.0	0.0	0.0	0.0
Guatemala	..	..	..	..	..	..	..	..
Honduras	..	13.8	25.6	23.1	..	..	62.7	59.6
Hong Kong, China	..	..	..	..	..	..	..	..
Hungary	..	..	..	..	..	..	..	..
India	..	..	..	0.0	..	0.1	..	..
Indonesia	..	..	..	..	..	..	..	..
Iceland	..	..	..	..	..	..	..	..
Ireland	3.9	4.9	4.5	4.7	..	5.3	2.5	1.3
Israel[1]	..	..	..	..	..	..	..	..
Italy	0.0	0.0	0.0	0.0	0.0	0.0	..	..
Japan	5.5	4.9	4.2	4.1	4.3	4.5	0.1	0.1
Korea	2.2	2.2	2.4	0.2	2.0	2.1	2.3	..
Latvia	55.7	56.3	58.5	59.3	61.4	63.1	65.5	44.8
Lithuania	41.5	41.6	43.1	41.8	40.8	41.4	43.3	62.2
Luxembourg	0.3	0.5	0.1	0.1	0.1	0.1	0.1	5.1
Malaysia	0.4	0.5	0.5	0.5	0.5	0.6	0.7	..
Mexico	..	..	..	..	..	..	..	..
Morocco	..	..	..	..	..	..	..	..
Netherlands	2.7	2.0	0.0	0.0	..	..	..	..
New Zealand	..	..	..	..	..	..	..	20.8
Nicaragua	..	..	..	..	..	..	..	..
Norway	0.8	1.3	1.4	0.7	0.7	0.7	0.5	0.4
Panama	10.3	10.0	..	..	..	..	..	39.3
Paraguay	..	..	..	0.0	0.0	..	..	0.0
Peru	..	..	..	..	..	..	..	..
Poland	..	..	..	..	..	..	..	..
Portugal	0.0	0.0	0.0	0.0	0.0	0.0	0.0	0.0
Puerto Rico	..	..	..	..	..	..	..	..
Russia	..	..	..	..	..	0.0	0.0	0.0
Singapore	15.1	15.0	32.6	30.7	32.3	8.7	..	15.2
Slovak Republic	4.3	5.4	4.4	4.8	..	5.6	..	15.3
Slovenia	..	..	..	..	..	..	..	..
South Africa	..	0.0	..	..	..	..	..	..
Spain	0.2	0.0	0.0	0.0	..	..	..	..
Sri Lanka	..	..	..	0.0	..	..	..	..
Sweden	..	..	0.7	..	..	..	..	..
Switzerland	2.1	1.5	0.0	0.0	0.0	0.0	0.0	0.1
Thailand	..	..	..	..	..	..	..	..
Tunisia	..	..	..	..	..	..	..	..
Turkey	..	..	..	..	0.0	0.0	0.0	..
United Kingdom	0.0	0.0	0.0	0.0	..	0.0	..	0.0
United States	..	..	..	..	0.0	0.0	0.0	0.0
Uruguay	..	0.0	0.0	0.0	..	0.0	..	0.0

.. Not available

Note: Detailed metadata at: *http://metalinks.oecd.org/ins/20210324/7de6*.

1. Information on data for Israel: *http://oe.cd/israel-disclaimer*.

Source: *Insurance activity indicators, OECD Insurance Statistics (database)*

Table 29. Market share of foreign companies in the domestic market (Non-life)

Per cent

	2012	2013	2014	2015	2016	2017	2018	2019
Argentina	17.6	20.1	21.1	22.0	23.4	30.5	30.0	29.6
Australia	27.1	27.7	28.7	28.2	28.7	29.5	34.8	37.3
Austria	..	35.2	37.5	36.9	36.6	33.2	32.9	33.1
Belgium	..	..	..	..	..	..	..	..
Bolivia	..	..	..	..	27.9	29.1	25.5	25.1
Brazil	..	..	51.3	32.4	35.7	39.4	53.9	43.9
Canada	29.0	27.9	44.8	41.6	40.9	41.3	37.5	..
Chile	65.7	63.7	63.5	62.7	79.0	75.6	73.8	73.5
Colombia	47.1	46.2	55.4	52.7	50.8	47.7	45.8	45.8
Costa Rica	7.6	10.0	14.2	17.5	20.5	22.8	25.4	25.4
Cuba	..	..	..	..	..	..	..	..
Czech Republic	88.6	88.2	89.4	90.0	89.1	88.6	87.8	86.9
Denmark	16.6	16.4	27.5	27.9	28.3	25.3	23.1	21.9
Dominican Republic	..	..	..	..	..	..	28.4	..
Ecuador	..	..	..	..	0.4	..	..	0.0
Egypt	..	..	..	..	..	..	..	..
El Salvador	2.4	0.0	0.0	0.0	0.0	..	4.5	4.2
Estonia	92.7	94.3	95.1	95.2	94.8	100.0	95.4	95.6
Finland	25.0	23.8	23.7	100.0	..	..	..	..
France	0.1	0.1	0.1	0.1	..	..	..	..
Germany	13.2	14.0	14.5	14.3	13.3	13.6	14.4	13.6
Greece	41.2	34.5	41.2	43.0	57.3	57.3	56.4	55.7
Guatemala	..	..	..	..	..	..	..	..
Honduras	..	10.5	40.3	42.8	..	..	49.3	47.3
Hong Kong, China	..	..	..	..	..	..	..	..
Hungary	95.7	94.9	94.7	92.8	91.7	91.4	91.4	91.4
India	..	..	..	..	..	2.9	..	..
Indonesia	..	..	..	..	..	..	..	..
Iceland	9.9	10.4	10.9	11.3	..	..	..	..
Ireland	17.6	14.3	24.3	22.2	..	17.1	16.6	22.8
Israel[1]	3.3	3.3	3.4	4.0	3.8	3.8	3.8	18.9
Italy	27.5	27.8	28.9	32.2	31.8	31.1	30.0	31.4
Japan	..	..	..	..	9.4	7.5	9.4	8.7
Korea	3.8	4.0	3.7	3.7	3.7	3.8	4.1	..
Latvia	48.1	49.4	48.7	57.1	79.0	77.2	79.5	83.5
Lithuania	98.5	98.8	99.0	99.0	99.3	99.5	99.5	99.6
Luxembourg	58.9	52.1	53.3	52.8	51.7	51.1	50.2	63.7
Malaysia	43.9	45.8	46.6	47.8	48.5	51.9	52.9	53.4
Mexico	52.4	9.7	48.7	52.2	48.5	50.3	48.1	49.5
Morocco	..	..	..	..	..	..	..	..
Netherlands	29.4	22.7	11.6	16.3	2.6	2.3	1.7	..
New Zealand	..	..	..	..	..	..	..	74.7
Nicaragua	24.6	25.7	24.7	25.7	26.0	..	29.4	..
Norway	43.9	43.4	41.1	40.2	40.3	37.8	37.3	37.3
Panama	39.2	47.0	..	..	..	..	..	43.4
Paraguay	0.0	26.4	..	0.0	22.8	24.7	..	27.5
Peru	19.1	19.9	20.6	45.9	24.8	25.7	25.0	40.1
Poland	62.8	61.3	61.3	61.8	59.1	58.4	59.1	60.0
Portugal	26.5	26.6	84.2	84.3	91.0	91.6	91.0	91.1
Puerto Rico	..	52.6	51.8	41.0	55.6	..	..	..
Russia	..	..	2.2	13.7	13.7	14.0	13.9	14.6
Singapore	86.8	86.2	89.0	89.2	90.2	80.0	..	79.0
Slovak Republic	94.0	93.8	93.6	93.2	..	8.3	..	96.8
Slovenia	4.9	5.1	5.2	5.3	5.7	5.9	5.8	18.3
South Africa	63.5	45.2	39.5	34.6	37.4	..	..	..
Spain	32.2	29.1	28.8	23.6	..	..	..	..
Sri Lanka	..	..	4.7	4.8	..	16.0	10.6	..
Sweden	63.8	57.6	55.4	44.8	46.7	48.0	52.6	52.3
Switzerland	20.4	20.6	19.6	20.3	20.1	18.7	17.4	16.9
Thailand	..	..	..	..	..	..	..	..
Tunisia	..	..	..	..	..	..	..	..
Turkey	53.8	62.2	59.3	66.7	63.7	57.1	54.2	52.9
United Kingdom	55.2	58.0	57.8	57.5	0.3	0.4	0.4	1.0
United States	10.1	10.4	9.4	9.5	10.2	10.0	0.8	5.5
Uruguay	31.3	31.4	32.2	33.6	..	34.7	..	34.6

.. Not available

Note: Detailed metadata at: *http://metalinks.oecd.org/ins/20210324/7de6*.

1. Information on data for Israel: *http://oe.cd/israel-disclaimer*.

Source: *Insurance activity indicators, OECD Insurance Statistics (database)*

INTERNATIONAL COMPARISONS

Table 30. Market share of foreign undertakings in total domestic business (Non-life)

Branches or agencies

Per cent

	2012	2013	2014	2015	2016	2017	2018	2019
Argentina	0.1	0.1	3.2	2.5	2.4	2.6	2.1	2.2
Australia	9.7	9.7	10.1	9.1	9.9	9.6	11.9	13.2
Austria	..	0.1	0.1	0.0	0.0	0.1	0.1	0.1
Belgium	..	..	..	..	..	..	..	..
Bolivia	..	..	..	..	..	..	..	..
Brazil	..	..	..	0.0	0.0	0.0	0.0	0.0
Canada	13.4	13.1	23.2	21.0	19.4	19.0	15.1	..
Chile	..	..	..	..	..	..	..	..
Colombia	..	..	0.0	..	..	..	..	..
Costa Rica	0.1	0.3	0.4	0.8	1.3	1.5	1.7	1.7
Cuba	..	..	..	..	..	..	..	..
Czech Republic	2.7	3.7	4.7	4.9	5.3	5.4	4.4	4.8
Denmark	..	..	..	..	..	..	..	..
Dominican Republic	..	..	..	..	..	..	..	..
Ecuador	..	..	..	..	..	..	..	0.0
Egypt	..	..	..	..	..	..	..	..
El Salvador	2.4	0.0	0.0	0.0	0.0	..	4.5	4.2
Estonia	14.5	13.6	14.8	13.5	15.0	15.1	15.3	15.9
Finland	..	..	..	..	..	..	..	..
France	0.1	0.1	0.1	0.1	..	..	..	..
Germany	3.1	2.7	3.2	3.5	3.1	3.8	4.0	3.6
Greece	7.9	0.0	0.0	0.0	0.0	0.0	0.0	0.0
Guatemala	..	..	..	..	..	..	..	..
Honduras	..	10.5	4.4	3.6	..	..	49.3	47.3
Hong Kong, China	..	..	..	..	..	..	..	..
Hungary	..	..	..	..	..	..	..	..
India	..	..	..	..	..	2.9	..	..
Indonesia	..	..	..	..	..	..	..	..
Iceland	..	..	..	..	..	..	..	..
Ireland	17.6	14.3	24.3	22.2	..	17.1	16.6	22.8
Israel[1]	..	..	..	..	..	..	..	..
Italy	1.1	1.1	1.1	1.4	1.6	1.5	1.6	1.7
Japan	..	..	..	..	2.3	2.5	2.8	2.3
Korea	2.0	3.1	2.3	2.3	2.3	2.4	2.8	..
Latvia	13.3	18.5	20.4	20.2	22.6	27.0	28.1	29.6
Lithuania	39.7	52.9	53.1	53.9	46.8	48.4	51.4	51.5
Luxembourg	7.5	6.5	3.6	3.6	3.5	3.3	3.6	11.7
Malaysia	5.8	6.7	7.3	8.4	9.6	8.9	8.8	10.0
Mexico	..	..	..	..	..	..	..	..
Morocco	..	..	..	..	..	..	..	..
Netherlands	1.9	0.3	0.3	0.0	..	..	..	..
New Zealand	..	..	..	..	..	..	..	13.0
Nicaragua	..	..	..	..	..	..	..	..
Norway	43.2	43.4	41.1	40.2	40.3	37.8	37.3	37.3
Panama	7.9	7.7	..	..	..	..	..	41.4
Paraguay	..	..	..	0.0	0.0	..	..	0.0
Peru	..	..	..	..	..	..	..	..
Poland	..	..	..	..	..	..	..	..
Portugal	0.0	0.0	0.0	0.0	0.0	0.0	0.0	0.0
Puerto Rico	..	..	..	..	..	..	..	..
Russia	..	..	..	..	0.1	0.0	0.0	0.0
Singapore	42.7	46.8	39.6	38.2	37.4	36.5	..	31.7
Slovak Republic	7.1	8.0	8.7	8.5	..	8.3	..	7.7
Slovenia	..	..	..	..	..	..	..	..
South Africa	..	0.0	..	..	..	..	..	..
Spain	0.2	0.0	0.0	0.0	..	..	..	..
Sri Lanka	..	..	..	0.0	..	..	..	..
Sweden	..	..	8.2	..	..	..	..	..
Switzerland	4.9	5.0	5.5	6.0	7.1	7.5	5.8	5.2
Thailand	..	..	..	..	..	..	..	..
Tunisia	..	..	..	..	..	..	..	..
Turkey	0.3	0.3	0.3	0.4	0.4	0.5	0.7	1.0
United Kingdom	4.7	3.7	4.1	4.6	0.3	0.4	0.4	1.0
United States	0.1	0.0	0.0	0.1	0.1	0.1	0.1	0.0
Uruguay	..	0.0	0.0	0.0	..	0.0	..	0.0

.. Not available

Note: Detailed metadata at: *http://metalinks.oecd.org/ins/20210324/7de6*.

1. Information on data for Israel: *http://oe.cd/israel-disclaimer*.

Source: *Insurance activity indicators, OECD Insurance Statistics (database)*

Country tables

AUSTRALIA

Table 1. Selected aggregates

Million AUD

	2012	2013	2014	2015	2016	2017	2018	2019
1.1 Insurance business written in the reporting country								
1.1.1 Insurance business, by ownership								
Gross premiums								
Domestic undertakings	79 230	86 754	103 414	100 992	95 348	90 032	88 064	81 517
Foreign controlled undertakings	13 757	15 722	17 983	19 150	19 836	21 498	24 659	26 308
Foreign companies (branches)	3 713	3 977	4 206	3 893	4 393	4 353	5 613	6 630
All undertakings	82 943	90 731	107 620	104 885	99 741	94 385	93 677	88 147
Premiums ceded								
Domestic undertakings	11 507	12 121	13 268	15 209	17 826	19 711	18 794	20 650
Foreign controlled undertakings	4 111	4 666	5 483	5 986	6 268	8 647	8 223	8 676
Foreign companies (branches)	1 659	1 947	1 842	1 739	1 759	1 873	1 875	2 155
All undertakings	13 166	14 068	15 110	16 948	19 585	21 584	20 669	22 805
Net written premiums								
Domestic undertakings	67 724	74 633	90 147	85 783	77 522	70 321	69 270	60 869
Foreign controlled undertakings	9 646	11 055	12 500	13 164	13 568	12 851	16 436	17 632
Foreign companies (branches)	2 054	2 030	2 365	2 154	2 634	2 480	3 738	4 475
All undertakings	69 778	76 663	92 511	87 937	80 156	72 801	73 008	65 344
1.1.2 Insurance business on foreign risks, gross premiums								
Life	491	574	686	701	711	706	880	1 176
Non-life	..	..	..	..	..	..	..	..
Composite total	..	..	..	..	..	..	..	..
Total	491	574	686	701	711	706	880	1 176
1.1.3 Life insurance payments, by class, gross premiums								
Annuities	..	..	..	..	..	..	..	..
Unit linked	..	..	..	..	..	..	..	..
Other life insurance	..	..	..	..	..	..	..	..
Total life insurance	41 091	45 794	60 881	56 868	49 890	43 141	39 741	31 149
***of which:** Pension contracts*	..	..	..	..	..	..	..	..
1.1.4 Non-life insurance payments, by class, gross premiums								
Motor vehicle insurance	12 114	12 924	13 467	13 749	14 512	15 447	15 789	16 471
Marine, aviation and other transport insurance	1 484	1 523	1 598	1 673	1 648	1 739	1 871	1 899
Freight insurance	..	..	..	..	..	..	..	..
Fire and other property damage insurance	10 918	12 038	11 836	12 031	12 297	12 713	13 428	14 391
Pecuniary loss insurance	1 207	1 258	1 454	1 493	1 443	1 352	1 230	1 169
General liability insurance	5 008	5 283	5 418	5 435	5 348	5 491	5 893	6 391
Accident and health	1 049	1 134	1 124	1 130	1 064	1 021	1 006	1 022
***of which:** Health*	..	..	..	..	..	..	..	..
Other non-life insurance	835	900	951	1 029	1 071	1 205	1 325	1 444
Treaty reinsurance	5 836	5 823	5 970	6 271	7 115	6 269	6 742	7 273
Total non-life insurance	38 450	40 884	41 818	42 811	44 498	45 237	47 283	50 060
1.2 Gross claims payments								
Life								
Domestic undertakings	45 777	47 647	64 828	56 547	59 350	47 307	46 989	43 814
Foreign controlled undertakings	4 181	5 212	5 876	6 681	7 133	9 207	8 564	9 141
Foreign companies (branches)	..	..	..	..	..	..	..	..
All undertakings	45 777	47 647	64 828	56 547	59 350	47 307	46 989	43 814
Non-life								
Domestic undertakings	22 048	24 141	26 293	29 311	28 026	29 946	30 252	33 037
Foreign controlled undertakings	4 538	4 542	5 446	6 183	5 534	6 453	8 199	8 425
Foreign companies (branches)	1 749	1 984	3 318	2 585	3 217	3 124	3 853	5 088
All undertakings	23 797	26 126	29 611	31 896	31 243	33 070	34 105	38 125
Composite, all undertakings	..	..	..	..	..	..	..	..
Total								
Domestic undertakings	67 825	71 788	91 121	85 858	87 376	77 253	77 241	76 851
Foreign controlled undertakings	8 719	9 754	11 322	12 864	12 667	15 660	16 763	17 566
Foreign companies (branches)	1 749	1 984	3 318	2 585	3 217	3 124	3 853	5 088
All undertakings	69 574	73 773	94 439	88 443	90 593	80 377	81 094	81 939
1.3 Commissions								
Life								
Domestic undertakings	3 007	3 015	3 118	3 087	3 129	2 514	2 402	2 052
Foreign controlled undertakings	252	447	451	460	464	494	483	470
Foreign companies (branches)	..	..	..	..	..	..	..	..
All undertakings	3 007	3 015	3 118	3 087	3 129	2 514	2 402	2 052
Non-life								
Domestic undertakings	..	506	566	816	1 038	1 070	1 310	1 338
Foreign controlled undertakings	..	239	270	276	308	341	418	452
Foreign companies (branches)	..	264	287	301	327	324	250	280
All undertakings	..	770	853	1 117	1 364	1 394	1 560	1 618
Composite, all undertakings	..	..	..	..	..	..	..	..
Total								
Domestic undertakings	3 007	3 521	3 684	3 903	4 167	3 584	3 712	3 390
Foreign controlled undertakings	252	686	721	736	772	835	901	923
Foreign companies (branches)	..	264	287	301	327	324	250	280
All undertakings	3 007	3 785	3 971	4 204	4 493	3 908	3 962	3 671

AUSTRALIA

Table 1. Selected aggregates *(cont.)*

Million AUD

	2012	2013	2014	2015	2016	2017	2018	2019
1.4 Gross operating expenses								
Life								
Domestic undertakings	7 274	7 830	8 128	8 041	8 666	8 457	9 370	8 045
Foreign controlled undertakings	1 430	2 392	2 393	2 487	3 038	3 239	4 439	3 546
Foreign companies (branches)	..	..	..	..	..	..	..	..
All undertakings	7 274	7 830	8 128	8 041	8 666	8 457	9 370	8 045
Non-life								
Domestic undertakings	7 197	7 361	7 502	7 497	7 368	7 475	7 517	7 979
Foreign controlled undertakings	1 490	1 618	1 704	1 850	1 829	1 975	2 378	2 710
Foreign companies (branches)	559	597	629	660	618	563	790	1 003
All undertakings	7 756	7 959	8 131	8 157	7 987	8 038	8 307	8 982
Composite, all undertakings	..	..	..	..	..	..	..	..
Total								
Domestic undertakings	14 471	15 191	15 630	15 538	16 034	15 932	16 887	16 024
Foreign controlled undertakings	2 920	4 010	4 097	4 337	4 867	5 214	6 817	6 256
Foreign companies (branches)	559	597	629	660	618	563	790	1 003
All undertakings	15 030	15 789	16 259	16 198	16 653	16 495	17 677	17 027
1.5 Insurance business written abroad by branches, gross premiums								
Life								
Branches and agencies	..	..	..	..	..	..	..	..
Subsidaries	..	..	..	..	..	..	..	..
Total	..	..	..	..	..	..	..	..
Non-life								
Branches and agencies	..	..	..	..	..	..	..	..
Subsidaries	..	..	..	..	..	..	..	..
Total	..	..	..	..	..	..	..	..
Composite total	..	..	..	..	..	..	..	..
Total								
Branches and agencies	..	..	..	..	..	..	..	..
Subsidaries	..	..	..	..	..	..	..	..
Total	..	..	..	..	..	..	..	..

.. Not available

Note: Detailed metadata at: *http://metalinks.oecd.org/ins/20210324/19e6.*

Source: *OECD Insurance Statistics (database)*

AUSTRALIA

Table 2. Number of companies and employees

	2012	2013	2014	2015	2016	2017	2018	2019
2.1 Number of companies								
Life								
Domestic undertakings	28	28	28	28	29	29	29	28
Foreign controlled undertakings	14	14	14	13	13	13	14	13
Foreign companies (branches)	..	..	..	..	..	..	..	..
All undertakings	28	28	28	28	29	29	29	28
Non-life								
Domestic undertakings	79	75	74	70	68	58	58	58
Foreign controlled undertakings	17	18	19	19	17	15	17	16
Foreign companies (branches)	30	29	29	29	31	28	28	27
All undertakings	109	104	103	99	99	86	86	85
Composite, all undertakings	..	..	..	0	..	..	..	..
Reinsurance								
Domestic undertakings	3	3	3	2	2	2	2	2
Foreign controlled undertakings	1	1	1	1	1	1	1	2
Foreign companies (branches)	9	9	9	9	8	8	8	9
All undertakings	12	12	12	11	10	10	10	11
Total								
Domestic undertakings	110	106	105	100	99	89	89	88
Foreign controlled undertakings	32	33	34	33	31	29	32	31
Foreign companies (branches)	39	38	38	38	39	36	36	36
All undertakings	149	144	143	138	138	125	125	124
2.2 Number of employees								
Insurance undertakings	..	..	..	..	..	..	..	..
Intermediaries	..	..	..	..	..	..	..	..
Total	..	..	..	..	..	..	..	..

.. Not available

Note: Detailed metadata at: *http://metalinks.oecd.org/ins/20210324/19e6.*

Source: *OECD Insurance Statistics (database)*

AUSTRIA

Table 1. Selected aggregates

Million EUR

	2012	2013	2014	2015	2016	2017	2018	2019
1.1 Insurance business written in the reporting country								
1.1.1 Insurance business, by ownership								
Gross premiums								
Domestic undertakings	..	18 879	18 889	19 003	18 647	18 126	18 520	18 831
Foreign controlled undertakings	..	6 781	7 196	7 060	6 979	6 390	6 467	6 549
Foreign companies (branches)	..	8	6	6	6	7	8	8
All undertakings	..	18 887	18 895	19 009	18 653	18 134	18 527	18 839
Premiums ceded								
Domestic undertakings	..	3 539	3 102	2 996	3 521	3 130	2 376	2 570
Foreign controlled undertakings	..	1 127	1 171	1 113	1 636	1 280	475	549
Foreign companies (branches)	..	0	0	0	0	0	0	0
All undertakings	..	3 539	3 102	2 996	3 522	3 131	2 376	2 571
Net written premiums								
Domestic undertakings	..	15 340	15 787	16 007	15 126	14 996	16 144	16 261
Foreign controlled undertakings	..	5 654	6 024	5 948	5 343	5 110	5 991	6 000
Foreign companies (branches)	..	8	6	6	6	7	7	8
All undertakings	..	15 348	15 793	16 013	15 131	15 003	16 151	16 268
1.1.2 Insurance business on foreign risks, gross premiums								
Life	72	157	22	20	14	3	4	23
Non-life	662	717	726	702	753	777	931	858
Composite	626	595	489	391	371	363	358	387
of which:								
Life	188	202	158	111	95	89	82	80
Non-life	438	393	331	280	276	274	276	306
Total	1 360	1 469	1 237	1 114	1 138	1 143	1 293	1 268
1.1.3 Life insurance payments, by class, gross premiums								
Annuities	..	1 441	1 822	1 946	1 531	1 434	1 367	1 361
Unit linked	1 846	1 248	1 011	933	864	812	972	1 013
Other life insurance	4 588	3 738	3 852	3 812	3 646	3 488	3 188	3 029
Total life insurance	6 434	6 427	6 685	6 692	6 041	5 735	5 527	5 403
***of which:** Pension contracts*	..	997	1 116	1 031	940	964	923	831
1.1.4 Non-life insurance payments, by class, gross premiums								
Motor vehicle insurance	1 386	1 487	1 447	3 920	4 043	3 980	4 207	4 292
Marine, aviation and other transport insurance	165	174	138	11	9	10	9	6
Freight insurance	..	..	..	155	148	137	165	164
Fire and other property damage insurance	1 008	1 081	1 058	3 153	3 178	3 013	3 030	3 170
Pecuniary loss insurance	167	174	183	178	176	166	169	168
General liability insurance	834	860	886	889	905	868	903	932
Accident and health	3 024	3 150	3 143	3 257	3 391	3 473	3 627	3 780
***of which:** Health*	1 762	1 841	1 905	2 007	2 096	2 167	2 264	2 374
Other non-life insurance	5 672	5 517	5 340	742	749	739	877	910
Treaty reinsurance	..	..	..	..	..	..	..	..
Total non-life insurance	12 255	12 444	12 195	12 303	12 599	12 386	12 987	13 421
1.2 Gross claims payments								
Life								
Domestic undertakings	360	358	1 110	1 254	947	977	933	956
Foreign controlled undertakings	145	140	714	837	920	959	914	938
Foreign companies (branches)	..	0	0	0	0	0	0	0
All undertakings	360	358	1 110	1 254	947	977	933	956
Non-life								
Domestic undertakings	2 675	1 107	1 632	2 072	2 203	1 939	1 936	1 995
Foreign controlled undertakings	1 490	905	873	1 288	2 620	1 893	1 862	1 936
Foreign companies (branches)	5	4	3	2	3	3	3	4
All undertakings	2 681	1 111	1 636	2 075	2 206	1 942	1 939	2 000
Composite								
Domestic undertakings	11 652	11 676	11 289	12 780	12 440	12 173	11 700	12 554
Foreign controlled undertakings	3 829	3 846	3 026	3 760	10 479	9 813	9 865	11 072
Foreign companies (branches)	..	0	0	0	0	0	0	0
All undertakings	11 652	11 676	11 289	12 780	12 440	12 173	11 700	12 554
of which:								
Life	6 047	6 011	5 955	7 193	6 817	6 194	5 688	6 294
Domestic undertakings	6 047	6 011	5 955	7 193	6 817	6 194	5 688	6 294
Foreign controlled undertakings	2 281	2 274	1 630	2 235	3 500	3 281	3 307	3 710
Foreign companies (branches)	..	0	0	0	0	0	0	0
All undertakings	6 047	6 011	5 955	7 193	6 817	6 194	5 688	6 294
Non-life	5 605	5 665	5 335	5 588	5 623	5 980	6 012	6 261
Domestic undertakings	5 605	5 665	5 335	5 588	5 623	5 980	6 012	6 261
Foreign controlled undertakings	1 549	1 572	1 396	1 525	6 979	6 532	6 558	7 362
Foreign companies (branches)	..	0	0	0	0	0	0	0
All undertakings	5 605	5 665	5 335	5 588	5 623	5 980	6 012	6 261
Total								
Domestic undertakings	14 687	13 141	14 032	16 107	15 590	15 089	14 568	15 506
Foreign controlled undertakings	5 464	4 891	4 613	5 885	14 018	12 665	12 641	13 945
Foreign companies (branches)	5	4	3	2	3	3	3	4
All undertakings	14 692	13 145	14 036	16 109	15 593	15 092	14 572	15 510

AUSTRIA

Table 1. Selected aggregates *(cont.)*

Million EUR

	2012	2013	2014	2015	2016	2017	2018	2019
1.3 Commissions								
Life								
Domestic undertakings	75	99	98	98	80	73	73	73
Foreign controlled undertakings	17	5	70	70	79	72	72	72
Foreign companies (branches)	..	0	0	0	0	0	0	0
All undertakings	75	99	98	98	80	73	73	73
Non-life								
Domestic undertakings	338	354	398	386	399	408	411	416
Foreign controlled undertakings	309	319	329	341	348	352	350	350
Foreign companies (branches)	2	2	1	1	1	2	2	2
All undertakings	340	356	399	387	400	410	413	418
Composite								
Domestic undertakings	2 309	2 285	2 279	2 354	2 392	2 365	2 335	2 402
Foreign controlled undertakings	750	752	666	739	734	725	706	747
Foreign companies (branches)	..	0	0	0	0	0	0	0
All undertakings	2 309	2 285	2 279	2 354	2 392	2 365	2 335	2 402
of which:								
Life	692	644	624	623	579	538	454	463
Domestic undertakings	692	644	624	623	579	538	454	463
Foreign controlled undertakings	253	238	163	188	163	149	106	112
Foreign companies (branches)	..	0	0	0	0	0	0	0
All undertakings	692	644	624	623	579	538	454	463
Non-life	1 616	1 641	1 655	1 731	1 812	1 827	1 881	1 939
Domestic undertakings	1 616	1 641	1 655	1 731	1 812	1 827	1 881	1 939
Foreign controlled undertakings	497	514	503	551	571	576	600	635
Foreign companies (branches)	..	0	0	0	0	0	0	0
All undertakings	1 616	1 641	1 655	1 731	1 812	1 827	1 881	1 939
Total								
Domestic undertakings	2 722	2 738	2 775	2 839	2 871	2 846	2 819	2 891
Foreign controlled undertakings	1 077	1 076	1 065	1 150	1 161	1 149	1 128	1 170
Foreign companies (branches)	2	2	1	1	1	2	2	2
All undertakings	2 724	2 740	2 776	2 840	2 872	2 848	2 821	2 893
1.4 Gross operating expenses								
Life								
Domestic undertakings	95	120	43	40	37	42	37	34
Foreign controlled undertakings	0	14	30	30	36	41	37	33
Foreign companies (branches)	..	0	0	0	0	0	0	0
All undertakings	95	120	43	40	37	42	37	34
Non-life								
Domestic undertakings	860	697	153	143	192	191	210	218
Foreign controlled undertakings	447	414	116	92	111	105	103	99
Foreign companies (branches)	3	3	1	1	1	1	1	1
All undertakings	863	700	154	144	193	192	210	219
Composite								
Domestic undertakings	1 918	2 306	623	678	702	696	741	777
Foreign controlled undertakings	695	699	167	185	177	181	178	183
Foreign companies (branches)	..	0	0	0	0	0	0	0
All undertakings	1 918	2 306	623	678	702	696	741	777
of which:								
Life	513	848	194	202	223	224	236	238
Domestic undertakings	513	848	194	202	223	224	236	238
Foreign controlled undertakings	339	323	61	68	63	58	60	63
Foreign companies (branches)	..	0	0	0	0	0	0	0
All undertakings	513	848	194	202	223	224	236	238
Non-life	1 405	1 458	428	476	479	472	505	539
Domestic undertakings	1 405	1 458	428	476	479	472	505	539
Foreign controlled undertakings	356	376	106	117	114	123	118	120
Foreign companies (branches)	..	0	0	0	0	0	0	0
All undertakings	1 405	1 458	428	476	479	472	505	539
Total								
Domestic undertakings	2 873	3 124	819	861	930	929	988	1 028
Foreign controlled undertakings	1 143	1 128	313	308	324	328	318	315
Foreign companies (branches)	3	3	1	1	1	1	1	1
All undertakings	2 876	3 127	820	862	931	930	989	1 029

AUSTRIA

Table 1. Selected aggregates *(cont.)*

Million EUR

	2012	2013	2014	2015	2016	2017	2018	2019
1.5 Insurance business written abroad by branches, gross premiums								
Life								
Branches and agencies	72	157	22	19	13	11	10	29
Subsidaries	..	..	..	..	..	..	..	..
Total	72	157	22	19	13	11	10	29
Non-life								
Branches and agencies	149	159	198	204	217	215	220	245
Subsidaries	..	..	..	..	..	..	..	..
Total	149	159	198	204	217	215	220	245
Composite								
Branches and agencies	557	480	368	284	251	275	279	261
Subsidaries	..	..	..	..	..	..	..	..
Total	557	480	368	284	251	275	279	261
of which:								
Life	168	140	103	78	83	78	73	71
Branches and agencies	168	140	103	78	83	78	73	71
Subsidaries	..	..	..	..	..	..	..	..
Total	168	140	103	78	83	78	73	71
Non-life	389	340	266	206	168	198	206	190
Branches and agencies	389	340	266	206	168	198	206	190
Subsidaries	..	..	..	..	..	..	..	..
Total	389	340	266	206	168	198	206	190
Total								
Branches and agencies	778	796	587	507	481	501	510	535
Subsidaries	..	..	..	..	..	..	..	..
Total	778	796	587	507	481	501	510	535

.. Not available

Note: Detailed metadata at: *http://metalinks.oecd.org/ins/20210324/4cd9.*

Source: *OECD Insurance Statistics (database)*

AUSTRIA

Table 2. Number of companies and employees

	2012	2013	2014	2015	2016	2017	2018	2019
2.1 Number of companies								
Life								
Domestic undertakings	3	3	7	7	6	6	6	6
Foreign controlled undertakings	1	1	3	3	4	4	4	4
Foreign companies (branches)	0	0	0	0	0	0	0	0
All undertakings	3	3	7	7	6	6	6	6
Non-life								
Domestic undertakings	14	14	12	12	12	12	12	12
Foreign controlled undertakings	7	7	8	8	8	8	7	7
Foreign companies (branches)	1	1	1	1	1	1	1	1
All undertakings	15	15	13	13	13	13	13	13
Composite								
Domestic undertakings	27	26	21	20	17	17	16	16
Foreign controlled undertakings	10	9	6	5	4	4	4	4
Foreign companies (branches)	0	0	0	0	0	0	0	0
All undertakings	27	26	21	20	17	17	16	16
Reinsurance								
Domestic undertakings	3	3	3	2	3	2	1	1
Foreign controlled undertakings	2	1	2	1	1	0	0	0
Foreign companies (branches)	0	0	0	0	0	0	0	0
All undertakings	3	3	3	2	3	2	1	1
Total								
Domestic undertakings	47	46	43	41	38	37	35	35
Foreign controlled undertakings	20	18	19	17	17	16	15	15
Foreign companies (branches)	1	1	1	1	1	1	1	1
All undertakings	48	47	44	42	39	38	36	36
2.2 Number of employees								
Insurance undertakings	27 430	27 738	27 791	27 911	28 336	28 367	27 804	27 903
Intermediaries	9 255	..	..	..	..	..	..	..
Total	27 430	27 738	27 791	27 911	28 336	28 367	27 804	27 903

.. Not available

Note: Detailed metadata at: *http://metalinks.oecd.org/ins/20210324/4cd9.*

Source: *OECD Insurance Statistics (database)*

BELGIUM

Table 1. Selected aggregates

Million EUR

	2012	2013	2014	2015	2016	2017	2018	2019
1.1 Insurance business written in the reporting country								
1.1.1 Insurance business, by ownership								
Gross premiums								
Domestic undertakings	32 640	28 251	28 863	27 712	27 493	27 299	28 539	31 400
Foreign controlled undertakings	..	..	..	..	..	..	..	..
Foreign companies (branches)	..	..	..	..	..	..	..	..
All undertakings	32 640	28 251	28 863	27 712	27 493	27 299	28 539	31 400
Premiums ceded								
Domestic undertakings	2 417	2 474	3 251	3 183	3 520	3 412	3 656	7 478
Foreign controlled undertakings	..	..	..	..	..	..	..	..
Foreign companies (branches)	..	..	..	..	..	..	..	..
All undertakings	2 417	2 474	3 251	3 183	3 520	3 412	3 656	7 478
Net written premiums								
Domestic undertakings	30 223	25 777	25 612	24 529	23 973	23 887	24 882	23 923
Foreign controlled undertakings	..	..	..	..	..	..	..	..
Foreign companies (branches)	..	..	..	..	..	..	..	..
All undertakings	30 223	25 777	25 612	24 529	23 973	23 887	24 882	23 923
1.1.2 Insurance business on foreign risks, gross premiums								
Life	31	25	15	24	20	17	6	15
Non-life	242	268	563	436	515	553	611	453
Composite	230	218	223	321	331	331	378	580
of which:								
Life	77	53	39	38	23	17	14	15
Non-life	153	165	184	282	308	313	364	565
Total	502	511	801	781	866	901	995	1 048
1.1.3 Life insurance payments, by class, gross premiums								
Annuities	..	..	..	..	..	..	..	..
Unit linked	4 844	2 743	2 524	3 008	2 221	3 182	3 520	3 341
Other life insurance	16 235	13 501	13 723	12 302	12 674	11 424	12 051	12 826
Total life insurance	21 078	16 244	16 247	15 310	14 895	14 606	15 571	16 167
***of which:** Pension contracts*	..	..	..	..	..	..	..	..
1.1.4 Non-life insurance payments, by class, gross premiums								
Motor vehicle insurance	3 459	3 487	3 542	3 585	..	..	..	..
Marine, aviation and other transport insurance	78	71	69	81	..	..	..	..
Freight insurance	116	104	100	73	..	..	..	..
Fire and other property damage insurance	2 573	2 696	2 755	2 708	..	..	..	..
Pecuniary loss insurance	407	404	725	598	..	..	..	..
General liability insurance	780	770	785	762	..	..	..	..
Accident and health	3 361	3 592	3 695	3 653	..	..	..	..
***of which:** Health*	1 517	1 618	1 708	1 849	..	..	..	..
Other non-life insurance	737	825	885	888	..	..	..	..
Treaty reinsurance	7	..	..	..	..	..	..	..
Total non-life insurance	11 516	11 949	12 556	12 349	12 532	12 652	12 926	15 159
1.2 Gross claims payments								
Life								
Domestic undertakings	592	528	626	469	642	521	731	694
Foreign controlled undertakings	..	..	..	..	..	..	..	..
Foreign companies (branches)	..	..	..	..	..	..	..	..
All undertakings	592	528	626	469	642	521	731	694
Non-life								
Domestic undertakings	1 898	1 960	2 272	2 363	2 539	2 316	1 489	1 989
Foreign controlled undertakings	..	..	..	..	..	..	..	..
Foreign companies (branches)	..	..	..	..	..	..	..	..
All undertakings	1 898	1 960	2 272	2 363	2 539	2 316	1 489	1 989
Composite								
Domestic undertakings	23 438	23 890	24 323	25 926	25 229	24 184	22 308	22 683
Foreign controlled undertakings	..	..	..	..	..	..	..	..
Foreign companies (branches)	..	..	..	..	..	..	..	..
All undertakings	23 438	23 890	24 323	25 926	25 229	24 184	22 308	22 683
of which:								
Life	17 427	17 746	17 418	19 244	18 328	17 466	16 063	15 914
Domestic undertakings	17 427	17 746	17 418	19 244	18 328	17 466	16 063	15 914
Foreign controlled undertakings	..	..	..	..	..	..	..	..
Foreign companies (branches)	..	..	..	..	..	..	..	..
All undertakings	17 427	17 746	17 418	19 244	18 328	17 466	16 063	15 914
Non-life	6 010	6 144	6 905	6 682	6 901	6 717	6 244	6 770
Domestic undertakings	6 010	6 144	6 905	6 682	6 901	6 717	6 244	6 770
Foreign controlled undertakings	..	..	..	..	..	..	..	..
Foreign companies (branches)	..	..	..	..	..	..	..	..
All undertakings	6 010	6 144	6 905	6 682	6 901	6 717	6 244	6 770
Total								
Domestic undertakings	25 928	26 378	27 222	28 758	28 410	27 020	24 527	25 366
Foreign controlled undertakings	..	..	..	..	..	..	..	..
Foreign companies (branches)	..	..	..	..	..	..	..	..
All undertakings	25 928	26 378	27 222	28 758	28 410	27 020	24 527	25 366

BELGIUM

Table 1. Selected aggregates *(cont.)*

Million EUR

	2012	2013	2014	2015	2016	2017	2018	2019
1.3 Commissions								
Life								
Domestic undertakings	59	55	45	47	55	56	64	67
Foreign controlled undertakings	..	..	..	..	..	..	..	..
Foreign companies (branches)	..	..	..	..	..	..	..	..
All undertakings	59	55	45	47	55	56	64	67
Non-life								
Domestic undertakings	394	391	450	550	616	607	303	287
Foreign controlled undertakings	..	..	..	..	..	..	..	..
Foreign companies (branches)	..	..	..	..	..	..	..	..
All undertakings	394	391	450	550	616	607	303	287
Composite								
Domestic undertakings	2 397	2 446	2 478	2 493	2 484	2 536	2 161	2 442
Foreign controlled undertakings	..	..	..	..	..	..	..	..
Foreign companies (branches)	..	..	..	..	..	..	..	..
All undertakings	2 397	2 446	2 478	2 493	2 484	2 536	2 161	2 442
of which:								
Life	905	875	852	833	765	756	730	735
Domestic undertakings	905	875	852	833	765	756	730	735
Foreign controlled undertakings	..	..	..	..	..	..	..	..
Foreign companies (branches)	..	..	..	..	..	..	..	..
All undertakings	905	875	852	833	765	756	730	735
Non-life	1 493	1 572	1 626	1 660	1 719	1 779	1 431	1 707
Domestic undertakings	1 493	1 572	1 626	1 660	1 719	1 779	1 431	1 707
Foreign controlled undertakings	..	..	..	..	..	..	..	..
Foreign companies (branches)	..	..	..	..	..	..	..	..
All undertakings	1 493	1 572	1 626	1 660	1 719	1 779	1 431	1 707
Total								
Domestic undertakings	2 851	2 892	2 973	3 090	3 155	3 198	2 529	2 797
Foreign controlled undertakings	..	..	..	..	..	..	..	..
Foreign companies (branches)	..	..	..	..	..	..	..	..
All undertakings	2 851	2 892	2 973	3 090	3 155	3 198	2 529	2 797
1.4 Gross operating expenses								
Life								
Domestic undertakings	118	58	41	45	47	51	61	60
Foreign controlled undertakings	..	..	..	..	..	..	..	..
Foreign companies (branches)	..	..	..	..	..	..	..	..
All undertakings	118	58	41	45	47	51	61	60
Non-life								
Domestic undertakings	806	386	643	618	641	678	382	363
Foreign controlled undertakings	..	..	..	..	..	..	..	..
Foreign companies (branches)	..	..	..	..	..	..	..	..
All undertakings	806	386	643	618	641	678	382	363
Composite								
Domestic undertakings	4 401	2 084	2 197	2 205	2 320	2 402	2 306	2 425
Foreign controlled undertakings	..	..	..	..	..	..	..	..
Foreign companies (branches)	..	..	..	..	..	..	..	..
All undertakings	4 401	2 084	2 197	2 205	2 320	2 402	2 306	2 425
of which:								
Life	1 702	830	833	824	859	869	883	895
Domestic undertakings	1 702	830	833	824	859	869	883	895
Foreign controlled undertakings	..	..	..	..	..	..	..	..
Foreign companies (branches)	..	..	..	..	..	..	..	..
All undertakings	1 702	830	833	824	859	869	883	895
Non-life	2 699	1 254	1 364	1 382	1 461	1 533	1 423	1 529
Domestic undertakings	2 699	1 254	1 364	1 382	1 461	1 533	1 423	1 529
Foreign controlled undertakings	..	..	..	..	..	..	..	..
Foreign companies (branches)	..	..	..	..	..	..	..	..
All undertakings	2 699	1 254	1 364	1 382	1 461	1 533	1 423	1 529
Total								
Domestic undertakings	5 325	2 528	2 881	2 868	3 008	3 130	2 749	2 847
Foreign controlled undertakings	..	..	..	..	..	..	..	..
Foreign companies (branches)	..	..	..	..	..	..	..	..
All undertakings	5 325	2 528	2 881	2 868	3 008	3 130	2 749	2 847

BELGIUM

Table 1. Selected aggregates *(cont.)*

Million EUR

	2012	2013	2014	2015	2016	2017	2018	2019
1.5 Insurance business written abroad by branches, gross premiums								
Life								
Branches and agencies	2	2	2	0	0	0	0	0
Subsidaries	..	..	..	..	..	..	..	..
Total	2	2	2	..	0	0	0	0
Non-life								
Branches and agencies	698	727	1 572	1 931	1 854	1 843	1 912	991
Subsidaries	..	..	..	..	..	..	..	..
Total	698	727	1 572	1 931	1 854	1 843	1 912	991
Composite								
Branches and agencies	442	448	1 121	1 156	1 197	1 337	1 246	2 622
Subsidaries	..	..	..	..	..	..	..	..
Total	442	448	1 121	1 156	1 197	1 337	1 246	2 622
of which:								
Life	32	28	16	16	14	61	57	559
Branches and agencies	32	28	16	16	14	61	57	559
Subsidaries	..	..	..	..	..	..	..	..
Total	32	28	16	16	14	61	57	559
Non-life	409	421	1 105	1 141	1 183	1 276	1 189	2 063
Branches and agencies	409	421	1 105	1 141	1 183	1 276	1 189	2 063
Subsidaries	..	..	..	..	..	..	..	..
Total	409	421	1 105	1 141	1 183	1 276	1 189	2 063
Total								
Branches and agencies	1 142	1 178	2 696	3 087	3 051	3 181	3 158	3 614
Subsidaries	..	..	..	..	..	..	..	..
Total	1 142	1 178	2 696	3 087	3 051	3 181	3 158	3 614

.. Not available

Note: Detailed metadata at: *http://metalinks.oecd.org/ins/20210324/3459*.

Source: *OECD Insurance Statistics (database)*

BELGIUM

Table 2. Number of companies and employees

	2012	2013	2014	2015	2016	2017	2018	2019
2.1 Number of companies								
Life								
Domestic undertakings	17	16	15	15	12	10	9	9
Foreign controlled undertakings	..	..	..	..	..	..	..	..
Foreign companies (branches)	7	7	8	8	10	10	7	7
All undertakings	24	23	23	23	22	20	16	16
Non-life								
Domestic undertakings	49	44	42	41	38	34	36	35
Foreign controlled undertakings	..	..	..	..	..	..	..	..
Foreign companies (branches)	36	36	36	32	32	33	36	36
All undertakings	85	80	78	73	70	67	72	71
Composite								
Domestic undertakings	23	23	23	23	22	23	22	22
Foreign controlled undertakings	..	..	..	..	..	..	..	..
Foreign companies (branches)	2	2	2	2	2	2	2	2
All undertakings	25	25	25	25	24	25	24	24
Reinsurance								
Domestic undertakings	1	1	1	1	1	1	2	2
Foreign controlled undertakings	..	..	..	..	..	..	..	..
Foreign companies (branches)	1	1	1	1	1	1	1	0
All undertakings	2	2	2	2	2	2	3	2
Total								
Domestic undertakings	90	84	81	80	73	68	69	68
Foreign controlled undertakings	..	..	..	..	..	..	..	..
Foreign companies (branches)	46	46	47	43	45	46	46	45
All undertakings	136	130	128	123	118	114	115	113
2.2 Number of employees								
Insurance undertakings	..	..	..	..	..	..	..	..
Intermediaries	..	..	..	..	..	..	..	..
Total	..	..	..	..	..	..	..	..

.. Not available

Note: Detailed metadata at: *http://metalinks.oecd.org/ins/20210324/3459*.

Source: *OECD Insurance Statistics (database)*

CANADA

Table 1. Selected aggregates

Million CAD

	2012	2013	2014	2015	2016	2017	2018	2019
1.1 Insurance business written in the reporting country								
1.1.1 Insurance business, by ownership								
Gross premiums								
Domestic undertakings	87 337	91 830	81 347	86 082	89 439	93 962	97 815	..
Foreign controlled undertakings	11 465	11 237	18 957	17 321	18 250	19 658	19 804	..
Foreign companies (branches)	9 621	9 651	21 604	20 840	19 141	19 488	14 937	..
All undertakings	96 958	101 481	102 951	106 922	108 580	113 450	112 752	..
Premiums ceded								
Domestic undertakings	23 483	25 176	22 771	25 855	23 885	26 759	19 135	..
Foreign controlled undertakings	2 413	2 504	5 070	4 912	5 107	7 154	6 751	..
Foreign companies (branches)	2 405	2 094	4 469	4 735	4 370	4 568	4 467	..
All undertakings	25 888	27 270	27 240	30 590	28 255	31 327	23 602	..
Net written premiums								
Domestic undertakings	63 854	66 655	58 576	60 227	65 554	67 204	78 680	..
Foreign controlled undertakings	9 052	8 733	13 888	12 410	13 142	12 504	13 053	..
Foreign companies (branches)	7 216	7 557	17 135	16 104	14 771	14 920	10 470	..
All undertakings	71 070	74 212	75 710	76 331	80 325	82 123	89 150	..
1.1.2 Insurance business on foreign risks, gross premiums								
Life	..	..	..	..	..	..	..	..
Non-life	..	..	..	..	..	..	..	..
Composite	..	..	..	..	..	..	..	..
of which:								
Life	..	..	..	..	..	..	..	..
Non-life	..	..	..	..	..	..	..	..
Total	..	..	..	..	..	..	..	..
1.1.3 Life insurance payments, by class, gross premiums								
Annuities	5 276	6 263	5 562	5 539	5 966	6 558	7 390	..
Unit linked	..	..	..	..	..	..	..	..
Other life insurance	..	..	..	..	..	..	..	..
Total life insurance	..	..	..	..	..	..	..	..
***of which:** Pension contracts*	..	..	..	..	..	..	..	..
1.1.4 Non-life insurance payments, by class, gross premiums								
Motor vehicle insurance	21 805	22 857	21 007	21 426	21 938	23 234	24 519	..
Marine, aviation and other transport insurance	672	630	773	716	769	700	1 143	..
Freight insurance	..	..	..	..	..	..	..	..
Fire and other property damage insurance	16 577	16 687	18 994	19 992	20 599	21 593	28 429	..
Pecuniary loss insurance	1 785	1 748	2 271	2 613	2 659	2 708	2 559	..
General liability insurance	5 197	5 267	5 830	6 289	6 339	6 398	10 463	..
Accident and health	19 672	20 262	25 708	26 370	25 944	26 471	24 315	..
***of which:** Health*	..	..	..	..	..	..	..	..
Other non-life insurance	14	32	138	275	368	440	170	..
Treaty reinsurance	..	..	..	..	..	..	..	..
Total non-life insurance	65 723	67 482	74 721	77 682	78 616	81 545	91 598	..
1.2 Gross claims payments								
Life								
Domestic undertakings	0	0	0	0	3	..	3	..
Foreign controlled undertakings	0	0	0	0	0	..	0	..
Foreign companies (branches)	28	36	41	13	3	3	3	..
All undertakings	28	36	41	13	6	3	6	..
Non-life								
Domestic undertakings	24 435	28 506	25 194	25 500	30 110	29 433	30 596	..
Foreign controlled undertakings	4 939	5 566	8 332	8 552	11 171	11 043	11 435	..
Foreign companies (branches)	4 875	5 242	5 901	4 694	6 748	4 566	6 479	..
All undertakings	29 310	33 748	31 095	30 193	36 858	33 999	37 075	..
Composite								
Domestic undertakings	10 851	11 227	9 477	10 030	11 984	12 753	18 600	..
Foreign controlled undertakings	731	736	881	303	336	396	435	..
Foreign companies (branches)	163	159	7 182	7 161	5 671	5 797	1 025	..
All undertakings	11 014	11 386	16 659	17 190	17 654	18 549	19 626	..
of which:								
Life	4 749	4 969	5 480	5 747	5 919	6 342	6 699	..
Domestic undertakings	4 650	4 869	3 858	4 186	4 581	4 981	6 073	..
Foreign controlled undertakings	189	190	344	188	210	256	301	..
Foreign companies (branches)	99	99	1 622	1 561	1 339	1 361	626	..
All undertakings	4 749	4 969	5 480	5 747	5 919	6 342	6 699	..
Non-life	6 264	6 417	11 179	11 444	11 735	12 207	12 927	..
Domestic undertakings	6 201	6 357	5 620	5 844	7 403	7 772	12 528	..
Foreign controlled undertakings	542	546	537	115	127	139	134	..
Foreign companies (branches)	63	60	5 560	5 600	4 332	4 435	399	..
All undertakings	6 264	6 417	11 179	11 444	11 735	12 207	12 927	..
Total								
Domestic undertakings	35 286	39 733	34 671	35 529	42 097	42 186	49 199	..
Foreign controlled undertakings	5 670	6 301	9 213	8 854	11 508	11 439	11 870	..
Foreign companies (branches)	5 066	5 437	13 124	11 867	12 422	10 366	7 507	..
All undertakings	40 351	45 170	47 795	47 396	54 518	52 552	56 706	..

CANADA

Table 1. Selected aggregates *(cont.)*

Million CAD

	2012	2013	2014	2015	2016	2017	2018	2019
1.3 Commissions								
Life								
Domestic undertakings	0	0	..	0	0	0	..	..
Foreign controlled undertakings	0	0	..	..	..	..	..	..
Foreign companies (branches)	12	10	..	0	0	0	..	..
All undertakings	12	10	..	0	0	0	..	..
Non-life								
Domestic undertakings	4 719	4 781	..	5 441	5 666	5 434	6 103	..
Foreign controlled undertakings	1 115	1 092	..	1 882	1 938	2 087	2 182	..
Foreign companies (branches)	1 077	1 095	..	1 104	1 177	1 299	1 492	..
All undertakings	5 796	5 876	..	6 545	6 843	6 733	7 595	..
Composite								
Domestic undertakings	5 505	5 558	..	4 787	5 363	5 218	5 127	..
Foreign controlled undertakings	258	239	..	97	94	97	150	..
Foreign companies (branches)	147	145	..	193	156	197	174	..
All undertakings	5 652	5 703	..	4 980	5 519	5 416	5 301	..
of which:								
Life	4 239	4 291	..	3 572	4 059	3 893	3 812	..
Domestic undertakings	4 150	4 213	..	3 457	3 982	3 801	3 734	..
Foreign controlled undertakings	172	173	..	65	72	75	93	..
Foreign companies (branches)	89	78	..	115	77	93	78	..
All undertakings	4 239	4 291	..	3 572	4 059	3 893	3 812	..
Non-life	1 413	1 412	..	1 408	1 460	1 522	1 489	..
Domestic undertakings	1 355	1 345	..	1 330	1 381	1 418	1 393	..
Foreign controlled undertakings	86	66	..	32	22	22	57	..
Foreign companies (branches)	58	67	..	78	79	105	97	..
All undertakings	1 413	1 412	..	1 408	1 460	1 522	1 489	..
Total								
Domestic undertakings	10 224	10 339	..	10 228	11 029	10 653	11 230	..
Foreign controlled undertakings	1 373	1 331	..	1 979	2 032	2 184	2 332	..
Foreign companies (branches)	1 235	1 249	..	1 298	1 333	1 496	1 666	..
All undertakings	11 460	11 588	..	11 526	12 362	12 149	12 896	..
1.4 Gross operating expenses								
Life								
Domestic undertakings	22	23	24	22	30	29	25	..
Foreign controlled undertakings	0	..	0	0	0	0	0	..
Foreign companies (branches)	32	27	28	15	10	9	10	..
All undertakings	53	50	52	37	40	38	36	..
Non-life								
Domestic undertakings	5 774	6 023	4 032	4 493	4 725	4 694	4 658	..
Foreign controlled undertakings	1 465	1 409	1 385	1 488	1 756	1 635	1 548	..
Foreign companies (branches)	1 001	1 017	855	689	673	672	704	..
All undertakings	6 775	7 040	4 887	5 182	5 398	5 366	5 362	..
Composite								
Domestic undertakings	12 274	13 728	12 612	14 400	17 159	17 966	19 399	..
Foreign controlled undertakings	557	571	736	187	194	248	251	..
Foreign companies (branches)	110	117	206	272	518	713	259	..
All undertakings	12 384	13 845	12 818	14 672	17 677	18 679	19 658	..
of which:								
Life	..	..	..	..	..	..	..	..
Domestic undertakings	..	..	..	..	..	..	..	..
Foreign controlled undertakings	..	..	..	..	..	..	..	..
Foreign companies (branches)	..	..	..	..	..	..	..	..
All undertakings	..	..	..	..	..	..	..	..
Non-life	..	..	..	..	..	..	..	..
Domestic undertakings	..	..	..	..	..	..	..	..
Foreign controlled undertakings	..	..	..	..	..	..	..	..
Foreign companies (branches)	..	..	..	..	..	..	..	..
All undertakings	..	..	..	..	..	..	..	..
Total								
Domestic undertakings	18 069	19 774	16 668	18 915	21 914	22 689	24 082	..
Foreign controlled undertakings	2 021	1 981	2 121	1 675	1 950	1 883	1 799	..
Foreign companies (branches)	1 143	1 161	1 089	976	1 201	1 394	973	..
All undertakings	19 212	20 934	17 757	19 891	23 115	24 083	25 055	..

CANADA

Table 1. Selected aggregates *(cont.)*

Million CAD

	2012	2013	2014	2015	2016	2017	2018	2019
1.5 Insurance business written abroad by branches, gross premiums								
Life								
Branches and agencies	..	..	..	..	..	..	..	..
Subsidaries	..	..	..	..	..	..	..	..
Total	..	..	0	0	0	0	0	..
Non-life								
Branches and agencies	..	..	..	..	..	..	..	..
Subsidaries	..	..	..	..	..	..	..	..
Total	548	1 018	1 320	1 500	1 502	1 522	2 658	..
Composite								
Branches and agencies	..	..	..	..	..	..	..	..
Subsidaries	..	..	..	..	..	..	..	..
Total	37 741	7 942	31 162	40 235	50 713	54 040	57 636	..
of which:								
Life	..	..	27 224	..	..	..	..	..
Branches and agencies	..	..	..	..	..	..	..	..
Subsidaries	..	..	..	..	..	..	..	..
Total	..	..	27 224	..	..	..	..	..
Non-life	..	..	3 939	..	..	..	..	..
Branches and agencies	..	..	..	..	..	..	..	..
Subsidaries	..	..	..	..	..	..	..	..
Total	..	..	3 939	..	..	..	..	..
Total								
Branches and agencies	..	..	..	..	..	..	..	..
Subsidaries	..	..	..	..	..	..	..	..
Total	38 289	8 959	32 482	41 736	52 215	55 562	60 294	..

.. Not available

Note: Detailed metadata at: *http://metalinks.oecd.org/ins/20210324/8992.*

Source: *OECD Insurance Statistics (database)*

CANADA

Table 2. Number of companies and employees

	2012	2013	2014	2015	2016	2017	2018	2019
2.1 Number of companies								
Life								
Domestic undertakings	1	1	1	1	3	3	3	..
Foreign controlled undertakings	0	0	0	0	0	0	0	..
Foreign companies (branches)	5	5	5	5	2	2	2	..
All undertakings	6	6	6	6	5	5	5	..
Non-life								
Domestic undertakings	84	60	66	66	63	61	57	..
Foreign controlled undertakings	23	22	28	28	27	27	25	..
Foreign companies (branches)	60	60	60	58	54	54	54	..
All undertakings	144	120	126	124	117	115	111	..
Composite								
Domestic undertakings	43	34	34	33	31	31	29	..
Foreign controlled undertakings	10	10	9	7	7	8	7	..
Foreign companies (branches)	21	26	23	22	20	20	20	..
All undertakings	64	60	57	55	51	51	49	..
Reinsurance								
Domestic undertakings	6	6	5	5	5	5	5	..
Foreign controlled undertakings	6	6	5	5	5	5	5	..
Foreign companies (branches)	27	28	25	26	28	28	28	..
All undertakings	33	34	30	31	33	33	33	..
Total								
Domestic undertakings	134	101	106	105	102	100	94	..
Foreign controlled undertakings	39	38	42	40	39	40	37	..
Foreign companies (branches)	113	119	113	111	104	104	104	..
All undertakings	247	220	219	216	206	204	198	..
2.2 Number of employees								
Insurance undertakings	..	..	..	..	..	..	..	..
Intermediaries	..	..	..	..	..	..	..	..
Total	..	..	..	..	..	..	..	..

.. Not available

Note: Detailed metadata at: *http://metalinks.oecd.org/ins/20210324/8992.*

Source: *OECD Insurance Statistics (database)*

CHILE

Table 1. Selected aggregates

Million CLP

	2012	2013	2014	2015	2016	2017	2018	2019
1.1 Insurance business written in the reporting country								
1.1.1 Insurance business, by ownership								
Gross premiums								
Domestic undertakings	5 496 223	5 832 221	6 260 019	7 465 743	8 394 971	8 344 320	8 981 504	9 062 220
Foreign controlled undertakings	2 821 041	3 056 166	3 211 682	3 614 011	4 422 880	4 504 671	4 722 316	4 929 006
Foreign companies (branches)	..	..	..	..	..	..	..	..
All undertakings	5 496 223	5 832 221	6 260 019	7 465 743	8 394 971	8 344 320	8 981 504	9 062 220
Premiums ceded								
Domestic undertakings	930 906	906 942	998 507	1 135 872	1 310 392	1 382 346	1 428 339	1 561 858
Foreign controlled undertakings	671 333	647 814	676 439	749 522	953 240	901 373	921 260	1 052 698
Foreign companies (branches)	..	..	..	..	..	..	..	..
All undertakings	930 906	906 942	998 507	1 135 872	1 310 392	1 382 346	1 428 339	1 561 858
Net written premiums								
Domestic undertakings	4 565 317	4 925 279	5 261 513	6 329 871	7 084 578	6 961 974	7 553 165	7 500 362
Foreign controlled undertakings	2 149 709	2 408 352	2 535 243	2 864 489	3 469 640	3 603 299	3 801 056	3 876 308
Foreign companies (branches)	..	..	..	..	..	..	..	..
All undertakings	4 565 317	4 925 279	5 261 513	6 329 871	7 084 578	6 961 974	7 553 165	7 500 362
1.1.2 Insurance business on foreign risks, gross premiums								
Life	..	..	..	..	..	..	..	..
Non-life	..	..	..	..	..	..	..	..
Composite total	..	..	..	..	..	..	..	..
Total	..	..	..	..	..	..	..	..
1.1.3 Life insurance payments, by class, gross premiums								
Annuities	1 623 894	1 729 819	1 692 693	2 343 736	2 759 473	2 456 649	2 767 820	2 455 785
Unit linked	213 028	318 975	475 508	613 110	712 539	728 441	582 074	547 256
Other life insurance	1 761 476	1 827 419	1 948 628	2 123 123	2 373 130	2 560 094	2 775 274	3 016 938
Total life insurance	3 598 399	3 876 213	4 116 829	5 079 969	5 845 142	5 745 185	6 125 167	6 019 980
***of which:** Pension contracts*	..	..	..	..	..	..	..	..
1.1.4 Non-life insurance payments, by class, gross premiums								
Motor vehicle insurance	480 767	467 370	509 632	554 020	607 928	658 852	741 818	776 970
Marine, aviation and other transport insurance	93 208	117 884	129 698	148 074	132 318	134 870	152 066	172 407
Freight insurance	0	0	0	0	0	0	0	0
Fire and other property damage insurance	726 707	711 066	788 536	901 636	926 988	899 548	999 817	1 123 188
Pecuniary loss insurance	62 661	55 877	62 708	73 291	81 763	83 750	89 411	93 093
General liability insurance	80 035	52 154	56 828	41 342	34 468	30 188	41 483	46 072
Accident and health	117 127	25 789	30 296	46 180	53 105	66 796	74 322	78 869
***of which:** Health*	1 362	1 349	6 186	2 268	8 145	7 442	15 661	4 707
Other non-life insurance	335 850	524 059	561 863	602 569	651 596	675 973	705 464	697 812
Treaty reinsurance	0	0	0	0	0	0	0	0
Total non-life insurance	1 896 354	1 954 198	2 139 562	2 367 113	2 488 165	2 549 976	2 804 382	2 988 410
1.2 Gross claims payments								
Life								
Domestic undertakings	3 393 850	3 714 398	4 027 828	2 853 170	3 342 724	3 838 076	4 106 073	4 387 098
Foreign controlled undertakings	1 353 122	1 551 286	1 580 430	1 020 903	1 219 666	1 524 203	1 999 198	1 833 862
Foreign companies (branches)	..	..	..	..	..	..	..	..
All undertakings	3 393 850	3 714 398	4 027 828	2 853 170	3 342 724	3 838 076	4 106 073	4 387 098
Non-life								
Domestic undertakings	874 913	896 672	260 092	1 421 296	1 491 740	1 515 015	1 432 942	1 475 444
Foreign controlled undertakings	524 939	541 982	157 970	889 183	1 193 951	1 168 469	1 032 572	1 053 771
Foreign companies (branches)	..	..	..	..	..	..	..	..
All undertakings	874 913	896 672	260 092	1 421 296	1 491 740	1 515 015	1 432 942	1 475 444
Composite, all undertakings	..	..	..	..	..	..	..	..
Total								
Domestic undertakings	4 268 763	4 611 070	4 287 920	4 274 466	4 834 464	5 353 090	5 539 015	5 862 542
Foreign controlled undertakings	1 878 061	2 093 268	1 738 400	1 910 087	2 413 617	2 692 672	3 031 770	2 887 633
Foreign companies (branches)	..	..	..	..	..	..	..	..
All undertakings	4 268 763	4 611 070	4 287 920	4 274 466	4 834 464	5 353 090	5 539 015	5 862 542
1.3 Commissions								
Life								
Domestic undertakings	228 573	248 645	263 060	301 418	318 445	330 472	360 325	349 461
Foreign controlled undertakings	118 560	131 550	139 650	164 172	159 299	171 055	186 888	181 279
Foreign companies (branches)	..	..	..	..	..	..	..	..
All undertakings	228 573	248 645	263 060	301 418	318 445	330 472	360 325	349 461
Non-life								
Domestic undertakings	224 665	230 945	260 092	287 918	312 001	322 793	360 936	368 082
Foreign controlled undertakings	142 291	140 238	157 970	171 469	242 835	238 778	261 147	261 710
Foreign companies (branches)	..	..	..	..	..	..	..	..
All undertakings	224 665	230 945	260 092	287 918	312 001	322 793	360 936	368 082
Composite, all undertakings	..	..	..	..	..	..	..	..
Total								
Domestic undertakings	453 238	479 590	523 153	589 336	630 445	653 265	721 261	717 542
Foreign controlled undertakings	260 851	271 787	297 621	335 641	402 134	409 832	448 035	442 989
Foreign companies (branches)	..	..	..	..	..	..	..	..
All undertakings	453 238	479 590	523 153	589 336	630 445	653 265	721 261	717 542

CHILE

Table 1. Selected aggregates *(cont.)*

Million CLP

	2012	2013	2014	2015	2016	2017	2018	2019
1.4 Gross operating expenses								
Life								
Domestic undertakings	519 184	549 344	583 313	612 178	664 997	732 176	776 679	883 091
Foreign controlled undertakings	250 271	268 515	284 692	308 320	316 103	364 993	390 610	413 417
Foreign companies (branches)	..	..	..	..	..	..	..	..
All undertakings	519 184	549 344	583 313	612 178	664 997	732 176	776 679	883 091
Non-life								
Domestic undertakings	339 044	359 066	382 886	412 676	457 861	501 804	533 252	569 035
Foreign controlled undertakings	239 100	251 791	266 721	288 658	367 114	406 682	414 288	431 095
Foreign companies (branches)	..	..	..	..	..	..	..	..
All undertakings	339 044	359 066	382 886	412 676	457 861	501 804	533 252	569 035
Composite, all undertakings	..	..	..	..	..	..	..	..
Total								
Domestic undertakings	858 228	908 410	966 199	1 024 854	1 122 857	1 233 980	1 309 931	1 452 126
Foreign controlled undertakings	489 370	520 306	551 413	596 978	683 216	771 674	804 898	844 512
Foreign companies (branches)	..	..	..	..	..	..	..	..
All undertakings	858 228	908 410	966 199	1 024 854	1 122 857	1 233 980	1 309 931	1 452 126
1.5 Insurance business written abroad by branches, gross premiums								
Life								
Branches and agencies	..	..	..	..	..	..	..	..
Subsidaries	..	..	..	..	..	..	..	..
Total	..	..	..	..	..	..	..	..
Non-life								
Branches and agencies	..	..	..	..	..	..	..	..
Subsidaries	..	..	..	..	..	..	..	..
Total	..	..	..	..	..	..	..	..
Composite total	..	..	..	..	..	..	..	..
Total								
Branches and agencies	..	..	..	..	..	..	..	..
Subsidaries	..	..	..	..	..	..	..	..
Total	..	..	..	..	..	..	..	..

.. Not available

Note: Detailed metadata at: *http://metalinks.oecd.org/ins/20210324/536a*.

Source: *OECD Insurance Statistics (database)*

CHILE

Table 2. Number of companies and employees

	2012	2013	2014	2015	2016	2017	2018	2019
2.1 Number of companies								
Life								
Domestic undertakings	32	33	34	36	36	36	37	37
Foreign controlled undertakings	11	12	12	13	13	15	16	13
Foreign companies (branches)	..	..	..	..	0	..	..	..
All undertakings	32	33	34	36	36	36	37	37
Non-life								
Domestic undertakings	28	29	29	30	30	32	32	34
Foreign controlled undertakings	16	18	17	18	11	19	17	18
Foreign companies (branches)	..	..	..	..	0	..	..	..
All undertakings	28	29	29	30	30	32	32	34
Composite, all undertakings	**0**	**0**	**0**	**0**	**0**	**..**	**..**	**..**
Reinsurance								
Domestic undertakings	1	1	1	1	1	1	1	1
Foreign controlled undertakings	1	1	1	..	1	1	1	1
Foreign companies (branches)	..	..	..	..	0	..	..	..
All undertakings	1	1	1	1	1	1	1	1
Total								
Domestic undertakings	61	63	64	67	67	69	70	72
Foreign controlled undertakings	28	31	30	31	25	35	33	32
Foreign companies (branches)	..	..	..	..	0	..	..	..
All undertakings	61	63	64	67	67	69	70	72
2.2 Number of employees								
Insurance undertakings	16 304	16 686	17 039	15 368	16 414	16 859	16 908	16 891
Intermediaries	6 828	7 046	6 959	7 499	7 599	7 663	7 945	7 997
Total	23 132	23 732	23 998	22 867	24 013	24 522	24 853	24 888

.. Not available

Note: Detailed metadata at: *http://metalinks.oecd.org/ins/20210324/536a*.

Source: *OECD Insurance Statistics (database)*

COLOMBIA

Table 1. Selected aggregates

Million COP

	2012	2013	2014	2015	2016	2017	2018	2019
1.1 Insurance business written in the reporting country								
1.1.1 Insurance business, by ownership								
Gross premiums								
Domestic undertakings	16 431 445	19 075 213	19 396 882	21 943 459	24 585 330	26 496 734	27 809 761	30 812 229
Foreign controlled undertakings	6 083 355	6 665 400	7 635 672	8 309 246	8 622 786	8 718 250	8 981 678	9 654 677
Foreign companies (branches)	..	..	0	..	..	..	..	..
All undertakings	16 431 445	19 075 213	19 396 882	21 943 459	24 585 330	26 496 734	27 809 761	30 812 229
Premiums ceded								
Domestic undertakings	3 072 740	3 264 752	3 392 593	4 062 439	4 883 531	4 863 385	5 257 745	6 045 450
Foreign controlled undertakings	1 554 934	1 537 641	1 762 391	1 871 332	2 075 143	1 676 354	1 762 454	2 052 794
Foreign companies (branches)	..	..	0	..	..	..	..	..
All undertakings	3 072 740	3 264 752	3 392 593	4 062 439	4 883 531	4 863 385	5 257 745	6 045 450
Net written premiums								
Domestic undertakings	13 358 704	15 810 461	16 004 289	17 881 020	19 701 798	21 633 350	22 552 017	24 766 779
Foreign controlled undertakings	4 528 421	5 127 759	5 873 280	6 437 914	6 547 643	7 041 896	7 219 224	7 601 883
Foreign companies (branches)	..	..	0	..	..	..	..	..
All undertakings	13 358 704	15 810 461	16 004 289	17 881 020	19 701 798	21 633 350	22 552 017	24 766 779
1.1.2 Insurance business on foreign risks, gross premiums								
Life	..	..	..	..	..	..	..	..
Non-life	..	..	..	..	..	..	..	..
Composite	..	..	..	..	..	..	..	..
of which:								
Life	..	..	..	..	..	..	..	..
Non-life	..	..	..	..	..	..	..	..
Total	..	..	..	..	..	..	..	..
1.1.3 Life insurance payments, by class, gross premiums								
Annuities	2 437 934	2 437 934	814 432	1 096 967	1 759 549	2 019 643	2 204 084	2 452 253
Unit linked	..	..	..	..	..	..	..	..
Other life insurance	5 254 056	7 301 890	8 389 995	9 114 695	10 077 271	11 453 593	11 714 575	13 136 500
Total life insurance	7 691 990	9 739 824	9 204 427	10 211 663	11 836 820	13 473 236	13 918 659	15 588 754
of which: *Pension contracts*	888 794	2 278 534	642 645	904 089	1 559 392	1 854 412	2 031 168	2 264 302
1.1.4 Non-life insurance payments, by class, gross premiums								
Motor vehicle insurance	2 150 299	2 198 323	2 389 604	2 628 864	2 982 278	3 365 337	3 491 141	3 668 192
Marine, aviation and other transport insurance	135 109	55 827	96 118	134 015	140 118	142 304	135 408	183 512
Freight insurance	272 930	266 931	264 282	285 223	301 591	290 964	293 469	315 021
Fire and other property damage insurance	1 415 031	1 394 129	1 984 995	2 388 974	2 596 551	2 592 128	2 787 985	2 992 325
Pecuniary loss insurance	1 154 461	1 210 196	1 876 165	2 171 112	2 173 155	2 035 235	2 188 222	2 421 701
General liability insurance	659 355	738 250	782 424	834 365	913 075	922 751	1 073 809	1 273 279
Accident and health	285 684	343 025	431 508	480 854	588 263	543 225	482 136	610 901
of which: *Health*	52 586	52 173	55 613	59 071	60 349	60 216	62 250	63 711
Other non-life insurance	2 659 433	3 124 590	2 359 305	2 800 552	3 044 763	3 126 668	3 436 491	3 758 816
Treaty reinsurance	0	0	..	..	..	..	..	..
Total non-life insurance	8 732 302	9 331 270	10 184 400	11 723 960	12 739 794	13 018 612	13 888 659	15 223 747
1.2 Gross claims payments								
Life								
Domestic undertakings	3 756 858	4 208 328	4 732 708	5 219 437	5 850 532	6 614 108	7 506 898	7 797 284
Foreign controlled undertakings	903 570	1 074 648	1 102 287	1 246 232	1 223 887	1 289 528	1 379 180	1 393 943
Foreign companies (branches)	..	..	..	..	..	..	..	..
All undertakings	3 756 858	4 208 328	4 732 708	5 219 437	5 850 532	6 614 108	7 506 898	7 797 284
Non-life								
Domestic undertakings	3 948 527	4 219 440	4 266 391	5 013 568	6 555 550	6 355 609	6 662 371	8 175 580
Foreign controlled undertakings	1 954 653	1 811 255	2 261 082	2 565 529	3 043 646	2 668 837	2 829 971	3 777 045
Foreign companies (branches)	..	..	..	..	..	..	..	..
All undertakings	3 948 527	4 219 441	4 266 391	5 013 568	6 555 550	6 355 609	6 662 371	8 175 580
Composite								
Domestic undertakings	..	..	..	..	..	..	..	..
Foreign controlled undertakings	..	..	..	..	..	..	..	..
Foreign companies (branches)	..	..	..	..	..	..	..	..
All undertakings	..	..	..	..	..	..	..	..
of which:								
Life								
Domestic undertakings	..	..	..	..	..	..	..	..
Foreign controlled undertakings	..	..	..	..	..	..	..	..
Foreign companies (branches)	..	..	..	..	..	..	..	..
All undertakings	..	..	..	..	..	..	..	..
Non-life	..	..	..	..	..	..	..	..
Domestic undertakings	..	..	..	..	..	..	..	..
Foreign controlled undertakings	..	..	..	..	..	..	..	..
Foreign companies (branches)	..	..	..	..	..	..	..	..
All undertakings	..	..	..	..	..	..	..	..
Total								
Domestic undertakings	7 705 385	8 427 768	8 999 099	10 233 005	12 406 082	12 969 717	14 169 269	15 972 864
Foreign controlled undertakings	2 858 223	2 885 903	3 363 369	3 811 761	4 267 533	3 958 365	4 209 152	5 170 989
Foreign companies (branches)	..	..	..	..	..	..	..	..
All undertakings	7 705 385	8 427 768	8 999 099	10 233 005	12 406 082	12 969 717	14 169 269	15 972 864

COLOMBIA

Table 1. Selected aggregates (cont.)

Million COP

	2012	2013	2014	2015	2016	2017	2018	2019
1.3 Commissions								
Life								
Domestic undertakings	..	..	..	..	..	..	..	..
Foreign controlled undertakings	..	..	..	..	..	..	..	..
Foreign companies (branches)	..	..	..	..	..	..	..	..
All undertakings	..	..	..	..	..	..	..	..
Non-life								
Domestic undertakings	..	..	..	..	..	..	..	..
Foreign controlled undertakings	..	..	..	..	..	..	..	..
Foreign companies (branches)	..	..	..	..	..	..	..	..
All undertakings	..	..	..	..	..	..	..	..
Composite								
Domestic undertakings	..	..	..	..	..	..	..	..
Foreign controlled undertakings	..	..	..	..	..	..	..	..
Foreign companies (branches)	..	..	..	..	..	..	..	..
All undertakings	..	..	..	..	..	..	..	..
of which:								
Life	..	..	..	..	..	..	..	..
Domestic undertakings	..	..	..	..	..	..	..	..
Foreign controlled undertakings	..	..	..	..	..	..	..	..
Foreign companies (branches)	..	..	..	..	..	..	..	..
All undertakings	..	..	..	..	..	..	..	..
Non-life	..	..	..	..	..	..	..	..
Domestic undertakings	..	..	..	..	..	..	..	..
Foreign controlled undertakings	..	..	..	..	..	..	..	..
Foreign companies (branches)	..	..	..	..	..	..	..	..
All undertakings	..	..	..	..	..	..	..	..
Total								
Domestic undertakings	..	..	..	..	..	..	..	..
Foreign controlled undertakings	..	..	..	..	..	..	..	..
Foreign companies (branches)	..	..	..	..	..	..	..	..
All undertakings	..	..	..	..	..	..	..	..
1.4 Gross operating expenses								
Life								
Domestic undertakings	1 237 926	1 324 845	3 306 113	3 596 035	3 847 673	4 227 762	4 582 318	5 170 933
Foreign controlled undertakings	359 450	384 239	708 464	1 077 766	1 100 785	1 280 372	1 383 239	1 421 144
Foreign companies (branches)	..	..	..	..	..	..	..	..
All undertakings	1 237 926	1 324 845	3 306 113	3 596 035	3 847 673	4 227 762	4 582 318	5 170 933
Non-life								
Domestic undertakings	1 718 330	1 957 574	3 907 054	4 067 473	4 555 295	4 738 383	4 996 774	5 709 898
Foreign controlled undertakings	1 052 070	1 052 070	2 331 832	2 418 659	2 624 752	2 729 921	2 665 162	3 071 224
Foreign companies (branches)	..	..	..	..	..	..	..	..
All undertakings	1 718 330	1 957 574	3 907 054	4 067 473	4 555 295	4 738 383	4 996 774	5 709 898
Composite								
Domestic undertakings	..	..	..	..	..	..	..	..
Foreign controlled undertakings	..	..	..	..	..	..	..	..
Foreign companies (branches)	..	..	..	..	..	..	..	..
All undertakings	..	..	..	..	..	..	..	..
of which:								
Life	..	..	..	..	..	..	..	..
Domestic undertakings	..	..	..	..	..	..	..	..
Foreign controlled undertakings	..	..	..	..	..	..	..	..
Foreign companies (branches)	..	..	..	..	..	..	..	..
All undertakings	..	..	..	..	..	..	..	..
Non-life	..	..	..	..	..	..	..	..
Domestic undertakings	..	..	..	..	..	..	..	..
Foreign controlled undertakings	..	..	..	..	..	..	..	..
Foreign companies (branches)	..	..	..	..	..	..	..	..
All undertakings	..	..	..	..	..	..	..	..
Total								
Domestic undertakings	2 956 256	3 282 419	7 213 167	7 663 508	8 402 968	8 966 145	9 579 092	10 880 831
Foreign controlled undertakings	1 411 520	1 436 309	3 040 295	3 496 425	3 725 536	4 010 293	4 048 401	4 492 368
Foreign companies (branches)	..	..	..	..	..	..	..	..
All undertakings	2 956 256	3 282 419	7 213 167	7 663 508	8 402 968	8 966 145	9 579 092	10 880 831

COLOMBIA

Table 1. Selected aggregates *(cont.)*

Million COP

	2012	2013	2014	2015	2016	2017	2018	2019
1.5 Insurance business written abroad by branches, gross premiums								
Life								
Branches and agencies	..	..	..	..	..	..	..	..
Subsidaries	..	..	..	..	..	..	..	..
Total	..	..	..	..	..	..	..	..
Non-life								
Branches and agencies	..	..	..	..	..	..	..	..
Subsidaries	..	..	..	..	..	..	..	..
Total	..	..	..	..	..	..	..	..
Composite								
Branches and agencies	..	..	..	..	..	..	..	..
Subsidaries	..	..	..	..	..	..	..	..
Total	..	..	..	..	..	..	..	..
of which:								
Life	..	..	..	..	..	..	..	..
Branches and agencies	..	..	..	..	..	..	..	..
Subsidaries	..	..	..	..	..	..	..	..
Total	..	..	..	..	..	..	..	..
Non-life	..	..	..	..	..	..	..	..
Branches and agencies	..	..	..	..	..	..	..	..
Subsidaries	..	..	..	..	..	..	..	..
Total	..	..	..	..	..	..	..	..
Total								
Branches and agencies	..	..	..	..	..	..	..	..
Subsidaries	..	..	..	..	..	..	..	..
Total	..	..	..	..	..	..	..	..

.. Not available

Note: Detailed metadata at: *http://metalinks.oecd.org/ins/20210324/cb10.*

Source: *OECD Insurance Statistics (database)*

COLOMBIA

Table 2. Number of companies and employees

	2012	2013	2014	2015	2016	2017	2018	2019
2.1 Number of companies								
Life								
Domestic undertakings	19	19	19	19	19	20	20	18
Foreign controlled undertakings	8	8	9	9	9	10	10	9
Foreign companies (branches)	..	..	0	0	0	0	0	0
All undertakings	19	19	19	19	19	20	20	18
Non-life								
Domestic undertakings	26	25	26	28	26	26	26	26
Foreign controlled undertakings	14	15	18	19	17	17	17	17
Foreign companies (branches)	..	..	0	0	0	0	0	0
All undertakings	26	25	26	28	26	26	26	26
Composite								
Domestic undertakings	..	..	..	..	..	..	..	..
Foreign controlled undertakings	..	..	..	..	..	..	..	..
Foreign companies (branches)	..	..	..	..	..	..	..	..
All undertakings	..	..	..	..	..	..	..	..
Reinsurance								
Domestic undertakings	..	..	0	0	0	..	..	0
Foreign controlled undertakings	..	..	0	0	0	..	..	0
Foreign companies (branches)	..	..	..	..	0	..	..	..
All undertakings	..	..	0	0	0	..	..	0
Total								
Domestic undertakings	45	44	45	47	45	46	46	44
Foreign controlled undertakings	22	23	27	28	26	27	27	26
Foreign companies (branches)	..	..	0	0	0	0	0	0
All undertakings	45	44	45	47	45	46	46	44
2.2 Number of employees								
Insurance undertakings	..	..	18 913	20 862	22 734	24 073	28 043	27 322
Intermediaries	..	..	..	..	..	..	..	..
Total	..	..	18 913	20 862	22 734	..	..	..

.. Not available

Note: Detailed metadata at: *http://metalinks.oecd.org/ins/20210324/cb10.*

Source: *OECD Insurance Statistics (database)*

CZECH REPUBLIC

Table 1. Selected aggregates

Million CZK

	2012	2013	2014	2015	2016	2017	2018	2019
1.1 Insurance business written in the reporting country								
1.1.1 Insurance business, by ownership								
Gross premiums								
Domestic undertakings	145 572	147 955	148 755	140 688	135 581	138 186	142 473	152 231
Foreign controlled undertakings	134 114	135 671	137 200	129 432	124 165	125 585	128 377	136 031
Foreign companies (branches)	8 026	8 567	9 164	11 159	11 102	11 459	10 768	13 208
All undertakings	153 597	156 522	157 919	151 846	146 683	149 645	153 241	165 439
Premiums ceded								
Domestic undertakings	27 730	29 333	29 915	29 857	28 913	30 449	31 057	32 569
Foreign controlled undertakings	24 826	26 054	26 601	26 578	25 450	26 230	26 704	27 639
Foreign companies (branches)	984	1 016	1 250	1 561	1 993	1 484	1 048	1 450
All undertakings	28 714	30 349	31 165	31 418	30 905	31 933	32 105	34 018
Net written premiums								
Domestic undertakings	117 842	118 623	118 839	110 831	106 669	107 737	111 416	119 662
Foreign controlled undertakings	109 288	109 617	110 598	102 854	98 714	99 356	101 673	108 393
Foreign companies (branches)	7 041	7 550	7 914	9 598	9 109	9 976	9 720	11 758
All undertakings	124 884	126 173	126 754	120 429	115 778	117 713	121 136	131 421
1.1.2 Insurance business on foreign risks, gross premiums								
Life	3	0	0	0	0	0	0	0
Non-life	931	741	993	524	274	738	874	1 906
Composite	1 681	1 780	2 121	1 867	1 843	2 777	3 561	3 503
of which:								
Life	0	37	360	4	0	1 805	1 897	2 099
Non-life	1 681	1 742	1 761	1 863	1 843	972	1 664	1 404
Total	2 614	2 521	3 113	2 390	2 117	3 515	4 435	5 408
1.1.3 Life insurance payments, by class, gross premiums								
Annuities	1 810	1 775	1 505	1 413	..	..	..	..
Unit linked	37 799	34 764	37 632	35 125	26 131	25 608	25 199	19 296
Other life insurance	32 437	35 030	32 042	25 876	33 110	31 425	30 653	33 652
Total life insurance	72 046	71 569	71 179	62 414	59 240	57 033	55 852	52 948
***of which:** Pension contracts*	..	..	..	..	..	0	0	0
1.1.4 Non-life insurance payments, by class, gross premiums								
Motor vehicle insurance	34 350	35 804	37 855	39 633	38 212	40 533	44 078	48 204
Marine, aviation and other transport insurance	243	214	294	331	912	1 073	1 072	1 056
Freight insurance	336	393	461	466	0	..	..	..
Fire and other property damage insurance	20 832	21 442	21 687	22 655	23 042	24 244	24 997	26 621
Pecuniary loss insurance	5 190	5 920	4 933	3 770	3 959	4 030	3 309	3 805
General liability insurance	12 420	12 869	13 164	13 810	13 609	14 559	15 207	16 661
Accident and health	5 523	5 482	5 342	5 393	5 136	5 460	5 802	13 242
***of which:** Health*	0	0	0	0	0	2 474	2 575	3 260
Other non-life insurance	2 656	2 825	3 002	3 374	2 223	2 364	2 489	2 432
Treaty reinsurance	0	0	0	0	0	..	..	..
Total non-life insurance	81 550	84 950	86 738	89 431	87 092	92 263	96 954	112 021
1.2 Gross claims payments								
Life								
Domestic undertakings	968	765	1 307	702	.. c	.. c	.. c	.. c
Foreign controlled undertakings	968	765	1 307	702	.. c	.. c	.. c	.. c
Foreign companies (branches)	4 402	7 219	6 044	6 376	6 094	6 249	5 572	6 169
All undertakings	5 370	7 984	7 352	7 077	6 456	6 567	5 875	6 176
Non-life								
Domestic undertakings	3 594	5 208	6 045	2 285	2 103	2 172	2 681	3 159
Foreign controlled undertakings	1 648	2 171	1 734	1 288	1 072	1 070	1 349	1 507
Foreign companies (branches)	746	1 184	1 353	1 216	1 674	1 764	1 344	1 778
All undertakings	4 340	6 392	7 398	3 501	3 777	3 936	4 025	4 937
Composite								
Domestic undertakings	78 484	86 244	90 284	84 909	81 024	80 221	80 773	87 779
Foreign controlled undertakings	74 012	81 355	84 712	79 681	75 835	75 301	75 653	82 528
Foreign companies (branches)	0	0	0	0	0	0	0	..
All undertakings	78 484	86 244	90 284	84 909	81 024	80 221	80 773	87 779
of which:								
Life	41 040	43 395	50 972	44 105	37 676	36 087	37 421	37 517
Domestic undertakings	41 040	43 395	50 972	44 105	37 676	36 087	37 421	37 517
Foreign controlled undertakings	39 685	42 174	49 092	42 631	36 570	35 018	36 422	37 483
Foreign companies (branches)	0	0	0	0	0	0	0	..
All undertakings	41 040	43 395	50 972	44 105	37 676	36 087	37 421	37 517
Non-life	37 444	42 849	39 312	40 805	43 348	44 134	43 352	50 263
Domestic undertakings	37 444	42 849	39 312	40 805	43 348	44 134	43 352	50 263
Foreign controlled undertakings	34 327	39 180	35 620	37 050	39 265	40 283	39 231	45 044
Foreign companies (branches)	0	0	0	0	0	0	0	..
All undertakings	37 444	42 849	39 312	40 805	43 348	44 134	43 352	50 263
Total								
Domestic undertakings	83 046	92 217	97 636	87 896	83 490	82 712	83 757	90 945
Foreign controlled undertakings	76 628	84 291	87 754	81 671	77 269	76 690	77 305	84 035
Foreign companies (branches)	5 148	8 403	7 397	7 592	7 767	8 012	6 916	7 947
All undertakings	88 194	100 620	105 033	95 488	91 257	90 724	90 673	98 892

CZECH REPUBLIC

Table 1. Selected aggregates *(cont.)*

Million CZK

	2012	2013	2014	2015	2016	2017	2018	2019
1.3 Commissions								
Life								
Domestic undertakings	..	..	..	..	..	..	..	..
Foreign controlled undertakings	..	..	..	..	..	..	..	..
Foreign companies (branches)	..	..	..	..	..	..	..	..
All undertakings	..	..	..	..	..	..	..	..
Non-life								
Domestic undertakings	..	..	..	..	..	..	..	..
Foreign controlled undertakings	..	..	..	..	..	..	..	..
Foreign companies (branches)	..	..	..	..	..	..	..	..
All undertakings	..	..	..	..	..	..	..	..
Composite								
Domestic undertakings	..	..	..	..	..	..	..	..
Foreign controlled undertakings	..	..	..	..	..	..	..	..
Foreign companies (branches)	..	..	..	..	..	..	..	..
All undertakings	..	..	..	..	..	..	..	..
of which:								
Life	..	..	..	..	..	..	..	..
Domestic undertakings	..	..	..	..	..	..	..	..
Foreign controlled undertakings	..	..	..	..	..	..	..	..
Foreign companies (branches)	..	..	..	..	..	..	..	..
All undertakings	..	..	..	..	..	..	..	..
Non-life	..	..	..	..	..	..	..	..
Domestic undertakings	..	..	..	..	..	..	..	..
Foreign controlled undertakings	..	..	..	..	..	..	..	..
Foreign companies (branches)	..	..	..	..	..	..	..	..
All undertakings	..	..	..	..	..	..	..	..
Total								
Domestic undertakings	..	..	..	..	..	..	..	..
Foreign controlled undertakings	..	..	..	..	..	..	..	..
Foreign companies (branches)	..	..	..	..	..	..	..	..
All undertakings	..	..	..	..	..	..	..	..
1.4 Gross operating expenses								
Life								
Domestic undertakings	1 132	748	759	739	.. c	.. c	.. c	.. c
Foreign controlled undertakings	1 132	748	759	739	.. c	.. c	.. c	.. c
Foreign companies (branches)	1 659	1 587	1 459	2 036	2 015	1 894	1 905	2 451
All undertakings	2 791	2 335	2 219	2 775	2 520	2 251	2 232	2 485
Non-life								
Domestic undertakings	1 970	1 795	1 805	1 571	1 203	2 170	2 988	2 902
Foreign controlled undertakings	1 152	987	937	883	622	979	1 044	1 424
Foreign companies (branches)	277	715	841	1 203	1 224	1 412	1 401	1 767
All undertakings	2 247	2 510	2 646	2 773	2 427	3 582	4 389	4 669
Composite								
Domestic undertakings	21 405	21 863	22 207	20 341	21 319	36 095	41 260	40 228
Foreign controlled undertakings	20 417	20 499	21 233	19 120	19 893	32 685	36 930	36 082
Foreign companies (branches)	0	0	0	0	0	0	0	..
All undertakings	21 405	21 863	22 207	20 341	21 319	36 095	41 260	40 228
of which:								
Life	12 009	11 670	11 475	9 613	9 217	11 707	12 405	10 887
Domestic undertakings	12 009	11 670	11 475	9 613	9 217	11 707	12 405	10 887
Foreign controlled undertakings	11 604	11 231	11 050	9 059	8 637	10 795	11 445	10 249
Foreign companies (branches)	0	0	0	0	0	0	0	..
All undertakings	12 009	11 670	11 475	9 613	9 217	11 707	12 405	10 887
Non-life	9 396	10 193	10 733	10 728	12 102	24 388	28 855	29 341
Domestic undertakings	9 396	10 193	10 733	10 728	12 102	24 388	28 855	29 341
Foreign controlled undertakings	8 814	9 268	10 184	10 061	11 256	21 890	25 485	25 833
Foreign companies (branches)	0	0	0	0	0	0	0	..
All undertakings	9 396	10 193	10 733	10 728	12 102	24 388	28 855	29 341
Total								
Domestic undertakings	24 507	24 407	24 772	22 650	23 027	38 621	44 574	43 164
Foreign controlled undertakings	22 701	22 234	22 929	20 742	21 020	34 020	38 301	37 505
Foreign companies (branches)	1 936	2 302	2 301	3 239	3 239	3 307	3 307	4 218
All undertakings	26 443	26 708	27 072	25 889	26 266	41 928	47 881	47 382

CZECH REPUBLIC

Table 1. Selected aggregates *(cont.)*

Million CZK

	2012	2013	2014	2015	2016	2017	2018	2019
1.5 Insurance business written abroad by branches, gross premiums								
Life								
Branches and agencies	0	0	0	0	0	0	0	0
Subsidaries	..	..	..	..	..	..	..	..
Total	0	0	0	0	..	0	0	0
Non-life								
Branches and agencies	307	323	313	351	377	596	804	1 076
Subsidaries	..	..	..	..	..	..	..	..
Total	307	323	313	351	377	596	804	1 076
Composite								
Branches and agencies	1 359	3 714	4 528	5 164	1 697	1 805	1 897	2 099
Subsidaries	..	..	..	..	..	..	..	..
Total	1 359	3 714	4 528	5 164	1 697	1 805	1 897	2 099
of which:								
Life	1 317	1 737	1 434	1 460	1 697	1 805	1 897	2 099
Branches and agencies	1 317	1 737	1 434	1 460	1 697	1 805	1 897	2 099
Subsidaries	..	..	..	..	..	..	..	..
Total	1 317	1 737	1 434	1 460	1 697	1 805	1 897	2 099
Non-life	42	1 977	3 095	3 704	..	0	0	0
Branches and agencies	42	1 977	3 095	3 704	0	0	0	0
Subsidaries	..	..	..	..	..	..	..	..
Total	42	1 977	3 095	3 704	..	0	0	0
Total								
Branches and agencies	1 666	4 037	4 841	5 516	2 074	2 401	2 700	3 175
Subsidaries	..	..	..	..	..	..	..	..
Total	1 666	4 037	4 841	5 516	2 074	2 401	2 700	3 175

.. Not available; c Confidential data

Note: Detailed metadata at: *http://metalinks.oecd.org/ins/20210324/46a3*.

Source: *OECD Insurance Statistics (database)*

CZECH REPUBLIC

Table 2. Number of companies and employees

	2012	2013	2014	2015	2016	2017	2018	2019
2.1 Number of companies								
Life								
Domestic undertakings	3	2	2	2	1	1	1	1
Foreign controlled undertakings	3	2	2	2	1	1	1	0
Foreign companies (branches)	3	3	4	5	5	5	6	6
All undertakings	6	5	6	7	6	6	7	7
Non-life								
Domestic undertakings	16	16	15	15	13	11	11	11
Foreign controlled undertakings	8	8	7	5	4	3	3	3
Foreign companies (branches)	15	15	16	18	19	17	14	13
All undertakings	31	31	31	33	32	28	25	24
Composite								
Domestic undertakings	15	15	15	14	14	14	14	13
Foreign controlled undertakings	12	12	12	11	11	11	11	10
Foreign companies (branches)	0	0	0	0	0	0	0	1
All undertakings	15	15	15	14	14	14	14	14
Reinsurance								
Domestic undertakings	1	1	1	1	1	1	1	1
Foreign controlled undertakings	1	1	1	1	1	1	1	1
Foreign companies (branches)	..	..	..	..	..	0	0	0
All undertakings	1	1	1	1	1	1	1	1
Total								
Domestic undertakings	35	34	33	32	29	27	27	26
Foreign controlled undertakings	24	23	22	19	17	16	16	14
Foreign companies (branches)	18	18	20	23	24	22	20	20
All undertakings	53	52	53	55	53	49	47	46
2.2 Number of employees								
Insurance undertakings	..	..	..	..	..	..	..	11 545
Intermediaries	..	..	..	..	..	..	..	..
Total	..	..	..	..	..	..	..	..

.. Not available

Note: Detailed metadata at: *http://metalinks.oecd.org/ins/20210324/46a3*.

Source: *OECD Insurance Statistics (database)*

DENMARK

Table 1. Selected aggregates

Million DKK

	2012	2013	2014	2015	2016	2017	2018	2019
1.1 Insurance business written in the reporting country								
1.1.1 Insurance business, by ownership								
Gross premiums								
Domestic undertakings	189 673	1 268 025	208 213	215 276	225 500	247 934	258 749	257 368
Foreign controlled undertakings	34 996	39 736	46 022	46 192	49 042	53 373	53 706	41 503
Foreign companies (branches)	..	..	..	..	..	..	..	..
All undertakings	189 673	1 268 025	208 213	215 276	225 500	247 934	258 749	257 368
Premiums ceded								
Domestic undertakings	7 009	7 417	5 875	6 309	6 943	8 079	7 160	5 780
Foreign controlled undertakings	3 293	3 199	2 080	2 462	2 355	2 024	1 666	794
Foreign companies (branches)	..	..	..	..	..	..	..	..
All undertakings	7 009	7 417	5 875	6 309	6 943	8 079	7 160	5 780
Net written premiums								
Domestic undertakings	182 664	1 260 608	202 338	208 966	218 557	239 855	251 589	251 588
Foreign controlled undertakings	31 703	36 537	43 942	43 730	46 687	51 349	52 040	40 709
Foreign companies (branches)	..	..	..	..	..	..	..	..
All undertakings	182 664	1 260 608	202 338	208 966	218 557	239 855	251 589	251 588
1.1.2 Insurance business on foreign risks, gross premiums								
Life	3 530	1 125	631	631	..	..	..	..
Non-life	14 359	14 611	23 099	22 611	..	..	..	..
Composite total	..	..	..	..	..	..	..	..
Total	17 889	15 737	23 730	23 242	..	..	..	..
1.1.3 Life insurance payments, by class, gross premiums								
Annuities	..	..	..	..	..	..	..	..
Unit linked	..	..	..	..	..	..	..	..
Other life insurance	..	..	..	..	..	..	..	..
Total life insurance	129 477	133 294	140 314	147 662	153 907	170 623	180 289	182 733
***of which:** Pension contracts*	..	..	..	..	..	..	..	..
1.1.4 Non-life insurance payments, by class, gross premiums								
Motor vehicle insurance	16 511	16 304	19 310	19 146	21 247	23 487	25 929	21 607
Marine, aviation and other transport insurance	1 397	1 263	1 174	1 105	1 857	1 844	1 769	1 763
Freight insurance	..	..	..	0	..	..	..	..
Fire and other property damage insurance	20 461	20 737	22 855	22 642	25 107	26 732	26 184	26 145
Pecuniary loss insurance	359	372	402	417	1 113	2 045	1 921	2 086
General liability insurance	2 023	2 061	2 377	2 314	3 203	3 411	3 494	3 659
Accident and health	13 553	12 611	15 063	15 282	15 965	16 727	16 051	16 759
***of which:** Health*	1 013	1 051	1 265	1 337	4 498	4 657	4 129	4 641
Other non-life insurance	4 465	4 659	5 156	5 052	1 635	1 759	1 710	1 808
Treaty reinsurance	638	653	867	937	538	616	687	11
Total non-life insurance	59 407	58 661	67 204	66 895	70 665	76 621	77 745	73 838
1.2 Gross claims payments								
Life								
Domestic undertakings	92 230	111 119	124 323	98 376	115 270	112 996	128 844	128 044
Foreign controlled undertakings	22 286	24 154	24 385	20 765	23 573	22 740	25 299	19 923
Foreign companies (branches)	..	..	..	..	..	..	..	..
All undertakings	92 230	111 119	124 323	98 376	115 270	112 996	128 844	128 044
Non-life								
Domestic undertakings	40 906	43 547	46 601	47 833	44 773	45 620	46 939	47 270
Foreign controlled undertakings	6 308	6 731	13 007	13 316	11 816	11 605	11 136	10 436
Foreign companies (branches)	..	..	..	..	..	..	..	..
All undertakings	40 906	43 547	46 601	47 833	44 773	45 620	46 939	47 270
Composite, all undertakings	..	..	..	..	..	..	..	..
Total								
Domestic undertakings	133 136	154 666	170 924	146 209	160 043	158 616	175 783	175 314
Foreign controlled undertakings	28 594	30 885	37 392	34 081	35 389	34 345	36 435	30 359
Foreign companies (branches)	..	..	..	..	..	..	..	..
All undertakings	133 136	154 666	170 924	146 209	160 043	158 616	175 783	175 314
1.3 Commissions								
Life								
Domestic undertakings	194	182	195	199	175	207	246	209
Foreign controlled undertakings	59	43	60	36	34	26	30	0
Foreign companies (branches)	..	..	..	..	..	..	..	..
All undertakings	194	182	195	199	175	207	246	209
Non-life								
Domestic undertakings	1 434	1 380	1 613	1 879	1 361	1 320	1 262	1 350
Foreign controlled undertakings	367	361	579	891	494	463	446	465
Foreign companies (branches)	..	..	..	..	..	..	..	..
All undertakings	1 434	1 380	1 613	1 879	1 361	1 320	1 262	1 350
Composite, all undertakings	..	..	..	..	..	..	..	..
Total								
Domestic undertakings	1 629	1 562	1 808	2 079	1 536	1 527	1 508	1 559
Foreign controlled undertakings	426	405	639	927	528	489	476	465
Foreign companies (branches)	..	..	..	..	..	..	..	..
All undertakings	1 629	1 562	1 808	2 079	1 536	1 527	1 508	1 559

DENMARK

Table 1. Selected aggregates *(cont.)*

Million DKK

	2012	2013	2014	2015	2016	2017	2018	2019
1.4 Gross operating expenses								
Life								
Domestic undertakings	5 088	4 954	4 887	4 570	4 788	4 971	5 138	5 428
Foreign controlled undertakings	1 316	1 326	1 377	1 284	1 268	1 386	1 349	1 133
Foreign companies (branches)	..	..	..	..	..	..	..	..
All undertakings	5 088	4 954	4 887	4 570	4 788	4 971	5 138	5 428
Non-life								
Domestic undertakings	10 292	10 391	11 564	11 856	12 050	12 003	11 298	11 258
Foreign controlled undertakings	2 124	2 200	3 867	4 065	3 780	3 542	2 778	2 666
Foreign companies (branches)	..	..	..	..	..	..	..	..
All undertakings	10 292	10 391	11 564	11 856	12 050	12 003	11 322	11 258
Composite, all undertakings	..	..	..	..	..	..	..	..
Total								
Domestic undertakings	15 380	15 345	16 451	16 426	16 838	16 974	16 436	16 686
Foreign controlled undertakings	3 440	3 526	5 244	5 349	5 048	4 928	4 127	3 799
Foreign companies (branches)	..	..	..	..	..	..	..	..
All undertakings	15 380	15 345	16 451	16 426	16 838	16 974	16 460	16 686
1.5 Insurance business written abroad by branches, gross premiums								
Life								
Branches and agencies	..	..	..	..	..	..	..	..
Subsidaries	..	..	..	..	..	..	..	..
Total	..	..	..	..	..	..	..	..
Non-life								
Branches and agencies	10 646	10 031	9 286	8 607	19 043	19 072	18 499	18 804
Subsidaries	..	..	..	..	..	..	..	..
Total	10 646	10 031	9 286	8 607	19 043	19 072	18 499	18 804
Composite total	..	..	..	..	..	..	..	..
Total								
Branches and agencies	10 646	10 031	9 286	8 607	19 043	19 072	18 499	18 804
Subsidaries	..	..	..	..	..	..	..	..
Total	10 646	10 031	9 286	8 607	19 043	19 072	18 499	18 804

.. Not available

Note: Detailed metadata at: *http://metalinks.oecd.org/ins/20210324/9827*.

Source: *OECD Insurance Statistics (database)*

DENMARK

Table 2. Number of companies and employees

	2012	2013	2014	2015	2016	2017	2018	2019
2.1 Number of companies								
Life								
Domestic undertakings	47	39	37	33	33	33	31	29
Foreign controlled undertakings	7	5	4	4	4	4	4	3
Foreign companies (branches)	6	1	1	1	1	2	2	3
All undertakings	53	40	38	34	34	35	33	32
Non-life								
Domestic undertakings	76	77	63	63	63	59	55	52
Foreign controlled undertakings	6	6	6	6	6	6	5	4
Foreign companies (branches)	38	48	49	49	53	56	67	58
All undertakings	114	125	112	112	116	115	122	110
Composite, all undertakings	**0**	**0**	**0**	**0**	**0**	..	..	..
Reinsurance								
Domestic undertakings	9	7	7	7	5	6	5	5
Foreign controlled undertakings	..	..	..	..	0	..	..	..
Foreign companies (branches)	..	..	..	..	..	..	..	..
All undertakings	9	7	7	7	5	6	5	5
Total								
Domestic undertakings	132	123	107	103	101	98	91	86
Foreign controlled undertakings	13	11	10	10	10	10	9	7
Foreign companies (branches)	44	49	50	50	54	58	69	61
All undertakings	176	172	157	153	155	156	160	147
2.2 Number of employees								
Insurance undertakings	15 835	15 377	17 057	16 472	16 112	13 640	11 568	14 391
Intermediaries	..	..	..	..	..	..	..	..
Total	15 835	15 377	17 057	16 472	16 112	13 640	11 568	14 391

.. Not available

Note: Detailed metadata at: *http://metalinks.oecd.org/ins/20210324/9827*.

Source: *OECD Insurance Statistics (database)*

ESTONIA

Table 1. Selected aggregates

Million EUR

	2012	2013	2014	2015	2016	2017	2018	2019
1.1 Insurance business written in the reporting country								
1.1.1 Insurance business, by ownership								
Gross premiums								
Domestic undertakings	430	523	561	619	654	721	807	847
Foreign controlled undertakings	407	499	539	596	627	721	775	815
Foreign companies (branches)	51	60	70	70	82	97	118	137
All undertakings	480	583	631	689	736	818	925	984
Premiums ceded								
Domestic undertakings	..	27	28	29	31	31	45	48
Foreign controlled undertakings	..	18	2	20	22	22	34	38
Foreign companies (branches)	..	..	..	..	..	..	..	..
All undertakings	..	..	..	..	..	..	..	..
Net written premiums								
Domestic undertakings	..	496	534	590	624	690	762	799
Foreign controlled undertakings	..	481	217	576	605	670	741	777
Foreign companies (branches)	..	..	..	..	..	..	..	..
All undertakings	..	..	..	..	..	..	..	..
1.1.2 Insurance business on foreign risks, gross premiums								
Life	..	..	..	..	..	..	..	..
Non-life	..	..	..	..	..	..	..	..
Composite	..	..	..	..	..	..	..	..
of which:								
Life	..	..	..	..	..	..	..	..
Non-life	..	..	..	..	..	..	..	..
Total	..	..	..	..	..	..	..	..
1.1.3 Life insurance payments, by class, gross premiums								
Annuities	10	17	19	24	27	27	..	..
Unit linked	27	87	109	118	116	116	120	137
Other life insurance	30	66	63	72	80	80	113	116
Total life insurance	68	171	191	215	221	223	233	253
***of which:** Pension contracts*	30	33	37	36	40	39	39	..
1.1.4 Non-life insurance payments, by class, gross premiums								
Motor vehicle insurance	143	229	244	259	292	345	404	409
Marine, aviation and other transport insurance	3	2	2	2	6	6	6	8
Freight insurance	..	3	4	4	..	..	..	..
Fire and other property damage insurance	59	99	107	115	127	140	159	174
Pecuniary loss insurance	5	8	9	9	12	17	21	27
General liability insurance	6	15	16	19	21	22	26	27
Accident and health	15	40	42	42	54	43	70	81
***of which:** Health*	..	9	..	..	..	..	20	25
Other non-life insurance	1	9	16	23	4	7	6	5
Treaty reinsurance	..	8	..	..	..	..	..	0
Total non-life insurance	231	412	440	474	515	580	692	731
1.2 Gross claims payments								
Life								
Domestic undertakings	112	101	..	97	87	.. c	.. c	.. c
Foreign controlled undertakings	112	101	..	97	87	.. c	.. c	.. c
Foreign companies (branches)	..	..	..	..	0	2	12	6
All undertakings	112	101	..	97	87	93	80	78
Non-life								
Domestic undertakings	147	197	..	230	243	270	315	343
Foreign controlled undertakings	134	184	..	217	228	253	297	323
Foreign companies (branches)	..	33	..	40	43	49	55	67
All undertakings	147	230	246	271	287	319	370	410
Composite								
Domestic undertakings	..	..	..	..	38	36	48	53
Foreign controlled undertakings	..	..	..	..	38	36	48	53
Foreign companies (branches)	..	..	..	..	3	4	4	8
All undertakings	..	..	..	..	42	40	52	61
of which:								
Life	..	..	..	..	34	40	39	46
Domestic undertakings	..	..	..	..	31	36	35	38
Foreign controlled undertakings	..	..	..	..	31	36	35	38
Foreign companies (branches)	..	..	..	..	3	4	4	8
All undertakings	..	..	..	..	34	40	39	46
Non-life	..	..	..	..	8	0	13	15
Domestic undertakings	..	..	..	..	8	0	13	15
Foreign controlled undertakings	..	..	..	..	8	0	13	15
Foreign companies (branches)	..	..	..	..	0	0	0	0
All undertakings	..	..	..	..	8	0	13	15
Total								
Domestic undertakings	259	298	..	328	369	397	431	468
Foreign controlled undertakings	246	285	..	314	354	380	413	448
Foreign companies (branches)	..	33	..	40	47	55	71	81
All undertakings	259	331	246	368	416	452	502	549

ESTONIA

Table 1. Selected aggregates *(cont.)*

Million EUR

	2012	2013	2014	2015	2016	2017	2018	2019
1.3 Commissions								
Life								
Domestic undertakings	9	19	21	23	..	..	..	..
Foreign controlled undertakings	9	19	21	23	..	..	..	..
Foreign companies (branches)	..	..	..	..	..	..	..	..
All undertakings	9	19	..	23	..	..	..	..
Non-life								
Domestic undertakings	4	72	73	78	..	..	..	..
Foreign controlled undertakings	2	67	69	73	..	..	..	..
Foreign companies (branches)	..	..	..	..	..	..	..	..
All undertakings	4	72	..	78	..	..	..	..
Composite								
Domestic undertakings	..	..	..	..	..	..	..	..
Foreign controlled undertakings	..	..	..	..	..	..	..	..
Foreign companies (branches)	..	..	..	..	..	..	..	..
All undertakings	..	..	..	..	..	..	..	..
of which:								
Life	..	..	..	..	..	..	..	..
Domestic undertakings	..	..	..	..	..	..	..	..
Foreign controlled undertakings	..	..	..	..	..	..	..	..
Foreign companies (branches)	..	..	..	..	..	..	..	..
All undertakings	..	..	..	..	..	..	..	..
Non-life	..	..	..	..	..	..	..	..
Domestic undertakings	..	..	..	..	..	..	..	..
Foreign controlled undertakings	..	..	..	..	..	..	..	..
Foreign companies (branches)	..	..	..	..	..	..	..	..
All undertakings	..	..	..	..	..	..	..	..
Total								
Domestic undertakings	13	90	94	101	..	..	..	..
Foreign controlled undertakings	11	86	89	95	..	..	..	..
Foreign companies (branches)	..	..	..	..	..	..	..	..
All undertakings	13	90	..	101	..	..	..	..
1.4 Gross operating expenses								
Life								
Domestic undertakings	23	9	9	11	..	..	.. c	.. c
Foreign controlled undertakings	23	9	9	11	..	..	.. c	.. c
Foreign companies (branches)	..	..	..	..	..	..	..	..
All undertakings	23	9	..	11	..	..	..	..
Non-life								
Domestic undertakings	73	27	30	27	115	137	153	157
Foreign controlled undertakings	67	25	29	26	..	..	142	148
Foreign companies (branches)	..	..	..	..	..	..	..	..
All undertakings	73	27	..	27	..	..	..	..
Composite								
Domestic undertakings	..	..	..	..	..	..	25	25
Foreign controlled undertakings	..	..	..	..	..	..	25	25
Foreign companies (branches)	..	..	..	..	..	..	..	..
All undertakings	..	..	..	..	..	..	..	..
of which:								
Life	..	..	..	..	..	..	..	..
Domestic undertakings	..	..	..	..	..	..	21	21
Foreign controlled undertakings	..	..	..	..	..	..	21	21
Foreign companies (branches)	..	..	..	..	..	..	..	..
All undertakings	..	..	..	..	..	..	..	..
Non-life	..	..	..	..	..	..	..	..
Domestic undertakings	..	..	..	..	..	..	4	4
Foreign controlled undertakings	..	..	..	..	..	..	4	4
Foreign companies (branches)	..	..	..	..	..	..	..	..
All undertakings	..	..	..	..	..	..	..	..
Total								
Domestic undertakings	96	37	40	38	115	137	188	191
Foreign controlled undertakings	90	35	38	36	..	..	177	182
Foreign companies (branches)	..	..	..	..	..	..	..	..
All undertakings	96	37	..	38	..	..	..	..

ESTONIA

Table 1. Selected aggregates *(cont.)*

Million EUR

	2012	2013	2014	2015	2016	2017	2018	2019
1.5 Insurance business written abroad by branches, gross premiums								
Life								
Branches and agencies	85	94	114	130	96	..	84	94
Subsidaries	..	..	..	..	..	..	..	..
Total	85	94	114	130	96	..	..	94
Non-life								
Branches and agencies	96	170	174	190	201	243	289	307
Subsidaries	..	..	..	..	..	..	..	..
Total	96	170	174	190	201	243	289	307
Composite								
Branches and agencies	..	..	..	..	52	..	73	88
Subsidaries	..	..	..	..	..	..	..	..
Total	..	..	..	..	52	..	..	88
of which:								
Life	..	..	..	..	42	..	..	67
Branches and agencies	..	..	..	..	42	..	56	67
Subsidaries	..	..	..	..	..	..	..	..
Total	..	..	..	..	42	..	..	67
Non-life	..	..	..	..	10	..	..	21
Branches and agencies	..	..	..	..	10	..	17	21
Subsidaries	..	..	..	..	..	..	..	..
Total	..	..	..	..	10	..	..	21
Total								
Branches and agencies	181	264	288	320	349	243	446	489
Subsidaries	..	..	..	..	..	..	..	..
Total	181	264	288	320	349	243	289	489

.. Not available; c Confidential data

Note: Detailed metadata at: *http://metalinks.oecd.org/ins/20210324/578a*.

Source: *OECD Insurance Statistics (database)*

ESTONIA

Table 2. Number of companies and employees

	2012	2013	2014	2015	2016	2017	2018	2019
2.1 Number of companies								
Life								
Domestic undertakings	4	4	4	4	2	1	1	1
Foreign controlled undertakings	4	4	4	4	2	1	1	1
Foreign companies (branches)	1	1	1	1	0	1	1	1
All undertakings	5	5	5	5	2	2	2	2
Non-life								
Domestic undertakings	8	8	8	8	8	7	7	7
Foreign controlled undertakings	5	5	5	5	5	4	4	4
Foreign companies (branches)	4	4	4	3	4	4	6	6
All undertakings	12	12	12	11	12	11	13	13
Composite								
Domestic undertakings	0	0	0	0	2	2	2	1
Foreign controlled undertakings	0	0	0	0	2	2	2	1
Foreign companies (branches)	0	0	0	0	1	1	1	2
All undertakings	0	0	0	0	3	3	3	3
Reinsurance								
Domestic undertakings	..	0	0	0	0	0	0	0
Foreign controlled undertakings	..	0	0	0	0	..	0	0
Foreign companies (branches)	..	..	..	0	0	..	0	0
All undertakings	..	..	..	0	0	..	0	0
Total								
Domestic undertakings	12	12	12	12	12	10	10	9
Foreign controlled undertakings	9	9	9	9	9	7	7	6
Foreign companies (branches)	5	5	5	4	5	6	8	9
All undertakings	17	17	17	16	17	16	18	18
2.2 Number of employees								
Insurance undertakings	1 903	2 596	2 561	2 581	..	..	..	..
Intermediaries	849	1 271	1 217	1 232	..	..	..	..
Total	2 752	3 867	3 778	3 813	..	..	..	..

.. Not available

Note: Detailed metadata at: *http://metalinks.oecd.org/ins/20210324/578a*.

Source: *OECD Insurance Statistics (database)*

FINLAND

Table 1. Selected aggregates

Million EUR

	2012	2013	2014	2015	2016	2017	2018	2019
1.1 Insurance business written in the reporting country								
1.1.1 Insurance business, by ownership								
Gross premiums								
Domestic undertakings	7 279	9 834	10 632	10 741	9 045	8 926	7 922	9 620
Foreign controlled undertakings	2 317	3 357	3 698	6 892	..	..	..	..
Foreign companies (branches)	..	..	..	..	..	..	..	..
All undertakings	7 279	9 834	10 632	10 741	9 045	8 926	4 366	6 024
Premiums ceded								
Domestic undertakings	240	257	259	246	241	230	-251	341
Foreign controlled undertakings	20	19	15	217	..	..	..	..
Foreign companies (branches)	..	..	..	..	..	..	..	..
All undertakings	240	257	259	246	241	230	-24	24
Net written premiums								
Domestic undertakings	7 039	9 577	10 373	10 495	8 804	8 696	7 671	9 271
Foreign controlled undertakings	2 297	3 338	3 683	6 675	..	..	..	..
Foreign companies (branches)	..	..	..	..	..	..	..	..
All undertakings	7 039	9 577	10 373	10 495	8 804	8 696	4 342	5 992
1.1.2 Insurance business on foreign risks, gross premiums								
Life	..	..	..	..	..	..	..	..
Non-life	..	..	..	..	..	..	..	..
Composite total	..	..	..	..	..	..	..	..
Total	..	..	..	..	..	..	..	..
1.1.3 Life insurance payments, by class, gross premiums								
Annuities	1 988	2 458	2 544	2 287	694	621	608	2 235
Unit linked	1 255	2 509	2 929	3 224	2 446	2 265	1 757	2 230
Other life insurance	505	614	619	745	1 433	1 641	2 000	1 554
Total life insurance	3 749	5 581	6 092	6 256	4 573	4 527	4 365	6 020
***of which:** Pension contracts*	828	819	756	597	675	2 265	593	638
1.1.4 Non-life insurance payments, by class, gross premiums								
Motor vehicle insurance	1 474	1 520	1 591	1 639	1 639	1 586	1 213	1 228
Marine, aviation and other transport insurance	68	70	70	68	73	69	69	84
Freight insurance	53	55	56	52	57	55	43	45
Fire and other property damage insurance	864	929	985	1 030	1 028	972	790	800
Pecuniary loss insurance	33	33	30	28	22	20	19	19
General liability insurance	191	239	392	385	234	218	193	79
Accident and health	1 024	1 048	1 060	1 058	1 119	1 183	957	1 029
***of which:** Health*	245	264	299	290	368	395	343	387
Other non-life insurance	131	144	152	88	163	151	124	129
Treaty reinsurance	149	149	135	135	136	144	148	150
Total non-life insurance	3 986	4 187	4 471	4 483	4 471	4 398	3 556	3 563
1.2 Gross claims payments								
Life								
Domestic undertakings	3 917	3 927	3 871	3 957	4 324	4 233	4 632	7 239
Foreign controlled undertakings	1 479	1 399	1 160	1 124	.. c	.. c	.. c	.. c
Foreign companies (branches)	..	..	..	..	..	..	..	..
All undertakings	3 917	3 927	3 871	3 957	4 324	4 233	4 632	7 239
Non-life								
Domestic undertakings	2 873	2 858	2 939	2 872	3 103	3 179	2 538	2 625
Foreign controlled undertakings	696	741	724	2 872	.. c	.. c	.. c	.. c
Foreign companies (branches)	..	..	..	..	..	..	.. c	.. c
All undertakings	2 873	2 858	2 939	2 872	3 103	3 179	.. c	.. c
Composite, all undertakings	..	..	..	..	..	..	..	..
Total								
Domestic undertakings	6 790	6 785	6 810	6 829	7 427	7 412	7 170	9 864
Foreign controlled undertakings	2 175	2 140	1 884	3 996	..	..	..	..
Foreign companies (branches)	..	..	..	..	..	..	..	..
All undertakings	6 790	6 785	6 810	6 829	7 427	7 412	4 632	7 239
1.3 Commissions								
Life								
Domestic undertakings	68	90	-83	101	126	121	116	113
Foreign controlled undertakings	6	9	-10	15	.. c	.. c	.. c	.. c
Foreign companies (branches)	..	..	..	..	..	..	..	..
All undertakings	68	90	-83	101	126	121	..	..
Non-life								
Domestic undertakings	102	58	-142	113	166	160	131	142
Foreign controlled undertakings	16	21	-18	23	.. c	.. c	.. c	.. c
Foreign companies (branches)	..	..	..	..	..	..	..	..
All undertakings	102	58	-142	113	166	160	..	..
Composite, all undertakings	..	..	..	..	..	..	..	..
Total								
Domestic undertakings	170	148	-225	214	292	281	247	255
Foreign controlled undertakings	22	30	-28	38	..	..	..	..
Foreign companies (branches)	..	..	..	..	..	..	..	..
All undertakings	170	148	-225	214	292	281	..	..

FINLAND

Table 1. Selected aggregates *(cont.)*

Million EUR

	2012	2013	2014	2015	2016	2017	2018	2019
1.4 Gross operating expenses								
Life								
Domestic undertakings	283	302	317	316	341	355	359	385
Foreign controlled undertakings	36	34	36	34	.. c	.. c	.. c	.. c
Foreign companies (branches)	..	..	..	..	..	..	..	..
All undertakings	283	302	317	316	341	355	359	385
Non-life								
Domestic undertakings	778	827	844	847	876	884	746	832
Foreign controlled undertakings	143	161	158	847	.. c	.. c	.. c	.. c
Foreign companies (branches)	..	..	..	..	..	..	..	..
All undertakings	778	827	844	847	876	884	..	..
Composite, all undertakings	..	..	..	..	..	..	..	..
Total								
Domestic undertakings	1 061	1 129	1 161	1 163	1 217	1 239	1 105	1 217
Foreign controlled undertakings	179	195	194	881	..	..	..	..
Foreign companies (branches)	..	..	..	..	..	..	..	..
All undertakings	1 061	1 129	1 161	1 163	1 217	1 239	359	385
1.5 Insurance business written abroad by branches, gross premiums								
Life								
Branches and agencies	203	162	107	17	..	..	..	..
Subsidaries	..	..	..	..	..	..	..	..
Total	203	162	107	17	..	..	..	..
Non-life								
Branches and agencies	..	..	..	..	..	..	..	..
Subsidaries	..	..	..	..	..	..	..	..
Total	..	..	..	..	..	..	..	..
Composite total	..	..	..	..	..	..	..	..
Total								
Branches and agencies	203	162	107	17	..	..	..	..
Subsidaries	..	..	..	..	..	..	..	..
Total	203	162	107	17	..	..	..	..

.. Not available; c Confidential data

Note: Detailed metadata at: *http://metalinks.oecd.org/ins/20210324/ed97*.

Source: *OECD Insurance Statistics (database)*

FINLAND

Table 2. Number of companies and employees

	2012	2013	2014	2015	2016	2017	2018	2019
2.1 Number of companies								
Life								
Domestic undertakings	13	13	13	13	11	10	10	11
Foreign controlled undertakings	1	1	1	1	1	1	1	1
Foreign companies (branches)	..	..	..	..	..	..	10	10
All undertakings	13	13	13	13	11	10	20	21
Non-life								
Domestic undertakings	42	42	38	38	37	37	40	37
Foreign controlled undertakings	1	1	1	1	2	2	1	1
Foreign companies (branches)	..	..	..	..	..	..	8	8
All undertakings	42	42	38	38	37	37	48	46
Composite, all undertakings	..	..	..	..	..	..	0	..
Reinsurance								
Domestic undertakings	..	..	..	..	..	..	0	..
Foreign controlled undertakings	..	..	..	..	..	..	0	..
Foreign companies (branches)	..	..	..	..	..	..	0	..
All undertakings	..	..	..	..	..	..	0	..
Total								
Domestic undertakings	55	55	51	51	48	47	50	48
Foreign controlled undertakings	2	2	2	2	3	3	2	2
Foreign companies (branches)	..	..	..	..	..	..	18	18
All undertakings	55	55	51	51	48	47	68	67
2.2 Number of employees								
Insurance undertakings	9 321	9 231	8 980	8 750	8 815	7 751	7 866	6 893
Intermediaries	342	203	216	221	244	265	265	86
Total	9 663	9 434	9 196	8 971	9 059	8 016	8 131	6 979

.. Not available

Note: Detailed metadata at: *http://metalinks.oecd.org/ins/20210324/ed97*.

Source: *OECD Insurance Statistics (database)*

FRANCE

Table 1. Selected aggregates

Million EUR

	2012	2013	2014	2015	2016	2017	2018	2019
1.1 Insurance business written in the reporting country								
1.1.1 Insurance business, by ownership								
Gross premiums								
Domestic undertakings	201 207	207 521	221 223	226 000	..	..	286 809	296 989
Foreign controlled undertakings	..	..	..	..	..	..	..	..
Foreign companies (branches)	104	103	103	111	..	..	..	..
All undertakings	201 310	207 624	221 327	226 111	283 901	278 237	286 809	296 989
Premiums ceded								
Domestic undertakings	21 638	22 115	19 932	25 840	..	..	35 307	38 657
Foreign controlled undertakings	..	..	..	..	..	..	..	..
Foreign companies (branches)	18	19	22	21	..	..	..	..
All undertakings	21 657	22 135	19 954	25 861	43 153	33 277	35 307	38 657
Net written premiums								
Domestic undertakings	179 568	185 406	201 291	200 160	..	..	251 502	258 332
Foreign controlled undertakings	..	..	..	..	..	..	..	..
Foreign companies (branches)	85	84	82	90	..	..	..	..
All undertakings	179 654	185 490	201 373	200 250	240 747	244 960	251 502	258 332
1.1.2 Insurance business on foreign risks, gross premiums								
Life	83	259	73	60	..	..	..	..
Non-life	1 589	1 735	1 876	2 188	..	..	..	..
Composite	206	636	468	485	..	..	..	..
of which:								
Life	206	167	456	482	..	..	..	..
Non-life	1	469	12	3	..	..	..	..
Total	1 879	2 631	2 416	2 734	..	..	..	..
1.1.3 Life insurance payments, by class, gross premiums								
Annuities	..	..	..	..	..	..	..	..
Unit linked	..	..	..	..	28 208	38 135	38 569	39 657
Other life insurance	..	..	..	..	111 059	102 007	106 170	110 125
Total life insurance	..	..	..	..	139 267	140 142	144 740	149 781
***of which:** Pension contracts*	..	..	..	..	..	..	..	..
1.1.4 Non-life insurance payments, by class, gross premiums								
Motor vehicle insurance	..	..	..	..	..	..	..	..
Marine, aviation and other transport insurance	..	..	..	..	..	..	..	..
Freight insurance	..	..	..	..	..	..	..	..
Fire and other property damage insurance	..	..	..	..	..	..	..	..
Pecuniary loss insurance	..	..	..	..	..	..	..	..
General liability insurance	..	..	..	..	..	..	..	..
Accident and health	..	..	..	..	..	..	..	..
***of which:** Health*	..	..	..	..	..	..	..	..
Other non-life insurance	..	..	..	..	..	..	..	..
Treaty reinsurance	..	..	..	..	..	..	..	..
Total non-life insurance	76 295	..	..	..	119 104	124 560	128 064	131 451
1.2 Gross claims payments								
Life								
Domestic undertakings	31 131	25 663	26 144	26 794	..	..	21 986	23 357
Foreign controlled undertakings	..	..	..	..	..	..	..	..
Foreign companies (branches)	..	..	..	..	..	..	..	..
All undertakings	31 131	25 663	26 144	26 794	133 135	145 577	21 986	23 357
Non-life								
Domestic undertakings	50 472	45 317	61 895	63 029	..	..	56 407	60 336
Foreign controlled undertakings	..	..	..	..	..	..	..	..
Foreign companies (branches)	59	59	52	51	..	..	..	..
All undertakings	50 531	45 376	61 947	63 080	95 217	101 007	56 407	60 336
Composite								
Domestic undertakings	98 016	97 287	86 518	91 862	..	..	158 076	158 713
Foreign controlled undertakings	..	..	..	..	..	..	..	..
Foreign companies (branches)	..	..	..	..	..	..	..	..
All undertakings	98 016	97 287	86 518	91 862	..	..	158 076	158 713
of which:								
Life	..	88 620	..	..	..	..	111 830	112 716
Domestic undertakings	..	88 620	..	..	..	..	111 830	112 716
Foreign controlled undertakings	..	..	..	..	..	..	..	..
Foreign companies (branches)	..	..	..	..	..	..	..	..
All undertakings	..	88 620	..	..	..	..	111 830	112 716
Non-life	..	8 667	..	..	..	..	46 246	45 996
Domestic undertakings	..	8 667	..	..	..	..	46 246	45 996
Foreign controlled undertakings	..	..	..	..	..	..	..	..
Foreign companies (branches)	..	..	..	..	..	..	..	..
All undertakings	..	8 667	..	..	..	..	46 246	45 996
Total								
Domestic undertakings	179 619	168 267	174 557	181 685	..	..	236 469	242 406
Foreign controlled undertakings	..	..	..	..	..	..	..	..
Foreign companies (branches)	59	59	52	51	..	..	..	..
All undertakings	179 678	168 326	174 608	181 736	228 352	246 584	236 469	242 406

Table 1. Selected aggregates *(cont.)*

Million EUR

	2012	2013	2014	2015	2016	2017	2018	2019
1.3 Commissions								
Life								
Domestic undertakings	1 705	..	..	..	..	..	..	..
Foreign controlled undertakings	..	..	..	..	..	..	..	..
Foreign companies (branches)	..	..	..	..	..	..	..	..
All undertakings	1 705	..	..	..	..	..	..	..
Non-life								
Domestic undertakings	10 610	..	..	..	..	..	..	..
Foreign controlled undertakings	..	..	..	..	..	..	..	..
Foreign companies (branches)	22	..	..	..	..	..	..	..
All undertakings	10 633	..	..	..	..	..	..	..
Composite								
Domestic undertakings	5 717	..	..	..	..	..	..	..
Foreign controlled undertakings	..	..	..	..	..	..	..	..
Foreign companies (branches)	..	..	..	..	..	..	..	..
All undertakings	5 717	..	..	..	..	..	..	..
of which:								
Life	4 677	..	..	..	..	..	..	..
Domestic undertakings	4 677	..	..	..	..	..	..	..
Foreign controlled undertakings	..	..	..	..	..	..	..	..
Foreign companies (branches)	..	..	..	..	..	..	..	..
All undertakings	4 677	..	..	..	..	..	..	..
Non-life	1 041	..	..	..	..	..	..	..
Domestic undertakings	1 041	..	..	..	..	..	..	..
Foreign controlled undertakings	..	..	..	..	..	..	..	..
Foreign companies (branches)	..	..	..	..	..	..	..	..
All undertakings	1 041	..	..	..	..	..	..	..
Total								
Domestic undertakings	18 033	..	..	..	..	..	..	..
Foreign controlled undertakings	..	..	..	..	..	..	..	..
Foreign companies (branches)	22	..	..	..	..	..	..	..
All undertakings	18 055	..	..	..	..	..	..	..
1.4 Gross operating expenses								
Life								
Domestic undertakings	2 982	2 828	2 893	2 914	..	..	2 545	2 697
Foreign controlled undertakings	..	..	..	..	..	..	..	..
Foreign companies (branches)	..	..	..	..	..	..	..	..
All undertakings	2 982	2 828	2 893	2 914	15 848	16 123	2 545	2 697
Non-life								
Domestic undertakings	15 726	15 969	16 156	15 936	..	..	18 654	20 368
Foreign controlled undertakings	..	..	..	..	..	..	..	..
Foreign companies (branches)	9	..	8	..	..	..	..	..
All undertakings	15 726	15 969	16 164	15 936	27 415	27 948	18 654	20 368
Composite								
Domestic undertakings	12 392	12 957	13 439	14 727	..	..	24 734	25 749
Foreign controlled undertakings	..	..	..	..	..	..	..	..
Foreign companies (branches)	..	..	..	..	..	..	..	..
All undertakings	12 392	12 957	13 439	14 727	..	..	24 734	25 749
of which:								
Life	..	10 533	10 808	11 414	..	..	13 366	16 771
Domestic undertakings	..	10 533	..	..	..	..	13 366	16 771
Foreign controlled undertakings	..	..	..	..	..	..	..	..
Foreign companies (branches)	..	..	..	..	..	..	..	..
All undertakings	..	10 533	10 808	11 414	..	..	13 366	16 771
Non-life	..	2 424	2 631	3 313	..	..	11 368	8 979
Domestic undertakings	..	2 424	..	..	..	..	11 368	8 979
Foreign controlled undertakings	..	..	..	..	..	..	..	..
Foreign companies (branches)	..	..	..	..	..	..	..	..
All undertakings	..	2 424	2 631	3 313	..	..	11 368	8 979
Total								
Domestic undertakings	31 100	31 754	32 488	33 578	..	..	45 933	48 814
Foreign controlled undertakings	..	..	..	..	..	..	..	..
Foreign companies (branches)	9	..	8	..	..	..	..	..
All undertakings	31 100	31 754	32 497	33 578	43 263	44 071	45 933	48 814

FRANCE

Table 1. Selected aggregates *(cont.)*

Million EUR

	2012	2013	2014	2015	2016	2017	2018	2019
1.5 Insurance business written abroad by branches, gross premiums								
Life								
Branches and agencies	1 895	2 691	2 860	3 373	4 393	5 050	..	..
Subsidaries	..	..	..	..	..	..	..	..
Total	1 895	2 691	2 860	3 373	4 393	5 050	..	..
Non-life								
Branches and agencies	4 107	4 176	4 960	5 460	8 837	9 719	..	..
Subsidaries	..	..	..	..	..	..	..	..
Total	4 107	4 176	4 960	5 460	8 837	9 719	..	..
Composite								
Branches and agencies	..	..	..	..	..	..	..	..
Subsidaries	..	..	..	..	..	..	..	..
Total	..	..	..	..	..	..	..	..
of which:								
Life	..	..	..	..	..	..	..	..
Branches and agencies	..	..	..	..	..	..	..	..
Subsidaries	..	..	..	..	..	..	..	..
Total	..	..	..	..	..	..	..	..
Non-life	..	..	..	..	..	..	..	..
Branches and agencies	..	..	..	..	..	..	..	..
Subsidaries	..	..	..	..	..	..	..	..
Total	..	..	..	..	..	..	..	..
Total								
Branches and agencies	6 001	6 867	7 820	8 834	13 230	14 769	..	..
Subsidaries	..	..	..	..	..	..	..	..
Total	6 001	6 867	7 820	8 834	13 230	14 769	..	..

.. Not available

Note: Detailed metadata at: *http://metalinks.oecd.org/ins/20210324/126f.*

Source: *OECD Insurance Statistics (database)*

FRANCE

Table 2. Number of companies and employees

	2012	2013	2014	2015	2016	2017	2018	2019
2.1 Number of companies								
Life								
Domestic undertakings	62	59	55	51	..	..	..	..
Foreign controlled undertakings	..	..	..	..	..	..	..	..
Foreign companies (branches)	..	..	..	..	..	..	..	..
All undertakings	62	59	55	51	..	..	..	..
Non-life								
Domestic undertakings	221	212	206	191	..	..	..	..
Foreign controlled undertakings	5	..	..	..	..	..	..	..
Foreign companies (branches)	..	4	4	4	..	..	..	..
All undertakings	221	216	210	195	394	381	364	345
Composite								
Domestic undertakings	40	38	38	39	..	..	..	..
Foreign controlled undertakings	..	..	..	..	..	..	..	..
Foreign companies (branches)	..	..	..	..	..	..	..	..
All undertakings	40	38	38	39	239	236	239	243
Reinsurance								
Domestic undertakings	16	16	15	16	..	..	..	..
Foreign controlled undertakings	..	..	..	..	..	..	..	..
Foreign companies (branches)	..	..	..	..	..	..	..	..
All undertakings	16	16	15	16	14	14	12	10
Total								
Domestic undertakings	339	325	314	297	..	..	..	..
Foreign controlled undertakings	5	..	..	..	..	..	..	..
Foreign companies (branches)	..	4	4	4	..	..	..	..
All undertakings	339	329	318	301	647	631	615	598
2.2 Number of employees								
Insurance undertakings	..	..	..	..	..	..	..	..
Intermediaries	..	..	..	..	..	..	..	..
Total	..	..	..	..	..	..	..	..

.. Not available

Note: Detailed metadata at: *http://metalinks.oecd.org/ins/20210324/126f.*

Source: *OECD Insurance Statistics (database)*

GERMANY

Table 1. Selected aggregates

Million EUR

	2012	2013	2014	2015	2016	2017	2018	2019
1.1 Insurance business written in the reporting country								
1.1.1 Insurance business, by ownership								
Gross premiums								
Domestic undertakings	233 661	243 304	246 201	254 407	257 208	264 933	273 036	296 378
Foreign controlled undertakings	37 194	39 396	38 694	39 170	36 978	36 644	39 215	40 551
Foreign companies (branches)	8 062	7 963	8 796	9 751	8 994	10 550	11 199	11 148
All undertakings	235 634	251 267	254 997	264 158	266 203	275 483	284 235	307 527
Premiums ceded								
Domestic undertakings	23 045	25 709	27 853	32 499	31 990	34 336	39 483	41 736
Foreign controlled undertakings	3 947	4 645	4 615	4 593	4 041	4 046	4 482	4 167
Foreign companies (branches)	100	108	103	114	112	132	127	83
All undertakings	23 145	25 817	27 956	32 613	32 102	34 469	39 609	41 819
Net written premiums								
Domestic undertakings	210 616	217 596	218 348	221 907	225 218	230 596	233 553	254 643
Foreign controlled undertakings	33 247	34 751	34 078	34 577	32 937	32 598	34 732	36 383
Foreign companies (branches)	1 873	7 854	8 693	9 637	8 882	10 418	11 073	11 065
All undertakings	212 489	225 450	227 041	231 545	234 100	241 014	244 626	265 707
1.1.2 Insurance business on foreign risks, gross premiums								
Life	..	..	..	..	..	..	..	..
Non-life	..	..	..	..	..	..	..	..
Composite total	..	..	..	..	..	..	..	..
Total	..	..	..	..	..	..	..	..
1.1.3 Life insurance payments, by class, gross premiums								
Annuities	29 443	32 863	34 019	31 782	31 215	30 000	31 730	36 776
Unit linked	12 721	12 919	13 863	13 863	15 351	15 994	17 293	18 685
Other life insurance	40 822	41 934	40 891	41 214	38 845	41 612	40 959	44 755
Total life insurance	82 986	87 716	88 774	86 859	85 411	87 606	89 982	100 217
***of which:** Pension contracts*	..	..	..	..	..	..	..	..
1.1.4 Non-life insurance payments, by class, gross premiums								
Motor vehicle insurance	27 577	28 592	31 425	32 589	36 521	40 579	44 565	46 631
Marine, aviation and other transport insurance	4 537	4 476	4 379	5 116	4 749	4 933	5 050	5 786
Freight insurance	..	..	..	..	..	..	..	..
Fire and other property damage insurance	34 420	36 832	35 422	38 830	42 499	46 541	50 056	55 618
Pecuniary loss insurance	2 754	2 815	2 088	2 197	2 376	3 872	3 857	4 134
General liability insurance	12 623	13 265	14 213	15 425	16 126	17 517	18 440	20 008
Accident and health	48 823	49 395	48 811	49 176	49 721	52 572	52 301	54 040
***of which:** Health*	41 036	41 747	40 924	41 627	37 178	39 328	40 220	41 217
Other non-life insurance	4 794	4 841	4 865	31 030	25 991	21 153	19 528	20 628
Treaty reinsurance	..	..	..	..	..	..	..	..
Total non-life insurance	135 526	140 215	141 203	174 363	177 983	187 167	193 798	206 844
1.2 Gross claims payments								
Life								
Domestic undertakings	66 288	69 267	74 625	73 307	78 596	69 073	70 871	75 975
Foreign controlled undertakings	15 284	17 017	17 510	17 929	17 942	16 501	16 759	17 071
Foreign companies (branches)	..	..	..	..	..	..	..	..
All undertakings	66 288	69 267	74 625	73 307	78 596	69 073	70 871	75 975
Non-life								
Domestic undertakings	101 839	113 293	72 709	77 667	78 086	84 787	87 989	139 877
Foreign controlled undertakings	12 192	12 402	8 955	3 653	9 227	9 500	10 110	13 369
Foreign companies (branches)	..	..	..	..	..	..	..	..
All undertakings	101 839	113 293	72 709	77 667	78 086	84 787	87 989	139 877
Composite, all undertakings	..	..	..	..	..	..	..	..
Total								
Domestic undertakings	168 127	182 560	147 334	150 974	156 682	153 859	158 861	215 852
Foreign controlled undertakings	27 475	29 419	26 465	21 581	27 169	26 001	26 869	30 440
Foreign companies (branches)	..	..	..	..	..	..	..	..
All undertakings	168 127	182 560	147 334	150 974	156 682	153 859	158 861	215 852
1.3 Commissions								
Life								
Domestic undertakings	6 005	5 367	5 583	5 069	4 987	4 794	4 961	5 618
Foreign controlled undertakings	1 771	1 604	1 533	1 488	1 238	1 138	1 211	1 306
Foreign companies (branches)	..	..	..	..	..	..	..	..
All undertakings	6 005	5 367	5 583	5 069	4 987	4 794	4 961	5 618
Non-life								
Domestic undertakings	10 069	10 048	10 221	10 740	11 105	12 173	12 647	13 656
Foreign controlled undertakings	1 985	1 720	1 626	257	1 594	1 623	1 806	1 940
Foreign companies (branches)	..	..	..	..	..	..	..	..
All undertakings	10 069	10 048	10 221	10 740	11 105	12 173	12 647	13 656
Composite, all undertakings	..	..	..	..	..	..	..	..
Total								
Domestic undertakings	16 074	15 416	15 805	15 810	16 092	16 967	17 609	19 273
Foreign controlled undertakings	3 756	3 323	3 159	1 745	2 832	2 760	3 017	3 247
Foreign companies (branches)	..	..	..	..	..	..	..	..
All undertakings	16 074	15 416	15 805	15 810	16 092	16 967	17 609	19 273

GERMANY

Table 1. Selected aggregates *(cont.)*

Million EUR

	2012	2013	2014	2015	2016	2017	2018	2019
1.4 Gross operating expenses								
Life								
Domestic undertakings	4 051	3 954	3 963	4 008	3 902	3 907	3 901	3 769
Foreign controlled undertakings	925	921	894	1 036	938	952	1 001	974
Foreign companies (branches)	..	..	..	..	..	..	..	..
All undertakings	4 051	3 954	3 963	4 008	3 902	3 907	3 901	3 769
Non-life								
Domestic undertakings	11 593	11 599	10 296	10 627	10 807	11 161	11 390	13 638
Foreign controlled undertakings	1 528	1 400	1 187	324	1 183	1 210	1 297	1 448
Foreign companies (branches)	..	..	..	..	..	..	..	..
All undertakings	11 593	11 599	10 296	10 627	10 807	11 161	11 390	13 638
Composite, all undertakings	..	..	..	..	..	..	..	..
Total								
Domestic undertakings	15 644	15 553	14 259	14 635	14 709	15 068	15 291	17 406
Foreign controlled undertakings	2 453	2 321	2 081	1 361	2 121	2 163	2 297	2 421
Foreign companies (branches)	..	..	..	..	..	..	..	..
All undertakings	15 644	15 553	14 259	14 635	14 709	15 068	15 291	17 406
1.5 Insurance business written abroad by branches, gross premiums								
Life								
Branches and agencies	..	..	..	..	..	..	200	481
Subsidaries	..	..	..	..	..	..	..	..
Total	..	..	..	..	..	..	200	481
Non-life								
Branches and agencies	..	..	..	..	..	..	22 495	25 723
Subsidaries	..	..	..	..	..	..	..	..
Total	..	..	..	..	..	..	22 495	25 723
Composite total	..	..	..	..	..	..	..	..
Total								
Branches and agencies	..	..	..	..	..	..	22 695	26 203
Subsidaries	..	..	..	..	..	..	..	..
Total	..	..	..	..	..	..	22 695	26 203

.. Not available

Note: Detailed metadata at: *http://metalinks.oecd.org/ins/20210324/61ad*.

Source: *OECD Insurance Statistics (database)*

GERMANY

Table 2. Number of companies and employees

	2012	2013	2014	2015	2016	2017	2018	2019
2.1 Number of companies								
Life								
Domestic undertakings	90	91	91	85	85	86	86	84
Foreign controlled undertakings	19	17	17	14	14	15	16	16
Foreign companies (branches)	19	2	2	2	2	1	1	1
All undertakings	109	93	93	87	87	87	87	85
Non-life								
Domestic undertakings	256	259	255	257	252	251	250	254
Foreign controlled undertakings	25	23	21	22	18	17	21	23
Foreign companies (branches)	62	3	3	3	2	2	1	1
All undertakings	318	262	258	260	254	253	251	255
Composite, all undertakings	**0**	**0**	**0**	**0**	**0**	..	..	..
Reinsurance								
Domestic undertakings	30	29	27	27	27	27	28	29
Foreign controlled undertakings	6	4	3	3	3	3	3	3
Foreign companies (branches)	7	1	1	1	1	1	1	1
All undertakings	37	30	28	28	28	28	29	30
Total								
Domestic undertakings	376	379	373	369	364	364	364	367
Foreign controlled undertakings	50	44	41	39	35	35	40	42
Foreign companies (branches)	88	6	6	6	5	4	3	3
All undertakings	464	385	379	375	369	368	367	370
2.2 Number of employees								
Insurance undertakings	126 625	128 755	126 755	128 784	..	..	..	..
Intermediaries	27 407	27 331	26 982	25 917	..	..	..	..
Total	154 032	156 086	153 737	154 701	156 675	154 262	152 888	150 886

.. Not available

Note: Detailed metadata at: *http://metalinks.oecd.org/ins/20210324/61ad*.

Source: *OECD Insurance Statistics (database)*

GREECE

Table 1. Selected aggregates

Million EUR

	2012	2013	2014	2015	2016	2017	2018	2019
1.1 Insurance business written in the reporting country								
1.1.1 Insurance business, by ownership								
Gross premiums								
Domestic undertakings	4 289	4 071	3 806	3 573	3 531	3 729	3 798	4 053
Foreign controlled undertakings	2 071	1 730	1 696	1 766	2 350	2 450	2 458	2 487
Foreign companies (branches)	211	0	0	0	0	0	0	0
All undertakings	4 499	4 071	3 806	3 573	3 531	3 729	3 798	4 053
Premiums ceded								
Domestic undertakings	534	824	471	459	396	402	429	423
Foreign controlled undertakings	235	214	206	201	244	260	274	270
Foreign companies (branches)	0	0	0	0	0	0	0	0
All undertakings	534	824	471	459	396	402	429	423
Net written premiums								
Domestic undertakings	3 754	3 247	3 334	3 114	3 135	3 328	3 369	3 631
Foreign controlled undertakings	1 836	1 516	1 490	1 565	2 106	2 190	2 183	2 218
Foreign companies (branches)	211	0	0	0	0	0	0	0
All undertakings	3 965	3 247	3 335	3 114	3 135	3 328	3 369	3 631
1.1.2 Insurance business on foreign risks, gross premiums								
Life	..	..	..	..	..	..	..	..
Non-life	..	..	..	..	..	..	..	..
Composite	..	..	..	..	..	..	..	..
of which:								
Life	..	..	..	..	..	..	..	..
Non-life	..	..	..	..	..	..	..	..
Total	..	..	..	..	..	..	..	..
1.1.3 Life insurance payments, by class, gross premiums								
Annuities	165	142	129	125	0	0	0	0
Unit linked	368	240	396	326	250	347	380	363
Other life insurance	1 406	1 299	1 353	1 348	1 416	1 533	1 499	1 700
Total life insurance	1 939	1 681	1 879	1 799	1 666	1 881	1 879	2 064
***of which:** Pension contracts*	205	143	151	156	..	..	..	..
1.1.4 Non-life insurance payments, by class, gross premiums								
Motor vehicle insurance	1 569	1 417	1 154	1 006	911	938	948	968
Marine, aviation and other transport insurance	21	19	19	20	32	34	38	38
Freight insurance	24	24	21	21	..	0	0	0
Fire and other property damage insurance	538	529	448	440	410	398	409	402
Pecuniary loss insurance	78	69	30	30	40	28	31	36
General liability insurance	78	76	67	68	65	63	75	83
Accident and health	68	64	57	57	300	242	263	298
***of which:** Health*	20	0	0	..	..	0	0	0
Other non-life insurance	179	188	128	129	137	146	153	165
Treaty reinsurance	0	0	0	..	..	0	0	0
Total non-life insurance	2 556	2 386	1 924	1 770	1 896	1 848	1 918	1 990
1.2 Gross claims payments								
Life								
Domestic undertakings	1 300	1 072	900	744	..	..	..	..
Foreign controlled undertakings	1 017	707	1	502	..	..	..	..
Foreign companies (branches)	0	0	0	0	..	..	..	..
All undertakings	1 300	1 072	900	744	..	..	..	..
Non-life								
Domestic undertakings	431	373	355	314	..	..	..	..
Foreign controlled undertakings	142	121	224	109	..	..	..	..
Foreign companies (branches)	0	1	1	0	..	..	..	..
All undertakings	431	375	356	314	..	..	..	..
Composite								
Domestic undertakings	1 291	1 096	1 018	931	..	..	..	..
Foreign controlled undertakings	441	364	412	347	..	..	..	..
Foreign companies (branches)	0	0	0	0	..	..	..	..
All undertakings	1 291	1 096	1 018	931	..	..	..	..
of which:								
Life	791	669	613	573	..	..	..	..
Domestic undertakings	791	669	613	573	..	..	..	..
Foreign controlled undertakings	282	226	7	220	..	..	..	..
Foreign companies (branches)	0	0	0	0	..	..	..	..
All undertakings	791	669	613	573	..	..	..	..
Non-life	501	426	405	358	..	..	..	..
Domestic undertakings	501	426	405	358	..	..	..	..
Foreign controlled undertakings	159	138	405	126	..	..	..	..
Foreign companies (branches)	0	0	0	0	..	..	..	..
All undertakings	501	426	405	358	..	..	..	..
Total								
Domestic undertakings	3 022	2 541	2 273	1 989	..	..	..	..
Foreign controlled undertakings	1 600	1 192	637	957	..	..	..	..
Foreign companies (branches)	0	1	1	0	..	..	..	..
All undertakings	3 022	2 542	2 274	1 989	..	..	..	..

GREECE

Table 1. Selected aggregates *(cont.)*

Million EUR

	2012	2013	2014	2015	2016	2017	2018	2019
1.3 Commissions								
Life								
Domestic undertakings	..	..	95	91	..	..	..	..
Foreign controlled undertakings	..	..	70	70	..	..	..	..
Foreign companies (branches)	..	..	0	0	..	..	..	..
All undertakings	..	..	95	91	..	..	..	..
Non-life								
Domestic undertakings	..	..	161	158	..	..	..	..
Foreign controlled undertakings	..	..	63	66	..	..	..	..
Foreign companies (branches)	..	..	0	0	..	..	..	..
All undertakings	..	..	162	158	..	..	..	..
Composite								
Domestic undertakings	..	..	276	709	..	..	..	..
Foreign controlled undertakings	..	..	115	115	..	..	..	..
Foreign companies (branches)	..	..	0	0	..	..	..	..
All undertakings	..	..	276	709	..	..	..	..
of which:								
Life	..	..	102	544	..	..	..	..
Domestic undertakings	..	..	102	544	..	..	..	..
Foreign controlled undertakings	..	..	39	40	..	..	..	..
Foreign companies (branches)	..	..	0	0	..	..	..	..
All undertakings	..	..	102	544	..	..	..	..
Non-life	..	..	174	164	..	..	..	..
Domestic undertakings	..	..	174	164	..	..	..	..
Foreign controlled undertakings	..	..	76	75	..	..	..	..
Foreign companies (branches)	..	..	0	0	..	..	..	..
All undertakings	..	..	174	164	..	..	..	..
Total								
Domestic undertakings	..	..	532	957	..	..	..	..
Foreign controlled undertakings	..	..	248	251	..	..	..	..
Foreign companies (branches)	..	..	0	0	..	..	..	..
All undertakings	..	..	532	957	..	..	..	..
1.4 Gross operating expenses								
Life								
Domestic undertakings	82	79	176	163	35	38	39	46
Foreign controlled undertakings	75	66	141	132	32	35	35	40
Foreign companies (branches)	0	0	0	..	0	0	0	0
All undertakings	82	79	176	163	35	38	39	46
Non-life								
Domestic undertakings	104	124	264	247	248	301	242	256
Foreign controlled undertakings	59	61	115	116	145	168	104	112
Foreign companies (branches)	1	0	0	0	0	0	0	0
All undertakings	106	124	264	247	248	301	242	256
Composite								
Domestic undertakings	67	169	404	371	700	701	811	774
Foreign controlled undertakings	16	57	154	150	448	438	550	495
Foreign companies (branches)	0	0	0	..	0	0	0	0
All undertakings	67	169	404	371	700	701	811	774
of which:								
Life	36	53	144	145	315	322	312	283
Domestic undertakings	36	53	144	145	315	322	312	283
Foreign controlled undertakings	11	21	53	52	231	223	219	216
Foreign companies (branches)	0	0	0	..	0	0	0	0
All undertakings	36	53	144	145	315	322	312	283
Non-life	31	116	260	226	385	379	499	492
Domestic undertakings	31	116	260	226	385	379	499	492
Foreign controlled undertakings	4	36	101	98	217	215	331	279
Foreign companies (branches)	0	0	0	..	0	0	0	0
All undertakings	31	116	260	226	385	379	499	492
Total								
Domestic undertakings	253	372	844	781	983	1 041	1 092	1 076
Foreign controlled undertakings	150	184	410	398	625	641	689	647
Foreign companies (branches)	1	0	0	0	0	0	0	0
All undertakings	254	372	844	781	983	1 041	1 092	1 076

GREECE

Table 1. Selected aggregates *(cont.)*

Million EUR

	2012	2013	2014	2015	2016	2017	2018	2019
1.5 Insurance business written abroad by branches, gross premiums								
Life								
Branches and agencies	..	..	..	..	..	0	0	0
Subsidaries	..	..	..	..	..	0	0	0
Total	..	..	..	..	..	0	0	0
Non-life								
Branches and agencies	..	..	..	..	..	1	3	6
Subsidaries	..	..	..	..	..	0	0	0
Total	..	..	..	..	..	1	3	6
Composite								
Branches and agencies	..	..	..	..	..	0	18	4
Subsidaries	..	..	..	..	..	0	0	0
Total	..	..	..	..	..	0	18	4
of which:								
Life	..	..	..	..	..	0	0	0
Branches and agencies	..	..	..	..	..	0	0	0
Subsidaries	..	..	..	..	..	0	0	0
Total	..	..	..	..	..	0	0	0
Non-life	..	..	..	..	..	0	17	4
Branches and agencies	..	..	..	..	..	0	17	4
Subsidaries	..	..	..	..	..	0	0	0
Total	..	..	..	..	..	0	17	4
Total								
Branches and agencies	..	..	..	..	..	1	21	10
Subsidaries	..	..	..	..	..	0	0	0
Total	..	..	..	..	..	1	21	10

.. Not available

Note: Detailed metadata at: *http://metalinks.oecd.org/ins/20210324/e4b0*.

Source: *OECD Insurance Statistics (database)*

GREECE

Table 2. Number of companies and employees

	2012	2013	2014	2015	2016	2017	2018	2019
2.1 Number of companies								
Life								
Domestic undertakings	11	11	11	11	4	3	2	2
Foreign controlled undertakings	7	7	7	7	2	2	1	1
Foreign companies (branches)	0	0	0	0	0	0	0	0
All undertakings	11	11	11	11	4	3	2	2
Non-life								
Domestic undertakings	31	28	24	24	24	22	20	19
Foreign controlled undertakings	7	7	6	5	7	6	5	5
Foreign companies (branches)	2	2	2	2	0	0	0	0
All undertakings	33	30	26	26	24	22	20	19
Composite								
Domestic undertakings	11	11	11	11	17	17	17	17
Foreign controlled undertakings	4	4	4	4	10	10	10	10
Foreign companies (branches)	0	0	0	0	0	0	0	0
All undertakings	11	11	11	11	17	17	17	17
Reinsurance								
Domestic undertakings	0	0	0	0	0	0	0	0
Foreign controlled undertakings	0	0	0	0	0	0	0	0
Foreign companies (branches)	0	0	0	0	0	0	0	0
All undertakings	0	0	0	0	0	0	0	0
Total								
Domestic undertakings	53	50	46	46	45	42	39	38
Foreign controlled undertakings	18	18	17	16	19	18	16	16
Foreign companies (branches)	2	2	2	2	0	0	0	0
All undertakings	55	52	48	48	45	42	39	38
2.2 Number of employees								
Insurance undertakings	..	..	..	..	..	..	..	..
Intermediaries	..	..	..	..	..	..	..	..
Total	..	..	..	..	..	..	..	..

.. Not available

Note: Detailed metadata at: *http://metalinks.oecd.org/ins/20210324/e4b0.*

Source: *OECD Insurance Statistics (database)*

HUNGARY

Table 1. Selected aggregates

Million HUF

	2012	2013	2014	2015	2016	2017	2018	2019
1.1 Insurance business written in the reporting country								
1.1.1 Insurance business, by ownership								
Gross premiums								
Domestic undertakings	760 249	801 210	833 664	835 428	885 781	956 006	1 017 779	1 149 523
Foreign controlled undertakings	718 932	763 286	796 332	788 248	835 272	897 699	953 320	1 075 690
Foreign companies (branches)	..	..	..	..	..	..	..	..
All undertakings	760 249	801 210	833 664	835 428	885 781	956 006	1 017 779	1 149 523
Premiums ceded								
Domestic undertakings	127 261	111 755	116 117	115 801	118 081	120 524	126 479	139 265
Foreign controlled undertakings	118 373	104 254	108 557	104 464	107 021	106 729	113 942	128 554
Foreign companies (branches)	..	..	..	..	..	..	..	..
All undertakings	127 261	111 755	116 117	115 801	118 081	120 524	126 479	139 265
Net written premiums								
Domestic undertakings	632 989	689 455	717 547	719 627	767 700	835 482	891 300	1 010 258
Foreign controlled undertakings	600 559	659 032	687 774	683 784	728 251	790 970	839 379	947 137
Foreign companies (branches)	..	..	..	..	..	..	..	..
All undertakings	632 989	689 455	717 547	719 627	767 700	835 482	891 300	1 010 258
1.1.2 Insurance business on foreign risks, gross premiums								
Life	3 284	3 358	3 533	4 234	4 317	4 630	5 116	5 343
Non-life	1 257	1 840	1 923	1 052	2 308	2 657	2 100	2 517
Composite	7 943	4 500	2 829	4 368	8 142	9 004	8 816	7 724
of which:								
Life	279	781	228	216	177	172	199	808
Non-life	7 665	3 719	2 602	4 152	7 965	8 832	8 617	6 916
Total	12 484	9 698	8 285	9 654	14 767	16 291	16 033	15 584
1.1.3 Life insurance payments, by class, gross premiums								
Annuities	3 529	2 975	3 147	3 479	..	..	..	..
Unit linked	261 098	286 919	282 059	266 857	..	..	..	..
Other life insurance	138 251	146 439	171 738	156 617	..	..	..	..
Total life insurance	402 878	436 333	456 944	426 953	438 718	460 791	470 685	509 033
of which: *Pension contracts*	..	19	..	10	..	..	..	..
1.1.4 Non-life insurance payments, by class, gross premiums								
Motor vehicle insurance	147 428	144 515	152 283	175 045	203 396	232 622	263 731	332 134
Marine, aviation and other transport insurance	663	661	793	879	142	172	201	354
Freight insurance	2 405	2 552	2 856	3 165	5 733	6 143	6 313	6 159
Fire and other property damage insurance	152 904	159 562	158 219	161 160	168 736	179 697	188 516	203 660
Pecuniary loss insurance	2 930	3 739	3 672	4 822	5 430	5 027	6 051	6 737
General liability insurance	18 856	20 074	21 904	23 585	21 274	24 525	26 379	27 271
Accident and health	23 361	25 922	28 358	29 859	22 389	24 898	31 241	36 837
of which: *Health*	7 128	8 559	9 558	8 668	4 250	5 557	8 909	11 827
Other non-life insurance	8 758	7 781	8 557	9 909	19 916	22 112	24 662	27 338
Treaty reinsurance	..	..	..	..	..	..	..	..
Total non-life insurance	357 305	364 806	376 641	408 424	447 017	495 197	547 094	640 490
1.2 Gross claims payments								
Life								
Domestic undertakings	153 649	139 994	130 633	150 198	155 047	172 359	156 899	185 600
Foreign controlled undertakings	150 320	129 594	121 318	139 595	147 047	160 787	146 733	171 402
Foreign companies (branches)	..	..	..	..	..	..	..	..
All undertakings	153 649	139 994	130 633	150 198	155 047	172 359	156 899	185 600
Non-life								
Domestic undertakings	22 516	25 692	27 416	30 571	34 112	32 258	34 114	32 143
Foreign controlled undertakings	11 387	12 611	13 973	14 605	16 056	12 917	12 308	11 636
Foreign companies (branches)	..	..	..	..	..	..	..	..
All undertakings	22 516	25 692	27 416	30 571	34 112	32 258	34 114	32 143
Composite								
Domestic undertakings	413 298	422 789	379 879	356 926	361 448	389 622	413 120	463 620
Foreign controlled undertakings	413 298	422 789	379 879	356 926	361 448	389 622	413 120	463 620
Foreign companies (branches)	..	..	..	..	..	..	..	..
All undertakings	413 298	422 789	379 879	356 926	361 448	389 622	413 120	463 620
of which:								
Life	240 059	242 802	212 244	180 098	176 820	185 216	205 734	230 696
Domestic undertakings	240 059	242 802	212 244	180 098	176 820	185 216	205 734	230 696
Foreign controlled undertakings	240 059	242 802	212 244	180 098	176 820	185 216	205 734	230 696
Foreign companies (branches)	..	..	..	..	..	..	..	..
All undertakings	240 059	242 802	212 244	180 098	176 820	185 216	205 734	230 696
Non-life	173 240	179 988	167 635	176 829	184 628	204 406	207 386	232 924
Domestic undertakings	173 240	179 988	167 635	176 829	184 628	204 406	207 386	232 924
Foreign controlled undertakings	173 240	179 988	167 635	176 829	184 628	204 406	207 386	232 924
Foreign companies (branches)	..	..	..	..	..	..	..	..
All undertakings	173 240	179 988	167 635	176 829	184 628	204 406	207 386	232 924
Total								
Domestic undertakings	589 464	588 475	537 928	537 695	550 607	594 239	604 133	681 363
Foreign controlled undertakings	575 006	564 995	515 171	511 127	524 551	563 326	572 162	646 658
Foreign companies (branches)	..	..	..	..	..	..	..	..
All undertakings	589 464	588 475	537 928	537 695	550 607	594 239	604 133	681 363

HUNGARY

Table 1. Selected aggregates *(cont.)*

Million HUF

	2012	2013	2014	2015	2016	2017	2018	2019
1.3 Commissions								
Life								
Domestic undertakings	20 760	14 900	14 024	13 526	16 531	17 513	15 243	16 536
Foreign controlled undertakings	14 215	11 559	11 559	11 089	14 360	15 017	12 599	13 254
Foreign companies (branches)	..	..	..	..	..	..	..	..
All undertakings	20 760	14 900	14 024	13 526	16 531	17 513	15 243	16 536
Non-life								
Domestic undertakings	6 319	7 349	7 243	9 161	10 325	13 383	14 338	15 392
Foreign controlled undertakings	4 457	4 813	4 948	5 986	5 650	6 550	6 809	7 114
Foreign companies (branches)	..	..	..	..	..	..	..	..
All undertakings	6 319	7 349	7 243	9 161	10 325	13 383	14 338	15 392
Composite								
Domestic undertakings	69 058	75 007	72 592	79 086	108 207	114 286	123 934	138 745
Foreign controlled undertakings	69 058	75 007	72 592	79 086	108 207	114 286	123 934	138 745
Foreign companies (branches)	..	..	..	..	..	..	..	..
All undertakings	69 058	75 007	72 592	79 086	108 207	114 286	123 934	138 745
of which:								
Life	26 909	29 847	30 235	29 116	39 083	38 017	36 194	39 422
Domestic undertakings	26 909	29 847	30 235	29 116	39 083	38 017	36 194	39 422
Foreign controlled undertakings	26 909	29 847	30 235	29 116	39 083	38 017	36 194	39 422
Foreign companies (branches)	..	..	..	..	..	..	..	..
All undertakings	26 909	29 847	30 235	29 116	39 083	38 017	36 194	39 422
Non-life	42 148	45 160	42 357	49 970	69 124	76 269	87 740	99 323
Domestic undertakings	42 148	45 160	42 357	49 970	69 124	76 269	87 740	99 323
Foreign controlled undertakings	42 148	45 160	42 357	49 970	69 124	76 269	87 740	99 323
Foreign companies (branches)	..	..	..	..	..	..	..	..
All undertakings	42 148	45 160	42 357	49 970	69 124	76 269	87 740	99 323
Total								
Domestic undertakings	96 136	97 256	93 859	101 773	135 063	145 182	153 515	170 673
Foreign controlled undertakings	87 729	91 380	89 099	96 162	128 218	135 853	143 341	159 113
Foreign companies (branches)	..	..	..	..	..	..	..	..
All undertakings	96 136	97 256	93 859	101 773	135 063	145 182	153 515	170 673
1.4 Gross operating expenses								
Life								
Domestic undertakings	37 846	32 595	35 399	32 897	34 946	34 955	32 702	34 429
Foreign controlled undertakings	32 963	27 473	30 053	29 279	31 818	30 865	28 684	31 147
Foreign companies (branches)	..	..	..	..	..	..	..	..
All undertakings	37 846	32 595	35 399	32 897	34 946	34 955	32 702	34 429
Non-life								
Domestic undertakings	16 277	17 413	17 638	20 337	21 977	21 528	19 122	24 892
Foreign controlled undertakings	10 465	11 126	11 890	14 690	13 298	10 965	11 520	12 934
Foreign companies (branches)	..	..	..	..	..	..	..	..
All undertakings	16 277	17 413	17 638	20 337	21 977	21 528	19 122	24 892
Composite								
Domestic undertakings	155 577	172 680	181 142	167 842	176 431	185 944	203 460	226 949
Foreign controlled undertakings	155 577	172 680	181 142	167 842	176 431	185 944	203 460	226 949
Foreign companies (branches)	..	..	..	..	..	..	..	..
All undertakings	155 577	172 680	181 142	167 842	176 431	185 944	203 460	226 949
of which:								
Life	55 125	56 633	70 675	55 349	56 859	50 779	55 001	63 365
Domestic undertakings	55 125	56 633	70 675	55 349	56 859	50 779	55 001	63 365
Foreign controlled undertakings	55 125	56 633	70 675	55 349	56 859	50 779	55 001	63 365
Foreign companies (branches)	..	..	..	..	..	..	..	..
All undertakings	55 125	56 633	70 675	55 349	56 859	50 779	55 001	63 365
Non-life	100 451	116 047	110 467	112 493	119 571	135 165	148 459	163 584
Domestic undertakings	100 451	116 047	110 467	112 493	119 571	135 165	148 459	163 584
Foreign controlled undertakings	100 451	116 047	110 467	112 493	119 571	135 165	148 459	163 584
Foreign companies (branches)	..	..	..	..	..	..	..	..
All undertakings	100 451	116 047	110 467	112 493	119 571	135 165	148 459	163 584
Total								
Domestic undertakings	209 699	222 687	234 179	221 076	233 354	242 427	255 284	286 269
Foreign controlled undertakings	199 004	211 279	223 085	211 811	221 547	227 774	243 664	271 030
Foreign companies (branches)	..	..	..	..	..	..	..	..
All undertakings	209 699	222 687	234 179	221 076	233 354	242 427	255 284	286 269

HUNGARY

Table 1. Selected aggregates *(cont.)*

Million HUF

	2012	2013	2014	2015	2016	2017	2018	2019
1.5 Insurance business written abroad by branches, gross premiums								
Life								
Branches and agencies	..	..	..	..	..	..	..	..
Subsidaries	..	..	..	..	..	..	..	..
Total	..	..	..	..	..	..	..	..
Non-life								
Branches and agencies	..	..	..	..	..	..	..	..
Subsidaries	..	..	..	..	..	..	..	..
Total	..	..	..	..	..	..	..	..
Composite								
Branches and agencies	..	..	..	..	..	..	..	..
Subsidaries	..	..	..	..	..	..	..	..
Total	..	..	..	..	..	..	..	..
of which:								
Life	..	..	..	..	..	..	..	..
Branches and agencies	..	..	..	..	..	..	..	..
Subsidaries	..	..	..	..	..	..	..	..
Total	..	..	..	..	..	..	..	..
Non-life	..	..	..	..	..	..	..	..
Branches and agencies	..	..	..	..	..	..	..	..
Subsidaries	..	..	..	..	..	..	..	..
Total	..	..	..	..	..	..	..	..
Total								
Branches and agencies	..	..	..	..	..	..	..	..
Subsidaries	..	..	..	..	..	..	..	..
Total	..	..	..	..	..	..	..	..

.. Not available

Note: Detailed metadata at: *http://metalinks.oecd.org/ins/20210324/93fb*.

Source: *OECD Insurance Statistics (database)*

HUNGARY

Table 2. Number of companies and employees

	2012	2013	2014	2015	2016	2017	2018	2019
2.1 Number of companies								
Life								
Domestic undertakings	12	10	10	10	8	7	6	5
Foreign controlled undertakings	9	7	7	7	7	6	5	4
Foreign companies (branches)	..	..	..	0	0	0	0	0
All undertakings	12	10	10	10	8	7	6	5
Non-life								
Domestic undertakings	13	12	12	11	10	9	9	9
Foreign controlled undertakings	7	6	6	6	6	5	5	5
Foreign companies (branches)	14	14	14	13	14	13	12	11
All undertakings	27	26	26	24	24	22	21	20
Composite								
Domestic undertakings	10	10	10	9	9	9	8	8
Foreign controlled undertakings	10	10	10	9	9	9	8	8
Foreign companies (branches)	1	1	1	2	2	2	2	1
All undertakings	11	11	11	11	11	11	10	9
Reinsurance								
Domestic undertakings	..	..	..	..	..	..	..	..
Foreign controlled undertakings	..	..	..	..	..	..	..	..
Foreign companies (branches)	..	..	..	..	..	..	..	..
All undertakings	..	..	..	..	..	..	..	..
Total								
Domestic undertakings	35	32	32	30	27	25	23	22
Foreign controlled undertakings	26	23	23	22	22	20	18	17
Foreign companies (branches)	15	15	15	15	16	15	14	12
All undertakings	50	47	47	45	43	40	37	34
2.2 Number of employees								
Insurance undertakings	9 701	9 363	9 229	8 728	8 542	8 133	11 116	8 858
Intermediaries	13 572	13 083	12 768	11 392	9 822	12 287	7 791	13 186
Total	23 273	22 445	21 997	20 121	18 364	20 420	18 907	22 044

.. Not available

Note: Detailed metadata at: *http://metalinks.oecd.org/ins/20210324/93fb*.

Source: *OECD Insurance Statistics (database)*

ICELAND

Table 1. Selected aggregates

Million ISK

	2012	2013	2014	2015	2016	2017	2018	2019
1.1 Insurance business written in the reporting country								
1.1.1 Insurance business, by ownership								
Gross premiums								
Domestic undertakings	50 490	51 142	51 849	55 346	58 777	65 274	70 561	74 978
Foreign controlled undertakings	4 788	5 088	5 401	6 010	..	..	..	..
Foreign companies (branches)	..	..	..	..	..	..	..	..
All undertakings	50 490	51 142	51 849	55 346	58 777	65 274	70 561	74 978
Premiums ceded								
Domestic undertakings	3 371	3 136	2 918	2 882	2 725	2 613	2 869	2 802
Foreign controlled undertakings	318	310	310	272	..	..	..	..
Foreign companies (branches)	..	..	..	..	..	..	..	..
All undertakings	3 371	3 136	2 918	2 882	2 725	2 613	2 869	2 802
Net written premiums								
Domestic undertakings	47 118	48 005	48 931	52 465	56 052	62 662	67 693	72 176
Foreign controlled undertakings	4 470	4 779	5 091	5 737	..	..	..	..
Foreign companies (branches)	..	..	..	..	..	..	..	..
All undertakings	47 118	48 005	48 931	52 465	56 052	62 662	67 693	72 176
1.1.2 Insurance business on foreign risks, gross premiums								
Life	0	0	0	0	0	0	0	0
Non-life	2 632	2 156	2 563	3 018	1 010	1 737	3 444	1 735
Composite total	..	..	..	..	..	..	..	..
Total	2 632	2 156	2 563	3 018	1 010	1 737	3 444	1 735
1.1.3 Life insurance payments, by class, gross premiums								
Annuities	61	61	111	473	..	..	..	..
Unit linked	87	86	87	91	20	32	23	17
Other life insurance	3 532	3 913	4 042	4 087	5 141	5 789	5 815	6 199
Total life insurance	3 680	4 061	4 240	4 651	5 161	5 821	5 837	6 217
***of which:** Pension contracts*	0	0	0	0	0	0	0	0
1.1.4 Non-life insurance payments, by class, gross premiums								
Motor vehicle insurance	21 226	21 522	22 084	23 952	28 398	33 127	35 842	38 310
Marine, aviation and other transport insurance	2 746	3 372	3 419	3 690	3 631	3 139	3 251	3 130
Freight insurance	667	638	646	751	0	0	0	0
Fire and other property damage insurance	14 028	13 816	13 903	13 911	12 484	13 048	14 472	15 552
Pecuniary loss insurance	77	45	23	27	33	26	59	70
General liability insurance	2 932	2 556	2 565	2 672	3 078	3 561	3 974	4 163
Accident and health	5 108	5 102	4 947	5 646	5 960	6 509	7 093	7 507
***of which:** Health*	..	..	..	..	..	..	..	..
Other non-life insurance	27	30	22	42	32	42	33	29
Treaty reinsurance	0	0	0	0	0	0	0	0
Total non-life insurance	46 809	47 081	47 608	50 690	53 616	59 453	64 724	68 761
1.2 Gross claims payments								
Life								
Domestic undertakings	1 434	1 381	1 529	1 325	1 690	1 755	1 752	2 380
Foreign controlled undertakings	56	47	30	58	..	..	..	..
Foreign companies (branches)	..	..	..	..	..	..	..	..
All undertakings	1 434	1 381	1 529	1 325	1 690	1 755	1 752	2 380
Non-life								
Domestic undertakings	30 190	31 417	32 554	36 082	41 655	43 781	51 533	52 944
Foreign controlled undertakings	2 931	3 412	3 520	4 169	..	..	..	..
Foreign companies (branches)	..	..	..	..	..	..	..	..
All undertakings	30 190	31 417	32 554	36 082	41 655	43 781	51 533	52 944
Composite, all undertakings	..	..	..	..	..	..	..	..
Total								
Domestic undertakings	31 624	32 798	34 083	37 407	43 345	45 536	53 285	55 324
Foreign controlled undertakings	2 987	3 459	3 550	4 227	..	..	..	..
Foreign companies (branches)	..	..	..	..	..	..	..	..
All undertakings	31 624	32 798	34 083	37 407	43 345	45 536	53 285	55 324
1.3 Commissions								
Life								
Domestic undertakings	71	66	118	90	..	..	..	..
Foreign controlled undertakings	12	20	42	3	..	..	..	..
Foreign companies (branches)	..	..	..	..	..	..	..	..
All undertakings	71	66	118	90	..	..	..	..
Non-life								
Domestic undertakings	122	102	39	36	..	..	..	..
Foreign controlled undertakings	0	0	0	0	..	..	..	..
Foreign companies (branches)	..	..	..	..	..	..	..	..
All undertakings	122	102	39	36	..	..	..	..
Composite, all undertakings	..	..	..	..	..	..	..	..
Total								
Domestic undertakings	193	168	157	126	..	..	..	..
Foreign controlled undertakings	12	20	42	3	..	..	..	..
Foreign companies (branches)	..	..	..	..	..	..	..	..
All undertakings	193	168	157	126	..	..	..	..

ICELAND

Table 1. Selected aggregates *(cont.)*

Million ISK

	2012	2013	2014	2015	2016	2017	2018	2019
1.4 Gross operating expenses								
Life								
Domestic undertakings	1 119	1 384	1 098	1 498	1 231	1 528	1 394	1 411
Foreign controlled undertakings	77	90	18	161	..	..	..	..
Foreign companies (branches)	..	..	..	..	..	..	..	..
All undertakings	1 119	1 384	1 098	1 498	1 231	1 528	1 394	1 411
Non-life								
Domestic undertakings	9 987	9 860	9 680	4 314	6 931	7 422	11 994	12 605
Foreign controlled undertakings	996	1 084	1 086	1 225	..	..	..	..
Foreign companies (branches)	..	..	..	..	..	..	..	..
All undertakings	9 987	9 860	9 680	4 314	6 931	7 422	12 026	12 605
Composite, all undertakings	..	..	..	..	..	..	..	..
Total								
Domestic undertakings	11 106	11 244	10 778	5 812	8 162	8 950	13 389	14 016
Foreign controlled undertakings	1 072	1 173	1 104	1 387	..	..	..	..
Foreign companies (branches)	..	..	..	..	..	..	..	..
All undertakings	11 106	11 244	10 778	5 812	8 162	8 950	13 421	14 016
1.5 Insurance business written abroad by branches, gross premiums								
Life								
Branches and agencies	0	..	..	..	..	..	..	..
Subsidaries	0	..	..	..	..	..	..	..
Total	0	..	..	..	..	..	..	..
Non-life								
Branches and agencies	914	..	..	..	..	..	..	..
Subsidaries	0	..	..	..	..	..	..	..
Total	914	..	..	..	..	..	..	..
Composite total	..	..	..	..	..	..	..	..
Total								
Branches and agencies	914	..	..	..	..	..	..	..
Subsidaries	0	..	..	..	..	..	..	..
Total	914	..	..	..	..	..	..	..

.. Not available

Note: Detailed metadata at: *http://metalinks.oecd.org/ins/20210324/f5ef.*

Source: *OECD Insurance Statistics (database)*

ICELAND

Table 2. Number of companies and employees

	2012	2013	2014	2015	2016	2017	2018	2019
2.1 Number of companies								
Life								
Domestic undertakings	5	5	5	5	4	4	4	4
Foreign controlled undertakings	1	1	1	1	..	..	..	..
Foreign companies (branches)	1	1	1	1	..	..	..	..
All undertakings	6	6	6	6	4	4	4	4
Non-life								
Domestic undertakings	6	5	5	5	4	4	4	4
Foreign controlled undertakings	1	1	1	1	..	..	..	..
Foreign companies (branches)	1	1	1	1	..	..	..	..
All undertakings	7	6	6	6	4	4	4	4
Composite, all undertakings	**0**	**0**	**0**	**0**	**0**	**0**	**0**	**0**
Reinsurance								
Domestic undertakings	2	2	2	2	0	0	0	0
Foreign controlled undertakings	0	..	..	..	..	..	..	..
Foreign companies (branches)	0	..	..	..	..	..	..	..
All undertakings	2	2	2	2	0	0	0	0
Total								
Domestic undertakings	13	12	12	12	8	8	8	8
Foreign controlled undertakings	2	2	2	2	0	0	0	0
Foreign companies (branches)	2	2	2	2	0	0	0	0
All undertakings	15	14	14	14	8	8	8	8
2.2 Number of employees								
Insurance undertakings	641	614	..	582	..	..	..	..
Intermediaries	..	..	592	..	..	..	..	..
Total	..	614	592	582	..	..	..	..

.. Not available

Note: Detailed metadata at: *http://metalinks.oecd.org/ins/20210324/f5ef.*

Source: *OECD Insurance Statistics (database)*

IRELAND

Table 1. Selected aggregates

Million EUR

	2012	2013	2014	2015	2016	2017	2018	2019
1.1 Insurance business written in the reporting country								
1.1.1 Insurance business, by ownership								
Gross premiums								
Domestic undertakings	33 133	31 818	36 377	40 340	48 949	40 281	36 998	40 282
Foreign controlled undertakings	..	..	..	..	..	..	..	..
Foreign companies (branches)	2 348	2 301	3 184	3 645	..	3 821	3 756	4 283
All undertakings	35 481	34 119	39 561	43 985	48 949	44 102	40 754	44 565
Premiums ceded								
Domestic undertakings	3 755	3 908	3 891	4 933	9 985	..	..	..
Foreign controlled undertakings	..	..	..	..	..	..	..	..
Foreign companies (branches)	356	268	371	359	..	..	..	..
All undertakings	4 111	4 176	4 262	5 292	9 985	..	..	..
Net written premiums								
Domestic undertakings	29 379	27 910	32 486	35 407	38 964	..	..	..
Foreign controlled undertakings	..	..	..	..	..	..	..	..
Foreign companies (branches)	1 992	2 033	2 813	3 286	..	..	..	..
All undertakings	31 371	29 943	35 299	38 693	38 964	..	..	..
1.1.2 Insurance business on foreign risks, gross premiums								
Life	15 038	16 125	21 410	23 192	..	19 774	16 644	16 606
Non-life	3 676	3 826	3 960	4 263	..	2 277	2 671	3 032
Composite	..	..	..	..	..	6	191	180
of which:								
Life	..	..	..	..	..	..	..	..
Non-life	..	..	..	..	..	..	..	..
Total	18 714	19 951	25 370	27 455	..	22 057	19 506	19 818
1.1.3 Life insurance payments, by class, gross premiums								
Annuities	..	..	..	..	0	0	0	0
Unit linked	..	..	..	..	28 838	30 737	26 568	27 840
Other life insurance	..	..	..	..	4 477	4 279	4 102	4 135
Total life insurance	28 140	27 207	32 171	34 587	33 315	35 016	30 670	31 975
***of which:** Pension contracts*	..	..	..	..	..	..	..	..
1.1.4 Non-life insurance payments, by class, gross premiums								
Motor vehicle insurance	1 486	1 435	1 599	1 795	3 905	2 086	2 067	2 900
Marine, aviation and other transport insurance	243	183	143	163	421	144	219	292
Freight insurance	..	..	..	..	0	0	..	0
Fire and other property damage insurance	1 906	1 763	1 758	1 768	4 023	1 401	1 503	2 156
Pecuniary loss insurance	..	105	124	92	332	830	848	1 152
General liability insurance	1 147	1 127	1 301	1 400	2 887	1 288	1 296	1 967
Accident and health	1 288	1 171	1 235	2 750	1 935	2 396	2 323	2 575
***of which:** Health*	..	..	..	..	..	..	..	..
Other non-life insurance	563	504	494	585	1 159	158	217	139
Treaty reinsurance	374	330	373	414	746	217	..	0
Total non-life insurance	7 007	6 618	7 027	8 967	15 408	8 520	8 473	11 181
1.2 Gross claims payments								
Life								
Domestic undertakings	27 921	28 263	27 434	28 474	32 280	26 726	25 196	26 254
Foreign controlled undertakings	..	..	..	..	..	..	..	..
Foreign companies (branches)	..	1 235	1 114	1 356	..	2 435	2 052	836
All undertakings	27 921	29 498	28 548	29 830	32 280	29 161	27 248	27 090
Non-life								
Domestic undertakings	4 842	4 369	3 853	5 343	15 941	8 482	8 283	9 604
Foreign controlled undertakings	..	..	..	..	..	..	..	..
Foreign companies (branches)	983	677	1 177	1 179	..	725	871	1 714
All undertakings	5 825	5 046	5 030	6 522	15 941	9 207	9 154	11 318
Composite								
Domestic undertakings	..	..	..	..	..	..	..	..
Foreign controlled undertakings	..	..	..	..	..	..	..	..
Foreign companies (branches)	..	..	..	..	..	357	983	974
All undertakings	..	..	..	..	..	357	983	974
of which:								
Life								
Domestic undertakings	..	..	..	..	..	..	..	..
Foreign controlled undertakings	..	..	..	..	..	..	..	..
Foreign companies (branches)	..	..	..	..	..	..	..	..
All undertakings	..	..	..	..	..	..	..	..
Non-life								
Domestic undertakings	..	..	..	..	..	..	..	..
Foreign controlled undertakings	..	..	..	..	..	..	..	..
Foreign companies (branches)	..	..	..	..	..	..	..	..
All undertakings	..	..	..	..	..	..	..	..
Total								
Domestic undertakings	32 763	32 632	31 287	33 817	48 221	35 208	33 479	35 858
Foreign controlled undertakings	..	..	..	..	..	..	..	..
Foreign companies (branches)	983	1 912	2 291	2 535	..	3 517	3 906	3 524
All undertakings	33 746	34 544	33 578	36 352	48 221	38 725	37 385	39 382

IRELAND

Table 1. Selected aggregates *(cont.)*

Million EUR

	2012	2013	2014	2015	2016	2017	2018	2019
1.3 Commissions								
Life								
Domestic undertakings	1 593	1 844	2 051	2 281	2 198	1 517	1 625	1 497
Foreign controlled undertakings	..	..	..	..	..	..	..	..
Foreign companies (branches)	..	43	64	59	..	94	44	-10
All undertakings	1 593	1 887	2 115	2 340	2 198	1 611	1 669	1 487
Non-life								
Domestic undertakings	657	737	764	896	2 292	957	1 012	1 187
Foreign controlled undertakings	..	..	..	..	..	..	..	..
Foreign companies (branches)	171	130	248	299	..	194	221	227
All undertakings	828	867	1 012	1 195	2 292	1 511	1 233	1 414
Composite								
Domestic undertakings	..	..	..	..	..	..	..	..
Foreign controlled undertakings	..	..	..	..	..	..	..	..
Foreign companies (branches)	..	..	..	..	..	80	110	94
All undertakings	..	..	..	..	..	80	110	94
of which:								
Life	..	..	..	..	..	..	..	..
Domestic undertakings	..	..	..	..	..	..	..	..
Foreign controlled undertakings	..	..	..	..	..	..	..	..
Foreign companies (branches)	..	..	..	..	..	..	..	..
All undertakings	..	..	..	..	..	..	..	..
Non-life	..	..	..	..	..	..	..	..
Domestic undertakings	..	..	..	..	..	..	..	..
Foreign controlled undertakings	..	..	..	..	..	..	..	..
Foreign companies (branches)	..	..	..	..	..	..	..	..
All undertakings	..	..	..	..	..	..	..	..
Total								
Domestic undertakings	2 250	2 581	2 815	3 177	4 490	2 474	2 637	2 684
Foreign controlled undertakings	..	..	..	..	..	..	..	..
Foreign companies (branches)	171	173	312	358	..	368	375	311
All undertakings	2 420	2 754	3 127	3 535	4 490	3 202	3 012	2 995
1.4 Gross operating expenses								
Life								
Domestic undertakings	1 268	1 346	1 429	1 437	1 319	444	..	..
Foreign controlled undertakings	..	..	..	..	..	..	..	..
Foreign companies (branches)	..	154	657	158	..	..	..	..
All undertakings	1 268	1 500	2 086	1 595	1 319	444	..	..
Non-life								
Domestic undertakings	622	650	589	484	1 873	932	..	..
Foreign controlled undertakings	..	..	..	..	..	..	..	..
Foreign companies (branches)	295	159	223	224	..	..	..	..
All undertakings	917	809	812	708	1 873	932	..	..
Composite								
Domestic undertakings	..	..	..	..	..	..	..	..
Foreign controlled undertakings	..	..	..	..	..	..	..	..
Foreign companies (branches)	..	..	..	..	..	..	..	..
All undertakings	..	..	..	..	..	..	..	..
of which:								
Life	..	..	..	..	..	..	..	..
Domestic undertakings	..	..	..	..	..	..	..	..
Foreign controlled undertakings	..	..	..	..	..	..	..	..
Foreign companies (branches)	..	..	..	..	..	..	..	..
All undertakings	..	..	..	..	..	..	..	..
Non-life	..	..	..	..	..	..	..	..
Domestic undertakings	..	..	..	..	..	..	..	..
Foreign controlled undertakings	..	..	..	..	..	..	..	..
Foreign companies (branches)	..	..	..	..	..	..	..	..
All undertakings	..	..	..	..	..	..	..	..
Total								
Domestic undertakings	1 891	1 996	2 018	1 921	3 192	1 376	..	..
Foreign controlled undertakings	..	..	..	..	..	..	..	..
Foreign companies (branches)	295	313	880	382	..	..	..	..
All undertakings	2 185	2 309	2 898	2 303	3 192	1 376	..	..

IRELAND

Table 1. Selected aggregates *(cont.)*

Million EUR

	2012	2013	2014	2015	2016	2017	2018	2019
1.5 Insurance business written abroad by branches, gross premiums								
Life								
Branches and agencies	3 422	5 563	5 970	6 234	..	6 438	5 266	6 513
Subsidaries	..	..	..	..	..	..	..	..
Total	3 422	5 563	5 970	6 234	..	6 438	5 266	6 513
Non-life								
Branches and agencies	9 599	9 228	9 640	9 835	..	8 739	9 029	11 204
Subsidaries	..	..	..	..	..	..	..	..
Total	9 599	9 228	9 640	9 835	..	8 739	9 029	11 204
Composite								
Branches and agencies	..	..	..	..	..	..	..	..
Subsidaries	..	..	..	..	..	..	..	..
Total	..	..	..	..	..	..	..	..
of which:								
Life	..	..	..	..	..	..	..	..
Branches and agencies	..	..	..	..	..	..	..	..
Subsidaries	..	..	..	..	..	..	..	..
Total	..	..	..	..	..	..	..	..
Non-life	..	..	..	..	..	..	..	..
Branches and agencies	..	..	..	..	..	..	..	..
Subsidaries	..	..	..	..	..	..	..	..
Total	..	..	..	..	..	..	..	..
Total								
Branches and agencies	13 021	14 791	15 610	16 069	..	15 177	14 295	17 717
Subsidaries	..	..	..	..	..	..	..	..
Total	13 021	14 791	15 610	16 069	..	15 177	14 295	17 717

.. Not available

Note: Detailed metadata at: *http://metalinks.oecd.org/ins/20210324/f71d.*

Source: *OECD Insurance Statistics (database)*

IRELAND

Table 2. Number of companies and employees

	2012	2013	2014	2015	2016	2017	2018	2019
2.1 Number of companies								
Life								
Domestic undertakings	55	53	51	48	44	45	42	43
Foreign controlled undertakings	0	..	..	..	0	0	..	..
Foreign companies (branches)	8	8	8	11	11	12	13	15
All undertakings	63	61	59	59	55	57	55	58
Non-life								
Domestic undertakings	111	104	102	101	90	99	95	95
Foreign controlled undertakings	0	..	..	..	0	0	..	..
Foreign companies (branches)	28	27	30	32	31	30	38	33
All undertakings	139	131	132	133	121	129	133	128
Composite								
Domestic undertakings	0	0	0	0	0	1	0	..
Foreign controlled undertakings	0	0	0	0	0	0	..	..
Foreign companies (branches)	0	0	0	0	0	0	0	..
All undertakings	0	0	0	0	0	1	0	..
Reinsurance								
Domestic undertakings	87	77	75	67	61	64	63	59
Foreign controlled undertakings	0	..	..	..	0	0	..	..
Foreign companies (branches)	0	0	0	0	0	0	0	..
All undertakings	87	77	75	67	61	64	63	59
Total								
Domestic undertakings	253	234	228	216	196	209	200	197
Foreign controlled undertakings	..	..	..	..	0	0	..	..
Foreign companies (branches)	36	35	38	43	42	42	51	48
All undertakings	289	269	266	259	238	251	251	245
2.2 Number of employees								
Insurance undertakings	8 682	8 887	8 095	9 404	..	..	..	..
Intermediaries	..	..	..	..	..	..	..	..
Total	8 682	8 887	..	..	..	..	..	..

.. Not available

Note: Detailed metadata at: *http://metalinks.oecd.org/ins/20210324/f71d.*

Source: *OECD Insurance Statistics (database)*

ISRAEL

Table 1. Selected aggregates

Million ILS

	2012	2013	2014	2015	2016	2017	2018	2019
1.1 Insurance business written in the reporting country								
1.1.1 Insurance business, by ownership								
Gross premiums								
Domestic undertakings	48 086	50 339	51 400	54 869	58 153	62 730	66 640	68 881
Foreign controlled undertakings	840	889	953	1 135	1 165	1 234	1 296	12 576
Foreign companies (branches)	..	..	..	..	..	..	..	..
All undertakings	48 086	50 339	51 400	54 869	58 153	62 730	66 640	68 881
Premiums ceded								
Domestic undertakings	6 877	6 418	5 934	6 356	8 756	8 468	9 454	10 098
Foreign controlled undertakings	185	164	162	232	225	228	249	1 646
Foreign companies (branches)	..	..	..	..	..	..	..	..
All undertakings	6 877	6 418	5 934	6 356	8 756	8 468	9 454	10 098
Net written premiums								
Domestic undertakings	41 209	43 921	45 466	48 512	49 398	54 263	57 186	58 782
Foreign controlled undertakings	656	726	791	903	940	1 006	1 047	10 930
Foreign companies (branches)	..	..	..	..	..	..	..	..
All undertakings	41 209	43 921	45 466	48 512	49 398	54 263	57 186	58 782
1.1.2 Insurance business on foreign risks, gross premiums								
Life	..	..	..	..	..	..	..	..
Non-life	..	..	..	..	..	..	..	..
Composite	..	..	..	..	..	..	..	..
of which:								
Life	..	..	..	..	..	..	..	..
Non-life	..	..	..	..	..	..	..	..
Total	..	..	..	..	..	..	..	..
1.1.3 Life insurance payments, by class, gross premiums								
Annuities	1 542	1 361	1 194	1 084	1 273	1 125	1 118	1 108
Unit linked	17 673	18 557	18 236	20 266	20 897	23 867	25 433	26 378
Other life insurance	6 242	6 709	7 141	8 066	8 492	8 730	9 412	10 352
Total life insurance	25 458	26 627	26 571	29 416	30 662	33 722	35 963	37 838
***of which:** Pension contracts*	..	..	..	..	..	..	..	..
1.1.4 Non-life insurance payments, by class, gross premiums								
Motor vehicle insurance	10 673	11 040	11 439	11 775	13 053	13 396	14 129	13 976
Marine, aviation and other transport insurance	41	38	38	39	38	36	40	43
Freight insurance	180	169	170	174	176	187	174	173
Fire and other property damage insurance	4 082	4 283	4 292	4 238	4 375	4 481	4 549	4 720
Pecuniary loss insurance	277	284	278	307	335	348	480	359
General liability insurance	2 487	2 575	2 697	2 814	2 917	3 094	3 250	3 402
Accident and health	4 396	4 869	5 425	5 678	6 086	6 961	7 548	7 826
***of which:** Health*	3 580	3 859	4 189	4 203	4 448	5 144	5 614	5 908
Other non-life insurance	492	452	492	426	502	506	506	545
Treaty reinsurance	..	..	0	0	0	..	0	0
Total non-life insurance	22 628	23 712	24 830	25 452	27 483	29 009	30 676	31 043
1.2 Gross claims payments								
Life								
Domestic undertakings	..	0	3	6	8	.. c	..	..
Foreign controlled undertakings	..	..	..	..	0	..	..	..
Foreign companies (branches)	..	..	..	..	..	..	..	..
All undertakings	..	0	3	6	8	.. c	..	..
Non-life								
Domestic undertakings	1 395	2 013	2 470	2 589	2 180	2 124	2 189	2 368
Foreign controlled undertakings	..	..	..	39	72	22	30	36
Foreign companies (branches)	..	..	..	..	..	..	..	..
All undertakings	1 395	2 013	2 470	2 589	2 180	2 124	2 189	2 368
Composite								
Domestic undertakings	25 830	24 594	27 644	30 828	31 879	35 461	36 580	40 374
Foreign controlled undertakings	393	280	462	640	538	0	578	6 432
Foreign companies (branches)	..	..	..	..	..	..	..	..
All undertakings	25 830	24 594	27 644	30 828	31 879	35 461	36 580	40 374
of which:								
Life	12 472	12 644	13 825	15 363	16 243	18 411	19 489	23 113
Domestic undertakings	12 472	12 644	13 825	15 363	16 243	18 411	19 489	23 113
Foreign controlled undertakings	27	18	26	39	36	42	50	3 257
Foreign companies (branches)	..	..	..	..	..	..	..	..
All undertakings	12 472	12 644	13 825	15 363	16 243	18 411	19 489	23 113
Non-life	13 358	11 949	13 819	15 465	15 636	17 051	17 091	17 261
Domestic undertakings	13 358	11 949	13 819	15 465	15 636	17 051	17 091	17 261
Foreign controlled undertakings	366	262	436	600	502	575	528	3 175
Foreign companies (branches)	..	..	..	..	..	..	..	..
All undertakings	13 358	11 949	13 819	15 465	15 636	17 051	17 091	17 261
Total								
Domestic undertakings	27 225	26 607	30 117	33 422	34 067	37 598	38 769	42 742
Foreign controlled undertakings	393	280	462	679	609	22	608	6 469
Foreign companies (branches)	..	..	..	..	..	..	..	..
All undertakings	27 225	26 607	30 117	33 422	34 067	37 598	38 769	42 742

Table 1. Selected aggregates *(cont.)*

Million ILS

	2012	2013	2014	2015	2016	2017	2018	2019
1.3 Commissions								
Life								
Domestic undertakings	..	0	6	15	19	.. c	..	..
Foreign controlled undertakings	..	..	..	..	0	..	..	..
Foreign companies (branches)	..	..	..	..	..	..	..	..
All undertakings	..	0	6	15	19	.. c	..	..
Non-life								
Domestic undertakings	175	248	281	317	291	341	358	347
Foreign controlled undertakings	..	..	..	0	0	0	0	0
Foreign companies (branches)	..	..	..	..	..	..	..	..
All undertakings	175	248	281	317	291	341	358	347
Composite								
Domestic undertakings	5 512	5 688	5 940	6 296	6 709	7 109	7 592	7 630
Foreign controlled undertakings	41	39	..	42	40	..	38	1 429
Foreign companies (branches)	..	..	..	..	..	..	..	..
All undertakings	5 512	5 688	5 940	6 296	6 709	7 109	7 592	7 630
of which:								
Life	2 577	2 571	2 639	2 912	3 097	3 215	3 531	3 507
Domestic undertakings	2 577	2 571	2 639	2 912	3 097	3 215	3 531	3 507
Foreign controlled undertakings	1	1	1	1	1	1	1	461
Foreign companies (branches)	..	..	..	..	..	..	..	..
All undertakings	2 577	2 571	2 639	2 912	3 097	3 215	3 531	3 507
Non-life	2 936	3 118	3 300	3 384	3 612	3 893	4 061	4 123
Domestic undertakings	2 936	3 118	3 300	3 384	3 612	3 893	4 061	4 123
Foreign controlled undertakings	40	38	38	41	39	37	37	968
Foreign companies (branches)	..	..	..	..	..	..	..	..
All undertakings	2 936	3 118	3 300	3 384	3 612	3 893	4 061	4 123
Total								
Domestic undertakings	5 688	5 936	6 226	6 628	7 019	7 464	7 950	7 976
Foreign controlled undertakings	41	39	..	42	40	0	38	1 429
Foreign companies (branches)	..	..	..	..	..	..	..	..
All undertakings	5 688	5 936	6 226	6 628	7 019	7 464	7 950	7 976
1.4 Gross operating expenses								
Life								
Domestic undertakings	..	1	10	32	32	.. c	..	..
Foreign controlled undertakings	..	..	..	..	0	..	..	..
Foreign companies (branches)	..	..	..	..	..	..	..	..
All undertakings	..	1	10	32	32	.. c	..	..
Non-life								
Domestic undertakings	305	449	322	402	380	417	32	33
Foreign controlled undertakings	..	..	..	30	29	33	36	37
Foreign companies (branches)	..	..	..	..	..	..	..	..
All undertakings	305	449	322	402	380	417	32	33
Composite								
Domestic undertakings	5 270	5 285	5 169	5 719	6 033	6 504	13 992	6 773
Foreign controlled undertakings	260	272	276	282	275	278	289	1 365
Foreign companies (branches)	..	..	..	..	..	..	..	..
All undertakings	5 270	5 285	5 169	5 719	6 033	6 504	13 992	6 773
of which:								
Life	2 323	2 542	2 608	2 790	2 707	2 849	2 946	3 041
Domestic undertakings	2 323	2 542	2 608	2 790	2 707	2 849	2 946	3 041
Foreign controlled undertakings	53	61	56	54	55	51	51	641
Foreign companies (branches)	..	..	..	..	..	..	..	..
All undertakings	2 323	2 542	2 608	2 790	2 707	2 849	2 946	3 041
Non-life	2 373	2 502	2 561	2 721	2 785	3 002	3 185	3 297
Domestic undertakings	2 373	2 502	2 561	2 721	2 785	3 002	3 185	3 297
Foreign controlled undertakings	208	212	220	228	220	227	239	724
Foreign companies (branches)	..	..	..	..	..	..	..	..
All undertakings	2 373	2 502	2 561	2 721	2 785	3 002	3 185	3 297
Total								
Domestic undertakings	5 574	5 736	5 501	6 153	6 445	6 940	14 024	6 806
Foreign controlled undertakings	260	272	276	312	304	311	325	1 402
Foreign companies (branches)	..	..	..	..	..	..	..	..
All undertakings	5 574	5 736	5 501	6 153	6 445	6 940	14 024	6 806

Table 1. Selected aggregates *(cont.)*

Million ILS

	2012	2013	2014	2015	2016	2017	2018	2019
1.5 Insurance business written abroad by branches, gross premiums								
Life								
Branches and agencies	..	..	..	..	..	..	..	..
Subsidaries	..	..	..	..	..	..	..	..
Total	..	..	..	..	..	..	..	..
Non-life								
Branches and agencies	..	..	..	..	..	..	..	..
Subsidaries	..	..	..	..	..	..	..	..
Total	..	..	..	..	..	..	..	..
Composite								
Branches and agencies	..	..	..	..	..	..	..	..
Subsidaries	..	..	..	..	..	..	..	..
Total	..	..	..	..	..	..	..	..
of which:								
Life	..	..	..	..	..	..	..	..
Branches and agencies	..	..	..	..	..	..	..	..
Subsidaries	..	..	..	..	..	..	..	..
Total	..	..	..	..	..	..	..	..
Non-life	..	..	..	..	..	..	..	..
Branches and agencies	..	..	..	..	..	..	..	..
Subsidaries	..	..	..	..	..	..	..	..
Total	..	..	..	..	..	..	..	..
Total								
Branches and agencies	..	..	..	..	..	..	..	..
Subsidaries	..	..	..	..	..	..	..	..
Total	..	..	..	..	..	..	..	..

.. Not available; c Confidential data

Note: Detailed metadata at: *http://metalinks.oecd.org/ins/20210324/24ce.*

The statistical data for Israel are supplied by and under the responsibility of the relevant Israeli authorities. The use of such data by the OECD is without prejudice to the status of the Golan Heights, East Jerusalem and Israeli settlements in the West Bank under the terms of international law.

Source: *OECD Insurance Statistics (database)*

ISRAEL

Table 2. Number of companies and employees

	2012	2013	2014	2015	2016	2017	2018	2019
2.1 Number of companies								
Life								
Domestic undertakings	..	1	1	2	2	1	0	0
Foreign controlled undertakings	..	..	..	0	..	..	0	0
Foreign companies (branches)	..	..	..	0	..	..	0	0
All undertakings	..	1	1	2	2	1	0	0
Non-life								
Domestic undertakings	10	12	12	10	10	10	12	12
Foreign controlled undertakings	..	..	..	1	1	1	1	1
Foreign companies (branches)	2	2	3	3	3	3	3	3
All undertakings	12	14	15	13	13	13	15	15
Composite								
Domestic undertakings	13	10	10	11	10	10	10	10
Foreign controlled undertakings	1	1	1	1	1	1	1	2
Foreign companies (branches)	..	..	..	0	..	..	0	0
All undertakings	13	10	10	11	10	10	10	10
Reinsurance								
Domestic undertakings	..	..	..	0	..	..	0	0
Foreign controlled undertakings	..	..	..	0	..	..	0	0
Foreign companies (branches)	..	..	..	0	..	..	0	0
All undertakings	..	..	0	0	0	..	0	0
Total								
Domestic undertakings	23	23	23	23	22	21	22	22
Foreign controlled undertakings	1	1	1	2	..	2	2	3
Foreign companies (branches)	2	2	3	3	3	3	3	3
All undertakings	25	25	26	26	25	24	25	25
2.2 Number of employees								
Insurance undertakings	..	..	..	..	..	..	..	..
Intermediaries	..	..	..	..	..	..	..	..
Total	..	..	..	..	..	..	..	..

.. Not available

Note: Detailed metadata at: *http://metalinks.oecd.org/ins/20210324/24ce.*

The statistical data for Israel are supplied by and under the responsibility of the relevant Israeli authorities. The use of such data by the OECD is without prejudice to the status of the Golan Heights, East Jerusalem and Israeli settlements in the West Bank under the terms of international law.

Source: *OECD Insurance Statistics (database)*

ITALY

Table 1. Selected aggregates

Million EUR

	2012	2013	2014	2015	2016	2017	2018	2019
1.1 Insurance business written in the reporting country								
1.1.1 Insurance business, by ownership								
Gross premiums								
Domestic undertakings	107 192	120 973	145 244	149 011	136 278	132 924	138 120	140 752
Foreign controlled undertakings	29 138	34 302	44 419	45 694	44 287	41 990	48 367	49 764
Foreign companies (branches)	399	373	375	473	521	504	565	601
All undertakings	107 591	121 345	145 619	149 484	136 799	133 429	138 685	141 353
Premiums ceded								
Domestic undertakings	5 178	4 513	4 203	4 079	4 914	4 939	5 213	4 904
Foreign controlled undertakings	1 392	1 116	991	983	1 822	1 829	1 867	1 940
Foreign companies (branches)	45	49	58	53	62	57	67	74
All undertakings	5 223	4 563	4 262	4 132	4 976	4 996	5 281	4 979
Net written premiums								
Domestic undertakings	102 014	116 459	141 041	144 932	131 364	127 986	132 907	135 847
Foreign controlled undertakings	27 746	33 186	43 428	44 711	42 465	40 160	46 500	47 824
Foreign companies (branches)	354	323	317	420	459	447	497	527
All undertakings	102 368	116 782	141 358	145 352	131 823	128 433	133 404	136 374
1.1.2 Insurance business on foreign risks, gross premiums								
Life	0	1	1	1	1	1	3	10
Non-life	50	53	59	54	59	57	72	85
Composite	1 935	2 044	1 904	2 016	2 070	2 037	2 008	3 652
of which:								
Life	1 327	1 232	1 073	1 166	1 255	1 252	1 215	1 538
Non-life	607	811	831	849	814	784	792	2 114
Total	1 984	2 098	1 963	2 071	2 130	2 095	2 082	3 747
1.1.3 Life insurance payments, by class, gross premiums								
Annuities	1 243	1 012	956	737	710	716	701	705
Unit linked	13 800	15 497	21 829	31 884	23 848	31 305	29 887	27 928
Other life insurance	54 597	68 501	87 639	82 220	77 596	66 709	71 545	77 445
Total life insurance	69 639	85 010	110 424	114 842	102 154	98 730	102 133	106 077
***of which:** Pension contracts*	4 296	3 825	4 873	5 492	5 848	6 308	6 631	7 536
1.1.4 Non-life insurance payments, by class, gross premiums								
Motor vehicle insurance	20 247	18 661	17 468	16 590	16 260	16 097	16 262	16 393
Marine, aviation and other transport insurance	366	327	334	326	417	387	288	349
Freight insurance	227	208	212	204	198	202	209	226
Fire and other property damage insurance	5 056	5 269	5 611	5 544	5 863	5 851	6 116	6 373
Pecuniary loss insurance	961	967	1 018	1 034	1 119	1 204	1 203	1 309
General liability insurance	2 972	2 905	2 879	2 952	3 073	3 094	3 198	3 427
Accident and health	5 151	5 144	5 221	5 415	5 868	6 200	6 471	7 004
***of which:** Health*	2 150	2 114	2 149	2 323	2 655	2 909	3 142	3 534
Other non-life insurance	698	1 163	988	1 082	1 217	1 293	1 373	1 528
Treaty reinsurance	417	0	0	0	0	0	0	..
Total non-life insurance	36 095	34 646	33 730	33 147	34 015	34 326	35 121	36 607
1.2 Gross claims payments								
Life								
Domestic undertakings	29 764	23 754	22 852	22 955	21 169	21 166	21 382	22 878
Foreign controlled undertakings	14 078	11 058	10 413	12 229	10 866	10 142	10 653	12 066
Foreign companies (branches)	0	0	0	0	0	0	0	0
All undertakings	29 764	23 754	22 852	22 955	21 169	21 166	21 382	22 878
Non-life								
Domestic undertakings	5 084	5 061	5 016	4 931	4 776	5 209	5 170	5 458
Foreign controlled undertakings	1 802	1 758	1 853	2 005	2 008	2 021	1 920	1 994
Foreign companies (branches)	257	231	257	308	369	364	357	394
All undertakings	5 341	5 292	5 273	5 240	5 144	5 574	5 527	5 852
Composite								
Domestic undertakings	67 451	64 138	61 204	65 892	59 690	68 163	69 576	71 806
Foreign controlled undertakings	16 282	16 899	14 972	16 842	16 097	17 146	17 740	18 704
Foreign companies (branches)	0	0	0	0	0	0	0	0
All undertakings	67 451	64 138	61 204	65 892	59 690	68 163	69 576	71 806
of which:								
Life	47 143	44 754	43 279	48 546	43 755	52 096	53 576	55 052
Domestic undertakings	47 143	44 754	43 279	48 546	43 755	52 096	53 576	55 052
Foreign controlled undertakings	11 858	12 685	11 217	12 693	12 061	13 358	13 790	14 438
Foreign companies (branches)	0	0	0	0	0	0	0	0
All undertakings	47 143	44 754	43 279	48 546	43 755	52 096	53 576	55 052
Non-life	20 308	19 384	17 925	17 346	15 935	16 067	16 000	16 754
Domestic undertakings	20 308	19 384	17 925	17 346	15 935	16 067	16 000	16 754
Foreign controlled undertakings	4 424	4 215	3 754	4 149	4 037	3 788	3 950	4 266
Foreign companies (branches)	0	0	0	0	0	0	0	0
All undertakings	20 308	19 384	17 925	17 346	15 935	16 067	16 000	16 754
Total								
Domestic undertakings	102 298	92 953	89 071	93 778	85 635	94 539	96 128	100 143
Foreign controlled undertakings	32 162	29 715	27 238	31 075	28 972	29 309	30 313	32 763
Foreign companies (branches)	257	231	257	308	369	364	357	394
All undertakings	102 555	93 185	89 328	94 087	86 003	94 904	96 485	100 536

ITALY

Table 1. Selected aggregates *(cont.)*

Million EUR

	2012	2013	2014	2015	2016	2017	2018	2019
1.3 Commissions								
Life								
Domestic undertakings	601	576	650	641	626	620	590	669
Foreign controlled undertakings	405	384	430	436	449	434	432	465
Foreign companies (branches)	0	0	0	0	0	0	..	..
All undertakings	601	576	650	641	626	620	590	1 134
Non-life								
Domestic undertakings	1 620	1 576	1 656	1 706	1 748	1 829	1 915	2 087
Foreign controlled undertakings	560	548	608	734	767	752	777	828
Foreign companies (branches)	78	73	72	93	107	108	123	136
All undertakings	1 698	1 649	1 729	1 799	1 855	1 937	2 038	3 051
Composite								
Domestic undertakings	7 101	7 278	7 573	7 699	7 571	7 600	7 673	7 791
Foreign controlled undertakings	1 778	1 830	1 978	2 106	2 006	2 073	2 139	2 153
Foreign companies (branches)	0	0	0	0	0	0	..	..
All undertakings	7 101	7 278	7 573	7 699	7 571	7 600	7 673	9 944
of which:								
Life	1 868	2 088	2 273	2 447	2 306	2 317	2 300	2 804
Domestic undertakings	1 868	2 088	2 273	2 447	2 306	2 317	2 300	2 253
Foreign controlled undertakings	413	450	510	542	504	550	608	550
Foreign companies (branches)	0	0	0	0	0	0	..	..
All undertakings	1 868	2 088	2 273	2 447	2 306	2 317	2 300	2 804
Non-life	5 232	5 190	5 300	5 251	5 265	5 283	5 372	7 141
Domestic undertakings	5 232	5 190	5 300	5 251	5 265	5 283	5 372	5 538
Foreign controlled undertakings	1 366	1 380	1 468	1 564	1 502	1 523	1 531	1 603
Foreign companies (branches)	0	0	0	0	0	0	..	..
All undertakings	5 232	5 190	5 300	5 251	5 265	5 283	5 372	7 141
Total								
Domestic undertakings	9 322	9 431	9 879	10 046	9 945	10 049	10 177	10 546
Foreign controlled undertakings	2 743	2 763	3 015	3 277	3 222	3 259	3 349	3 446
Foreign companies (branches)	78	73	72	93	107	108	123	136
All undertakings	9 399	9 504	9 952	10 139	10 052	10 157	10 300	14 129
1.4 Gross operating expenses								
Life								
Domestic undertakings	912	876	953	948	963	970	925	1 008
Foreign controlled undertakings	600	570	622	634	673	658	649	681
Foreign companies (branches)	0	0	0	0	0	0	..	..
All undertakings	912	876	953	948	963	970	925	1 689
Non-life								
Domestic undertakings	2 168	2 154	2 252	2 332	2 390	2 501	2 634	2 869
Foreign controlled undertakings	750	794	818	968	1 012	992	1 022	1 106
Foreign companies (branches)	115	112	110	144	176	174	183	197
All undertakings	2 283	2 266	2 362	2 476	2 565	2 676	2 817	4 172
Composite								
Domestic undertakings	9 321	9 490	9 686	9 829	9 860	9 929	10 069	10 269
Foreign controlled undertakings	2 304	2 294	2 443	2 632	2 566	2 658	2 742	2 707
Foreign companies (branches)	0	0	0	0	0	0	..	..
All undertakings	9 321	9 490	9 686	9 829	9 860	9 929	10 069	12 976
of which:								
Life	2 788	2 970	3 109	3 292	3 196	3 223	3 244	3 991
Domestic undertakings	2 788	2 970	3 109	3 292	3 196	3 223	3 244	3 213
Foreign controlled undertakings	635	628	696	743	708	773	833	778
Foreign companies (branches)	0	0	0	0	0	0	..	..
All undertakings	2 788	2 970	3 109	3 292	3 196	3 223	3 244	3 991
Non-life	6 532	6 520	6 577	6 537	6 664	6 706	6 825	8 985
Domestic undertakings	6 532	6 520	6 577	6 537	6 664	6 706	6 825	7 056
Foreign controlled undertakings	1 669	1 667	1 747	1 889	1 858	1 885	1 909	1 929
Foreign companies (branches)	0	0	0	0	0	0	..	..
All undertakings	6 532	6 520	6 577	6 537	6 664	6 706	6 825	8 985
Total								
Domestic undertakings	12 401	12 520	12 891	13 109	13 213	13 400	13 629	14 146
Foreign controlled undertakings	3 653	3 658	3 883	4 234	4 251	4 307	4 413	4 494
Foreign companies (branches)	115	112	110	144	176	174	183	197
All undertakings	12 516	12 633	13 001	13 253	13 388	13 574	13 812	18 837

ITALY

Table 1. Selected aggregates *(cont.)*

Million EUR

	2012	2013	2014	2015	2016	2017	2018	2019
1.5 Insurance business written abroad by branches, gross premiums								
Life								
Branches and agencies	0	0	1	1	3	1	2	0
Subsidaries	2 813	3 333	3 469	4 224	1 339	1 712	1 403	1 529
Total	2 813	3 333	3 469	4 226	1 342	1 713	1 404	1 529
Non-life								
Branches and agencies	9	12	12	9	10	13	7	15
Subsidaries	0	0	0	0	0	0	..	..
Total	9	12	12	9	10	13	7	15
Composite								
Branches and agencies	762	823	892	868	1 376	1 114	1 138	2 791
Subsidaries	57 155	56 340	54 902	58 541	57 863	60 367	56 485	56 132
Total	57 917	57 163	55 795	59 409	59 239	61 482	57 623	58 923
of which:								
Life	39 265	39 445	39 878	42 059	41 554	43 469	40 058	40 286
Branches and agencies	127	154	175	235	477	215	208	1 366
Subsidaries	39 138	39 291	39 703	41 824	41 077	43 254	39 850	38 920
Total	39 265	39 445	39 878	42 059	41 554	43 469	40 058	40 286
Non-life	18 652	17 718	15 917	17 350	17 685	18 012	17 565	18 637
Branches and agencies	634	668	718	633	899	899	930	1 425
Subsidaries	18 018	17 049	15 199	16 717	16 785	17 113	16 635	17 212
Total	18 652	17 718	15 917	17 350	17 685	18 012	17 565	18 637
Total								
Branches and agencies	771	835	905	878	1 390	1 128	1 147	2 806
Subsidaries	59 968	59 673	58 371	62 765	59 202	62 079	57 887	57 661
Total	60 739	60 508	59 276	63 643	60 592	63 207	59 034	60 467

.. Not available

Note: Detailed metadata at: *http://metalinks.oecd.org/ins/20210324/ab0f.*

Source: *OECD Insurance Statistics (database)*

ITALY

Table 2. Number of companies and employees

	2012	2013	2014	2015	2016	2017	2018	2019
2.1 Number of companies								
Life								
Domestic undertakings	41	41	38	35	32	30	26	26
Foreign controlled undertakings	23	23	20	19	17	13	11	11
Foreign companies (branches)	20	17	19	20	22	19	20	20
All undertakings	61	58	57	55	54	49	46	46
Non-life								
Domestic undertakings	69	67	63	58	54	50	51	52
Foreign controlled undertakings	21	20	18	19	18	16	16	17
Foreign companies (branches)	61	65	60	65	65	73	81	77
All undertakings	130	132	123	123	119	123	132	129
Composite								
Domestic undertakings	25	23	21	21	21	20	20	20
Foreign controlled undertakings	9	8	8	9	10	9	9	9
Foreign companies (branches)	12	13	14	14	13	14	13	13
All undertakings	37	36	35	35	34	34	33	33
Reinsurance								
Domestic undertakings	0	0	0	0	0	0	..	..
Foreign controlled undertakings	0	0	0	0	0	0	..	..
Foreign companies (branches)	7	7	7	7	7	7	7	6
All undertakings	7	7	7	7	7	7	7	6
Total								
Domestic undertakings	135	131	122	114	107	100	97	98
Foreign controlled undertakings	53	51	46	47	45	38	36	37
Foreign companies (branches)	100	102	100	106	107	113	121	116
All undertakings	235	233	222	220	214	213	218	214
2.2 Number of employees								
Insurance undertakings	40 798	39 887	40 259	40 588	40 872	40 386	40 028	39 733
Intermediaries	220 130	227 444	220 288	220 850	212 596	..	..	..
Total	260 928	267 331	260 547	261 438	253 468	..	..	..

.. Not available

Note: Detailed metadata at: *http://metalinks.oecd.org/ins/20210324/ab0f.*

Source: *OECD Insurance Statistics (database)*

JAPAN

Table 1. Selected aggregates

Million JPY

	2012	2013	2014	2015	2016	2017	2018	2019
1.1 Insurance business written in the reporting country								
1.1.1 Insurance business, by ownership								
Gross premiums								
Domestic undertakings	44 184 695	42 971 395	46 031 579	46 908 456	42 615 488	41 452 663	44 740 881	42 580 813
Foreign controlled undertakings	6 746 278	6 184 716	6 724 592	7 046 820	6 617 836	6 432 494	8 315 056	7 768 028
Foreign companies (branches)	2 028 538	1 699 621	1 548 143	1 537 624	1 703 444	1 739 958	348 167	314 078
All undertakings	37 140 563	34 738 150	37 222 352	37 748 110	44 318 932	43 192 621	45 089 048	42 894 891
Premiums ceded								
Domestic undertakings	3 820 152	3 823 919	4 207 229	4 127 260	4 449 638	4 176 204	4 817 685	6 191 736
Foreign controlled undertakings	2 083 368	1 802 239	2 084 233	1 890 218	2 143 727	1 733 566	2 285 450	2 793 927
Foreign companies (branches)	20 507	38 391	47 768	75 917	214 477	239 041	223 967	206 605
All undertakings	2 188 965	1 780 848	2 129 106	2 022 086	4 664 115	4 415 245	5 041 652	6 398 341
Net written premiums								
Domestic undertakings	40 364 544	39 147 476	41 824 350	42 781 196	38 165 836	37 276 448	39 923 181	36 388 692
Foreign controlled undertakings	4 662 910	4 382 477	4 640 359	5 156 602	4 474 105	4 698 925	6 029 602	4 974 097
Foreign companies (branches)	2 008 031	1 661 230	1 500 375	1 461 707	1 488 976	1 499 865	124 190	107 464
All undertakings	34 951 598	32 957 302	35 093 246	35 726 024	39 654 812	38 776 313	40 047 371	36 496 156
1.1.2 Insurance business on foreign risks, gross premiums								
Life	..	..	..	..	..	..	..	..
Non-life	..	..	..	..	..	..	..	..
Composite total	..	..	..	..	..	..	..	..
Total	..	..	..	..	..	..	..	..
1.1.3 Life insurance payments, by class, gross premiums								
Annuities	4 374 166	4 312 468	5 154 122	4 729 892	4 340 846	3 607 407	3 875 104	3 300 278
Unit linked	..	..	..	..	..	..	..	..
Other life insurance	29 076 673	27 864 772	30 015 418	31 464 495	27 968 949	27 990 703	29 370 822	27 589 307
Total life insurance	33 450 839	32 177 240	35 169 540	36 194 387	32 309 795	31 598 110	33 245 926	30 889 585
***of which:** Pension contracts*	3 683 892	3 851 878	4 175 622	4 562 867	3 057 696	2 953 431	2 861 906	2 833 705
1.1.4 Non-life insurance payments, by class, gross premiums								
Motor vehicle insurance	5 268 338	5 632 807	5 786 949	5 916 489	6 026 253	5 814 388	5 905 312	5 988 484
Marine, aviation and other transport insurance	149 531	170 502	170 115	186 542	159 142	152 632	150 286	177 296
Freight insurance	217 090	242 939	248 817	242 488	230 397	239 546	253 139	250 516
Fire and other property damage insurance	1 787 943	1 983 049	2 104 111	2 228 178	..	..	..	..
Pecuniary loss insurance	216 797	266 835	299 082	342 570	..	..	..	..
General liability insurance	519 985	584 318	598 945	615 167	633 290	657 637	692 945	713 193
Accident and health	780 078	897 507	979 477	982 614	..	..	..	..
***of which:** Health*	-216	76	214	-152	..	..	..	..
Other non-life insurance	132 908	154 909	169 874	183 922	..	..	..	..
Treaty reinsurance	..	..	..	..	..	..	..	..
Total non-life insurance	9 072 670	9 932 866	10 357 370	10 697 970	10 859 799	10 750 127	11 173 102	11 483 495
1.2 Gross claims payments								
Life								
Domestic undertakings	31 012 138	33 069 327	34 214 304	31 685 988	28 227 418	28 115 903	28 748 864	29 502 430
Foreign controlled undertakings	5 218 820	6 584 738	6 428 288	5 559 928	5 107 453	5 198 975	5 980 013	6 200 318
Foreign companies (branches)	673 623	709 471	738 243	768 206	786 644	827 193	37 839	45 369
All undertakings	31 685 761	33 778 798	34 952 547	32 454 194	29 014 062	28 943 096	28 786 703	29 547 799
Non-life								
Domestic undertakings	6 215 207	5 904 278	5 953 809	5 917 050	6 694 135	5 856 017	7 585 094	7 135 164
Foreign controlled undertakings	251 245	341 353	373 601	366 795	383 518	237 359	480 088	411 562
Foreign companies (branches)	..	..	..	..	104 648	98 935	222 146	200 874
All undertakings	..	..	..	..	6 798 783	5 954 952	7 807 240	7 336 038
Composite, all undertakings	..	..	..	..	..	..	..	..
Total								
Domestic undertakings	37 227 345	38 973 605	40 168 113	37 603 038	34 921 553	33 971 920	36 333 958	36 637 594
Foreign controlled undertakings	5 470 065	6 926 091	6 801 889	5 926 723	5 490 971	5 436 334	6 460 101	6 611 880
Foreign companies (branches)	673 623	709 471	738 243	768 206	891 292	926 128	259 985	246 243
All undertakings	31 685 761	33 778 798	34 952 547	32 454 194	35 812 845	34 898 048	36 593 943	36 883 837
1.3 Commissions								
Life								
Domestic undertakings	..	..	..	..	..	..	..	..
Foreign controlled undertakings	..	..	..	..	..	..	..	..
Foreign companies (branches)	..	..	..	..	..	..	..	..
All undertakings	..	..	..	..	..	..	..	..
Non-life								
Domestic undertakings	1 141 653	1 149 357	1 229 205	1 273 631	1 240 454	1 221 324	1 241 826	1 296 198
Foreign controlled undertakings	48 003	25 883	33 975	37 223	20 067	-15 311	-19 855	-27 941
Foreign companies (branches)	..	..	..	..	-19 897	-29 330	-33 799	-1 094
All undertakings	..	..	..	..	1 220 557	1 191 994	1 208 027	1 295 104
Composite, all undertakings	..	..	..	..	..	..	..	..
Total								
Domestic undertakings	1 141 653	1 149 357	1 229 205	1 273 631	1 240 454	1 221 324	1 241 826	1 296 198
Foreign controlled undertakings	48 003	25 883	33 975	37 223	20 067	-15 311	-19 855	-27 941
Foreign companies (branches)	..	..	..	..	-19 897	-29 330	-33 799	-1 094
All undertakings	..	..	..	..	1 220 557	1 191 994	1 208 027	1 295 104

JAPAN

Table 1. Selected aggregates *(cont.)*

Million JPY

	2012	2013	2014	2015	2016	2017	2018	2019
1.4 Gross operating expenses								
Life								
Domestic undertakings	4 030 195	4 068 896	4 178 568	4 356 425	4 369 595	4 385 030	4 856 591	4 691 017
Foreign controlled undertakings	838 416	862 622	893 811	945 921	948 132	965 055	1 353 249	1 282 164
Foreign companies (branches)	319 261	320 576	320 518	349 858	357 069	366 406	22 814	23 341
All undertakings	4 349 456	4 389 472	4 499 086	4 706 283	4 726 664	4 751 436	4 879 405	4 714 358
Non-life								
Domestic undertakings	1 229 758	3 034 716	3 189 416	3 275 358	3 247 478	3 206 606	3 318 518	3 389 286
Foreign controlled undertakings	69 136	176 725	238 092	249 835	207 689	125 459	185 822	158 127
Foreign companies (branches)	..	..	..	..	34 405	37 023	34 772	61 577
All undertakings	..	..	..	..	3 281 883	3 243 629	3 353 290	3 450 863
Composite, all undertakings	..	..	..	..	..	..	..	..
Total								
Domestic undertakings	5 259 953	7 103 612	7 367 984	7 631 783	7 617 073	7 591 636	8 175 109	8 080 303
Foreign controlled undertakings	907 552	1 039 347	1 131 903	1 195 756	1 155 821	1 090 514	1 539 071	1 440 291
Foreign companies (branches)	319 261	320 576	320 518	349 858	391 474	403 429	57 586	84 918
All undertakings	4 349 456	4 389 472	4 499 086	4 706 283	8 008 547	7 995 065	8 232 695	8 165 221
1.5 Insurance business written abroad by branches, gross premiums								
Life								
Branches and agencies	..	..	..	..	..	..	..	..
Subsidaries	..	..	..	..	..	..	..	..
Total	..	..	..	..	..	..	..	..
Non-life								
Branches and agencies	..	..	..	..	..	..	..	..
Subsidaries	..	..	..	..	..	..	..	..
Total	..	..	..	..	..	..	..	..
Composite total	..	..	..	..	..	..	..	..
Total								
Branches and agencies	..	..	..	..	..	..	..	..
Subsidaries	..	..	..	..	..	..	..	..
Total	..	..	..	..	..	..	..	..

.. Not available

Note: Detailed metadata at: *http://metalinks.oecd.org/ins/20210324/019e.*

Source: *OECD Insurance Statistics (database)*

JAPAN

Table 2. Number of companies and employees

	2012	2013	2014	2015	2016	2017	2018	2019
2.1 Number of companies								
Life								
Domestic undertakings	40	40	39	38	38	38	40	41
Foreign controlled undertakings	15	15	13	13	13	13	14	14
Foreign companies (branches)	3	3	3	3	3	3	1	1
All undertakings	43	43	42	41	41	41	41	42
Non-life								
Domestic undertakings	30	30	30	30	30	29	30	32
Foreign controlled undertakings	5	6	7	7	7	6	7	7
Foreign companies (branches)	23	22	22	22	21	23	21	21
All undertakings	53	52	52	52	51	52	51	53
Composite, all undertakings	**0**	**0**	**0**	**0**	**0**	..	..	..
Reinsurance								
Domestic undertakings	..	..	..	..	..	..	..	..
Foreign controlled undertakings	..	..	..	..	..	..	..	..
Foreign companies (branches)	..	..	..	..	..	..	..	..
All undertakings	..	..	..	..	..	..	..	..
Total								
Domestic undertakings	..	..	..	68	68	67	70	..
Foreign controlled undertakings	..	..	..	20	20	19	21	..
Foreign companies (branches)	..	..	..	25	24	26	22	..
All undertakings	..	..	..	93	92	93	92	..
2.2 Number of employees								
Insurance undertakings	447 435	221 675	226 043	120 353	..	..	..	..
Intermediaries	..	2 283 335	2 293 863	2 059 743	..	..	..	..
Total	..	2 505 010	2 519 906	2 080 096	..	345 582	..	..

.. Not available

Note: Detailed metadata at: *http://metalinks.oecd.org/ins/20210324/019e.*

Source: *OECD Insurance Statistics (database)*

KOREA

Table 1. Selected aggregates

Million KRW

	2012	2013	2014	2015	2016	2017	2018	2019
1.1 Insurance business written in the reporting country								
1.1.1 Insurance business, by ownership								
Gross premiums								
Domestic undertakings	179 792 881	180 479 019	192 380 611	205 460 047	210 800 275	209 464 937	206 866 894	..
Foreign controlled undertakings	16 543 211	15 928 630	13 324 532	15 765 302	16 670 208	17 513 911	14 930 441	..
Foreign companies (branches)	3 894 692	4 755 050	4 594 745	2 267 929	4 629 847	4 849 409	5 320 101	..
All undertakings	183 687 573	185 234 069	196 975 356	207 727 976	215 430 122	214 314 346	212 186 995	..
Premiums ceded								
Domestic undertakings	8 770 133	9 411 425	9 694 294	10 255 858	10 505 959	11 215 981	11 733 647	..
Foreign controlled undertakings	581 696	538 227	478 174	638 961	599 183	611 390	584 975	..
Foreign companies (branches)	448 135	456 049	651 726	732 347	817 712	990 510	1 035 820	..
All undertakings	9 218 268	9 867 474	10 346 020	10 988 205	11 323 671	12 206 491	12 769 467	..
Net written premiums								
Domestic undertakings	171 022 748	171 067 594	182 686 317	195 204 189	200 294 316	198 248 956	195 133 247	..
Foreign controlled undertakings	15 961 515	15 390 403	12 846 358	15 126 341	16 071 025	16 902 521	14 345 466	..
Foreign companies (branches)	3 446 557	4 299 001	3 943 019	1 535 582	3 812 135	3 858 899	4 284 281	..
All undertakings	174 469 305	175 366 595	186 629 336	196 739 771	204 106 451	202 107 855	199 417 528	..
1.1.2 Insurance business on foreign risks, gross premiums								
Life	..	..	..	..	..	..	..	..
Non-life	..	..	..	..	..	..	..	..
Composite total	..	..	..	..	..	..	..	..
Total	..	..	..	..	..	..	..	..
1.1.3 Life insurance payments, by class, gross premiums								
Annuities	29 118 668	25 867 249	23 905 884	24 586 649	21 347 503	19 558 128	17 605 227	..
Unit linked	21 003 522	21 073 957	20 670 949	20 643 073	19 406 180	19 623 687	18 834 528	..
Other life insurance	57 004 710	61 618 265	65 998 453	71 983 930	79 057 566	74 791 666	74 403 374	..
Total life insurance	107 126 900	108 559 471	110 575 286	117 213 652	119 811 249	113 973 481	110 843 129	..
***of which:** Pension contracts*	6 187 541	8 103 216	11 817 288	13 694 337	16 718 996	14 905 838	16 869 826	..
1.1.4 Non-life insurance payments, by class, gross premiums								
Motor vehicle insurance	13 667 642	13 692 186	14 188 378	15 635 198	16 975 333	17 426 917	17 276 192	..
Marine, aviation and other transport insurance	1 249 845	1 062 919	1 006 367	971 854	854 536	917 229	832 470	..
Freight insurance	..	0	0	..	..	..	..	..
Fire and other property damage insurance	509 590	515 217	484 799	472 624	471 017	428 560	373 175	..
Pecuniary loss insurance	1 697 064	1 637 782	1 601 517	1 672 799	1 693 861	1 858 689	2 133 544	..
General liability insurance	870 395	947 583	910 341	967 362	1 100 438	1 182 101	1 233 606	..
Accident and health	18 558 162	49 501 658	24 196 315	39 104 233	30 297 640	33 024 528	36 093 627	..
***of which:** Health*	7 171 480	83 983	10 090 810	11 740 294	13 406 917	14 799 985	16 444 106	..
Other non-life insurance	38 774 054	8 105 434	32 685 216	30 357 048	42 702 138	43 864 781	41 435 506	..
Treaty reinsurance	..	0	0	..	..	..	..	..
Total non-life insurance	75 326 752	75 462 779	85 163 744	89 181 118	94 094 963	98 702 805	99 378 120	..
1.2 Gross claims payments								
Life								
Domestic undertakings	50 571 293	51 098 146	61 070 702	65 751 692	77 155 805	78 055 802	77 155 805	..
Foreign controlled undertakings	7 981 965	8 103 569	69 035 817	6 945 034	9 505 582	10 803 105	9 505 582	..
Foreign companies (branches)	1 251 467	1 252 924	1 292 842	1 333 124	1 410 493	1 457 100	1 410 493	..
All undertakings	51 822 760	52 351 070	62 363 544	67 084 816	78 566 298	79 512 902	78 566 298	..
Non-life								
Domestic undertakings	26 319 367	22 119 519	30 233 735	30 895 053	32 747 964	35 060 020	40 091 995	..
Foreign controlled undertakings	833 963	516 770	844 722	843 763	802 729	767 651	824 571	..
Foreign companies (branches)	914 946	7 033 799	1 098 087	1 264 227	1 282 459	1 285 551	1 554 862	..
All undertakings	27 234 313	29 153 318	31 331 823	32 159 280	34 030 423	36 345 571	41 646 857	..
Composite, all undertakings	..	..	..	..	..	..	..	..
Total								
Domestic undertakings	76 890 660	73 217 665	91 304 438	96 646 745	109 903 769	113 115 822	117 247 800	..
Foreign controlled undertakings	8 815 928	8 620 339	69 880 539	7 788 797	10 308 311	11 570 756	10 330 153	..
Foreign companies (branches)	2 166 413	8 286 723	2 390 929	2 597 351	2 692 952	2 742 651	2 965 355	..
All undertakings	79 057 073	81 504 388	93 695 367	99 244 096	112 596 721	115 858 473	120 213 155	..
1.3 Commissions								
Life								
Domestic undertakings	..	..	..	..	..	..	..	..
Foreign controlled undertakings	..	..	..	..	..	..	..	..
Foreign companies (branches)	..	..	..	..	..	..	..	..
All undertakings	..	..	..	..	..	..	..	..
Non-life								
Domestic undertakings	..	..	..	..	..	..	..	..
Foreign controlled undertakings	..	..	..	..	..	..	..	..
Foreign companies (branches)	..	..	..	..	..	..	..	..
All undertakings	..	..	..	..	..	..	..	..
Composite, all undertakings	..	..	..	..	..	..	..	..
Total								
Domestic undertakings	..	..	..	..	..	..	..	..
Foreign controlled undertakings	..	..	..	..	..	..	..	..
Foreign companies (branches)	..	..	..	..	..	..	..	..
All undertakings	..	..	..	..	..	..	..	..

KOREA

Table 1. Selected aggregates (cont.)

Million KRW

	2012	2013	2014	2015	2016	2017	2018	2019
1.4 Gross operating expenses								
Life								
Domestic undertakings	23 307 641	25 608 456	27 511 983	28 987 407	28 236 989	28 574 504	36 539 562	..
Foreign controlled undertakings	5 189 114	5 278 175	806 034	756 903	5 074 779	5 675 330	5 878 573	..
Foreign companies (branches)	734 416	770 753	4 595 483	5 009 714	760 976	619 584	790 806	..
All undertakings	24 042 057	26 379 209	32 107 466	33 997 121	28 997 965	29 194 088	37 330 368	..
Non-life								
Domestic undertakings	11 569 785	11 294 192	16 760 436	13 511 865	14 238 364	15 685 551	16 637 805	..
Foreign controlled undertakings	320 770	129 781	245 017	182 669	163 724	225 860	254 141	..
Foreign companies (branches)	331 833	1 592 503	1 116 586	405 386	411 714	434 676	510 688	..
All undertakings	11 901 618	12 886 695	17 877 022	13 917 251	14 650 078	16 120 227	17 148 493	..
Composite, all undertakings	..	..	..	..	..	..	..	..
Total								
Domestic undertakings	34 877 426	36 902 648	44 272 419	42 499 272	42 475 353	44 260 055	53 177 367	..
Foreign controlled undertakings	5 509 884	5 407 956	1 051 051	939 572	5 238 503	5 901 190	6 132 714	..
Foreign companies (branches)	1 066 249	2 363 256	5 712 069	5 415 100	1 172 690	1 054 260	1 301 494	..
All undertakings	35 943 675	39 265 904	49 984 488	47 914 372	43 648 043	45 314 315	54 478 861	..
1.5 Insurance business written abroad by branches, gross premiums								
Life								
Branches and agencies	..	..	..	..	..	..	..	..
Subsidaries	..	..	..	..	..	..	..	..
Total	..	..	..	..	..	..	..	..
Non-life								
Branches and agencies	..	..	..	..	..	..	..	..
Subsidaries	..	..	..	..	..	..	..	..
Total	..	..	..	..	..	..	..	..
Composite total	..	..	..	..	..	..	..	..
Total								
Branches and agencies	..	..	..	..	..	..	..	..
Subsidaries	..	..	..	..	..	..	..	..
Total	..	..	..	..	..	..	..	..

.. Not available

Note: Detailed metadata at: *http://metalinks.oecd.org/ins/20210324/431e.*

Source: *OECD Insurance Statistics (database)*

KOREA

Table 2. Number of companies and employees

	2012	2013	2014	2015	2016	2017	2018	2019
2.1 Number of companies								
Life								
Domestic undertakings	23	24	24	24	24	24	24	..
Foreign controlled undertakings	8	8	7	7	8	8	8	..
Foreign companies (branches)	1	1	1	1	1	1	1	..
All undertakings	24	25	25	25	25	25	25	..
Non-life								
Domestic undertakings	16	16	17	17	17	18	17	..
Foreign controlled undertakings	6	3	4	4	4	5	4	..
Foreign companies (branches)	8	8	5	5	5	6	5	..
All undertakings	24	24	22	22	22	24	22	..
Composite, all undertakings	**0**	**0**	**0**	**0**	**0**	..	..	..
Reinsurance								
Domestic undertakings	1	1	1	1	1	1	1	..
Foreign controlled undertakings	..	..	0	0	0	0	0	..
Foreign companies (branches)	6	6	8	8	9	9	9	..
All undertakings	7	7	9	9	10	10	10	..
Total								
Domestic undertakings	40	41	42	42	42	43	42	..
Foreign controlled undertakings	14	11	11	11	12	13	12	..
Foreign companies (branches)	15	15	14	14	15	16	15	..
All undertakings	55	56	56	56	57	59	57	..
2.2 Number of employees								
Insurance undertakings	62 155	63 859	61 158	59 685	58 833	57 854	58 833	..
Intermediaries	288 362	280 087	245 127	235 319	229 292	222 411	229 292	..
Total	350 517	343 946	306 285	295 004	288 125	280 265	288 125	..

.. Not available

Note: Detailed metadata at: *http://metalinks.oecd.org/ins/20210324/431e.*

Source: *OECD Insurance Statistics (database)*

LATVIA

Table 1. Selected aggregates

Million EUR

	2012	2013	2014	2015	2016	2017	2018	2019
1.1 Insurance business written in the reporting country								
1.1.1 Insurance business, by ownership								
Gross premiums								
Domestic undertakings	354	350	371	379	364	419	489	569
Foreign controlled undertakings	155	150	151	188	267	293	352	446
Foreign companies (branches)	93	121	146	152	168	227	267	289
All undertakings	447	471	517	531	532	646	756	857
Premiums ceded								
Domestic undertakings	26	17	19	22	25	44	77	83
Foreign controlled undertakings	5	4	4	7	18	27	54	58
Foreign companies (branches)	..	..	..	..	..	..	..	..
All undertakings	26	17	19	22	25	44	77	83
Net written premiums								
Domestic undertakings	328	333	352	357	339	375	412	486
Foreign controlled undertakings	150	146	147	182	249	266	298	388
Foreign companies (branches)	93	121	146	152	168	227	267	289
All undertakings	421	454	498	509	507	602	679	774
1.1.2 Insurance business on foreign risks, gross premiums								
Life	..	..	..	..	0	0	..	..
Non-life	..	..	..	..	160	204	234	226
Composite	..	..	..	..	0	0	0	69
of which:								
Life	..	..	..	..	0	0	0	69
Non-life	..	..	..	..	..	0	..	..
Total	..	..	..	..	160	204	234	296
1.1.3 Life insurance payments, by class, gross premiums								
Annuities	0	0	0	0	11	18	25	41
Unit linked	21	23	34	43	45	57	55	102
Other life insurance	57	66	73	72	68	70	65	85
Total life insurance	79	89	107	115	124	145	145	228
***of which:** Pension contracts*	0	0	0	0	..	..	..	..
1.1.4 Non-life insurance payments, by class, gross premiums								
Motor vehicle insurance	204	221	222	221	229	301	381	370
Marine, aviation and other transport insurance	3	2	2	2	2	5	4	4
Freight insurance	6	5	3	3	3	1	3	3
Fire and other property damage insurance	63	67	86	84	76	84	90	104
Pecuniary loss insurance	12	11	13	14	12	11	16	20
General liability insurance	21	17	21	21	19	19	21	23
Accident and health	50	46	52	58	55	63	78	85
***of which:** Health*	42	38	42	48	45	54	64	71
Other non-life insurance	10	12	12	13	13	16	18	20
Treaty reinsurance	0	0	0	0	0	0	0	0
Total non-life insurance	368	382	411	416	409	501	611	629
1.2 Gross claims payments								
Life								
Domestic undertakings	19	31	26	29	0	0	..	..
Foreign controlled undertakings	18	26	24	27	0	0	0	..
Foreign companies (branches)	27	31	31	34	0	0	..	..
All undertakings	46	62	57	63	0	0	..	..
Non-life								
Domestic undertakings	169	165	184	198	180	193	229	303
Foreign controlled undertakings	75	68	77	92	139	126	170	231
Foreign companies (branches)	25	38	43	50	60	78	86	101
All undertakings	194	204	226	248	240	271	315	404
Composite								
Domestic undertakings	..	..	..	..	33	43	43	86
Foreign controlled undertakings	..	..	..	..	27	31	34	77
Foreign companies (branches)	..	..	..	..	40	47	48	59
All undertakings	..	..	..	..	72	90	91	145
of which:								
Life	..	..	..	..	72	90	91	145
Domestic undertakings	..	..	..	..	33	43	43	86
Foreign controlled undertakings	..	..	..	..	27	31	34	77
Foreign companies (branches)	..	..	..	..	40	47	48	59
All undertakings	..	..	..	..	72	90	91	145
Non-life	..	..	..	..	..	0	..	..
Domestic undertakings	..	..	..	..	..	0	..	..
Foreign controlled undertakings	..	..	..	..	..	0	..	..
Foreign companies (branches)	..	..	..	..	..	0	..	..
All undertakings	..	..	..	..	..	0	..	..
Total								
Domestic undertakings	188	196	209	227	213	236	272	388
Foreign controlled undertakings	93	94	102	119	166	158	203	308
Foreign companies (branches)	52	69	73	83	99	125	134	161
All undertakings	240	265	283	311	312	361	406	549

LATVIA

Table 1. Selected aggregates *(cont.)*

Million EUR

	2012	2013	2014	2015	2016	2017	2018	2019
1.3 Commissions								
Life								
Domestic undertakings	1	1	1	0	0	0	0	..
Foreign controlled undertakings	1	1	1	1	0	0	0	..
Foreign companies (branches)	4	5	5	6	..	..	..	..
All undertakings	5	5	6	6	0	0	0	..
Non-life								
Domestic undertakings	38	32	45	34	32	40	65	60
Foreign controlled undertakings	5	..	7	11	16	13	37	38
Foreign companies (branches)	4	10	12	13	..	..	..	..
All undertakings	41	42	58	47	32	40	65	60
Composite								
Domestic undertakings	..	..	..	..	0	1	1	6
Foreign controlled undertakings	..	..	..	..	0	0	1	6
Foreign companies (branches)	..	..	..	..	..	..	..	..
All undertakings	..	..	..	..	0	1	1	6
of which:								
Life	..	..	..	..	0	1	1	6
Domestic undertakings	..	..	..	..	0	1	1	6
Foreign controlled undertakings	..	..	..	..	0	0	1	6
Foreign companies (branches)	..	..	..	..	..	..	..	..
All undertakings	..	..	..	..	0	1	1	6
Non-life	..	..	..	..	..	0	..	..
Domestic undertakings	..	..	..	..	..	0	..	..
Foreign controlled undertakings	..	..	..	..	..	0	..	..
Foreign companies (branches)	..	..	..	..	..	..	..	..
All undertakings	..	..	..	..	..	0	..	..
Total								
Domestic undertakings	38	33	46	34	33	41	65	66
Foreign controlled undertakings	6	1	8	11	16	14	37	44
Foreign companies (branches)	8	15	17	19	..	..	..	..
All undertakings	46	48	64	53	33	41	65	66
1.4 Gross operating expenses								
Life								
Domestic undertakings	4	4	4	4	0	0	0	..
Foreign controlled undertakings	4	4	4	4	0	0	0	..
Foreign companies (branches)	..	..	..	..	..	..	..	..
All undertakings	4	4	4	4	0	0	0	..
Non-life								
Domestic undertakings	110	102	108	109	56	87	119	118
Foreign controlled undertakings	45	40	40	51	30	51	81	87
Foreign companies (branches)	..	..	..	..	..	..	..	..
All undertakings	110	102	108	109	56	87	119	118
Composite								
Domestic undertakings	..	..	..	..	4	5	5	17
Foreign controlled undertakings	..	..	..	..	4	4	5	16
Foreign companies (branches)	..	..	..	..	..	..	..	..
All undertakings	..	..	..	..	4	5	5	17
of which:								
Life	..	..	..	..	4	5	5	17
Domestic undertakings	..	..	..	..	4	5	5	17
Foreign controlled undertakings	..	..	..	..	4	4	5	16
Foreign companies (branches)	..	..	..	..	..	..	..	..
All undertakings	..	..	..	..	4	5	5	17
Non-life	..	..	..	..	..	0	..	..
Domestic undertakings	..	..	..	..	..	0	..	..
Foreign controlled undertakings	..	..	..	..	..	0	..	..
Foreign companies (branches)	..	..	..	..	..	..	..	..
All undertakings	..	..	..	..	..	0	..	..
Total								
Domestic undertakings	115	106	112	113	60	92	124	135
Foreign controlled undertakings	49	44	44	55	34	55	86	104
Foreign companies (branches)	..	..	..	..	..	..	..	..
All undertakings	115	106	112	113	60	92	124	135

LATVIA

Table 1. Selected aggregates *(cont.)*

Million EUR

	2012	2013	2014	2015	2016	2017	2018	2019
1.5 Insurance business written abroad by branches, gross premiums								
Life								
Branches and agencies	0	0	0	0	0	0	..	..
Subsidaries	..	..	..	..	..	..	..	..
Total	0	0	0	0	0	0	..	..
Non-life								
Branches and agencies	143	158	168	157	158	203	233	226
Subsidaries	..	..	..	..	..	..	..	..
Total	143	158	168	157	158	203	233	226
Composite								
Branches and agencies	..	..	..	..	0	0	..	69
Subsidaries	..	..	..	..	..	..	..	..
Total	..	..	..	..	0	0	..	69
of which:								
Life	..	..	..	..	0	0	..	69
Branches and agencies	..	..	..	..	0	0	..	69
Subsidaries	..	..	..	..	..	..	..	..
Total	..	..	..	..	0	0	..	69
Non-life	..	..	..	..	..	0	..	..
Branches and agencies	..	..	..	..	..	0	..	..
Subsidaries	..	..	..	..	..	..	..	..
Total	..	..	..	..	..	0	..	..
Total								
Branches and agencies	143	158	168	157	158	203	233	296
Subsidaries	..	..	..	..	..	..	..	..
Total	143	158	168	157	158	203	233	296

.. Not available

Note: Detailed metadata at: *http://metalinks.oecd.org/ins/20210324/1567*.

Source: *OECD Insurance Statistics (database)*

LATVIA

Table 2. Number of companies and employees

	2012	2013	2014	2015	2016	2017	2018	2019
2.1 Number of companies								
Life								
Domestic undertakings	2	2	2	2	..	0	0	0
Foreign controlled undertakings	1	1	1	1	..	0	0	0
Foreign companies (branches)	5	5	5	4	..	0	0	0
All undertakings	7	7	7	6	..	0	0	..
Non-life								
Domestic undertakings	7	5	5	6	5	4	4	4
Foreign controlled undertakings	3	2	2	3	3	2	2	2
Foreign companies (branches)	8	7	9	10	8	7	7	8
All undertakings	15	12	14	16	13	11	11	12
Composite								
Domestic undertakings	0	0	0	0	2	2	2	2
Foreign controlled undertakings	0	0	0	0	1	1	1	1
Foreign companies (branches)	0	0	0	0	4	4	4	4
All undertakings	0	0	0	0	6	6	6	6
Reinsurance								
Domestic undertakings	0	0	0	0	..	0	..	..
Foreign controlled undertakings	0	0	0	0	..	0	..	..
Foreign companies (branches)	0	0	0	0	..	0	..	..
All undertakings	0	0	0	0	..	0	..	..
Total								
Domestic undertakings	9	7	7	8	7	6	6	6
Foreign controlled undertakings	4	3	3	4	4	3	3	3
Foreign companies (branches)	13	12	14	14	12	11	11	12
All undertakings	22	19	21	22	19	17	17	18
2.2 Number of employees								
Insurance undertakings	2 749	2 300	2 121	1 047	..	..	..	..
Intermediaries	1 168	846	773	905	..	..	..	..
Total	3 917	3 146	2 894	1 952	..	..	..	..

.. Not available

Note: Detailed metadata at: *http://metalinks.oecd.org/ins/20210324/1567*.

Source: *OECD Insurance Statistics (database)*

LITHUANIA

Table 1. Selected aggregates

Million EUR

	2012	2013	2014	2015	2016	2017	2018	2019
1.1 Insurance business written in the reporting country								
1.1.1 Insurance business, by ownership								
Gross premiums								
Domestic undertakings	309	288	303	326	393	425	447	430
Foreign controlled undertakings	299	278	294	316	383	416	437	419
Foreign companies (branches)	208	280	298	319	317	367	432	516
All undertakings	518	567	601	645	710	793	878	946
Premiums ceded								
Domestic undertakings	14	10	8	8	21	27	29	23
Foreign controlled undertakings	13	10	8	8	21	27	29	23
Foreign companies (branches)	..	..	21	24	15	40	55	63
All undertakings	..	..	29	32	36	68	84	86
Net written premiums								
Domestic undertakings	296	277	295	318	372	398	418	407
Foreign controlled undertakings	285	268	285	308	362	388	408	397
Foreign companies (branches)	..	..	277	295	302	327	376	453
All undertakings	..	..	572	613	674	725	794	860
1.1.2 Insurance business on foreign risks, gross premiums								
Life	..	..	..	..	..	..	..	..
Non-life	..	..	..	..	..	..	..	..
Composite	..	..	..	..	..	..	..	..
of which:								
Life	..	..	..	..	..	..	..	..
Non-life	..	..	..	..	..	..	..	..
Total	..	..	..	..	..	..	..	..
1.1.3 Life insurance payments, by class, gross premiums								
Annuities	3	3	4	5	6	7	7	6
Unit linked	115	126	152	170	157	137	151	170
Other life insurance	48	52	59	60	84	88	90	94
Total life insurance	166	181	215	236	247	231	248	270
***of which:** Pension contracts*	..	..	..	..	1	..	..	..
1.1.4 Non-life insurance payments, by class, gross premiums								
Motor vehicle insurance	209	228	227	236	273	353	403	420
Marine, aviation and other transport insurance	2	2	2	2	2	2	2	1
Freight insurance	2	2	2	2	2	3	3	3
Fire and other property damage insurance	68	74	79	89	98	103	109	120
Pecuniary loss insurance	20	20	18	17	17	20	23	25
General liability insurance	16	19	20	20	20	21	22	24
Accident and health	34	40	37	42	49	56	65	78
***of which:** Health*	21	25	21	24	30	35	42	51
Other non-life insurance	1	1	1	1	2	3	3	4
Treaty reinsurance	..	..	..	..	..	0	0	0
Total non-life insurance	352	386	386	409	463	561	630	675
1.2 Gross claims payments								
Life								
Domestic undertakings	10	15	13	15	26	29	32	34
Foreign controlled undertakings	10	15	13	15	23	26	29	30
Foreign companies (branches)	60	41	47	42	45	56	48	45
All undertakings	70	57	60	57	71	85	80	79
Non-life								
Domestic undertakings	126	105	105	116	134	169	153	168
Foreign controlled undertakings	106	85	92	102	134	169	153	168
Foreign companies (branches)	74	104	111	113	117	126	158	184
All undertakings	200	209	216	229	251	295	311	353
Composite								
Domestic undertakings	43	40	35	40	43	65	46	20
Foreign controlled undertakings	41	38	33	38	43	65	46	20
Foreign companies (branches)	3	4	4	6	8	11	15	47
All undertakings	46	44	40	46	51	75	62	67
of which:								
Life	41	39	35	40	43	66	49	51
Domestic undertakings	39	37	32	36	39	60	42	15
Foreign controlled undertakings	37	35	30	34	39	60	42	15
Foreign companies (branches)	2	2	2	3	4	6	7	36
All undertakings	41	39	35	40	43	66	49	51
Non-life	5	5	5	6	8	9	13	16
Domestic undertakings	4	3	3	4	4	4	4	5
Foreign controlled undertakings	4	3	3	4	4	4	4	5
Foreign companies (branches)	1	2	2	2	4	5	9	11
All undertakings	5	5	5	6	8	9	13	16
Total								
Domestic undertakings	179	161	154	171	203	263	231	222
Foreign controlled undertakings	157	138	138	155	200	260	228	219
Foreign companies (branches)	137	149	163	161	170	193	221	277
All undertakings	316	310	316	332	373	456	453	499

LITHUANIA

Table 1. Selected aggregates *(cont.)*

Million EUR

	2012	2013	2014	2015	2016	2017	2018	2019
1.3 Commissions								
Life								
Domestic undertakings	0	0	0	0	0	0	0	0
Foreign controlled undertakings	0	0	0	0	0	0	0	0
Foreign companies (branches)	..	..	0	0	0	0	0	0
All undertakings	..	..	0	0	0	0	0	0
Non-life								
Domestic undertakings	1	0	1	0	2	5	7	5
Foreign controlled undertakings	1	0	1	0	2	5	7	5
Foreign companies (branches)	..	..	3	3	2	7	12	11
All undertakings	..	..	3	3	4	12	19	16
Composite								
Domestic undertakings	2	3	1	1	0	0	0	0
Foreign controlled undertakings	2	3	1	1	0	0	0	0
Foreign companies (branches)	..	..	0	1	1	1	1	1
All undertakings	..	..	1	1	1	1	2	2
of which:								
Life	..	..	..	1	1	1	2	2
Domestic undertakings	1	1	..	1	0	0	0	0
Foreign controlled undertakings	1	1	..	1	0	0	0	0
Foreign companies (branches)	..	..	..	1	1	1	1	1
All undertakings	..	..	..	1	1	1	2	2
Non-life	..	..	..	0	0	0	0	0
Domestic undertakings	1	2	..	0	0	0	0	0
Foreign controlled undertakings	1	2	..	0	0	0	0	0
Foreign companies (branches)	..	..	..	0	0	0	0	0
All undertakings	..	..	..	0	0	0	0	0
Total								
Domestic undertakings	3	3	1	1	3	5	7	6
Foreign controlled undertakings	3	3	1	1	3	5	7	6
Foreign companies (branches)	..	..	3	4	3	8	13	12
All undertakings	..	..	4	5	6	13	21	18
1.4 Gross operating expenses								
Life								
Domestic undertakings	8	9	9	12	16	16	16	17
Foreign controlled undertakings	8	9	9	12	14	14	15	15
Foreign companies (branches)	..	..	8	6	7	6	6	7
All undertakings	..	..	17	18	22	21	22	24
Non-life								
Domestic undertakings	79	72	71	97	87	90	94	98
Foreign controlled undertakings	75	68	68	94	85	89	92	96
Foreign companies (branches)	..	..	63	95	63	65	76	81
All undertakings	..	..	134	192	150	155	170	179
Composite								
Domestic undertakings	20	22	17	28	9	14	14	7
Foreign controlled undertakings	18	21	16	25	9	14	14	7
Foreign companies (branches)	..	..	9	29	12	13	14	23
All undertakings	..	..	27	56	22	26	28	30
of which:								
Life	..	..	26	55	20	24	25	27
Domestic undertakings	17	19	17	27	8	13	13	6
Foreign controlled undertakings	15	17	15	24	8	13	13	6
Foreign companies (branches)	..	..	9	28	12	11	12	21
All undertakings	..	..	26	55	20	24	25	27
Non-life	..	..	1	2	2	2	3	3
Domestic undertakings	3	3	1	1	1	1	1	1
Foreign controlled undertakings	3	3	1	1	1	1	1	1
Foreign companies (branches)	..	..	0	1	1	1	2	2
All undertakings	..	..	1	2	2	2	3	3
Total								
Domestic undertakings	107	102	97	137	111	120	124	122
Foreign controlled undertakings	101	98	93	131	108	116	121	118
Foreign companies (branches)	..	..	81	130	82	83	96	111
All undertakings	..	..	178	267	194	203	220	234

LITHUANIA

Table 1. Selected aggregates *(cont.)*

Million EUR

	2012	2013	2014	2015	2016	2017	2018	2019
1.5 Insurance business written abroad by branches, gross premiums								
Life								
Branches and agencies	0	0	0	0	0	0	0	0
Subsidaries	..	..	..	..	..	..	..	..
Total	0	0	0	0	0	0	0	0
Non-life								
Branches and agencies	0	1	17	40	65	115	142	150
Subsidaries	..	..	..	..	..	..	..	..
Total	0	1	17	40	65	115	142	150
Composite								
Branches and agencies	22	26	31	37	40	46	46	46
Subsidaries	..	..	..	..	..	..	..	..
Total	22	26	31	37	40	46	46	46
of which:								
Life	10	11	14	18	19	22	22	21
Branches and agencies	10	11	14	18	19	22	22	21
Subsidaries	..	..	..	..	..	..	..	..
Total	10	11	14	18	19	22	22	21
Non-life	12	15	17	20	21	24	24	25
Branches and agencies	12	15	17	20	21	24	24	25
Subsidaries	..	..	..	..	..	..	..	..
Total	12	15	17	20	21	24	24	25
Total								
Branches and agencies	22	27	48	77	105	161	188	196
Subsidaries	..	..	..	..	..	..	..	..
Total	22	27	48	77	105	161	188	196

.. Not available

Note: Detailed metadata at: *http://metalinks.oecd.org/ins/20210324/5919*.

Source: *OECD Insurance Statistics (database)*

LITHUANIA

Table 2. Number of companies and employees

	2012	2013	2014	2015	2016	2017	2018	2019
2.1 Number of companies								
Life								
Domestic undertakings	1	1	1	1	3	3	3	3
Foreign controlled undertakings	1	1	1	1	2	2	2	2
Foreign companies (branches)	4	3	3	3	2	2	2	2
All undertakings	5	4	4	4	5	5	5	5
Non-life								
Domestic undertakings	6	5	5	5	4	4	4	4
Foreign controlled undertakings	3	2	2	3	3	3	3	3
Foreign companies (branches)	9	10	10	10	9	9	8	8
All undertakings	15	15	15	15	13	13	12	12
Composite								
Domestic undertakings	4	4	4	4	2	2	2	1
Foreign controlled undertakings	3	3	3	3	2	2	2	1
Foreign companies (branches)	1	1	1	1	1	1	1	2
All undertakings	5	5	5	5	3	3	3	3
Reinsurance								
Domestic undertakings	..	..	..	..	..	..	..	..
Foreign controlled undertakings	..	..	..	..	..	..	..	..
Foreign companies (branches)	..	..	..	..	..	..	..	..
All undertakings	..	..	..	..	..	..	..	..
Total								
Domestic undertakings	11	10	10	10	9	9	9	8
Foreign controlled undertakings	7	6	6	7	7	7	7	6
Foreign companies (branches)	14	14	14	14	12	12	11	12
All undertakings	25	24	24	24	21	21	20	20
2.2 Number of employees								
Insurance undertakings	4 390	4 519	4 414	4 482	4 562	4 599	4 569	4 409
Intermediaries	1 320	1 320	1 433	1 441	1 480	1 463	1 459	1 480
Total	5 710	5 839	5 847	5 923	6 042	6 062	6 028	5 889

.. Not available

Note: Detailed metadata at: *http://metalinks.oecd.org/ins/20210324/5919.*

Source: *OECD Insurance Statistics (database)*

LUXEMBOURG

Table 1. Selected aggregates

Million EUR

	2012	2013	2014	2015	2016	2017	2018	2019
1.1 Insurance business written in the reporting country								
1.1.1 Insurance business, by ownership								
Gross premiums								
Domestic undertakings	19 445	18 410	21 712	19 100	18 259	21 446	20 702	23 692
Foreign controlled undertakings	17 930	17 036	20 356	17 075	13 690	18 728	18 360	21 280
Foreign companies (branches)	144	191	76	78	70	77	77	1 435
All undertakings	19 589	18 601	21 788	19 178	18 329	21 523	20 779	25 128
Premiums ceded								
Domestic undertakings	6 109	4 624	6 122	3 030	3 235	3 026	4 794	6 325
Foreign controlled undertakings	5 892	4 246	5 863	2 770	2 943	2 657	4 452	6 126
Foreign companies (branches)	40	37	33	26	31	27	33	456
All undertakings	6 149	4 661	6 155	3 056	3 267	3 053	4 827	6 781
Net written premiums								
Domestic undertakings	13 336	13 787	15 590	16 070	15 024	18 421	15 908	17 367
Foreign controlled undertakings	12 037	12 790	14 493	14 305	10 747	16 070	13 907	15 155
Foreign companies (branches)	104	153	43	52	39	50	44	980
All undertakings	13 440	13 940	15 633	16 122	15 063	18 470	15 952	18 347
1.1.2 Insurance business on foreign risks, gross premiums								
Life	17 115	15 837	18 455	16 383	15 071	18 182	17 356	19 705
Non-life	476	572	438	587	621	784	658	1 014
Composite	..	0	0	0	0	0	0	1 344
of which:								
Life	..	0	0	0	0	0	0	1 133
Non-life	..	0	0	0	0	0	0	211
Total	17 591	16 408	18 893	16 969	15 692	18 967	18 014	22 063
1.1.3 Life insurance payments, by class, gross premiums								
Annuities	..	..	..	..	..	..	..	..
Unit linked	11 224	10 516	11 086	12 874	11 949	15 426	12 966	14 616
Other life insurance	6 826	6 413	9 103	4 685	4 767	4 283	6 064	6 994
Total life insurance	18 050	16 929	20 190	17 559	16 716	19 709	19 030	21 610
***of which:** Pension contracts*	..	..	..	..	..	..	..	..
1.1.4 Non-life insurance payments, by class, gross premiums								
Motor vehicle insurance	..	..	..	..	..	..	..	..
Marine, aviation and other transport insurance	..	..	..	..	..	..	..	..
Freight insurance	..	..	..	..	..	..	..	..
Fire and other property damage insurance	..	..	..	..	..	..	..	..
Pecuniary loss insurance	..	..	..	..	..	..	..	..
General liability insurance	..	..	..	..	..	..	..	..
Accident and health	..	..	..	..	..	..	..	..
***of which:** Health*	..	..	..	..	..	..	..	..
Other non-life insurance	..	..	..	..	..	..	..	..
Treaty reinsurance	..	..	..	..	..	..	..	..
Total non-life insurance	1 300	1 501	1 339	1 476	1 554	1 767	1 707	2 339
1.2 Gross claims payments								
Life								
Domestic undertakings	11 111	11 696	10 597	9 995	11 802	12 002	11 103	11 861
Foreign controlled undertakings	10 823	11 179	10 214	9 032	11 035	11 291	10 262	10 534
Foreign companies (branches)	10	25	25	27	28	27	26	60
All undertakings	11 122	11 721	10 622	10 023	11 829	12 029	11 129	11 921
Non-life								
Domestic undertakings	623	1 105	809	900	860	961	987	1 192
Foreign controlled undertakings	348	691	428	512	766	500	488	552
Foreign companies (branches)	27	39	36	18	31	37	26	34
All undertakings	650	1 143	845	918	891	999	1 014	1 225
Composite								
Domestic undertakings	..	0	0	0	0	0	0	0
Foreign controlled undertakings	..	0	0	0	0	0	0	0
Foreign companies (branches)	38	27	133	17	8	8	9	754
All undertakings	38	27	133	17	8	8	9	754
of which:								
Life	20	15	130	17	8	8	9	624
Domestic undertakings	..	0	0	0	0	0	0	0
Foreign controlled undertakings	..	0	0	0	0	0	0	0
Foreign companies (branches)	20	15	130	17	8	8	9	624
All undertakings	20	15	130	17	8	8	9	624
Non-life	18	12	3	0	0	0	0	130
Domestic undertakings	..	0	0	0	0	0	0	0
Foreign controlled undertakings	..	0	0	0	0	0	0	0
Foreign companies (branches)	18	12	3	0	0	0	0	130
All undertakings	18	12	3	0	0	0	0	130
Total								
Domestic undertakings	11 734	12 801	11 406	10 896	12 661	12 964	12 091	13 053
Foreign controlled undertakings	11 171	11 869	10 642	9 544	11 802	11 791	10 751	11 086
Foreign companies (branches)	76	90	195	62	66	72	61	848
All undertakings	11 810	12 891	11 600	10 958	12 728	13 036	12 152	13 900

LUXEMBOURG

Table 1. Selected aggregates *(cont.)*

Million EUR

	2012	2013	2014	2015	2016	2017	2018	2019
1.3 Commissions								
Life								
Domestic undertakings	328	327	317	326	291	320	312	319
Foreign controlled undertakings	328	309	297	289	186	283	276	273
Foreign companies (branches)	0	0	0	0	0	0	0	0
All undertakings	328	328	317	326	292	320	312	319
Non-life								
Domestic undertakings	205	217	211	237	251	284	283	344
Foreign controlled undertakings	205	119	109	122	143	151	140	194
Foreign companies (branches)	11	12	9	9	9	8	7	9
All undertakings	217	229	221	246	260	292	290	353
Composite								
Domestic undertakings	..	0	0	0	0	0	0	0
Foreign controlled undertakings	..	0	0	0	0	0	0	0
Foreign companies (branches)	12	12	3	4	4	3	0	0
All undertakings	12	12	3	4	4	3	0	0
of which:								
Life	5	5	3	4	4	3	0	0
Domestic undertakings	..	0	0	0	0	0	0	0
Foreign controlled undertakings	..	0	0	0	0	0	0	0
Foreign companies (branches)	5	5	3	4	4	3	0	0
All undertakings	5	5	3	4	4	3	0	0
Non-life	7	7	0	0	0	0	0	0
Domestic undertakings	..	0	0	0	0	0	0	0
Foreign controlled undertakings	..	0	0	0	0	0	0	0
Foreign companies (branches)	7	7	0	0	0	0	0	0
All undertakings	7	7	0	0	0	0	0	0
Total								
Domestic undertakings	533	544	528	563	542	604	595	662
Foreign controlled undertakings	533	428	406	411	329	435	416	467
Foreign companies (branches)	24	25	13	14	14	11	7	9
All undertakings	557	569	541	576	556	615	602	672
1.4 Gross operating expenses								
Life								
Domestic undertakings	656	362	376	406	417	433	450	470
Foreign controlled undertakings	622	347	358	374	352	392	411	422
Foreign companies (branches)	0	0	1	0	1	1	1	0
All undertakings	656	362	376	406	418	433	450	470
Non-life								
Domestic undertakings	270	66	72	82	81	96	59	125
Foreign controlled undertakings	270	34	41	46	78	58	17	82
Foreign companies (branches)	14	3	2	2	3	3	5	6
All undertakings	285	69	74	84	84	99	64	131
Composite								
Domestic undertakings	..	0	0	0	0	0	0	0
Foreign controlled undertakings	..	0	0	0	0	0	0	0
Foreign companies (branches)	18	7	1	1	1	1	1	17
All undertakings	18	7	1	1	1	1	1	17
of which:								
Life	7	3	1	1	1	1	1	16
Domestic undertakings	..	0	0	0	0	0	0	0
Foreign controlled undertakings	..	0	0	0	0	0	0	0
Foreign companies (branches)	7	3	1	1	1	1	1	16
All undertakings	7	3	1	1	1	1	1	16
Non-life	11	4	0	0	0	0	0	1
Domestic undertakings	..	0	0	0	0	0	0	0
Foreign controlled undertakings	..	0	0	0	0	0	0	0
Foreign companies (branches)	11	4	0	0	0	0	0	1
All undertakings	11	4	0	0	0	0	0	1
Total								
Domestic undertakings	926	429	448	488	498	529	509	595
Foreign controlled undertakings	892	381	399	421	430	450	428	504
Foreign companies (branches)	33	9	4	3	4	5	6	23
All undertakings	959	438	451	491	502	534	515	618

LUXEMBOURG

Table 1. Selected aggregates *(cont.)*

Million EUR

	2012	2013	2014	2015	2016	2017	2018	2019
1.5 Insurance business written abroad by branches, gross premiums								
Life								
Branches and agencies	2 619	2 648	3 250	3 552	4 622	3 492	4 746	3 999
Subsidaries	0	..	..	..	..	..	..	..
Total	2 619	2 648	3 250	3 552	4 622	3 492	4 746	3 999
Non-life								
Branches and agencies	1 417	1 546	1 831	1 965	2 022	1 957	2 847	10 306
Subsidaries	0	..	..	..	..	..	..	..
Total	1 417	1 546	1 831	1 965	2 022	1 957	2 847	10 306
Composite								
Branches and agencies	..	0	0	0	0	0	0	0
Subsidaries	..	..	..	..	..	..	..	..
Total	..	0	0	0	0	0	0	0
of which:								
Life	..	0	0	0	0	0	0	0
Branches and agencies	..	0	0	0	0	0	0	0
Subsidaries	..	..	..	..	..	..	..	..
Total	..	0	0	0	0	0	0	0
Non-life	..	0	0	0	0	0	0	0
Branches and agencies	..	0	0	0	0	0	0	0
Subsidaries	..	..	..	..	..	..	..	..
Total	..	0	0	0	0	0	0	0
Total								
Branches and agencies	4 036	4 194	5 082	5 516	6 644	5 449	7 593	14 305
Subsidaries	0	..	..	..	..	..	..	..
Total	4 036	4 194	5 082	5 516	6 644	5 449	7 593	14 305

.. Not available

Note: Detailed metadata at: *http://metalinks.oecd.org/ins/20210324/4d0b*.

Source: *OECD Insurance Statistics (database)*

LUXEMBOURG

Table 2. Number of companies and employees

	2012	2013	2014	2015	2016	2017	2018	2019
2.1 Number of companies								
Life								
Domestic undertakings	43	42	44	43	40	39	38	36
Foreign controlled undertakings	39	34	39	38	34	35	30	30
Foreign companies (branches)	1	2	2	2	3	3	3	2
All undertakings	44	44	46	45	43	42	41	38
Non-life								
Domestic undertakings	31	34	34	32	33	34	41	42
Foreign controlled undertakings	27	27	8	21	24	25	33	31
Foreign companies (branches)	11	10	10	10	10	9	8	9
All undertakings	42	44	44	42	43	43	49	51
Composite								
Domestic undertakings	0	0	0	0	0	0	0	0
Foreign controlled undertakings	0	0	0	0	0	0	0	0
Foreign companies (branches)	3	3	3	3	3	2	3	3
All undertakings	3	3	3	3	3	2	3	3
Reinsurance								
Domestic undertakings	238	226	224	217	208	204	198	196
Foreign controlled undertakings	219	207	205	204	191	187	181	179
Foreign companies (branches)	0	0	0	0	0	0	0	0
All undertakings	238	226	224	217	208	204	198	196
Total								
Domestic undertakings	312	302	302	292	281	277	277	274
Foreign controlled undertakings	285	268	252	263	249	247	244	240
Foreign companies (branches)	15	15	15	15	16	14	14	14
All undertakings	327	317	317	307	297	291	291	288
2.2 Number of employees								
Insurance undertakings	4 326	5 692	6 057	6 484	6 484	7 446	8 034	10 295
Intermediaries	9 659	10 030	550	561	522	586	637	578
Total	13 985	15 722	6 607	7 045	7 006	8 032	8 671	10 873

Note: Detailed metadata at: *http://metalinks.oecd.org/ins/20210324/4d0b*.
Source: *OECD Insurance Statistics (database)*

MEXICO

Table 1. Selected aggregates

Million MXN

	2012	2013	2014	2015	2016	2017	2018	2019
1.1 Insurance business written in the reporting country								
1.1.1 Insurance business, by ownership								
Gross premiums								
Domestic undertakings	310 747	347 196	363 530	395 083	450 740	502 856	543 652	603 832
Foreign controlled undertakings	189 698	207 890	220 225	242 872	265 159	290 985	312 037	350 508
Foreign companies (branches)	..	..	..	..	..	..	..	..
All undertakings	310 747	347 196	363 530	395 083	450 740	502 856	543 652	603 832
Premiums ceded								
Domestic undertakings	50 188	60 551	58 378	67 135	70 420	93 577	91 472	112 667
Foreign controlled undertakings	24 728	26 822	29 932	40 217	40 674	58 977	51 768	68 212
Foreign companies (branches)	..	..	..	..	..	..	..	..
All undertakings	50 188	60 551	58 378	67 135	70 420	93 577	91 472	112 667
Net written premiums								
Domestic undertakings	260 559	286 645	305 152	327 947	380 320	409 279	452 180	491 165
Foreign controlled undertakings	164 970	181 068	190 293	202 655	224 485	232 008	260 270	282 295
Foreign companies (branches)	..	..	..	..	..	..	..	..
All undertakings	260 559	286 645	305 152	327 947	380 320	409 279	452 180	491 165
1.1.2 Insurance business on foreign risks, gross premiums								
Life	..	..	..	..	..	..	..	..
Non-life	425	402	..	..	..	..	..	..
Composite	1 787	1 692	..	..	..	..	..	..
of which:								
Life	..	..	..	..	..	..	..	..
Non-life	..	..	..	..	..	..	..	..
Total	2 212	2 093	..	..	..	..	..	..
1.1.3 Life insurance payments, by class, gross premiums								
Annuities	17 633	20 099	20 521	19 719	19 286	21 310	24 176	27 278
Unit linked	..	..	..	..	..	..	0	0
Other life insurance	125 175	138 959	148 624	162 199	189 860	193 587	218 641	243 178
Total life insurance	142 808	159 058	169 145	181 918	209 146	214 897	242 817	270 456
of which: *Pension contracts*	..	..	..	..	..	..	..	..
1.1.4 Non-life insurance payments, by class, gross premiums								
Motor vehicle insurance	62 944	66 562	68 735	75 858	91 375	103 014	110 405	115 377
Marine, aviation and other transport insurance	7 691	7 851	9 356	11 007	11 312	16 558	12 811	18 850
Freight insurance	..	..	..	..	..	..	..	..
Fire and other property damage insurance	9 980	16 520	12 232	13 815	14 497	18 115	37 929	46 830
Pecuniary loss insurance	749	5 210	501	947	1 131	12 278	1 774	1 933
General liability insurance	6 920	7 341	7 201	9 099	9 668	12 005	11 757	13 878
Accident and health	45 526	51 189	56 686	59 550	66 512	76 720	85 417	92 322
of which: *Health*	1 918	2 682	2 719	2 622	3 218	3 518	4 279	4 910
Other non-life insurance	33 390	32 581	38 511	42 081	45 976	48 006	39 687	42 678
Treaty reinsurance	..	..	..	..	..	..	..	..
Total non-life insurance	167 200	187 253	193 221	212 357	240 470	286 696	299 780	331 868
1.2 Gross claims payments								
Life								
Domestic undertakings	10 279	11 800	12 325	13 760	14 829	16 234	18 272	20 554
Foreign controlled undertakings	..	..	5 875	6 443	6 971	7 390	8 005	8 593
Foreign companies (branches)	..	..	..	..	..	..	..	..
All undertakings	10 279	11 800	12 325	13 760	14 829	16 234	18 272	20 554
Non-life								
Domestic undertakings	14 874	21 716	17 912	19 552	23 827	32 868	32 866	32 639
Foreign controlled undertakings	..	..	4 093	4 923	5 515	7 449	5 433	5 012
Foreign companies (branches)	..	..	..	..	..	..	..	..
All undertakings	14 874	21 716	17 912	19 552	23 827	32 868	32 866	32 639
Composite								
Domestic undertakings	115 041	159 315	148 932	162 803	185 481	204 354	224 193	256 776
Foreign controlled undertakings	..	..	104 822	109 465	125 575	136 316	151 138	179 902
Foreign companies (branches)	..	..	..	..	..	..	..	..
All undertakings	115 041	159 315	148 932	162 803	185 481	204 354	224 193	256 776
of which:								
Life	55 436	76 467	81 643	88 136	101 700	115 199	124 902	152 184
Domestic undertakings	55 436	76 467	81 643	88 136	101 700	115 199	124 902	152 184
Foreign controlled undertakings	..	..	67 855	70 802	81 029	89 726	97 155	122 938
Foreign companies (branches)	..	..	..	..	..	..	..	..
All undertakings	55 436	76 467	81 643	88 136	101 700	115 199	124 902	152 184
Non-life	59 605	82 848	67 289	74 667	83 781	89 154	99 291	104 592
Domestic undertakings	59 605	82 848	67 289	74 667	83 781	89 154	99 291	104 592
Foreign controlled undertakings	..	..	36 968	38 662	44 546	46 591	53 983	56 964
Foreign companies (branches)	..	..	..	..	..	..	..	..
All undertakings	59 605	82 848	67 289	74 667	83 781	89 154	99 291	104 592
Total								
Domestic undertakings	140 195	192 832	179 169	196 115	224 138	253 455	275 331	309 969
Foreign controlled undertakings	..	..	114 791	120 830	138 061	151 155	164 576	193 507
Foreign companies (branches)	..	..	..	..	..	..	..	..
All undertakings	140 195	192 832	179 169	196 115	224 138	253 455	275 331	309 969

MEXICO

Table 1. Selected aggregates *(cont.)*

Million MXN

	2012	2013	2014	2015	2016	2017	2018	2019
1.3 Commissions								
Life								
Domestic undertakings	1 133	1 075	749	1 045	1 155	..	..	..
Foreign controlled undertakings	277	251	74	192	247	..	..	..
Foreign companies (branches)	..	..	..	..	..	..	..	..
All undertakings	1 133	1 075	749	1 045	1 155	..	..	..
Non-life								
Domestic undertakings	6 911	8 410	9 458	7 257	9 473	..	..	..
Foreign controlled undertakings	2 721	3 523	3 808	1 888	1 618	..	..	..
Foreign companies (branches)	..	..	..	..	..	..	..	..
All undertakings	6 911	8 410	9 458	7 257	9 473	..	..	..
Composite								
Domestic undertakings	44 178	46 777	49 973	48 713	56 225	..	..	..
Foreign controlled undertakings	28 060	29 464	31 616	30 146	33 073	..	..	..
Foreign companies (branches)	..	..	..	..	..	..	..	..
All undertakings	44 178	46 777	49 973	48 713	56 225	..	..	..
of which:								
Life	18 508	19 316	21 023	22 507	26 955	..	..	..
Domestic undertakings	18 508	19 316	21 023	22 507	26 955	..	..	..
Foreign controlled undertakings	12 501	12 940	17 514	14 838	17 151	..	..	..
Foreign companies (branches)	..	..	..	..	..	..	..	..
All undertakings	18 508	19 316	21 023	22 507	26 955	..	..	..
Non-life	25 670	27 462	28 950	26 206	29 270	..	..	..
Domestic undertakings	25 670	27 462	28 950	26 206	29 270	..	..	..
Foreign controlled undertakings	15 559	16 524	14 103	15 308	15 922	..	..	..
Foreign companies (branches)	..	..	..	..	..	..	..	..
All undertakings	25 670	27 462	28 950	26 206	29 270	..	..	..
Total								
Domestic undertakings	52 222	56 263	60 180	57 016	66 853	..	..	..
Foreign controlled undertakings	31 058	33 239	35 498	32 226	34 937	..	..	..
Foreign companies (branches)	..	..	..	..	..	..	..	..
All undertakings	52 222	56 263	60 180	57 016	66 853	..	..	..
1.4 Gross operating expenses								
Life								
Domestic undertakings	1 313	1 486	1 156	1 336	1 705	1 617	1 480	1 699
Foreign controlled undertakings	..	..	570	661	723	759	734	704
Foreign companies (branches)	..	..	..	..	..	..	..	..
All undertakings	1 313	1 486	1 156	1 336	1 705	1 617	1 480	1 699
Non-life								
Domestic undertakings	2 968	3 545	4 198	4 924	5 852	7 490	8 280	9 060
Foreign controlled undertakings	..	..	2 010	3 137	3 249	4 041	3 412	4 004
Foreign companies (branches)	..	..	..	..	..	..	..	..
All undertakings	2 968	3 545	4 198	4 924	5 852	7 490	8 280	9 060
Composite								
Domestic undertakings	14 382	16 389	16 621	18 736	21 447	23 147	25 162	24 951
Foreign controlled undertakings	..	..	10 470	12 270	13 297	13 037	15 216	14 640
Foreign companies (branches)	..	..	..	..	..	..	..	..
All undertakings	14 382	16 389	16 621	18 736	21 447	23 147	25 162	24 951
of which:								
Life	7 085	8 530	8 486	9 990	11 792	11 674	12 701	12 400
Domestic undertakings	7 085	8 530	8 486	9 990	11 792	11 674	12 701	12 400
Foreign controlled undertakings	..	..	6 273	7 388	8 480	7 981	8 964	8 466
Foreign companies (branches)	..	..	..	..	..	..	..	..
All undertakings	7 085	8 530	8 486	9 990	11 792	11 674	12 701	12 400
Non-life	7 298	7 859	8 135	8 746	9 655	11 473	12 461	12 551
Domestic undertakings	7 298	7 859	8 135	8 746	9 655	11 473	12 461	12 551
Foreign controlled undertakings	..	..	4 198	4 882	4 818	5 055	6 252	6 174
Foreign companies (branches)	..	..	..	..	..	..	..	..
All undertakings	7 298	7 859	8 135	8 746	9 655	11 473	12 461	12 551
Total								
Domestic undertakings	18 662	21 420	21 974	24 996	29 004	32 254	34 923	35 709
Foreign controlled undertakings	..	..	13 050	16 068	17 270	17 837	19 363	19 349
Foreign companies (branches)	..	..	..	..	..	..	..	..
All undertakings	18 662	21 420	21 974	24 996	29 004	32 254	34 923	35 709

MEXICO

Table 1. Selected aggregates *(cont.)*

Million MXN

	2012	2013	2014	2015	2016	2017	2018	2019
1.5 Insurance business written abroad by branches, gross premiums								
Life								
Branches and agencies	..	..	..	..	..	..	..	..
Subsidaries	..	..	..	..	..	..	..	..
Total	..	..	..	..	..	..	..	..
Non-life								
Branches and agencies	..	..	..	..	..	..	..	..
Subsidaries	..	..	..	..	..	..	..	..
Total	..	..	..	..	..	..	..	..
Composite								
Branches and agencies	..	..	..	..	..	..	..	..
Subsidaries	..	..	..	..	..	..	..	..
Total	..	..	..	..	..	..	..	..
of which:								
Life	..	..	..	..	..	..	..	..
Branches and agencies	..	..	..	..	..	..	..	..
Subsidaries	..	..	..	..	..	..	..	..
Total	..	..	..	..	..	..	..	..
Non-life	..	..	..	..	..	..	..	..
Branches and agencies	..	..	..	..	..	..	..	..
Subsidaries	..	..	..	..	..	..	..	..
Total	..	..	..	..	..	..	..	..
Total								
Branches and agencies	..	..	..	..	..	..	..	..
Subsidaries	..	..	..	..	..	..	..	..
Total	..	..	..	..	..	..	..	..

.. Not available

Note: Detailed metadata at: *http://metalinks.oecd.org/ins/20210324/f949*.

Source: *OECD Insurance Statistics (database)*

MEXICO

Table 2. Number of companies and employees

	2012	2013	2014	2015	2016	2017	2018	2019
2.1 Number of companies								
Life								
Domestic undertakings	20	20	16	16	17	15	15	14
Foreign controlled undertakings	11	11	9	9	10	8	8	7
Foreign companies (branches)	..	..	..	..	..	..	..	..
All undertakings	20	20	16	16	17	15	15	14
Non-life								
Domestic undertakings	47	45	49	46	44	60	58	61
Foreign controlled undertakings	27	27	26	23	22	31	28	31
Foreign companies (branches)	..	..	..	..	..	..	..	..
All undertakings	47	45	49	46	44	60	58	61
Composite								
Domestic undertakings	35	37	38	37	37	38	36	35
Foreign controlled undertakings	21	21	22	21	20	21	20	19
Foreign companies (branches)	..	..	..	..	..	..	..	..
All undertakings	35	37	38	37	37	38	36	35
Reinsurance								
Domestic undertakings	2	2	2	3	2	2	2	2
Foreign controlled undertakings	0	0	0	0	0	0	..	..
Foreign companies (branches)	..	..	..	..	..	..	..	..
All undertakings	2	2	2	3	2	2	2	2
Total								
Domestic undertakings	104	104	105	102	100	115	111	112
Foreign controlled undertakings	59	59	57	53	52	60	56	57
Foreign companies (branches)	..	..	..	..	..	..	..	..
All undertakings	104	104	105	102	100	115	111	112
2.2 Number of employees								
Insurance undertakings	14 491	14 500	14 799	19 168	..	..	..	..
Intermediaries	36 190	46 712	51 780	55 005	57 900	61 695	..	..
Total	50 681	61 212	66 579	74 173	57 900	61 695	..	..

.. Not available

Note: Detailed metadata at: *http://metalinks.oecd.org/ins/20210324/f949*.

Source: *OECD Insurance Statistics (database)*

NETHERLANDS

Table 1. Selected aggregates

Million EUR

	2012	2013	2014	2015	2016	2017	2018	2019
1.1 Insurance business written in the reporting country								
1.1.1 Insurance business, by ownership								
Gross premiums								
Domestic undertakings	39 012	38 077	36 523	33 708	69 887	71 228	73 667	..
Foreign controlled undertakings	9 255	7 674	2 969	5 812	4 102	4 371	3 429	..
Foreign companies (branches)	891	430	62	0	..	..	..	..
All undertakings	39 903	38 507	36 585	33 708	69 887	71 228	73 667	..
Premiums ceded								
Domestic undertakings	3 109	2 951	3 880	2 814	1 198	1 698	1 460	..
Foreign controlled undertakings	1 706	1 484	1 615	1 365	287	353	84	..
Foreign companies (branches)	79	20	0	0	..	..	..	..
All undertakings	3 188	2 971	3 880	2 814	1 198	1 698	1 460	..
Net written premiums								
Domestic undertakings	35 903	35 126	32 643	30 894	68 689	69 530	72 207	..
Foreign controlled undertakings	7 549	6 190	1 354	4 447	3 815	4 018	3 345	..
Foreign companies (branches)	812	410	62	0	..	..	..	..
All undertakings	36 715	35 536	32 705	30 894	68 689	69 530	72 207	..
1.1.2 Insurance business on foreign risks, gross premiums								
Life	..	..	..	..	269	273	300	..
Non-life	..	..	..	..	534	452	1 102	..
Composite total	..	..	..	..	..	252	501	..
Total	..	..	..	..	803	977	1 903	..
1.1.3 Life insurance payments, by class, gross premiums								
Annuities	10 892	10 998	10 806	9 035	0	0	0	..
Unit linked	7 836	7 086	6 504	5 533	5 262	4 553	4 296	..
Other life insurance	247	188	150	122	8 465	8 411	7 674	..
Total life insurance	18 975	18 272	17 460	14 690	13 727	12 964	11 970	..
***of which:** Pension contracts*	6 034	5 810	5 552	5 208	334	157	38	..
1.1.4 Non-life insurance payments, by class, gross premiums								
Motor vehicle insurance	4 500	4 376	3 934	3 884	3 892	4 051	4 312	..
Marine, aviation and other transport insurance	596	525	435	404	361	283	273	..
Freight insurance	263	256	231	191	..	0	0	..
Fire and other property damage insurance	3 698	3 664	3 449	3 456	3 256	3 290	3 380	..
Pecuniary loss insurance	278	206	164	176	258	206	271	..
General liability insurance	1 116	1 125	1 064	1 033	882	883	919	..
Accident and health	8 560	8 167	7 867	7 851	46 459	47 499	50 393	..
***of which:** Health*	..	..	..	..	45 064	46 044	48 900	..
Other non-life insurance	1 907	1 919	1 976	2 016	1 049	1 165	1 099	..
Treaty reinsurance	..	..	..	..	..	0	0	..
Total non-life insurance	20 918	20 238	19 120	19 011	56 157	57 377	60 647	..
1.2 Gross claims payments								
Life								
Domestic undertakings	25 331	24 085	25 487	22 576	20 919	25 124	20 129	..
Foreign controlled undertakings	3 538	3 205	1 136	4 504	4 203	4 286	3 640	..
Foreign companies (branches)	401	420	0	0	..	..	..	..
All undertakings	25 732	24 505	25 487	22 576	20 919	25 124	20 129	..
Non-life								
Domestic undertakings	13 999	14 304	13 666	13 806	50 966	51 936	53 872	..
Foreign controlled undertakings	2 870	2 915	867	1 937	1 053	844	693	..
Foreign companies (branches)	41	41	149	0	..	..	..	..
All undertakings	14 040	14 345	13 815	13 806	50 966	51 936	53 872	..
Composite, all undertakings	**..**	**..**	**..**	**..**	**..**	**473**	**481**	**..**
Total								
Domestic undertakings	39 330	38 389	39 153	36 382	71 885	77 533	74 482	..
Foreign controlled undertakings	6 408	6 120	2 003	6 441	5 256	5 130	4 333	..
Foreign companies (branches)	442	461	149	0	..	..	..	..
All undertakings	39 772	38 850	39 302	36 382	71 885	77 533	74 482	..
1.3 Commissions								
Life								
Domestic undertakings	473	243	190	158	..	..	..	..
Foreign controlled undertakings	196	64	17	49	..	..	..	..
Foreign companies (branches)	17	12	0	0	..	..	..	..
All undertakings	490	255	190	158	..	..	..	..
Non-life								
Domestic undertakings	3 197	2 891	2 713	2 663	..	..	..	..
Foreign controlled undertakings	833	734	282	464	..	..	..	..
Foreign companies (branches)	22	22	21	0	..	..	..	..
All undertakings	3 219	2 913	2 734	2 663	..	..	..	..
Composite, all undertakings	**..**	**..**	**..**	**..**	**..**	**..**	**..**	**..**
Total								
Domestic undertakings	3 670	3 134	2 903	2 821	..	..	..	..
Foreign controlled undertakings	1 029	798	299	513	..	..	..	..
Foreign companies (branches)	39	34	21	0	..	..	..	..
All undertakings	3 709	3 168	2 924	2 821	..	..	..	..

NETHERLANDS

Table 1. Selected aggregates *(cont.)*

Million EUR

	2012	2013	2014	2015	2016	2017	2018	2019
1.4 Gross operating expenses								
Life								
Domestic undertakings	2 827	2 266	2 497	2 072	2 183	2 002	1 839	..
Foreign controlled undertakings	342	297	113	378	417	356	274	..
Foreign companies (branches)	37	44	0	0	..	..	..	..
All undertakings	2 864	2 310	2 497	2 072	2 183	2 002	1 839	..
Non-life								
Domestic undertakings	4 933	4 809	4 635	4 485	6 219	6 156	6 235	..
Foreign controlled undertakings	1 181	1 136	373	771	525	550	461	..
Foreign companies (branches)	24	25	23	0	..	..	..	..
All undertakings	4 957	4 834	4 658	4 485	6 219	6 156	6 235	..
Composite, all undertakings	**..**	**..**	**..**	**..**	**..**	**115**	**71**	**..**
Total								
Domestic undertakings	7 759	7 075	7 132	6 557	8 402	8 273	8 145	..
Foreign controlled undertakings	1 523	1 433	486	1 149	942	906	735	..
Foreign companies (branches)	61	69	23	0	..	..	..	..
All undertakings	7 820	7 144	7 155	6 557	8 402	8 273	8 145	..
1.5 Insurance business written abroad by branches, gross premiums								
Life								
Branches and agencies	540	370	276	..	253	260	291	..
Subsidaries	..	..	..	..	..	..	..	..
Total	540	370	276	267	253	260	291	..
Non-life								
Branches and agencies	1 276	1 132	1 289	..	175	163	153	..
Subsidaries	..	..	..	..	..	..	..	..
Total	1 276	1 132	1 289	1 487	175	163	153	..
Composite total	**..**	**..**	**..**	**..**	**..**	**0**	**477**	**..**
Total								
Branches and agencies	1 816	1 502	1 565	..	428	423	921	..
Subsidaries	..	..	..	..	..	..	..	..
Total	1 816	1 502	1 565	1 754	428	423	921	..

.. Not available

Note: Detailed metadata at: *http://metalinks.oecd.org/ins/20210324/956a*.

Source: *OECD Insurance Statistics (database)*

NETHERLANDS

Table 2. Number of companies and employees

	2012	2013	2014	2015	2016	2017	2018	2019
2.1 Number of companies								
Life								
Domestic undertakings	41	36	38	..	31	30	27	..
Foreign controlled undertakings	6	6	7	..	11	10	6	..
Foreign companies (branches)	4	4	0	..	..	..	..	..
All undertakings	45	40	38	..	31	30	27	..
Non-life								
Domestic undertakings	158	316	136	..	107	101	96	..
Foreign controlled undertakings	15	14	8	..	9	8	7	..
Foreign companies (branches)	2	1	2	..	..	..	..	..
All undertakings	160	317	138	..	107	101	96	..
Composite, all undertakings	**0**	**0**	**0**	**0**	**0**	**0**	..	..
Reinsurance								
Domestic undertakings	15	11	10	..	9	9	8	..
Foreign controlled undertakings	1	0	0	..	0	0	0	..
Foreign companies (branches)	0	0	0	..	..	..	..	..
All undertakings	15	11	10	..	9	9	8	..
Total								
Domestic undertakings	214	363	184	..	147	140	131	..
Foreign controlled undertakings	22	20	15	..	20	18	13	..
Foreign companies (branches)	6	5	2	..	..	..	..	..
All undertakings	220	368	186	..	147	140	131	..
2.2 Number of employees								
Insurance undertakings	..	..	..	..	..	..	..	..
Intermediaries	..	..	..	..	..	..	..	..
Total	..	..	..	..	..	..	..	..

.. Not available

Note: Detailed metadata at: *http://metalinks.oecd.org/ins/20210324/956a*.

Source: *OECD Insurance Statistics (database)*

NEW ZEALAND

Table 1. Selected aggregates

Million NZD

	2012	2013	2014	2015	2016	2017	2018	2019
1.1 Insurance business written in the reporting country								
1.1.1 Insurance business, by ownership								
Gross premiums								
Domestic undertakings	..	..	..	..	..	..	..	9 384
Foreign controlled undertakings	..	..	..	..	..	..	..	6 678
Foreign companies (branches)	..	..	..	..	..	..	..	1 634
All undertakings	5 665	6 266	6 460	6 678	6 828	7 240	..	11 017
Premiums ceded								
Domestic undertakings	..	..	..	..	..	..	..	2 548
Foreign controlled undertakings	..	..	..	..	..	..	..	2 148
Foreign companies (branches)	..	..	..	..	..	..	..	721
All undertakings	1 207	1 412	1 292	1 305	1 789	1 852	..	3 269
Net written premiums								
Domestic undertakings	..	..	..	..	..	..	..	6 836
Foreign controlled undertakings	..	..	..	..	..	..	..	4 530
Foreign companies (branches)	..	..	..	..	..	..	..	912
All undertakings	6 365	6 758	7 186	7 523	7 303	7 729	..	7 748
1.1.2 Insurance business on foreign risks, gross premiums								
Life	..	..	..	..	..	..	..	0
Non-life	..	..	..	..	..	..	..	0
Composite	..	..	..	..	..	..	..	0
of which:								
Life	..	..	..	..	..	..	..	0
Non-life	..	..	..	..	..	..	..	0
Total	..	..	..	..	..	..	..	0
1.1.3 Life insurance payments, by class, gross premiums								
Annuities	..	..	..	..	..	..	..	1
Unit linked	..	..	..	..	..	..	..	9
Other life insurance	..	..	..	..	..	..	..	2 587
Total life insurance	..	..	..	..	..	..	..	2 597
***of which:** Pension contracts*	..	..	..	..	..	..	..	0
1.1.4 Non-life insurance payments, by class, gross premiums								
Motor vehicle insurance	..	..	..	..	..	..	..	2 154
Marine, aviation and other transport insurance	..	..	..	..	..	..	..	149
Freight insurance	..	..	..	..	..	..	..	..
Fire and other property damage insurance	..	..	..	..	..	..	..	3 388
Pecuniary loss insurance	..	..	..	..	..	..	..	..
General liability insurance	..	..	..	..	..	..	..	593
Accident and health	..	..	..	..	..	..	..	1 678
***of which:** Health*	..	..	..	..	..	..	..	1 633
Other non-life insurance	..	..	..	..	..	..	..	455
Treaty reinsurance	..	..	..	..	..	..	..	..
Total non-life insurance	5 665	6 266	6 460	6 678	6 828	7 240	..	8 415
1.2 Gross claims payments								
Life								
Domestic undertakings	..	..	..	..	..	..	..	556
Foreign controlled undertakings	..	..	..	..	..	..	..	388
Foreign companies (branches)	..	..	..	..	..	..	..	355
All undertakings	1 360	1 303	1 399	1 544	1 598	1 579	..	911
Non-life								
Domestic undertakings	..	..	..	..	..	..	..	4 730
Foreign controlled undertakings	..	..	..	..	..	..	..	3 119
Foreign companies (branches)	..	..	..	..	..	..	..	588
All undertakings	9 531	4 539	5 642	6 302	4 864	6 662	..	5 318
Composite								
Domestic undertakings	..	..	..	..	..	..	..	755
Foreign controlled undertakings	..	..	..	..	..	..	..	590
Foreign companies (branches)	..	..	..	..	..	..	..	84
All undertakings	..	..	..	..	..	..	..	839
of which:								
Life	..	..	..	..	..	..	..	549
Domestic undertakings	..	..	..	..	..	..	..	478
Foreign controlled undertakings	..	..	..	..	..	..	..	372
Foreign companies (branches)	..	..	..	..	..	..	..	71
All undertakings	..	..	..	..	..	..	..	549
Non-life	..	..	..	..	..	..	..	291
Domestic undertakings	..	..	..	..	..	..	..	277
Foreign controlled undertakings	..	..	..	..	..	..	..	218
Foreign companies (branches)	..	..	..	..	..	..	..	13
All undertakings	..	..	..	..	..	..	..	291
Total								
Domestic undertakings	..	..	..	..	..	..	..	6 041
Foreign controlled undertakings	..	..	..	..	..	..	..	4 097
Foreign companies (branches)	..	..	..	..	..	..	..	1 027
All undertakings	10 891	5 842	7 041	7 846	6 462	8 241	..	7 068

NEW ZEALAND

Table 1. Selected aggregates *(cont.)*

Million NZD

	2012	2013	2014	2015	2016	2017	2018	2019
1.3 Commissions								
Life								
Domestic undertakings	..	..	..	..	..	..	..	169
Foreign controlled undertakings	..	..	..	..	..	..	..	105
Foreign companies (branches)	..	..	..	..	..	..	..	35
All undertakings	..	..	..	..	..	..	..	204
Non-life								
Domestic undertakings	..	..	..	..	..	..	..	659
Foreign controlled undertakings	..	..	..	..	..	..	..	618
Foreign companies (branches)	..	..	..	..	..	..	..	190
All undertakings	..	..	..	..	..	..	..	849
Composite								
Domestic undertakings	..	..	..	..	..	..	..	313
Foreign controlled undertakings	..	..	..	..	..	..	..	196
Foreign companies (branches)	..	..	..	..	..	..	..	31
All undertakings	..	..	..	..	..	..	..	343
of which:								
Life	..	..	..	..	..	..	..	267
Domestic undertakings	..	..	..	..	..	..	..	240
Foreign controlled undertakings	..	..	..	..	..	..	..	144
Foreign companies (branches)	..	..	..	..	..	..	..	27
All undertakings	..	..	..	..	..	..	..	267
Non-life	..	..	..	..	..	..	..	76
Domestic undertakings	..	..	..	..	..	..	..	73
Foreign controlled undertakings	..	..	..	..	..	..	..	52
Foreign companies (branches)	..	..	..	..	..	..	..	3
All undertakings	..	..	..	..	..	..	..	76
Total								
Domestic undertakings	..	..	..	..	..	..	..	1 140
Foreign controlled undertakings	..	..	..	..	..	..	..	918
Foreign companies (branches)	..	..	..	..	..	..	..	256
All undertakings	..	..	..	..	..	..	..	1 396
1.4 Gross operating expenses								
Life								
Domestic undertakings	..	..	..	..	..	..	..	291
Foreign controlled undertakings	..	..	..	..	..	..	..	206
Foreign companies (branches)	..	..	..	..	..	..	..	70
All undertakings	2 169	2 151	2 384	2 323	2 489	2 476	..	360
Non-life								
Domestic undertakings	..	..	..	..	..	..	..	989
Foreign controlled undertakings	..	..	..	..	..	..	..	655
Foreign companies (branches)	..	..	..	..	..	..	..	153
All undertakings	12 070	6 102	7 490	8 472	6 875	8 884	..	1 142
Composite								
Domestic undertakings	..	..	..	..	..	..	..	342
Foreign controlled undertakings	..	..	..	..	..	..	..	258
Foreign companies (branches)	..	..	..	..	..	..	..	38
All undertakings	..	..	..	..	..	..	..	380
of which:								
Life	..	..	..	..	..	..	..	294
Domestic undertakings	..	..	..	..	..	..	..	261
Foreign controlled undertakings	..	..	..	..	..	..	..	200
Foreign companies (branches)	..	..	..	..	..	..	..	33
All undertakings	..	..	..	..	..	..	..	294
Non-life	..	..	..	..	..	..	..	86
Domestic undertakings	..	..	..	..	..	..	..	81
Foreign controlled undertakings	..	..	..	..	..	..	..	58
Foreign companies (branches)	..	..	..	..	..	..	..	5
All undertakings	..	..	..	..	..	..	..	86
Total								
Domestic undertakings	..	..	..	..	..	..	..	1 622
Foreign controlled undertakings	..	..	..	..	..	..	..	1 119
Foreign companies (branches)	..	..	..	..	..	..	..	261
All undertakings	14 239	8 253	9 874	10 795	9 364	11 360	..	1 882

NEW ZEALAND

Table 1. Selected aggregates *(cont.)*

Million NZD

	2012	2013	2014	2015	2016	2017	2018	2019
1.5 Insurance business written abroad by branches, gross premiums								
Life								
Branches and agencies	..	..	..	..	..	..	..	0
Subsidaries	..	..	..	..	..	..	..	..
Total	..	..	..	..	..	..	..	0
Non-life								
Branches and agencies	..	..	..	..	..	..	..	22
Subsidaries	..	..	..	..	..	..	..	..
Total	..	..	..	..	..	..	..	22
Composite								
Branches and agencies	..	..	..	..	..	..	..	0
Subsidaries	..	..	..	..	..	..	..	..
Total	..	..	..	..	..	..	..	0
of which:								
Life	..	..	..	..	..	..	..	0
Branches and agencies	..	..	..	..	..	..	..	0
Subsidaries	..	..	..	..	..	..	..	..
Total	..	..	..	..	..	..	..	0
Non-life	..	..	..	..	..	..	..	0
Branches and agencies	..	..	..	..	..	..	..	0
Subsidaries	..	..	..	..	..	..	..	..
Total	..	..	..	..	..	..	..	0
Total								
Branches and agencies	..	..	..	..	..	..	..	22
Subsidaries	..	..	..	..	..	..	..	..
Total	..	..	..	..	..	..	..	22

.. Not available

Note: Detailed metadata at: *http://metalinks.oecd.org/ins/20210324/cbcd.*

Source: *OECD Insurance Statistics (database)*

NEW ZEALAND

Table 2. Number of companies and employees

	2012	2013	2014	2015	2016	2017	2018	2019
2.1 Number of companies								
Life								
Domestic undertakings	..	..	..	..	..	..	..	14
Foreign controlled undertakings	..	..	..	..	..	..	..	6
Foreign companies (branches)	..	..	..	..	..	..	..	3
All undertakings	43	37	43	30	30	30	..	17
Non-life								
Domestic undertakings	..	..	..	..	..	..	..	31
Foreign controlled undertakings	..	..	..	..	..	..	..	9
Foreign companies (branches)	..	..	..	..	..	..	..	20
All undertakings	142	130	145	102	90	87	..	51
Composite								
Domestic undertakings	..	..	..	..	..	..	..	10
Foreign controlled undertakings	..	..	..	..	..	..	..	3
Foreign companies (branches)	..	..	..	..	..	..	..	1
All undertakings	..	..	..	..	..	..	..	11
Reinsurance								
Domestic undertakings	..	..	..	..	..	..	..	0
Foreign controlled undertakings	..	..	..	..	..	..	..	0
Foreign companies (branches)	..	..	..	..	..	..	..	9
All undertakings	..	..	..	..	..	..	..	9
Total								
Domestic undertakings	..	..	..	..	..	..	..	55
Foreign controlled undertakings	..	..	..	..	..	..	..	18
Foreign companies (branches)	..	..	..	..	..	..	..	32
All undertakings	185	167	188	132	120	117	..	87
2.2 Number of employees								
Insurance undertakings	..	10 780	10 720	10 680	..	..	..	..
Intermediaries	..	..	..	..	..	..	..	..
Total	10 640	10 780	..	..	..	..	..	..

.. Not available

Note: Detailed metadata at: *http://metalinks.oecd.org/ins/20210324/cbcd.*

Source: *OECD Insurance Statistics (database)*

NORWAY

Table 1. Selected aggregates

Million NOK

	2012	2013	2014	2015	2016	2017	2018	2019
1.1 Insurance business written in the reporting country								
1.1.1 Insurance business, by ownership								
Gross premiums								
Domestic undertakings	119 751	119 149	134 884	135 864	138 612	139 748	148 945	161 842
Foreign controlled undertakings	8 589	8 948	11 029	13 195	..	..	..	..
Foreign companies (branches)	30 039	30 872	31 867	30 638	31 150	29 049	29 917	32 324
All undertakings	149 790	150 021	166 751	166 502	169 762	168 797	178 862	194 166
Premiums ceded								
Domestic undertakings	6 252	6 396	6 891	7 973	7 053	7 061	7 109	6 671
Foreign controlled undertakings	316	173	198	218	..	..	..	..
Foreign companies (branches)	4 290	4 219	4 653	4 976	5 362	4 814	4 868	5 613
All undertakings	10 542	10 614	11 544	12 950	12 415	11 876	11 976	12 284
Net written premiums								
Domestic undertakings	113 499	112 754	127 993	127 890	131 559	132 686	141 836	155 171
Foreign controlled undertakings	8 273	8 775	10 832	12 978	..	..	..	..
Foreign companies (branches)	25 749	26 653	27 213	25 662	25 788	24 235	25 049	26 711
All undertakings	139 248	139 407	155 206	153 552	157 347	156 921	166 885	181 882
1.1.2 Insurance business on foreign risks, gross premiums								
Life	31	..	..	9	7	6	4 144	2
Non-life	7 352	6 202	11 468	11 250	10 855	10 417	10 989	12 310
Composite total	..	..	..	..	..	..	..	..
Total	7 383	6 202	11 468	11 260	10 862	10 422	15 133	12 313
1.1.3 Life insurance payments, by class, gross premiums								
Annuities	..	..	..	..	..	..	..	..
Unit linked	..	..	..	..	..	..	..	..
Other life insurance	..	..	..	..	..	..	..	..
Total life insurance	81 742	81 299	92 185	91 794	94 093	93 577	99 961	108 693
***of which:** Pension contracts*	69 652	66 873	..	..	..	..	..	..
1.1.4 Non-life insurance payments, by class, gross premiums								
Motor vehicle insurance	19 403	..	20 378	20 706	20 897	21 029	22 316	24 811
Marine, aviation and other transport insurance	9 581	..	6 574	5 201	15 291	5 292	5 203	11 270
Freight insurance	..	..	..	..	0	..	..	..
Fire and other property damage insurance	17 738	..	18 195	19 041	23 135	22 553	23 487	25 120
Pecuniary loss insurance	585	..	127	97	432	92	98	..
General liability insurance	1 755	..	1 695	1 637	2 000	1 774	1 980	3 276
Accident and health	6 111	..	5 608	5 553	10 526	10 288	11 075	12 004
***of which:** Health*	..	..	..	..	0	..	..	..
Other non-life insurance	12 875	..	21 989	13 048	7 085	6 088	12 644	8 992
Treaty reinsurance	..	..	..	..	0	..	2 099	..
Total non-life insurance	68 048	..	74 566	65 283	79 366	67 116	78 901	85 472
1.2 Gross claims payments								
Life								
Domestic undertakings	45 033	45 143	45 742	49 007	51 548	54 419	58 887	60 593
Foreign controlled undertakings	3 120	3 186	3 150	4 796	.. c	..	..	.. c
Foreign companies (branches)	482	692	476	235	288	281	298	288
All undertakings	45 515	45 835	46 218	49 242	51 836	54 700	59 185	60 881
Non-life								
Domestic undertakings	28 356	23 486	30 742	34 587	32 537	31 896	34 370	37 564
Foreign controlled undertakings	542	.. c	.. c	.. c	.. c	..	..	.. c
Foreign companies (branches)	24 549	20 026	22 287	21 584	21 146	20 655	20 427	23 006
All undertakings	52 905	43 512	53 030	56 170	53 683	52 550	54 797	60 569
Composite, all undertakings	..	..	..	..	..	..	..	..
Total								
Domestic undertakings	73 389	68 629	76 485	83 593	84 085	86 315	93 257	98 157
Foreign controlled undertakings	3 662	3 186	3 150	4 796	..	..	..	..
Foreign companies (branches)	25 031	20 718	22 763	21 819	21 434	20 935	20 725	23 294
All undertakings	98 420	89 347	99 248	105 413	105 519	107 250	113 983	121 451
1.3 Commissions								
Life								
Domestic undertakings	692	774	839	916	890	783	737	913
Foreign controlled undertakings	152	179	202	227	.. c	.. c	.. c	.. c
Foreign companies (branches)	0	0	0	..	..	..	..	..
All undertakings	692	774	839	916	890	783	737	913
Non-life								
Domestic undertakings	1 507	1 536	2 204	2 119	1 956	2 105	2 309	2 684
Foreign controlled undertakings	35	.. c	.. c	..	.. c	.. c	.. c	.. c
Foreign companies (branches)	1 101	1 084	1 099	1 107	950	915	916	952
All undertakings	2 608	2 619	3 303	3 226	2 906	3 020	3 224	3 636
Composite, all undertakings	..	..	..	..	..	..	..	..
Total								
Domestic undertakings	2 199	2 310	3 043	3 035	2 846	2 889	3 046	3 597
Foreign controlled undertakings	187	179	202	227	..	..	..	..
Foreign companies (branches)	1 101	1 084	1 099	1 107	950	915	916	952
All undertakings	3 300	3 393	4 142	4 142	3 797	3 804	3 961	4 549

NORWAY

Table 1. Selected aggregates *(cont.)*

Million NOK

	2012	2013	2014	2015	2016	2017	2018	2019
1.4 Gross operating expenses								
Life								
Domestic undertakings	7 019	6 688	7 205	7 383	7 750	7 380	7 817	8 313
Foreign controlled undertakings	692	185	807	765	.. c	..	..	..
Foreign companies (branches)	0	126	162	..	157	143	126	83
All undertakings	7 019	6 814	7 367	7 383	7 907	7 523	7 943	8 396
Non-life								
Domestic undertakings	5 527	5 925	6 585	6 138	6 139	6 956	11 045	8 474
Foreign controlled undertakings	48	.. c	.. c	.. c	.. c	..	..	..
Foreign companies (branches)	4 765	4 203	5 318	5 574	5 465	4 732	5 207	4 862
All undertakings	10 292	10 128	11 903	11 712	11 605	11 688	16 252	13 336
Composite, all undertakings	..	..	..	..	..	..	..	..
Total								
Domestic undertakings	12 546	12 613	13 790	13 521	13 889	14 336	18 862	16 787
Foreign controlled undertakings	740	185	807	765	..	..	..	..
Foreign companies (branches)	4 765	4 329	5 480	5 574	5 623	4 875	5 333	4 945
All undertakings	17 311	16 942	19 270	19 095	19 512	19 211	24 195	21 732
1.5 Insurance business written abroad by branches, gross premiums								
Life								
Branches and agencies	..	.. c	..	..	..	..	..	..
Subsidaries	..	..	..	..	..	..	..	..
Total	..	.. c	..	..	..	..	..	..
Non-life								
Branches and agencies	2 454	1 134	4 636	1 569	7 141	2 493	2 431	4 073
Subsidaries	..	.. c	.. c	..	..	..	..	..
Total	2 454	1 134	4 636	1 569	7 141	2 493	2 431	4 073
Composite total	..	..	..	..	..	..	..	..
Total								
Branches and agencies	2 454	1 134	4 636	1 569	7 141	2 493	2 431	4 073
Subsidaries	..	..	..	..	..	..	..	..
Total	2 454	1 134	4 636	1 569	7 141	2 493	2 431	4 073

.. Not available; c Confidential data

Note: Detailed metadata at: *http://metalinks.oecd.org/ins/20210324/9a07*.

Source: *OECD Insurance Statistics (database)*

NORWAY

Table 2. Number of companies and employees

	2012	2013	2014	2015	2016	2017	2018	2019
2.1 Number of companies								
Life								
Domestic undertakings	10	12	10	10	10	13	12	11
Foreign controlled undertakings	2	2	2	2	2	3	3	3
Foreign companies (branches)	9	9	7	7	7	6	6	6
All undertakings	19	21	17	17	17	19	18	17
Non-life								
Domestic undertakings	63	59	59	58	59	58	56	55
Foreign controlled undertakings	1	1	1	2	2	2	1	1
Foreign companies (branches)	25	25	22	21	23	23	21	24
All undertakings	88	84	81	79	82	81	77	79
Composite, all undertakings	**0**	**0**	**0**	**0**	..	..	..	..
Reinsurance								
Domestic undertakings	..	..	..	..	..	..	..	..
Foreign controlled undertakings	..	..	..	..	..	..	..	..
Foreign companies (branches)	..	..	..	..	..	..	..	..
All undertakings	..	..	..	..	..	..	..	..
Total								
Domestic undertakings	73	71	69	68	69	71	68	66
Foreign controlled undertakings	3	3	3	4	4	5	4	4
Foreign companies (branches)	34	34	29	28	30	29	27	30
All undertakings	107	105	98	96	99	100	95	96
2.2 Number of employees								
Insurance undertakings	..	..	..	..	..	..	..	..
Intermediaries	..	..	..	..	..	..	..	..
Total	..	..	..	..	..	..	..	..

.. Not available

Note: Detailed metadata at: *http://metalinks.oecd.org/ins/20210324/9a07*.

Source: *OECD Insurance Statistics (database)*

POLAND

Table 1. Selected aggregates

Million PLN

	2012	2013	2014	2015	2016	2017	2018	2019
1.1 Insurance business written in the reporting country								
1.1.1 Insurance business, by ownership								
Gross premiums								
Domestic undertakings	62 627	57 863	54 927	54 804	56 039	62 339	62 161	63 838
Foreign controlled undertakings	35 100	31 562	30 425	30 801	31 961	33 189	33 452	35 129
Foreign companies (branches)	..	..	..	..	..	..	..	..
All undertakings	62 627	57 863	54 927	54 804	56 039	62 339	62 161	63 838
Premiums ceded								
Domestic undertakings	4 598	4 214	4 170	5 197	6 765	7 216	7 235	7 940
Foreign controlled undertakings	4 224	3 664	3 533	4 355	4 798	4 664	4 396	4 768
Foreign companies (branches)	..	..	..	..	..	..	..	..
All undertakings	4 598	4 214	4 170	5 197	6 765	7 216	7 235	7 940
Net written premiums								
Domestic undertakings	58 029	53 649	50 757	49 606	49 274	55 123	54 927	55 898
Foreign controlled undertakings	30 876	27 898	26 892	26 446	27 163	28 525	29 057	30 361
Foreign companies (branches)	..	..	..	..	..	..	..	..
All undertakings	58 029	53 649	50 757	49 606	49 274	55 123	54 927	55 898
1.1.2 Insurance business on foreign risks, gross premiums								
Life	..	..	..	..	..	118	100	215
Non-life	..	..	..	..	..	181	255	422
Composite total	..	..	..	..	..	..	..	..
Total	..	..	..	..	..	299	355	637
1.1.3 Life insurance payments, by class, gross premiums								
Annuities	99	107	114	131	138	0	0	0
Unit linked	12 046	13 052	12 600	12 996	10 325	10 955	7 487	6 440
Other life insurance	24 203	18 082	15 933	14 377	13 370	13 583	14 216	14 836
Total life insurance	36 348	31 241	28 646	27 505	23 833	24 539	21 702	21 275
***of which:** Pension contracts*	371	396	356	356	..	243	230	226
1.1.4 Non-life insurance payments, by class, gross premiums								
Motor vehicle insurance	14 780	13 945	13 397	13 910	18 744	23 249	24 295	24 638
Marine, aviation and other transport insurance	256	267	275	210	185	271	319	435
Freight insurance	119	117	126	116	120	..	..	0
Fire and other property damage insurance	5 441	5 973	5 715	5 938	6 246	6 877	7 618	8 249
Pecuniary loss insurance	1 526	1 858	2 149	1 893	1 805	1 713	1 812	2 203
General liability insurance	1 773	1 891	1 964	2 134	1 915	2 064	2 297	2 518
Accident and health	1 801	1 926	2 007	2 273	2 222	2 347	2 715	2 972
***of which:** Health*	513	612	656	613	618	561	872	942
Other non-life insurance	554	622	627	804	947	1 256	1 403	1 379
Treaty reinsurance	..	..	..	..	..	..	..	0
Total non-life insurance	26 250	26 599	26 260	27 278	32 182	37 777	40 459	42 392
1.2 Gross claims payments								
Life								
Domestic undertakings	25 917	23 087	20 360	19 358	18 284	20 315	21 401	17 292
Foreign controlled undertakings	13 331	10 927	9 783	8 795	9 543	9 295	10 029	7 810
Foreign companies (branches)	..	..	..	..	..	..	..	..
All undertakings	25 917	23 087	20 360	19 358	18 284	20 315	21 401	17 292
Non-life								
Domestic undertakings	14 046	13 711	13 811	15 488	18 393	19 931	21 011	22 605
Foreign controlled undertakings	8 890	8 434	8 579	9 515	10 911	11 453	12 435	13 797
Foreign companies (branches)	..	..	..	..	..	..	..	..
All undertakings	14 046	13 711	13 811	15 488	18 393	19 931	21 011	22 605
Composite, all undertakings	..	..	..	..	..	..	..	..
Total								
Domestic undertakings	39 963	36 798	34 171	34 846	36 677	40 246	42 412	39 896
Foreign controlled undertakings	22 221	19 362	18 363	18 310	20 454	20 748	22 464	21 607
Foreign companies (branches)	..	..	..	..	..	..	..	..
All undertakings	39 963	36 798	34 171	34 846	36 677	40 246	42 412	39 896
1.3 Commissions								
Life								
Domestic undertakings	70	93	203	231	222	183	2 854	2 719
Foreign controlled undertakings	69	70	191	223	218	179	1 754	1 594
Foreign companies (branches)	..	..	..	..	..	..	..	..
All undertakings	70	93	203	231	222	183	2 854	2 719
Non-life								
Domestic undertakings	657	740	651	719	1 115	1 545	6 720	7 131
Foreign controlled undertakings	648	606	594	657	929	1 122	4 641	4 826
Foreign companies (branches)	..	..	..	..	..	..	..	..
All undertakings	657	740	651	719	1 115	1 545	6 720	7 131
Composite, all undertakings	..	..	..	..	..	..	..	..
Total								
Domestic undertakings	727	833	854	950	1 337	1 727	9 574	9 850
Foreign controlled undertakings	717	676	785	880	1 147	1 301	6 396	6 420
Foreign companies (branches)	..	..	..	..	..	..	..	..
All undertakings	727	833	854	950	1 337	1 727	9 574	9 850

POLAND

Table 1. Selected aggregates *(cont.)*

Million PLN

	2012	2013	2014	2015	2016	2017	2018	2019
1.4 Gross operating expenses								
Life								
Domestic undertakings	6 416	6 146	6 588	6 476	5 647	5 963	5 697	5 230
Foreign controlled undertakings	4 244	3 831	4 369	4 182	3 797	3 491	3 276	2 708
Foreign companies (branches)	..	..	..	..	..	..	..	..
All undertakings	6 416	6 146	6 588	6 476	5 647	5 963	5 697	5 230
Non-life								
Domestic undertakings	7 733	7 775	8 018	8 335	9 104	12 793	14 073	14 974
Foreign controlled undertakings	5 225	5 090	5 135	5 569	5 978	7 938	8 744	9 193
Foreign companies (branches)	..	..	..	..	..	..	..	..
All undertakings	7 733	7 775	8 018	8 335	9 104	12 793	14 073	14 974
Composite, all undertakings	..	..	..	..	..	..	..	..
Total								
Domestic undertakings	14 149	13 921	14 606	14 811	14 751	18 756	19 770	20 204
Foreign controlled undertakings	9 469	8 921	9 504	9 751	9 776	11 429	12 021	11 901
Foreign companies (branches)	..	..	..	..	..	..	..	..
All undertakings	14 149	13 921	14 606	14 811	14 751	18 756	19 770	20 204
1.5 Insurance business written abroad by branches, gross premiums								
Life								
Branches and agencies	26	..	79	92	..	95	80	99
Subsidaries	..	..	..	..	..	..	..	..
Total	26	..	79	92	..	95	80	99
Non-life								
Branches and agencies	53	..	98	116	..	..	0	0
Subsidaries	..	..	..	..	..	..	..	..
Total	53	..	98	116	..	..	0	0
Composite total	..	..	..	..	..	..	..	..
Total								
Branches and agencies	79	..	177	208	..	95	80	99
Subsidaries	..	..	..	..	..	..	..	..
Total	79	..	177	208	..	95	80	99

.. Not available

Note: Detailed metadata at: *http://metalinks.oecd.org/ins/20210324/b462.*

Source: *OECD Insurance Statistics (database)*

POLAND

Table 2. Number of companies and employees

	2012	2013	2014	2015	2016	2017	2018	2019
2.1 Number of companies								
Life								
Domestic undertakings	28	27	26	28	27	27	26	26
Foreign controlled undertakings	23	21	19	21	21	20	18	17
Foreign companies (branches)	..	..	..	..	..	..	..	..
All undertakings	28	27	26	28	27	27	26	26
Non-life								
Domestic undertakings	30	30	30	32	33	33	33	32
Foreign controlled undertakings	21	19	19	22	20	19	19	18
Foreign companies (branches)	..	..	..	..	..	..	..	..
All undertakings	30	30	30	32	33	33	33	32
Composite, all undertakings	**0**	**0**	**0**	**0**	**0**	..	..	..
Reinsurance								
Domestic undertakings	1	1	1	1	1	1	1	1
Foreign controlled undertakings	1	1	1	1	1	1	1	1
Foreign companies (branches)	..	..	..	..	..	..	..	..
All undertakings	1	1	1	1	1	1	1	1
Total								
Domestic undertakings	59	58	57	61	61	61	60	59
Foreign controlled undertakings	45	41	39	44	42	40	38	36
Foreign companies (branches)	..	..	..	..	..	..	..	..
All undertakings	59	58	57	61	61	61	60	59
2.2 Number of employees								
Insurance undertakings	37 205	37 187	35 922	35 282	..	..	..	..
Intermediaries	58 879	69 621	58 004	49 126	..	..	..	..
Total	96 083	106 808	93 926	84 408	..	..	..	..

.. Not available

Note: Detailed metadata at: *http://metalinks.oecd.org/ins/20210324/b462.*

Source: *OECD Insurance Statistics (database)*

PORTUGAL

Table 1. Selected aggregates

Million EUR

	2012	2013	2014	2015	2016	2017	2018	2019
1.1 Insurance business written in the reporting country								
1.1.1 Insurance business, by ownership								
Gross premiums								
Domestic undertakings	10 553	12 802	14 051	12 568	10 913	11 455	12 590	11 915
Foreign controlled undertakings	1 553	1 617	8 737	8 890	9 048	10 640	11 441	10 457
Foreign companies (branches)	0	0	0	0	0	0	0	0
All undertakings	10 553	12 802	14 051	12 568	10 913	11 455	12 590	11 915
Premiums ceded								
Domestic undertakings	1 096	1 144	1 118	1 194	1 214	1 307	1 338	1 638
Foreign controlled undertakings	130	140	836	924	992	1 180	1 209	1 505
Foreign companies (branches)	0	0	0	0	0	0	0	0
All undertakings	1 096	1 144	1 118	1 194	1 214	1 307	1 338	1 638
Net written premiums								
Domestic undertakings	9 457	11 658	12 933	11 374	9 698	10 148	11 252	10 277
Foreign controlled undertakings	1 423	1 477	7 902	7 966	8 056	9 460	10 232	8 952
Foreign companies (branches)	0	0	0	0	0	0	0	0
All undertakings	9 457	11 658	12 933	11 374	9 698	10 148	11 252	10 277
1.1.2 Insurance business on foreign risks, gross premiums								
Life	2	3	13	8	11	8	0	0
Non-life	15	14	13	13	4	7	8	15
Composite	54	64	92	107	127	129	195	252
of which:								
Life	27	27	53	63	70	74	132	183
Non-life	27	38	39	44	57	55	63	69
Total	72	81	118	129	142	144	203	267
1.1.3 Life insurance payments, by class, gross premiums								
Annuities	46	79	64	109	142	183	142	40
Unit linked	1 999	1 851	1 966	2 119	1 655	2 077	1 703	1 647
Other life insurance	4 633	7 094	8 220	6 254	4 708	4 450	5 934	5 072
Total life insurance	6 678	9 023	10 249	8 481	6 504	6 710	7 779	6 759
***of which:** Pension contracts*	..	..	..	..	..	..	..	..
1.1.4 Non-life insurance payments, by class, gross premiums								
Motor vehicle insurance	1 353	1 277	1 256	1 316	1 399	1 482	1 429	1 517
Marine, aviation and other transport insurance	35	33	29	28	25	27	26	29
Freight insurance	25	25	24	23	22	22	0	21
Fire and other property damage insurance	702	700	699	745	771	795	764	820
Pecuniary loss insurance	63	69	70	73	84	83	47	95
General liability insurance	89	84	87	94	99	102	101	117
Accident and health	1 430	1 413	1 452	1 602	1 783	1 999	2 141	2 354
***of which:** Health*	838	862	896	973	1 084	1 208	1 307	1 429
Other non-life insurance	177	178	183	205	225	235	239	201
Treaty reinsurance	0	0	0	0	0	0	..	..
Total non-life insurance	3 874	3 778	3 802	4 086	4 408	4 745	4 747	5 155
1.2 Gross claims payments								
Life								
Domestic undertakings	4 875	4 518	5 254	6 133	6 568	3 940	3 306	3 141
Foreign controlled undertakings	461	374	2 667	2 724	2 252	2 853	2 749	2 547
Foreign companies (branches)	0	0	0	0	0	0	0	0
All undertakings	4 875	4 518	5 254	6 133	6 568	3 940	3 306	3 141
Non-life								
Domestic undertakings	1 471	1 446	1 407	1 520	1 336	1 413	1 530	1 550
Foreign controlled undertakings	385	376	1 174	1 278	1 070	1 130	1 200	1 246
Foreign companies (branches)	0	0	0	0	0	0	0	0
All undertakings	1 471	1 446	1 407	1 520	1 336	1 413	1 530	1 550
Composite								
Domestic undertakings	5 927	5 427	5 201	5 128	4 554	4 230	5 086	4 341
Foreign controlled undertakings	541	562	3 991	3 922	4 501	4 180	4 606	3 877
Foreign companies (branches)	0	0	0	0	0	0	0	0
All undertakings	5 927	5 427	5 201	5 128	4 554	4 230	5 086	4 341
of which:								
Life	4 616	4 067	3 895	3 840	2 867	2 479	3 320	2 568
Domestic undertakings	4 616	4 067	3 895	3 840	2 867	2 479	3 320	2 568
Foreign controlled undertakings	184	167	2 904	2 839	2 815	2 431	2 843	2 106
Foreign companies (branches)	0	0	0	0	0	0	0	0
All undertakings	4 616	4 067	3 895	3 840	2 867	2 479	3 320	2 568
Non-life	1 311	1 360	1 306	1 288	1 687	1 751	1 766	1 774
Domestic undertakings	1 311	1 360	1 306	1 288	1 687	1 751	1 766	1 774
Foreign controlled undertakings	357	395	1 087	1 083	1 686	1 749	1 763	1 771
Foreign companies (branches)	0	0	0	0	0	0	0	0
All undertakings	1 311	1 360	1 306	1 288	1 687	1 751	1 766	1 774
Total								
Domestic undertakings	12 274	11 391	11 861	12 782	12 458	9 582	9 922	9 032
Foreign controlled undertakings	1 387	1 312	7 832	7 923	7 822	8 163	8 555	7 670
Foreign companies (branches)	0	0	0	0	0	0	0	0
All undertakings	12 274	11 391	11 861	12 782	12 458	9 582	9 922	9 032

PORTUGAL

Table 1. Selected aggregates *(cont.)*

Million EUR

	2012	2013	2014	2015	2016	2017	2018	2019
1.3 Commissions								
Life								
Domestic undertakings	47	144	40	77	105	103	89	132
Foreign controlled undertakings	7	7	15	41	42	85	78	116
Foreign companies (branches)	0	0	0	0	0	0	0	0
All undertakings	47	144	40	77	105	103	89	132
Non-life								
Domestic undertakings	157	156	153	178	164	183	194	220
Foreign controlled undertakings	40	38	117	133	98	115	124	141
Foreign companies (branches)	0	0	0	0	0	0	0	0
All undertakings	157	156	153	178	164	183	194	220
Composite								
Domestic undertakings	272	291	301	295	286	351	350	393
Foreign controlled undertakings	81	99	208	222	283	344	333	373
Foreign companies (branches)	0	0	0	0	0	0	0	0
All undertakings	272	291	301	295	286	351	350	393
of which:								
Life	87	98	100	82	49	58	75	86
Domestic undertakings	87	98	100	82	49	58	75	86
Foreign controlled undertakings	21	28	42	44	47	52	58	66
Foreign companies (branches)	0	0	0	0	0	0	0	0
All undertakings	87	98	100	82	49	58	75	86
Non-life	185	193	201	214	237	293	275	307
Domestic undertakings	185	193	201	214	237	293	275	307
Foreign controlled undertakings	60	71	165	178	236	291	275	306
Foreign companies (branches)	0	0	0	0	0	0	0	0
All undertakings	185	193	201	214	237	293	275	307
Total								
Domestic undertakings	476	591	493	550	554	637	633	745
Foreign controlled undertakings	128	144	339	396	423	543	534	630
Foreign companies (branches)	0	0	0	0	0	0	0	0
All undertakings	476	591	493	550	554	637	633	745
1.4 Gross operating expenses								
Life								
Domestic undertakings	206	314	212	244	300	298	280	289
Foreign controlled undertakings	36	33	136	163	168	248	246	254
Foreign companies (branches)	0	0	0	0	0	0	0	0
All undertakings	206	314	212	244	300	298	280	289
Non-life								
Domestic undertakings	511	496	495	550	467	494	513	549
Foreign controlled undertakings	144	133	398	441	357	388	402	430
Foreign companies (branches)	0	0	0	0	0	0	0	0
All undertakings	511	496	495	550	467	494	513	549
Composite								
Domestic undertakings	723	715	717	720	711	851	823	859
Foreign controlled undertakings	200	198	541	571	702	839	790	821
Foreign companies (branches)	0	0	0	0	0	0	0	0
All undertakings	723	715	717	720	711	851	823	859
of which:								
Life	221	234	230	222	148	173	206	207
Domestic undertakings	221	234	230	222	148	173	206	207
Foreign controlled undertakings	49	48	125	145	140	162	175	170
Foreign companies (branches)	0	0	0	0	0	0	0	0
All undertakings	221	234	230	222	148	173	206	207
Non-life	502	481	487	497	562	678	617	652
Domestic undertakings	502	481	487	497	562	678	617	652
Foreign controlled undertakings	151	151	416	427	562	677	615	651
Foreign companies (branches)	0	0	0	0	0	0	0	0
All undertakings	502	481	487	497	562	678	617	652
Total								
Domestic undertakings	1 440	1 525	1 425	1 513	1 478	1 643	1 615	1 697
Foreign controlled undertakings	380	364	1 076	1 176	1 227	1 474	1 438	1 505
Foreign companies (branches)	0	0	0	0	0	0	0	0
All undertakings	1 440	1 525	1 425	1 513	1 478	1 643	1 615	1 697

PORTUGAL

Table 1. Selected aggregates *(cont.)*

Million EUR

	2012	2013	2014	2015	2016	2017	2018	2019
1.5 Insurance business written abroad by branches, gross premiums								
Life								
Branches and agencies	2	3	13	8	11	8	0	0
Subsidaries	0	0	0	0	0	0	0	0
Total	2	3	13	8	11	8	0	0
Non-life								
Branches and agencies	14	12	12	12	1	3	0	6
Subsidaries	0	0	0	0	0	0	0	0
Total	14	12	12	12	1	3	0	6
Composite								
Branches and agencies	54	64	92	107	127	129	195	252
Subsidaries	0	0	0	0	0	0	0	0
Total	54	64	92	107	127	129	195	252
of which:								
Life	27	27	53	63	70	74	132	183
Branches and agencies	27	27	53	63	70	74	132	183
Subsidaries	0	0	0	0	0	0	0	0
Total	27	27	53	63	70	74	132	183
Non-life	27	38	39	44	57	55	63	69
Branches and agencies	27	38	39	44	57	55	63	69
Subsidaries	0	0	0	0	0	0	0	0
Total	27	38	39	44	57	55	63	69
Total								
Branches and agencies	70	79	117	128	138	140	195	258
Subsidaries	0	0	0	0	0	0	0	0
Total	70	79	117	128	138	140	195	258

.. Not available

Note: Detailed metadata at: *http://metalinks.oecd.org/ins/20210324/9c4c.*

Source: *OECD Insurance Statistics (database)*

PORTUGAL

Table 2. Number of companies and employees

	2012	2013	2014	2015	2016	2017	2018	2019
2.1 Number of companies								
Life								
Domestic undertakings	14	14	16	16	14	13	12	12
Foreign controlled undertakings	5	5	10	10	9	9	10	10
Foreign companies (branches)	6	5	5	5	4	4	5	0
All undertakings	20	19	21	21	18	17	17	12
Non-life								
Domestic undertakings	21	21	21	24	23	23	23	22
Foreign controlled undertakings	4	4	15	16	15	15	16	15
Foreign companies (branches)	25	24	23	21	19	19	23	0
All undertakings	46	45	44	45	42	42	46	22
Composite								
Domestic undertakings	6	6	5	5	5	6	5	5
Foreign controlled undertakings	2	2	3	3	4	4	3	3
Foreign companies (branches)	5	6	6	7	7	7	9	0
All undertakings	11	12	11	12	12	13	14	5
Reinsurance								
Domestic undertakings	1	1	1	1	1	1	1	1
Foreign controlled undertakings	0	0	1	1	1	1	1	1
Foreign companies (branches)	0	0	0	0	0	0	0	0
All undertakings	1	1	1	1	1	1	1	1
Total								
Domestic undertakings	42	42	43	46	43	43	41	40
Foreign controlled undertakings	11	11	29	30	29	29	30	29
Foreign companies (branches)	36	35	34	33	30	30	37	0
All undertakings	78	77	77	79	73	73	78	40
2.2 Number of employees								
Insurance undertakings	8 807	9 224	9 252	9 441	9 387	9 381	8 781	8 781
Intermediaries	24 624	24 207	23 465	22 738	21 426	20 258	18 999	16 763
Total	33 431	33 431	32 717	32 179	30 813	29 639	27 780	25 544

Note: Detailed metadata at: *http://metalinks.oecd.org/ins/20210324/9c4c*.
Source: *OECD Insurance Statistics (database)*

SLOVAK REPUBLIC

Table 1. Selected aggregates

Million EUR

	2012	2013	2014	2015	2016	2017	2018	2019
1.1 Insurance business written in the reporting country								
1.1.1 Insurance business, by ownership								
Gross premiums								
Domestic undertakings	2 036	2 082	2 106	2 020	..	4 186	..	2 304
Foreign controlled undertakings	1 863	1 901	1 918	1 827	..	..	..	2 044
Foreign companies (branches)	121	146	142	143	..	282	..	287
All undertakings	2 157	2 228	2 248	2 163	..	4 468	..	2 522
Premiums ceded								
Domestic undertakings	294	298	314	319	..	319	..	363
Foreign controlled undertakings	267	268	283	287	..	..	..	280
Foreign companies (branches)	17	19	17	17	..	31	..	30
All undertakings	311	316	331	336	..	350	..	365
Net written premiums								
Domestic undertakings	1 742	1 785	1 792	1 701	..	3 868	..	1 941
Foreign controlled undertakings	1 596	1 633	1 635	1 540	..	..	..	1 765
Foreign companies (branches)	104	127	126	126	..	250	..	258
All undertakings	1 846	1 912	1 917	1 827	..	4 118	..	2 157
1.1.2 Insurance business on foreign risks, gross premiums								
Life	..	..	..	..	..	..	..	..
Non-life	..	..	..	..	..	..	..	..
Composite	..	..	..	..	..	..	..	..
of which:								
Life	..	..	..	..	..	..	..	..
Non-life	..	..	..	..	..	..	..	..
Total	..	..	..	..	..	..	..	..
1.1.3 Life insurance payments, by class, gross premiums								
Annuities	607	649	623	586	..	2	..	1
Unit linked	409	423	417	351	..	166	..	253
Other life insurance	146	164	180	171	..	950	..	947
Total life insurance	1 162	1 236	1 220	1 108	..	1 119	..	1 202
***of which:** Pension contracts*	13	12	12	12	..	..	..	..
1.1.4 Non-life insurance payments, by class, gross premiums								
Motor vehicle insurance	548	528	532	547	..	309	..	704
Marine, aviation and other transport insurance	7	6	6	6	..	10	..	12
Freight insurance	8	8	8	8	..	..	..	..
Fire and other property damage insurance	247	250	257	257	..	276	..	297
Pecuniary loss insurance	24	27	33	34	..	11	..	..
General liability insurance	68	73	78	78	..	80	..	79
Accident and health	40	45	49	44	..	..	..	..
***of which:** Health*	2	2	2	3	..	..	..	..
Other non-life insurance	32	34	35	39	..	397	..	100
Treaty reinsurance	21	21	32	42	..	..	..	..
Total non-life insurance	996	992	1 028	1 055	..	1 083	..	1 366
1.2 Gross claims payments								
Life								
Domestic undertakings	93	91	107	98	186	76	..	74
Foreign controlled undertakings	93	91	107	98	..	73	..	71
Foreign companies (branches)	0	0	0	2	..	117	..	102
All undertakings	93	91	108	100	..	193	..	176
Non-life								
Domestic undertakings	1	0	0	0	..	..	..	..
Foreign controlled undertakings	1	0	0	0	..	..	..	..
Foreign companies (branches)	44	27	29	32	..	21	..	18
All undertakings	45	27	29	32	..	..	..	18
Composite								
Domestic undertakings	1 083	1 117	1 084	1 057	2 291	..	..	..
Foreign controlled undertakings	948	979	948	911	1 909	76	..	1 171
Foreign companies (branches)	12	14	16	16	..	21	..	46
All undertakings	1 094	1 131	1 099	1 073	..	..	..	1 367
of which:								
Life	640	658	646	575	..	..	..	747
Domestic undertakings	632	647	634	563	1 794	..	..	..
Foreign controlled undertakings	527	544	533	457	1 459	72	..	615
Foreign companies (branches)	8	11	12	12	..	17	..	37
All undertakings	640	658	646	575	..	..	..	747
Non-life	455	473	453	497	..	..	..	620
Domestic undertakings	451	470	450	494	497	..	..	..
Foreign controlled undertakings	421	435	415	454	450	4	..	555
Foreign companies (branches)	4	4	3	3	..	5	..	9
All undertakings	455	473	453	497	..	..	..	620
Total								
Domestic undertakings	1 176	1 208	1 191	1 155	2 477	76	..	74
Foreign controlled undertakings	1 042	1 070	1 055	1 010	1 909	149	..	1 242
Foreign companies (branches)	55	42	44	49	..	159	..	166
All undertakings	1 232	1 249	1 236	1 205	..	193	..	1 561

SLOVAK REPUBLIC

Table 1. Selected aggregates *(cont.)*

Million EUR

	2012	2013	2014	2015	2016	2017	2018	2019
1.3 Commissions								
Life								
Domestic undertakings	28	29	33	37	..	..	..	..
Foreign controlled undertakings	28	29	33	37	..	..	..	..
Foreign companies (branches)	1	1	1	2	..	23	..	26
All undertakings	29	30	34	39	..	..	..	..
Non-life								
Domestic undertakings	1	0	0	0	..	..	..	..
Foreign controlled undertakings	1	0	0	0	..	..	..	..
Foreign companies (branches)	11	13	15	18	..	21	..	22
All undertakings	12	13	15	18	..	..	..	..
Composite								
Domestic undertakings	238	251	259	250	..	..	..	..
Foreign controlled undertakings	225	238	244	233	..	..	..	..
Foreign companies (branches)	17	18	4	16	..	20	..	22
All undertakings	255	269	264	266	..	..	..	..
of which:								
Life	102	107	95	89	..	..	..	..
Domestic undertakings	86	93	95	77	..	..	..	..
Foreign controlled undertakings	81	90	91	73	..	..	..	..
Foreign companies (branches)	16	14	0	12	..	13	..	12
All undertakings	102	107	95	89	..	..	..	..
Non-life	154	162	168	177	..	..	..	..
Domestic undertakings	152	158	164	173	..	..	..	..
Foreign controlled undertakings	143	149	153	160	..	..	..	..
Foreign companies (branches)	2	4	4	5	..	7	..	10
All undertakings	154	162	168	177	..	..	..	..
Total								
Domestic undertakings	266	279	292	287	..	..	..	..
Foreign controlled undertakings	253	267	277	270	..	..	..	..
Foreign companies (branches)	30	32	21	36	..	64	..	71
All undertakings	296	311	313	323	..	..	..	..
1.4 Gross operating expenses								
Life								
Domestic undertakings	58	57	63	72	..	55	..	107 361 381
Foreign controlled undertakings	58	57	63	72	..	..	..	53 819 969
Foreign companies (branches)	3	2	2	3	..	51	..	58
All undertakings	60	59	65	75	..	105	..	165
Non-life								
Domestic undertakings	2	0	0	0	..	..	..	..
Foreign controlled undertakings	2	0	0	0	..	..	..	..
Foreign companies (branches)	26	30	31	32	..	41	..	39
All undertakings	28	30	31	32	..	41	..	39
Composite								
Domestic undertakings	510	522	529	505	..	502	..	641 249 475
Foreign controlled undertakings	481	492	498	472	..	..	..	..
Foreign companies (branches)	29	28	7	25	..	29	..	32
All undertakings	539	549	536	531	..	531	..	673
of which:								
Life	231	228	212	187	..	179	..	191
Domestic undertakings	207	207	212	170	..	161	..	173 023 120
Foreign controlled undertakings	195	197	202	160	..	..	..	..
Foreign companies (branches)	24	21	1	17	..	19	..	18
All undertakings	231	228	212	187	..	179	..	191
Non-life	308	321	324	344	..	351	..	482
Domestic undertakings	303	314	317	336	..	341	..	468 226 356
Foreign controlled undertakings	286	295	295	312	..	..	..	..
Foreign companies (branches)	5	7	6	8	..	10	..	14
All undertakings	308	321	324	344	..	351	..	482
Total								
Domestic undertakings	569	578	592	578	..	556	..	748 610 856
Foreign controlled undertakings	541	549	561	544	..	..	..	53 819 969
Foreign companies (branches)	57	60	40	60	..	121	..	129
All undertakings	627	639	632	638	..	677	..	877

SLOVAK REPUBLIC

Table 1. Selected aggregates *(cont.)*

Million EUR

	2012	2013	2014	2015	2016	2017	2018	2019
1.5 Insurance business written abroad by branches, gross premiums								
Life								
Branches and agencies	0	0	0	1	..	..	..	..
Subsidaries	0	0	1	5	..	..	..	..
Total	0	0	1	6	..	..	..	..
Non-life								
Branches and agencies	0	0	0	0	..	..	..	..
Subsidaries	0	0	0	0	..	..	..	..
Total	0	0	0	0	..	..	..	..
Composite								
Branches and agencies	1	1	2	2	..	..	..	..
Subsidaries	3	3	4	6	..	..	..	..
Total	4	5	6	8	..	..	..	..
of which:								
Life	0	0	0	0	..	..	..	..
Branches and agencies	0	0	0	0	..	..	..	..
Subsidaries	0	0	0	0	..	..	..	..
Total	0	0	0	0	..	..	..	..
Non-life	4	5	6	8	..	..	..	..
Branches and agencies	1	1	2	2	..	..	..	..
Subsidaries	3	3	4	6	..	..	..	..
Total	4	5	6	8	..	..	..	..
Total								
Branches and agencies	1	1	2	3	..	..	..	..
Subsidaries	3	3	5	10	..	..	..	..
Total	4	5	7	14	..	..	..	..

.. Not available

Note: Detailed metadata at: *http://metalinks.oecd.org/ins/20210324/a5ab.*

Source: *OECD Insurance Statistics (database)*

SLOVAK REPUBLIC

Table 2. Number of companies and employees

	2012	2013	2014	2015	2016	2017	2018	2019
2.1 Number of companies								
Life								
Domestic undertakings	5	5	5	5	3	3	..	3
Foreign controlled undertakings	5	5	5	5	3	2	..	2
Foreign companies (branches)	1	1	1	1	2	2	..	..
All undertakings	6	6	6	6	5	5	..	5
Non-life								
Domestic undertakings	1	0	0	0	0	0	..	0
Foreign controlled undertakings	1	0	0	0	0	0	..	0
Foreign companies (branches)	16	17	17	17	19	19	..	..
All undertakings	17	17	17	17	19	19	..	0
Composite								
Domestic undertakings	12	12	12	12	12	12	..	10
Foreign controlled undertakings	10	10	10	10	12	10	..	8
Foreign companies (branches)	2	2	2	2	18	2	..	..
All undertakings	14	14	14	14	30	14	..	18
Reinsurance								
Domestic undertakings	0	0	0	0	0	0	..	0
Foreign controlled undertakings	0	0	0	0	0	0	..	0
Foreign companies (branches)	1	1	1	1	0	0	..	..
All undertakings	1	1	1	1	0	0	..	0
Total								
Domestic undertakings	18	17	17	17	15	15	..	13
Foreign controlled undertakings	16	15	15	15	15	12	..	10
Foreign companies (branches)	20	21	21	21	39	23	..	..
All undertakings	38	38	38	38	54	38	..	..
2.2 Number of employees								
Insurance undertakings	5 878	5 778	5 937	..	..	..	..	..
Intermediaries	1 373	..	1 358	..	..	..	..	25 066
Total	7 251	..	7 295	..	..	..	..	..

.. Not available

Note: Detailed metadata at: *http://metalinks.oecd.org/ins/20210324/a5ab.*

Source: *OECD Insurance Statistics (database)*

SLOVENIA

Table 1. Selected aggregates

Million EUR

	2012	2013	2014	2015	2016	2017	2018	2019
1.1 Insurance business written in the reporting country								
1.1.1 Insurance business, by ownership								
Gross premiums								
Domestic undertakings	2 192	2 114	2 095	2 150	2 182	2 298	2 424	2 647
Foreign controlled undertakings	166	166	166	172	180	186	191	522
Foreign companies (branches)	..	..	..	..	..	..	..	..
All undertakings	2 192	2 114	2 095	2 150	2 182	2 298	2 424	2 647
Premiums ceded								
Domestic undertakings	283	258	274	256	269	310	320	377
Foreign controlled undertakings	27	27	28	33	39	42	42	65
Foreign companies (branches)	..	..	..	..	..	..	..	..
All undertakings	283	258	274	256	269	310	320	377
Net written premiums								
Domestic undertakings	1 909	1 856	1 821	1 894	1 914	1 988	2 105	2 270
Foreign controlled undertakings	139	140	137	139	141	144	149	457
Foreign companies (branches)	..	..	..	..	..	..	..	..
All undertakings	1 909	1 856	1 821	1 894	1 914	1 988	2 105	2 270
1.1.2 Insurance business on foreign risks, gross premiums								
Life	0	..	..	..	..	..	..	..
Non-life	..	0	0	0	..	..	..	..
Composite	2	2	1	1	..	..	..	..
of which:								
Life	..	0	0	1	..	..	..	..
Non-life	2	1	1	0	..	..	..	..
Total	2	2	2	2	..	..	..	..
1.1.3 Life insurance payments, by class, gross premiums								
Annuities	..	..	..	..	..	..	..	..
Unit linked	219	201	195	215	213	223	225	258
Other life insurance	266	273	284	283	279	293	301	293
Total life insurance	485	473	479	498	492	516	526	551
of which: *Pension contracts*	65	45	37	37	39	41	41	50
1.1.4 Non-life insurance payments, by class, gross premiums								
Motor vehicle insurance	559	513	495	484	499	539	590	659
Marine, aviation and other transport insurance	18	15	16	18	18	19	21	24
Freight insurance	15	14	13	15	16	16	16	13
Fire and other property damage insurance	396	370	372	393	405	415	439	470
Pecuniary loss insurance	48	49	56	62	62	64	60	62
General liability insurance	61	63	65	64	72	73	79	87
Accident and health	580	585	574	591	591	623	661	738
of which: *Health*	467	480	470	484	489	522	556	628
Other non-life insurance	30	31	24	25	28	33	34	42
Treaty reinsurance	0	..	0	0	0	0	0	0
Total non-life insurance	1 706	1 641	1 616	1 652	1 690	1 782	1 898	2 096
1.2 Gross claims payments								
Life								
Domestic undertakings	40	31	36	52	50	46	..	..
Foreign controlled undertakings	0	0	1	0	2	..	..	..
Foreign companies (branches)	..	..	..	..	..	..	..	..
All undertakings	40	31	36	52	50	46	..	..
Non-life								
Domestic undertakings	463	482	449	499	491	532	556	595
Foreign controlled undertakings	..	..	..	1	0	..	0	6
Foreign companies (branches)	..	..	..	..	..	..	..	..
All undertakings	463	482	449	499	491	532	556	595
Composite								
Domestic undertakings	902	951	941	911	903	995	1 115	1 132
Foreign controlled undertakings	84	93	90	91	95	104	111	326
Foreign companies (branches)	..	..	..	..	..	..	..	..
All undertakings	902	951	941	911	903	995	1 115	1 132
of which:								
Life	259	299	304	305	314	347	402	424
Domestic undertakings	259	299	304	305	314	347	402	424
Foreign controlled undertakings	47	51	50	51	50	50	49	94
Foreign companies (branches)	..	..	..	..	..	..	..	..
All undertakings	259	299	304	305	314	347	402	424
Non-life	642	651	637	606	590	648	713	708
Domestic undertakings	642	651	637	606	590	648	713	708
Foreign controlled undertakings	38	42	41	40	45	54	62	232
Foreign companies (branches)	..	..	..	..	..	..	..	..
All undertakings	642	651	637	606	590	648	713	708
Total								
Domestic undertakings	1 404	1 464	1 426	1 461	1 445	1 573	1 670	1 727
Foreign controlled undertakings	85	93	91	91	97	104	111	331
Foreign companies (branches)	..	..	..	..	..	..	..	..
All undertakings	1 404	1 464	1 426	1 461	1 445	1 573	1 670	1 727

SLOVENIA

Table 1. Selected aggregates *(cont.)*

Million EUR

	2012	2013	2014	2015	2016	2017	2018	2019
1.3 Commissions								
Life								
Domestic undertakings	6	3	3	3	3	4	..	..
Foreign controlled undertakings	0	0	0	0	0	..	..	..
Foreign companies (branches)	..	..	..	..	..	..	..	..
All undertakings	6	3	3	3	3	4	..	..
Non-life								
Domestic undertakings	2	4	7	8	7	8	9	1
Foreign controlled undertakings	..	..	..	0	0	..	0	0
Foreign companies (branches)	..	..	..	..	..	..	..	..
All undertakings	2	4	7	8	7	8	9	1
Composite								
Domestic undertakings	80	84	86	89	86	92	104	115
Foreign controlled undertakings	19	19	20	21	28	22	23	49
Foreign companies (branches)	..	..	..	..	..	..	..	..
All undertakings	80	84	86	89	86	92	104	115
of which:								
Life	27	32	32	34	32	32	35	34
Domestic undertakings	27	32	32	34	32	32	35	34
Foreign controlled undertakings	10	10	10	10	15	9	9	13
Foreign companies (branches)	..	..	..	..	..	..	..	..
All undertakings	27	32	32	34	32	32	35	34
Non-life	53	52	54	56	54	60	68	81
Domestic undertakings	53	52	54	56	54	60	68	81
Foreign controlled undertakings	9	9	10	11	13	13	14	36
Foreign companies (branches)	..	..	..	..	..	..	..	..
All undertakings	53	52	54	56	54	60	68	81
Total								
Domestic undertakings	89	91	96	100	96	104	112	116
Foreign controlled undertakings	20	19	20	21	28	22	23	49
Foreign companies (branches)	..	..	..	..	..	..	..	..
All undertakings	89	91	96	100	96	104	112	116
1.4 Gross operating expenses								
Life								
Domestic undertakings	28	14	15	16	12	15	..	..
Foreign controlled undertakings	2	2	1	1	1	..	..	..
Foreign companies (branches)	..	..	..	..	..	..	..	..
All undertakings	28	14	15	16	12	15	..	..
Non-life								
Domestic undertakings	80	81	86	90	97	97	105	112
Foreign controlled undertakings	..	..	..	0	1	..	1	6
Foreign companies (branches)	..	..	..	..	..	..	..	..
All undertakings	80	81	86	90	97	97	105	112
Composite								
Domestic undertakings	361	366	362	368	378	388	418	442
Foreign controlled undertakings	56	47	57	60	60	66	68	146
Foreign companies (branches)	..	..	..	..	..	..	..	..
All undertakings	361	366	362	368	378	388	418	442
of which:								
Life	93	104	99	100	99	102	116	118
Domestic undertakings	93	104	99	100	99	102	116	118
Foreign controlled undertakings	28	26	27	28	26	27	27	43
Foreign companies (branches)	..	..	..	..	..	..	..	..
All undertakings	93	104	99	100	99	102	116	118
Non-life	269	263	263	268	279	286	302	324
Domestic undertakings	269	263	263	268	279	286	302	324
Foreign controlled undertakings	28	21	30	32	33	39	41	103
Foreign companies (branches)	..	..	..	..	..	..	..	..
All undertakings	269	263	263	268	279	286	302	324
Total								
Domestic undertakings	469	461	462	474	487	500	523	553
Foreign controlled undertakings	57	49	59	62	62	66	69	152
Foreign companies (branches)	..	..	..	..	..	..	..	..
All undertakings	469	461	462	474	487	500	523	553

SLOVENIA

Table 1. Selected aggregates *(cont.)*

Million EUR

	2012	2013	2014	2015	2016	2017	2018	2019
1.5 Insurance business written abroad by branches, gross premiums								
Life								
Branches and agencies	..	..	..	..	..	..	..	..
Subsidaries	..	..	..	..	..	..	..	..
Total	..	..	..	..	..	..	..	..
Non-life								
Branches and agencies	..	..	..	..	..	1	1	1
Subsidaries	..	..	..	..	..	..	..	..
Total	..	..	..	..	..	1	1	1
Composite								
Branches and agencies	..	..	..	2	..	31	44	65
Subsidaries	..	..	..	..	..	..	..	..
Total	..	..	..	2	..	31	44	65
of which:								
Life	..	..	..	2	..	6	7	7
Branches and agencies	..	..	..	2	..	6	7	7
Subsidaries	..	..	..	..	..	..	..	..
Total	..	..	..	2	..	6	7	7
Non-life	..	..	..	0	..	25	37	58
Branches and agencies	..	..	..	0	..	25	37	58
Subsidaries	..	..	..	..	..	..	..	..
Total	..	..	..	0	..	25	37	58
Total								
Branches and agencies	..	..	..	2	..	32	45	66
Subsidaries	..	..	..	..	..	..	..	..
Total	..	..	..	2	..	32	45	66

.. Not available

Note: Detailed metadata at: *http://metalinks.oecd.org/ins/20210324/4d24.*

Source: *OECD Insurance Statistics (database)*

SLOVENIA

Table 2. Number of companies and employees

	2012	2013	2014	2015	2016	2017	2018	2019
2.1 Number of companies								
Life								
Domestic undertakings	4	3	3	3	3	2	0	0
Foreign controlled undertakings	1	1	1	1	1	0	0	0
Foreign companies (branches)	0	0	0	0	0	0	0	0
All undertakings	4	3	3	3	3	2	0	0
Non-life								
Domestic undertakings	3	3	3	4	4	4	4	4
Foreign controlled undertakings	0	0	0	0	0	0	1	2
Foreign companies (branches)	3	4	4	4	4	4	3	3
All undertakings	6	7	7	8	8	8	7	7
Composite								
Domestic undertakings	8	8	8	8	7	7	9	9
Foreign controlled undertakings	3	3	3	3	3	3	3	4
Foreign companies (branches)	2	2	2	2	2	2	4	4
All undertakings	10	10	10	10	9	9	13	13
Reinsurance								
Domestic undertakings	2	2	2	2	2	2	2	2
Foreign controlled undertakings	0	0	0	0	0	0	0	0
Foreign companies (branches)	0	0	0	0	0	0	0	0
All undertakings	2	2	2	2	2	2	2	2
Total								
Domestic undertakings	17	16	16	17	16	15	15	15
Foreign controlled undertakings	4	4	4	4	4	3	4	6
Foreign companies (branches)	5	6	6	6	6	6	7	7
All undertakings	22	22	22	23	22	21	22	22
2.2 Number of employees								
Insurance undertakings	..	..	..	..	..	..	..	..
Intermediaries	..	..	..	..	..	..	..	..
Total	..	..	..	..	..	..	..	..

.. Not available

Note: Detailed metadata at: *http://metalinks.oecd.org/ins/20210324/4d24.*

Source: OECD *Insurance Statistics (database)*

SPAIN

Table 1. Selected aggregates

Million EUR

	2012	2013	2014	2015	2016	2017	2018	2019
1.1 Insurance business written in the reporting country								
1.1.1 Insurance business, by ownership								
Gross premiums								
Domestic undertakings	56 608	58 110	57 662	59 048	66 541	65 719	66 538	66 197
Foreign controlled undertakings	14 689	12 578	12 542	11 038	..	..	..	..
Foreign companies (branches)	117	0	0	0	..	..	..	..
All undertakings	56 725	58 110	57 662	59 048	66 541	65 719	66 538	66 197
Premiums ceded								
Domestic undertakings	4 235	5 831	5 019	5 161	6 014	6 206	6 020	6 885
Foreign controlled undertakings	1 094	1 058	923	736	..	..	..	..
Foreign companies (branches)	42	0	0	0	..	..	..	..
All undertakings	4 277	5 831	5 019	5 161	6 014	6 206	6 020	6 885
Net written premiums								
Domestic undertakings	52 373	52 279	52 643	53 886	60 527	59 513	60 518	59 312
Foreign controlled undertakings	13 594	11 520	11 620	10 301	..	..	..	..
Foreign companies (branches)	75	0	0	0	..	..	..	..
All undertakings	52 448	52 279	52 643	53 886	60 527	59 513	60 518	59 312
1.1.2 Insurance business on foreign risks, gross premiums								
Life	16	22	7	11	13	9	11	0
Non-life	138	79	73	59	45	20	3	326
Composite	54	52	44	61	49	26	147	150
of which:								
Life	39	42	34	46	35	2	28	46
Non-life	16	10	9	15	14	24	119	104
Total	209	153	123	130	107	55	160	476
1.1.3 Life insurance payments, by class, gross premiums								
Annuities	7 052	7 946	6 406	5 881	8 746	8 318	7 583	7 053
Unit linked	3 748	3 062	2 816	2 721	2 981	4 431	4 432	4 842
Other life insurance	15 828	14 865	16 021	17 128	19 330	16 270	16 559	15 144
Total life insurance	26 629	25 873	25 244	25 730	31 056	29 019	28 574	27 039
of which: *Pension contracts*	..	..	..	..	..	..	..	..
1.1.4 Non-life insurance payments, by class, gross premiums								
Motor vehicle insurance	9 961	9 610	9 445	9 695	10 451	10 918	11 212	11 734
Marine, aviation and other transport insurance	329	390	361	369	369	367	389	409
Freight insurance	194	294	268	261	270	281	301	320
Fire and other property damage insurance	913	2 246	2 315	2 610	2 895	2 770	3 425	3 379
Pecuniary loss insurance	311	175	178	208	283	247	252	221
General liability insurance	1 096	1 077	1 009	1 011	1 049	1 100	1 181	1 300
Accident and health	7 629	7 888	8 227	8 449	8 879	9 329	9 744	10 057
of which: *Health*	6 777	7 031	7 356	7 536	7 902	8 224	8 652	8 997
Other non-life insurance	10 502	10 531	10 558	10 729	11 001	11 264	11 029	11 281
Treaty reinsurance	0	0	0	0	0	..	..	..
Total non-life insurance	30 933	32 211	32 362	33 332	35 197	36 275	37 532	38 702
1.2 Gross claims payments								
Life								
Domestic undertakings	15 189	14 147	16 777	18 872	3 070	3 685	3 096	2 488
Foreign controlled undertakings	2 127	1 814	1 688	1 582	..	..	..	..
Foreign companies (branches)	0	0	0	0	..	..	..	..
All undertakings	15 189	14 147	16 777	18 872	3 070	3 685	3 096	2 488
Non-life								
Domestic undertakings	9 489	9 463	9 250	9 593	9 453	10 280	9 702	9 940
Foreign controlled undertakings	3 926	3 947	3 890	2 592	..	..	..	..
Foreign companies (branches)	0	0	0	0	..	..	..	..
All undertakings	9 489	9 463	9 250	9 593	9 453	10 280	9 702	9 940
Composite								
Domestic undertakings	22 204	21 477	21 596	20 659	32 425	35 292	35 464	37 506
Foreign controlled undertakings	6 495	5 208	5 230	5 136	..	..	..	..
Foreign companies (branches)	49	0	0	0	..	..	..	..
All undertakings	22 252	21 477	21 596	20 659	32 425	35 292	35 464	37 506
of which:								
Life	11 547	9 702	9 986	8 948	20 670	22 722	21 474	23 064
Domestic undertakings	11 511	9 702	9 986	8 948	20 670	22 722	21 474	23 064
Foreign controlled undertakings	3 836	2 320	2 497	2 292	..	..	..	..
Foreign companies (branches)	36	0	0	0	..	..	..	..
All undertakings	11 547	9 702	9 986	8 948	20 670	22 722	21 474	23 064
Non-life	10 705	11 775	11 610	11 711	11 755	12 571	13 989	14 442
Domestic undertakings	10 693	11 775	11 610	11 711	11 755	12 571	13 989	14 442
Foreign controlled undertakings	2 659	2 888	2 733	2 843	..	..	..	..
Foreign companies (branches)	12	0	0	0	..	..	..	..
All undertakings	10 705	11 775	11 610	11 711	11 755	12 571	13 989	14 442
Total								
Domestic undertakings	46 882	45 088	47 622	49 125	44 947	49 258	48 262	49 934
Foreign controlled undertakings	12 548	10 968	10 809	9 310	..	..	..	..
Foreign companies (branches)	49	0	0	0	..	..	..	..
All undertakings	46 930	45 088	47 622	49 125	44 947	49 258	48 262	49 934

SPAIN

Table 1. Selected aggregates *(cont.)*

Million EUR

	2012	2013	2014	2015	2016	2017	2018	2019
1.3 Commissions								
Life								
Domestic undertakings	..	..	660	712	234	257	273	225
Foreign controlled undertakings	..	..	86	71	..	..	..	..
Foreign companies (branches)	..	..	0	0	..	..	..	..
All undertakings	..	..	660	712	234	257	273	225
Non-life								
Domestic undertakings	..	..	1 472	1 436	1 433	1 522	1 524	1 565
Foreign controlled undertakings	..	..	642	517	..	..	..	..
Foreign companies (branches)	..	..	0	0	..	..	..	..
All undertakings	..	..	1 472	1 436	1 433	1 522	1 524	1 565
Composite								
Domestic undertakings	..	..	2 270	2 635	3 328	4 629	3 786	3 897
Foreign controlled undertakings	..	..	669	710	..	..	..	..
Foreign companies (branches)	..	..	0	0	..	..	..	..
All undertakings	..	..	2 270	2 635	3 328	4 629	3 786	3 897
of which:								
Life	..	..	418	379	979	1 185	1 114	1 169
Domestic undertakings	..	..	418	379	979	1 185	1 114	1 169
Foreign controlled undertakings	..	..	94	103	..	..	..	..
Foreign companies (branches)	..	..	0	0	..	..	..	..
All undertakings	..	..	418	379	979	1 185	1 114	1 169
Non-life	..	..	1 852	2 255	2 349	3 444	2 672	2 728
Domestic undertakings	..	..	1 852	2 255	2 349	3 444	2 672	2 728
Foreign controlled undertakings	..	..	576	607	..	..	..	..
Foreign companies (branches)	..	..	0	0	..	..	..	..
All undertakings	..	..	1 852	2 255	2 349	3 444	2 672	2 728
Total								
Domestic undertakings	..	..	4 403	4 782	4 995	6 408	5 583	5 687
Foreign controlled undertakings	..	..	1 398	1 298	..	..	..	..
Foreign companies (branches)	..	..	0	0	..	..	..	..
All undertakings	..	..	4 403	4 782	4 995	6 408	5 583	5 687
1.4 Gross operating expenses								
Life								
Domestic undertakings	220	968	994	1 075	425	455	484	409
Foreign controlled undertakings	39	201	190	192	..	..	..	..
Foreign companies (branches)	0	0	..	..	..	..	..	..
All undertakings	220	968	994	1 075	425	455	484	409
Non-life								
Domestic undertakings	491	3 046	2 880	2 832	2 876	3 081	3 065	3 092
Foreign controlled undertakings	242	1 272	1 289	947	..	..	..	..
Foreign companies (branches)	0	0	..	..	..	..	..	..
All undertakings	491	3 046	2 880	2 832	2 876	3 081	3 065	3 092
Composite								
Domestic undertakings	564	5 322	5 034	5 250	6 332	6 550	6 855	7 166
Foreign controlled undertakings	120	1 152	1 070	1 100	..	..	..	..
Foreign companies (branches)	5	1	..	4	..	..	..	..
All undertakings	569	5 323	5 034	5 254	6 332	6 550	6 855	7 166
of which:								
Life	87	809	797	729	1 489	1 546	1 677	1 816
Domestic undertakings	85	809	797	729	1 489	1 546	1 677	1 816
Foreign controlled undertakings	26	162	178	186	..	..	..	..
Foreign companies (branches)	2	0	..	..	..	..	..	..
All undertakings	87	809	797	729	1 489	1 546	1 677	1 816
Non-life	482	4 515	4 237	4 525	4 843	5 004	5 178	5 350
Domestic undertakings	479	4 514	4 237	4 521	4 843	5 004	5 178	5 350
Foreign controlled undertakings	94	990	892	913	..	..	..	..
Foreign companies (branches)	3	1	0	4	..	..	..	..
All undertakings	482	4 515	4 237	4 525	4 843	5 004	5 178	5 350
Total								
Domestic undertakings	1 275	9 337	8 907	9 157	9 633	10 087	10 405	10 667
Foreign controlled undertakings	401	2 625	2 549	2 239	..	..	..	..
Foreign companies (branches)	5	1	..	4	..	..	..	..
All undertakings	1 280	9 338	8 907	9 161	9 633	10 087	10 405	10 667

SPAIN

Table 1. Selected aggregates *(cont.)*

Million EUR

	2012	2013	2014	2015	2016	2017	2018	2019
1.5 Insurance business written abroad by branches, gross premiums								
Life								
Branches and agencies	323	274	0	0	0	0	1	0
Subsidaries	..	..	..	..	..	..	..	..
Total	..	..	..	..	0	0	1	0
Non-life								
Branches and agencies	419	592	654	701	1 694	1 841	1 537	1 606
Subsidaries	..	..	..	..	..	..	..	..
Total	..	..	..	..	1 694	1 841	1 537	1 606
Composite								
Branches and agencies	135	885	1 286	1 361	1 262	1 385	2 155	2 184
Subsidaries	..	..	..	..	..	..	..	..
Total	..	..	..	..	1 262	1 385	2 155	2 184
of which:								
Life	..	..	..	..	518	574	812	661
Branches and agencies	23	212	559	694	518	574	812	661
Subsidaries	..	..	..	..	..	..	..	..
Total	..	..	..	..	518	574	812	661
Non-life	..	..	..	..	744	812	1 344	1 523
Branches and agencies	113	673	728	667	744	812	1 344	1 523
Subsidaries	..	..	..	..	..	..	..	..
Total	..	..	..	..	744	812	1 344	1 523
Total								
Branches and agencies	878	1 751	1 940	2 062	2 955	3 226	3 693	3 790
Subsidaries	..	..	..	..	..	..	..	..
Total	..	..	..	..	2 955	3 226	3 693	3 790

.. Not available

Note: Detailed metadata at: *http://metalinks.oecd.org/ins/20210324/8670.*

Source: *OECD Insurance Statistics (database)*

SPAIN

Table 2. Number of companies and employees

	2012	2013	2014	2015	2016	2017	2018	2019
2.1 Number of companies								
Life								
Domestic undertakings	84	83	79	78	32	32	29	26
Foreign controlled undertakings	10	10	9	8	..	..	..	..
Foreign companies (branches)	0	0	0	0	..	..	..	..
All undertakings	84	83	79	78	32	32	29	26
Non-life								
Domestic undertakings	136	132	127	118	121	111	105	100
Foreign controlled undertakings	18	19	19	17	..	..	..	..
Foreign companies (branches)	0	0	0	1	..	..	..	..
All undertakings	136	132	127	119	121	111	105	100
Composite								
Domestic undertakings	46	47	45	41	75	74	74	74
Foreign controlled undertakings	10	8	8	8	..	..	..	..
Foreign companies (branches)	2	1	1	0	..	..	..	..
All undertakings	48	48	46	41	75	74	74	74
Reinsurance								
Domestic undertakings	2	2	3	3	3	3	3	4
Foreign controlled undertakings	0	0	0	0	..	..	..	..
Foreign companies (branches)	0	0	0	0	..	..	..	..
All undertakings	2	2	3	3	3	3	3	4
Total								
Domestic undertakings	268	264	254	240	231	220	211	204
Foreign controlled undertakings	38	37	36	33	..	..	..	..
Foreign companies (branches)	2	1	1	1	..	..	..	..
All undertakings	270	265	255	241	231	220	211	204
2.2 Number of employees								
Insurance undertakings	46 439	46 324	45 535	45 218	47 453	47 498	47 380	48 194
Intermediaries	..	121 427	129 549	..	..	..	..	..
Total	..	167 751	175 084	..	..	..	..	..

.. Not available

Note: Detailed metadata at: *http://metalinks.oecd.org/ins/20210324/8670*.

Source: *OECD Insurance Statistics (database)*

SWEDEN

Table 1. Selected aggregates

Million SEK

	2012	2013	2014	2015	2016	2017	2018	2019
1.1 Insurance business written in the reporting country								
1.1.1 Insurance business, by ownership								
Gross premiums								
Domestic undertakings	167 132	177 197	332 028	339 533	334 834	379 418	426 318	460 661
Foreign controlled undertakings	65 752	66 854	66 041	62 537	67 208	78 911	97 388	101 544
Foreign companies (branches)	..	..	10 260	..	..	..	..	..
All undertakings	167 132	177 197	342 288	339 533	334 834	379 418	426 318	460 661
Premiums ceded								
Domestic undertakings	13 068	12 967	15 157	10 306	9 139	10 693	11 095	14 223
Foreign controlled undertakings	5 428	4 727	3 870	4 441	4 296	5 538	6 138	8 471
Foreign companies (branches)	..	..	..	..	..	..	..	..
All undertakings	13 068	12 967	15 157	10 306	9 139	10 693	11 095	14 223
Net written premiums								
Domestic undertakings	154 064	164 230	316 871	329 227	325 695	368 725	415 223	446 438
Foreign controlled undertakings	60 324	62 127	62 171	58 096	62 912	73 373	91 250	93 073
Foreign companies (branches)	..	..	10 260	..	..	..	..	..
All undertakings	154 064	164 230	327 131	329 227	325 695	368 725	415 223	446 438
1.1.2 Insurance business on foreign risks, gross premiums								
Life	..	..	581	667	60	58	58	59
Non-life	..	..	28 134	27 121	26 941	30 482	40 549	44 517
Composite total	..	..	..	..	..	..	..	..
Total	..	..	28 715	27 788	27 001	30 540	40 607	44 576
1.1.3 Life insurance payments, by class, gross premiums								
Annuities	73 378	73 377	205 927	169 626	94 037	107 773	126 049	139 221
Unit linked	1 708	1 188	2 366	75 221	85 696	97 951	107 143	106 859
Other life insurance	13 229	13 591	29 900	3 957	71 084	82 841	89 138	102 063
Total life insurance	88 315	88 156	238 192	248 804	250 817	288 565	322 330	348 143
***of which:** Pension contracts*	..	..	..	..	..	..	..	..
1.1.4 Non-life insurance payments, by class, gross premiums								
Motor vehicle insurance	..	..	30 360	21 348	..	..	..	..
Marine, aviation and other transport insurance	..	..	2 627	749	..	..	..	..
Freight insurance	..	..	..	..	..	..	..	..
Fire and other property damage insurance	..	..	29 146	36 720	..	..	..	..
Pecuniary loss insurance	..	..	459	1 070	..	..	..	..
General liability insurance	..	..	4 045	4 119	..	..	..	..
Accident and health	..	..	5 674	5 155	..	..	..	..
***of which:** Health*	..	..	..	..	..	..	..	..
Other non-life insurance	..	..	9 165	21 483	..	..	..	..
Treaty reinsurance	..	..	13 811	..	..	..	..	..
Total non-life insurance	76 947	84 766	95 287	90 644	83 954	90 800	103 940	112 479
1.2 Gross claims payments								
Life								
Domestic undertakings	58 780	64 657	60 930	64 815	76 869	76 390	77 434	73 104
Foreign controlled undertakings	3 499	6 337	6 055	5 719	5 852	5 784	5 704	5 652
Foreign companies (branches)	..	..	5 999	..	..	..	..	..
All undertakings	58 780	64 657	66 929	64 815	76 869	76 390	77 434	73 104
Non-life								
Domestic undertakings	69 882	69 100	75 805	64 537	65 941	66 635	77 278	82 672
Foreign controlled undertakings	31 639	31 398	31 024	23 701	22 495	25 544	32 791	33 257
Foreign companies (branches)	..	..	5 328	..	..	..	..	..
All undertakings	69 882	69 100	81 133	64 537	65 941	66 635	77 278	82 672
Composite, all undertakings	..	..	..	..	..	..	..	..
Total								
Domestic undertakings	128 662	133 757	136 735	129 352	142 810	143 025	154 712	155 776
Foreign controlled undertakings	35 138	37 735	37 079	29 420	28 347	31 328	38 495	38 909
Foreign companies (branches)	..	..	11 327	..	..	..	..	..
All undertakings	128 662	133 757	148 062	129 352	142 810	143 025	154 712	155 776
1.3 Commissions								
Life								
Domestic undertakings	..	..	4 167	3 782	3 063	3 545	3 494	3 648
Foreign controlled undertakings	..	..	1 302	610	274	589	587	567
Foreign companies (branches)	..	..	121	..	..	..	..	..
All undertakings	..	..	4 288	3 782	3 063	3 545	3 494	3 648
Non-life								
Domestic undertakings	..	..	4 168	4 264	3 848	3 953	3 711	4 280
Foreign controlled undertakings	..	..	2 049	2 589	2 362	2 482	2 634	2 711
Foreign companies (branches)	..	..	786	..	..	..	..	..
All undertakings	..	..	4 954	4 264	3 848	3 953	3 711	4 280
Composite, all undertakings	..	..	..	..	..	..	..	..
Total								
Domestic undertakings	..	..	8 335	8 046	6 911	7 498	7 205	7 928
Foreign controlled undertakings	..	..	3 351	3 199	2 636	3 071	3 221	3 278
Foreign companies (branches)	..	..	907	..	..	..	..	..
All undertakings	..	..	9 242	8 046	6 911	7 498	7 205	7 928

SWEDEN

Table 1. Selected aggregates *(cont.)*

Million SEK

	2012	2013	2014	2015	2016	2017	2018	2019
1.4 Gross operating expenses								
Life								
Domestic undertakings	11 509	12 115	12 738	13 573	12 617	13 248	15 095	13 651
Foreign controlled undertakings	3 557	3 630	3 639	2 122	1 297	1 918	1 901	1 944
Foreign companies (branches)	..	..	..	..	..	..	..	..
All undertakings	11 509	12 115	12 738	13 573	12 617	13 248	15 095	13 651
Non-life								
Domestic undertakings	14 989	15 004	16 878	16 854	15 781	15 863	18 250	19 503
Foreign controlled undertakings	7 138	7 248	8 238	7 704	7 205	7 691	9 496	10 114
Foreign companies (branches)	..	..	..	..	..	..	..	..
All undertakings	14 989	15 004	16 878	16 854	15 781	15 863	18 250	19 503
Composite, all undertakings	..	..	..	..	..	..	..	..
Total								
Domestic undertakings	26 498	27 119	29 616	30 427	28 398	29 111	33 345	33 154
Foreign controlled undertakings	10 695	10 878	11 877	9 826	8 502	9 609	11 397	12 058
Foreign companies (branches)	..	..	..	..	..	..	..	..
All undertakings	26 498	27 119	29 616	30 427	28 398	29 111	33 345	33 154
1.5 Insurance business written abroad by branches, gross premiums								
Life								
Branches and agencies	234	..	243	279	347	347	447	421
Subsidaries	..	..	..	..	..	..	..	..
Total	234	..	243	279	347	347	447	421
Non-life								
Branches and agencies	18 948	..	18 630	18 207	24 226	24 226	34 479	33 631
Subsidaries	..	..	..	..	..	..	..	..
Total	18 948	..	18 630	18 207	24 226	24 226	34 479	33 631
Composite total	..	..	..	..	..	..	..	..
Total								
Branches and agencies	19 182	..	18 873	18 486	24 573	24 573	34 926	34 052
Subsidaries	..	..	..	..	..	..	..	..
Total	19 182	..	18 873	18 486	24 573	24 573	34 926	34 052

.. Not available

Note: Detailed metadata at: *http://metalinks.oecd.org/ins/20210324/060f.*

Source: *OECD Insurance Statistics (database)*

SWEDEN

Table 2. Number of companies and employees

	2012	2013	2014	2015	2016	2017	2018	2019
2.1 Number of companies								
Life								
Domestic undertakings	39	39	39	38	37	36	35	37
Foreign controlled undertakings	9	8	8	8	6	6	4	4
Foreign companies (branches)	5	5	6	8	6	4	4	4
All undertakings	44	44	45	46	43	46	39	41
Non-life								
Domestic undertakings	131	130	130	127	120	117	127	127
Foreign controlled undertakings	46	44	34	24	14	15	8	8
Foreign companies (branches)	32	32	28	33	31	25	9	9
All undertakings	163	162	158	160	151	157	136	136
Composite, all undertakings	**0**	**0**	**0**	**0**	**0**	..	..	..
Reinsurance								
Domestic undertakings	2	1	1	1	0	..	..	..
Foreign controlled undertakings	0	0	0	1	0	..	..	..
Foreign companies (branches)	0	..	0	0	..	..	..	..
All undertakings	2	1	1	1	..	..	..	..
Total								
Domestic undertakings	172	170	170	166	157	153	162	164
Foreign controlled undertakings	55	52	42	33	20	21	12	12
Foreign companies (branches)	37	37	34	41	37	29	13	13
All undertakings	209	207	204	207	194	203	175	176
2.2 Number of employees								
Insurance undertakings	19 158	19 059	19 573	18 792	20 600	21 900	20 865	22 000
Intermediaries	2 000	2 000	3 849	3 235	3 540	3 585	3 789	1 245
Total	21 158	21 059	23 422	22 027	..	25 485	24 654	23 245

.. Not available

Note: Detailed metadata at: *http://metalinks.oecd.org/ins/20210324/060f*.

Source: *OECD Insurance Statistics (database)*

SWITZERLAND

Table 1. Selected aggregates

Million CHF

	2012	2013	2014	2015	2016	2017	2018	2019
1.1 Insurance business written in the reporting country								
1.1.1 Insurance business, by ownership								
Gross premiums								
Domestic undertakings	63 507	66 569	66 312	65 628	63 975	63 967	65 722	67 482
Foreign controlled undertakings	14 322	15 423	14 214	13 846	12 578	11 699	12 241	7 760
Foreign companies (branches)	2 331	2 267	1 923	2 091	2 522	2 768	2 198	2 064
All undertakings	65 838	68 836	68 235	67 720	66 497	66 735	67 920	69 546
Premiums ceded								
Domestic undertakings	4 479	4 536	4 346	4 141	3 363	4 085	4 283	4 600
Foreign controlled undertakings	1 219	963	831	731	506	502	613	548
Foreign companies (branches)	487	532	533	553	813	874	776	772
All undertakings	4 965	5 068	4 879	4 694	4 176	4 959	5 059	5 372
Net written premiums								
Domestic undertakings	59 028	62 033	61 966	61 487	60 612	59 882	61 439	62 882
Foreign controlled undertakings	13 102	14 460	13 383	13 115	12 072	11 197	11 628	7 212
Foreign companies (branches)	1 845	1 735	1 390	1 539	1 709	1 894	1 422	1 292
All undertakings	60 873	63 768	63 356	63 026	62 321	61 776	62 861	64 174
1.1.2 Insurance business on foreign risks, gross premiums								
Life	..	..	..	..	..	..	..	..
Non-life	..	..	..	..	..	..	..	..
Composite total	..	..	..	..	..	..	..	..
Total	..	..	..	..	..	..	..	..
1.1.3 Life insurance payments, by class, gross premiums								
Annuities	677	564	441	495	428	317	246	281
Unit linked	2 637	2 403	1 730	1 755	1 738	1 861	1 947	2 202
Other life insurance	27 841	29 707	30 478	30 359	28 518	27 445	27 607	27 514
Total life insurance	31 155	32 675	32 649	32 609	30 684	29 623	29 800	29 997
***of which:** Pension contracts*	..	..	..	..	..	..	..	..
1.1.4 Non-life insurance payments, by class, gross premiums								
Motor vehicle insurance	6 526	6 556	6 580	6 595	6 598	6 742	6 804	6 909
Marine, aviation and other transport insurance	968	1 060	876	732	657	681	635	724
Freight insurance	..	..	..	..	..	..	..	..
Fire and other property damage insurance	8 150	8 206	8 123	7 909	7 411	7 397	7 804	8 297
Pecuniary loss insurance	932	1 042	1 096	897	1 095	1 108	1 055	1 024
General liability insurance	3 514	3 558	3 658	3 562	3 293	3 447	3 416	3 768
Accident and health	13 093	13 889	13 414	13 387	14 585	15 626	16 692	17 240
***of which:** Health*	9 656	9 911	9 934	10 266	10 606	11 361	11 901	12 099
Other non-life insurance	1 151	1 351	1 378	1 525	1 649	1 715	1 361	1 214
Treaty reinsurance	..	..	..	..	..	..	..	..
Total non-life insurance	34 334	35 661	35 125	34 607	35 288	36 716	37 767	39 176
1.2 Gross claims payments								
Life								
Domestic undertakings	25 817	27 624	27 943	27 794	29 083	29 352	44 908	58 408
Foreign controlled undertakings	7 060	8 854	7 917	8 123	8 578	8 159	11 255	29 424
Foreign companies (branches)	186	306	3	3	3	3	7	4
All undertakings	26 003	27 930	27 946	27 797	29 086	29 355	44 915	58 412
Non-life								
Domestic undertakings	20 279	19 735	20 149	20 621	20 498	20 716	42 021	44 831
Foreign controlled undertakings	2 292	2 171	2 281	2 671	2 471	2 299	4 534	4 308
Foreign companies (branches)	667	798	874	902	1 105	1 164	1 219	1 006
All undertakings	20 946	20 533	21 023	21 523	21 603	21 880	43 240	45 837
Composite, all undertakings	..	..	..	..	..	..	..	..
Total								
Domestic undertakings	46 096	47 359	48 092	48 415	49 581	50 068	86 929	103 239
Foreign controlled undertakings	9 352	11 025	10 198	10 794	11 049	10 458	15 789	33 732
Foreign companies (branches)	853	1 104	877	905	1 108	1 167	1 226	1 010
All undertakings	46 949	48 463	48 969	49 320	50 689	51 235	88 155	104 249
1.3 Commissions								
Life								
Domestic undertakings	875	904	920	856	856	836	829	850
Foreign controlled undertakings	103	148	114	169	169	163	163	139
Foreign companies (branches)	8	11	0	0	1	1	1	1
All undertakings	883	915	920	856	857	837	830	851
Non-life								
Domestic undertakings	1 955	2 067	1 597	2 188	2 289	2 078	1 403	2 410
Foreign controlled undertakings	442	372	381	441	450	453	458	469
Foreign companies (branches)	88	95	91	78	65	24	72	66
All undertakings	2 043	2 162	1 688	2 266	2 354	2 102	1 475	2 476
Composite, all undertakings	..	..	..	..	..	..	..	..
Total								
Domestic undertakings	2 830	2 971	2 517	3 044	3 145	2 914	2 232	3 260
Foreign controlled undertakings	545	520	495	610	619	616	621	608
Foreign companies (branches)	96	106	91	78	66	25	73	67
All undertakings	2 926	3 077	2 608	3 122	3 211	2 939	2 305	3 327

SWITZERLAND

Table 1. Selected aggregates *(cont.)*

Million CHF

	2012	2013	2014	2015	2016	2017	2018	2019
1.4 Gross operating expenses								
Life								
Domestic undertakings	1 390	1 289	1 364	1 078	1 085	1 091	1 117	1 097
Foreign controlled undertakings	239	176	209	156	156	160	186	186
Foreign companies (branches)	4	4	2	1	1	2	3	1
All undertakings	1 394	1 293	1 366	1 079	1 086	1 093	1 120	1 098
Non-life								
Domestic undertakings	3 835	3 745	5 520	2 975	2 981	3 185	3 388	3 590
Foreign controlled undertakings	371	416	420	341	310	316	353	337
Foreign companies (branches)	80	100	108	103	215	195	186	157
All undertakings	3 915	3 845	5 628	3 078	3 196	3 380	3 574	3 747
Composite, all undertakings	..	..	..	..	..	..	..	..
Total								
Domestic undertakings	5 225	5 034	6 884	4 053	4 066	4 276	4 505	4 687
Foreign controlled undertakings	610	592	629	497	466	476	539	523
Foreign companies (branches)	84	104	110	104	216	197	189	158
All undertakings	5 309	5 138	6 994	4 157	4 282	4 473	4 694	4 845
1.5 Insurance business written abroad by branches, gross premiums								
Life								
Branches and agencies	2 006	1 967	1 794	1 604	1 567	1 613	1 653	1 717
Subsidaries	..	..	..	..	..	..	..	..
Total	2 006	1 967	1 794	1 604	1 567	1 613	1 653	1 717
Non-life								
Branches and agencies	15 417	15 563	15 331	14 100	12 578	12 689	6 664	6 089
Subsidaries	..	..	..	..	..	..	..	..
Total	15 417	15 563	15 331	14 100	12 578	12 689	6 664	6 089
Composite total	..	..	..	..	..	..	..	..
Total								
Branches and agencies	17 423	17 531	17 125	15 704	14 145	14 302	8 317	7 806
Subsidaries	..	..	..	..	..	..	..	..
Total	17 423	17 531	17 125	15 704	14 145	14 302	8 317	7 806

.. Not available

Note: Detailed metadata at: *http://metalinks.oecd.org/ins/20210324/b975.*

Source: *OECD Insurance Statistics (database)*

SWITZERLAND

Table 2. Number of companies and employees

	2012	2013	2014	2015	2016	2017	2018	2019
2.1 Number of companies								
Life								
Domestic undertakings	19	19	18	17	16	16	16	16
Foreign controlled undertakings	1	1	1	1	1	1	1	1
Foreign companies (branches)	4	4	3	3	3	3	3	3
All undertakings	23	23	21	20	19	19	19	19
Non-life								
Domestic undertakings	81	80	79	76	74	73	70	72
Foreign controlled undertakings	6	6	6	6	5	5	5	5
Foreign companies (branches)	42	44	48	46	46	45	44	46
All undertakings	123	124	127	122	120	118	114	118
Composite, all undertakings	**0**	**0**	**0**	**0**	**0**	..	..	..
Reinsurance								
Domestic undertakings	61	62	62	59	55	55	54	50
Foreign controlled undertakings	7	7	7	7	7	6	6	6
Foreign companies (branches)	..	..	..	..	..	..	..	..
All undertakings	61	62	62	59	55	55	54	50
Total								
Domestic undertakings	161	161	159	152	145	144	140	138
Foreign controlled undertakings	14	14	14	14	13	12	12	12
Foreign companies (branches)	46	48	51	49	49	48	47	49
All undertakings	207	209	210	201	194	192	187	187
2.2 Number of employees								
Insurance undertakings	..	..	..	..	..	..	..	..
Intermediaries	..	..	..	..	..	..	..	..
Total	..	..	..	..	..	..	..	..

.. Not available

Note: Detailed metadata at: *http://metalinks.oecd.org/ins/20210324/b975*.

Source: *OECD Insurance Statistics (database)*

TURKEY

Table 1. Selected aggregates

Million TRY

	2012	2013	2014	2015	2016	2017	2018	2019
1.1 Insurance business written in the reporting country								
1.1.1 Insurance business, by ownership								
Gross premiums								
Domestic undertakings	20 427	25 084	26 872	31 903	41 280	47 495	54 416	68 247
Foreign controlled undertakings	10 122	14 981	15 528	20 981	25 640	26 984	29 792	35 819
Foreign companies (branches)	46	68	77	126	152	201	304	553
All undertakings	20 473	25 152	26 949	32 029	41 431	47 696	54 720	68 800
Premiums ceded								
Domestic undertakings	4 483	6 077	6 686	7 984	9 816	13 268	15 814	19 346
Foreign controlled undertakings	2 192	3 458	3 510	4 773	5 482	6 672	7 850	8 518
Foreign companies (branches)	33	49	57	74	76	96	131	288
All undertakings	4 516	6 126	6 743	8 059	9 892	13 364	15 945	19 634
Net written premiums								
Domestic undertakings	15 944	19 006	20 186	23 919	31 464	34 227	38 601	48 901
Foreign controlled undertakings	7 931	11 522	12 018	16 208	20 158	20 312	21 942	27 300
Foreign companies (branches)	13	20	20	52	76	105	173	265
All undertakings	15 957	19 026	20 206	23 971	31 540	34 332	38 774	49 166
1.1.2 Insurance business on foreign risks, gross premiums								
Life	..	..	3 280	..	6 166	..	..	..
Non-life	..	..	22 711	..	34 322	..	..	..
Composite	..	..	958	..	943	..	..	..
of which:								
Life	..	..	24	..	19	..	..	..
Non-life	..	..	934	..	924	..	..	..
Total	..	..	26 948	..	41 431	..	..	..
1.1.3 Life insurance payments, by class, gross premiums								
Annuities	..	..	..	..	..	..	..	..
Unit linked	..	..	..	..	..	..	..	..
Other life insurance	..	..	..	..	..	..	..	..
Total life insurance	3 107	3 354	3 895	3 720	5 916	6 766	6 835	13 340
***of which:** Pension contracts*	..	..	..	..	..	..	..	..
1.1.4 Non-life insurance payments, by class, gross premiums								
Motor vehicle insurance	8 091	10 411	10 648	13 102	19 156	19 981	23 614	26 466
Marine, aviation and other transport insurance	263	253	321	423	455	490	706	929
Freight insurance	378	416	530	580	585	652	828	922
Fire and other property damage insurance	4 390	5 512	6 992	8 105	9 032	10 101	12 208	14 193
Pecuniary loss insurance	228	302	318	443	439	549	666	901
General liability insurance	420	508	679	811	863	1 028	1 389	1 698
Accident and health	2 897	3 352	4 010	4 685	4 582	6 708	8 051	9 798
***of which:** Health*	2 227	2 472	0	0	..	5 025	6 245	8 190
Other non-life insurance	61	74	147	99	134	226	167	197
Treaty reinsurance	..	..	..	0	..	..	..	..
Total non-life insurance	16 727	20 828	23 645	28 249	35 246	39 735	47 628	55 104
1.2 Gross claims payments								
Life								
Domestic undertakings	2 037	2 355	2 085	2 557	2 957	3 293	3 609	4 776
Foreign controlled undertakings	483	1 128	760	1 194	1 485	1 757	2 061	2 685
Foreign companies (branches)	..	..	..	..	0	..	0	..
All undertakings	2 037	2 355	2 085	2 557	2 957	3 293	3 609	4 776
Non-life								
Domestic undertakings	9 163	9 440	11 314	13 322	15 041	18 341	23 049	27 354
Foreign controlled undertakings	5 327	6 301	7 496	8 700	-9 940	11 648	13 543	15 282
Foreign companies (branches)	3	11	10	34	128	77	121	86
All undertakings	9 166	9 451	11 325	13 356	15 168	18 417	23 170	27 440
Composite								
Domestic undertakings	..	619	592	664	572	617	771	..
Foreign controlled undertakings	..	..	..	..	..	1	5	..
Foreign companies (branches)	..	..	..	..	..	..	..	..
All undertakings	721	619	592	664	572	617	771	..
of which:								
Life	6	7	11	6	9	15	7	..
Domestic undertakings	..	7	11	6	9	15	7	..
Foreign controlled undertakings	..	..	..	..	..	0	0	..
Foreign companies (branches)	..	..	..	..	..	..	..	..
All undertakings	6	7	11	6	9	15	7	..
Non-life	715	612	581	657	564	602	764	..
Domestic undertakings	..	612	581	657	564	602	764	..
Foreign controlled undertakings	..	..	..	..	..	1	5	..
Foreign companies (branches)	..	..	..	..	..	..	..	..
All undertakings	715	612	581	657	564	602	764	..
Total								
Domestic undertakings	11 200	12 413	13 991	16 543	18 570	22 251	27 430	32 130
Foreign controlled undertakings	5 810	7 429	8 256	9 894	-8 455	13 406	15 609	17 967
Foreign companies (branches)	3	11	10	34	128	77	121	86
All undertakings	11 924	12 425	14 001	16 578	18 698	22 328	27 551	32 216

TURKEY

Table 1. Selected aggregates *(cont.)*

Million TRY

	2012	2013	2014	2015	2016	2017	2018	2019
1.3 Commissions								
Life								
Domestic undertakings	..	..	..	..	..	..	..	..
Foreign controlled undertakings	..	..	..	..	..	..	..	..
Foreign companies (branches)	..	..	..	..	..	..	..	..
All undertakings	..	..	..	..	..	..	..	..
Non-life								
Domestic undertakings	..	..	..	..	..	..	..	..
Foreign controlled undertakings	..	..	..	..	..	..	..	..
Foreign companies (branches)	..	..	..	..	..	..	..	..
All undertakings	..	..	..	..	..	..	..	..
Composite								
Domestic undertakings	..	..	..	..	..	..	..	..
Foreign controlled undertakings	..	..	..	..	..	..	..	..
Foreign companies (branches)	..	..	..	..	..	..	..	..
All undertakings	..	..	..	..	..	..	..	..
of which:								
Life	..	..	..	..	..	..	..	..
Domestic undertakings	..	..	..	..	..	..	..	..
Foreign controlled undertakings	..	..	..	..	..	..	..	..
Foreign companies (branches)	..	..	..	..	..	..	..	..
All undertakings	..	..	..	..	..	..	..	..
Non-life	..	..	..	..	..	..	..	..
Domestic undertakings	..	..	..	..	..	..	..	..
Foreign controlled undertakings	..	..	..	..	..	..	..	..
Foreign companies (branches)	..	..	..	..	..	..	..	..
All undertakings	..	..	..	..	..	..	..	..
Total								
Domestic undertakings	..	..	..	..	..	..	..	..
Foreign controlled undertakings	..	..	..	..	..	..	..	..
Foreign companies (branches)	..	..	..	..	..	..	..	..
All undertakings	..	..	..	..	..	..	..	..
1.4 Gross operating expenses								
Life								
Domestic undertakings	978	2 009	1 198	1 595	1 970	2 644	2 961	4 103
Foreign controlled undertakings	422	1 242	765	1 033	1 241	1 724	1 926	2 376
Foreign companies (branches)	..	..	..	..	..	..	..	..
All undertakings	978	2 009	1 198	1 595	1 970	2 644	2 961	4 103
Non-life								
Domestic undertakings	3 230	3 726	4 309	4 648	5 579	6 263	6 689	8 211
Foreign controlled undertakings	1 976	2 564	2 944	3 110	3 847	4 170	4 183	4 821
Foreign companies (branches)	12	19	20	24	26	30	44	122
All undertakings	3 242	3 745	4 329	4 672	5 604	6 293	6 733	8 333
Composite								
Domestic undertakings	..	..	..	309	316	333	436	..
Foreign controlled undertakings	..	..	..	..	5	2	3	..
Foreign companies (branches)	..	..	..	..	..	..	..	..
All undertakings	285	294	289	309	316	333	436	..
of which:								
Life	8	10	8	10	10	5	8	..
Domestic undertakings	..	..	..	10	10	5	8	..
Foreign controlled undertakings	..	..	..	..	..	0	0	..
Foreign companies (branches)	..	..	..	..	..	..	..	..
All undertakings	8	10	8	10	10	5	8	..
Non-life	277	284	281	299	306	328	429	..
Domestic undertakings	..	..	..	299	306	328	429	..
Foreign controlled undertakings	..	..	..	..	5	2	3	..
Foreign companies (branches)	..	..	..	..	..	..	..	..
All undertakings	277	284	281	299	306	328	429	..
Total								
Domestic undertakings	4 209	5 735	5 507	6 552	7 865	9 240	10 087	12 314
Foreign controlled undertakings	2 399	3 806	3 708	4 143	5 092	5 895	6 112	7 197
Foreign companies (branches)	12	19	20	24	26	30	44	122
All undertakings	4 506	6 048	5 816	6 576	7 890	9 270	10 130	12 436

TURKEY

Table 1. Selected aggregates (cont.)

Million TRY

	2012	2013	2014	2015	2016	2017	2018	2019
1.5 Insurance business written abroad by branches, gross premiums								
Life								
Branches and agencies	..	..	..	..	..	..	..	..
Subsidaries	..	..	..	..	..	..	..	..
Total	..	..	..	..	..	..	..	..
Non-life								
Branches and agencies	..	..	..	..	..	..	..	..
Subsidaries	..	..	..	..	..	..	..	..
Total	..	..	..	..	..	..	..	..
Composite								
Branches and agencies	..	..	..	..	..	..	..	..
Subsidaries	..	..	..	..	..	..	..	..
Total	..	..	..	..	..	..	..	..
of which:								
Life	..	..	..	..	..	..	..	..
Branches and agencies	..	..	..	..	..	..	..	..
Subsidaries	..	..	..	..	..	..	..	..
Total	..	..	..	..	..	..	..	..
Non-life	..	..	..	..	..	..	..	..
Branches and agencies	..	..	..	..	..	..	..	..
Subsidaries	..	..	..	..	..	..	..	..
Total	..	..	..	..	..	..	..	..
Total								
Branches and agencies	..	..	..	..	..	..	..	..
Subsidaries	..	..	..	..	..	..	..	..
Total	..	..	..	..	..	..	..	..

.. Not available

Note: Detailed metadata at: *http://metalinks.oecd.org/ins/20210324/4ca0*.

Source: *OECD Insurance Statistics (database)*

TURKEY

Table 2. Number of companies and employees

	2012	2013	2014	2015	2016	2017	2018	2019
2.1 Number of companies								
Life								
Domestic undertakings	23	24	25	23	22	22	22	22
Foreign controlled undertakings	13	16	16	15	15	15	15	15
Foreign companies (branches)	0	..	0	..	0	0	..	..
All undertakings	23	24	25	23	22	22	22	22
Non-life								
Domestic undertakings	33	34	36	36	35	37	36	37
Foreign controlled undertakings	22	22	24	22	23	23	20	19
Foreign companies (branches)	2	2	2	2	2	2	2	2
All undertakings	35	36	38	38	37	39	38	39
Composite								
Domestic undertakings	0	..	0	..	0	0	0	..
Foreign controlled undertakings	0	..	0	..	0	0	0	..
Foreign companies (branches)	0	..	0	..	0	0	0	..
All undertakings	0	..	0	..	0	0	0	..
Reinsurance								
Domestic undertakings	1	1	1	1	2	2	2	3
Foreign controlled undertakings	0	..	0	..	1	1	1	1
Foreign companies (branches)	0	..	0	..	0	0	0	..
All undertakings	1	1	1	1	2	2	2	3
Total								
Domestic undertakings	57	59	62	60	59	61	62	62
Foreign controlled undertakings	35	38	40	37	39	39	38	35
Foreign companies (branches)	2	2	2	2	2	2	2	2
All undertakings	59	61	64	62	61	63	62	64
2.2 Number of employees								
Insurance undertakings	17 304	18 297	19 305	19 274	19 240	19 883	19 117	14 228
Intermediaries	16 994	15 603	15 587	18 931	35 992	40 231	20 605	40 000
Total	34 298	33 900	34 892	38 205	55 232	60 114	39 722	54 228

.. Not available

Note: Detailed metadata at: *http://metalinks.oecd.org/ins/20210324/4ca0.*

Source: *OECD Insurance Statistics (database)*

UNITED KINGDOM

Table 1. Selected aggregates

Million GBP

	2012	2013	2014	2015	2016	2017	2018	2019
1.1 Insurance business written in the reporting country								
1.1.1 Insurance business, by ownership								
Gross premiums								
Domestic undertakings	230 559	215 494	219 832	217 673	298 817	305 746	352 480	326 970
Foreign controlled undertakings	75 289	69 361	57 959	58 471	..	..	..	..
Foreign companies (branches)	2 735	2 237	2 407	2 741	247	471	400	1 032
All undertakings	233 294	217 731	222 239	220 414	299 064	306 217	351 620	328 002
Premiums ceded								
Domestic undertakings	28 545	27 456	33 780	24 299	68 763	36 758	68 170	63 557
Foreign controlled undertakings	8 285	9 270	11 048	10 801	0	..	..	..
Foreign companies (branches)	179	53	47	52	115	199	113	565
All undertakings	28 724	27 509	33 827	24 351	68 878	36 957	68 283	64 122
Net written premiums								
Domestic undertakings	202 014	188 038	186 052	193 374	230 054	268 988	284 310	263 413
Foreign controlled undertakings	67 004	60 091	46 911	47 670	..	..	..	..
Foreign companies (branches)	2 555	2 184	2 361	2 689	132	272	287	468
All undertakings	204 570	190 222	188 412	196 062	230 186	269 260	283 337	263 881
1.1.2 Insurance business on foreign risks, gross premiums								
Life	..	..	..	..	..	..	..	..
Non-life	..	..	..	..	..	..	..	..
Composite	..	..	..	..	..	..	..	..
of which:								
Life	..	..	..	..	..	..	..	..
Non-life	..	..	..	..	..	..	..	..
Total	..	..	..	..	..	..	..	..
1.1.3 Life insurance payments, by class, gross premiums								
Annuities	..	20 899	22 295	17 278	..	..	..	..
Unit linked	..	112 727	114 296	117 452	..	..	..	..
Other life insurance	..	9 393	11 834	10 622	..	..	..	..
Total life insurance	163 481	143 018	148 425	145 353	121 964	187 390	204 870	198 322
***of which:** Pension contracts*	143 813	104 333	132 542	128 601	..	..	..	..
1.1.4 Non-life insurance payments, by class, gross premiums								
Motor vehicle insurance	12 643	12 133	12 069	12 883	18 956	16 564	15 520	19 010
Marine, aviation and other transport insurance	3 634	3 805	3 098	2 604	9 395	9 610	10 636	9 554
Freight insurance	778	942	885	808	..	..	..	..
Fire and other property damage insurance	16 087	16 500	15 969	15 544	30 491	32 392	33 815	28 933
Pecuniary loss insurance	5 707	5 717	5 966	5 791	5 064	5 921	6 018	2 269
General liability insurance	8 750	10 218	10 593	10 308	16 201	16 585	18 635	17 451
Accident and health	7 287	7 895	7 662	7 821	10 872	13 590	15 548	12 281
***of which:** Health*	..	..	..	..	8 287	7 817	11 055	10 454
Other non-life insurance	2 442	2 859	2 962	3 177	2 407	2 341	2 497	2 596
Treaty reinsurance	..	..	..	..	..	..	..	..
Total non-life insurance	57 328	60 070	59 206	58 936	93 387	97 003	102 669	92 094
1.2 Gross claims payments								
Life								
Domestic undertakings	166 655	166 084	161 503	172 514	131 443	227 698	263 732	224 133
Foreign controlled undertakings	51 269	42 535	26 653	29 078	..	..	..	..
Foreign companies (branches)	4	-1	4	5	..	..	..	5
All undertakings	166 658	166 083	161 507	172 518	131 443	227 698	263 732	224 138
Non-life								
Domestic undertakings	30 566	33 152	32 079	30 897	30 260	32 185	30 902	24 435
Foreign controlled undertakings	16 160	17 593	17 062	16 387	..	..	..	..
Foreign companies (branches)	1 785	1 405	1 469	1 871	43	..	280	293
All undertakings	32 351	34 557	33 548	32 768	30 303	32 185	31 182	24 728
Composite								
Domestic undertakings	20 735	21 625	22 527	23 077	50 234	64 884	65 265	63 458
Foreign controlled undertakings	615	754	2 170	2 734	..	..	..	..
Foreign companies (branches)	1 729	0	0	0	..	..	..	200
All undertakings	22 464	21 625	22 527	23 077	50 234	64 884	65 265	63 658
of which:								
Life	21 386	20 366	21 254	21 794	23 337	30 083	31 495	29 662
Domestic undertakings	19 657	20 366	21 254	21 794	23 337	30 083	31 495	29 462
Foreign controlled undertakings	342	326	1 876	2 413	..	..	..	..
Foreign companies (branches)	1 729	0	0	0	..	..	..	200
All undertakings	21 386	20 366	21 254	21 794	23 337	30 083	31 495	29 662
Non-life	1 077	1 259	1 273	1 283	26 897	34 801	33 770	33 996
Domestic undertakings	1 077	1 259	1 273	1 283	26 897	34 801	33 770	33 996
Foreign controlled undertakings	273	428	294	321	..	..	..	..
Foreign companies (branches)	0	0	0	0	..	..	..	..
All undertakings	1 077	1 259	1 273	1 283	26 897	34 801	33 770	33 996
Total								
Domestic undertakings	217 956	220 861	216 108	226 488	211 938	324 767	359 899	312 026
Foreign controlled undertakings	68 043	60 882	45 885	48 198	..	..	..	..
Foreign companies (branches)	3 517	1 404	1 474	1 875	43	..	280	498
All undertakings	221 473	222 265	217 582	228 363	211 981	324 767	360 179	312 525

Table 1. Selected aggregates *(cont.)*

Million GBP

	2012	2013	2014	2015	2016	2017	2018	2019
1.3 Commissions								
Life								
Domestic undertakings	..	..	..	..	..	..	..	..
Foreign controlled undertakings	..	..	..	..	..	..	..	..
Foreign companies (branches)	..	..	..	..	..	..	..	..
All undertakings	..	..	..	..	..	..	..	..
Non-life								
Domestic undertakings	..	..	..	..	..	..	..	..
Foreign controlled undertakings	..	..	..	..	..	..	..	..
Foreign companies (branches)	..	..	..	..	..	..	..	..
All undertakings	..	..	..	..	..	..	..	..
Composite								
Domestic undertakings	..	..	..	..	..	..	..	..
Foreign controlled undertakings	..	..	..	..	..	..	..	..
Foreign companies (branches)	..	..	..	..	..	..	..	..
All undertakings	..	..	..	..	..	..	..	..
of which:								
Life	..	..	..	..	..	..	..	..
Domestic undertakings	..	..	..	..	..	..	..	..
Foreign controlled undertakings	..	..	..	..	..	..	..	..
Foreign companies (branches)	..	..	..	..	..	..	..	..
All undertakings	..	..	..	..	..	..	..	..
Non-life	..	..	..	..	..	..	..	..
Domestic undertakings	..	..	..	..	..	..	..	..
Foreign controlled undertakings	..	..	..	..	..	..	..	..
Foreign companies (branches)	..	..	..	..	..	..	..	..
All undertakings	..	..	..	..	..	..	..	..
Total								
Domestic undertakings	..	..	..	..	..	..	..	..
Foreign controlled undertakings	..	..	..	..	..	..	..	..
Foreign companies (branches)	..	..	..	..	..	..	..	..
All undertakings	..	..	..	..	..	..	..	..
1.4 Gross operating expenses								
Life								
Domestic undertakings	6 511	6 453	6 694	6 794	8 085	3 332	8 978	8 251
Foreign controlled undertakings	961	976	929	850	..	..	..	..
Foreign companies (branches)	1	0	1	1	..	..	..	3
All undertakings	6 512	6 453	6 695	6 795	8 085	3 332	8 978	8 254
Non-life								
Domestic undertakings	6 843	7 125	6 782	6 639	15 414	15 040	16 657	12 334
Foreign controlled undertakings	3 168	3 589	3 549	3 562	..	..	..	..
Foreign companies (branches)	200	167	174	186	59	117	119	135
All undertakings	7 044	7 292	6 956	6 825	15 474	15 103	16 776	12 469
Composite								
Domestic undertakings	1 856	1 978	2 127	2 325	16 675	18 958	18 816	19 093
Foreign controlled undertakings	195	172	277	328	..	..	..	..
Foreign companies (branches)	22	0	0	0	..	..	..	..
All undertakings	1 877	1 978	2 127	2 325	16 675	18 958	18 816	19 093
of which:								
Life	1 637	1 736	1 874	2 038	3 140	2 574	2 916	3 512
Domestic undertakings	1 616	1 736	1 874	2 038	3 140	2 574	2 917	3 512
Foreign controlled undertakings	102	91	185	211	..	..	..	..
Foreign companies (branches)	22	0	0	0	..	..	..	..
All undertakings	1 637	1 736	1 874	2 038	3 140	2 574	2 916	3 512
Non-life	240	242	252	287	13 535	15 088	15 899	15 581
Domestic undertakings	240	242	252	287	13 535	15 088	15 899	15 581
Foreign controlled undertakings	94	82	92	117	..	..	..	..
Foreign companies (branches)	0	0	0	0	..	..	..	..
All undertakings	240	242	252	287	13 535	15 088	15 899	15 581
Total								
Domestic undertakings	15 209	15 556	15 602	15 759	40 174	37 330	44 451	39 678
Foreign controlled undertakings	4 324	4 737	4 754	4 740	..	..	..	..
Foreign companies (branches)	224	167	175	187	59	117	119	138
All undertakings	15 433	15 723	15 777	15 946	40 234	37 393	44 570	39 816

UNITED KINGDOM

Table 1. Selected aggregates *(cont.)*

Million GBP

	2012	2013	2014	2015	2016	2017	2018	2019
1.5 Insurance business written abroad by branches, gross premiums								
Life								
Branches and agencies	..	..	..	..	..	..	..	..
Subsidaries	..	..	..	..	..	..	..	..
Total	..	..	..	..	..	..	..	..
Non-life								
Branches and agencies	..	..	..	..	..	..	..	..
Subsidaries	..	..	..	..	..	..	..	..
Total	..	..	..	..	..	..	..	..
Composite								
Branches and agencies	..	..	..	..	..	..	..	..
Subsidaries	..	..	..	..	..	..	..	..
Total	..	..	..	..	..	..	..	..
of which:								
Life	..	..	..	..	..	..	..	..
Branches and agencies	..	..	..	..	..	..	..	..
Subsidaries	..	..	..	..	..	..	..	..
Total	..	..	..	..	..	..	..	..
Non-life	..	..	..	..	..	..	..	..
Branches and agencies	..	..	..	..	..	..	..	..
Subsidaries	..	..	..	..	..	..	..	..
Total	..	..	..	..	..	..	..	..
Total								
Branches and agencies	..	..	..	..	..	..	..	..
Subsidaries	..	..	..	..	..	..	..	..
Total	..	..	..	..	..	..	..	..

.. Not available

Note: Detailed metadata at: *http://metalinks.oecd.org/ins/20210324/8843*.

Source: *OECD Insurance Statistics (database)*

UNITED KINGDOM

Table 2. Number of companies and employees

	2012	2013	2014	2015	2016	2017	2018	2019
2.1 Number of companies								
Life								
Domestic undertakings	184	183	181	181	74	75	69	70
Foreign controlled undertakings	15	15	14	14	..	..	..	..
Foreign companies (branches)	1	1	1	1	1	1	0	1
All undertakings	185	184	182	182	75	76	69	71
Non-life								
Domestic undertakings	234	227	214	209	168	165	153	179
Foreign controlled undertakings	104	99	92	89	..	..	..	..
Foreign companies (branches)	15	10	12	7	13	11	12	14
All undertakings	249	237	226	216	181	176	165	193
Composite								
Domestic undertakings	21	21	25	25	21	22	19	15
Foreign controlled undertakings	7	7	8	8	..	..	..	..
Foreign companies (branches)	2	2	2	2	1	1	1	1
All undertakings	23	23	27	27	22	23	20	16
Reinsurance								
Domestic undertakings	31	30	29	26	16	19	17	14
Foreign controlled undertakings	19	18	16	13	..	..	..	..
Foreign companies (branches)	2	2	2	3	0	0	1	0
All undertakings	33	32	31	29	16	19	18	14
Total								
Domestic undertakings	470	461	449	441	279	281	258	278
Foreign controlled undertakings	145	139	130	124	..	..	..	..
Foreign companies (branches)	20	15	17	13	15	13	14	16
All undertakings	490	476	466	454	294	294	272	294
2.2 Number of employees								
Insurance undertakings	..	..	..	..	..	..	..	..
Intermediaries	..	..	..	..	..	..	..	..
Total	..	..	..	..	..	..	..	..

.. Not available

Note: Detailed metadata at: *http://metalinks.oecd.org/ins/20210324/8843.*

Source: *OECD Insurance Statistics (database)*

UNITED STATES

Table 1. Selected aggregates

Million USD

	2012	2013	2014	2015	2016	2017	2018	2019
1.1 Insurance business written in the reporting country								
1.1.1 Insurance business, by ownership								
Gross premiums								
Domestic undertakings	2 278 908	2 289 259	2 430 627	2 619 954	2 702 786	2 835 259	2 631 364	2 773 179
Foreign controlled undertakings	317 074	321 246	330 660	324 083	393 449	401 025	273 750	320 958
Foreign companies (branches)	909	662	696	1 129	1 007	1 034	920	737
All undertakings	2 279 817	2 289 921	2 431 323	2 621 083	2 703 793	2 836 293	2 632 284	2 773 916
Premiums ceded								
Domestic undertakings	601 133	657 662	609 531	713 961	743 307	810 265	429 234	430 891
Foreign controlled undertakings	140 316	175 424	134 223	139 675	195 708	226 256	108 845	175 820
Foreign companies (branches)	298	275	287	252	260	274	307	502
All undertakings	601 431	657 937	609 818	714 213	743 567	810 539	429 541	431 393
Net written premiums								
Domestic undertakings	1 677 776	1 631 597	1 821 096	1 905 993	1 959 479	2 024 995	2 202 129	2 342 288
Foreign controlled undertakings	176 758	145 822	196 437	184 408	197 742	174 769	164 906	145 138
Foreign companies (branches)	611	387	409	877	747	760	613	236
All undertakings	1 678 387	1 631 984	1 821 505	1 906 870	1 960 226	2 025 755	2 202 742	2 342 524
1.1.2 Insurance business on foreign risks, gross premiums								
Life	38 347	22 113	..	..	..	..	..	..
Non-life	..	..	..	..	..	..	..	..
Composite total	..	..	..	..	..	..	..	..
Total	38 347	22 113	..	..	..	..	..	..
1.1.3 Life insurance payments, by class, gross premiums								
Annuities	272 564	248 568	261 327	264 944	254 313	247 002	277 044	302 021
Unit linked	..	..	..	..	..	..	..	..
Other life insurance	557 259	533 515	527 280	561 674	581 948	612 083	632 578	666 265
Total life insurance	829 823	782 083	788 607	826 618	836 261	859 085	909 623	968 286
***of which:** Pension contracts*	..	..	..	..	..	..	..	..
1.1.4 Non-life insurance payments, by class, gross premiums								
Motor vehicle insurance	329 520	342 548	379 889	393 897	422 808	459 200	297 284	309 499
Marine, aviation and other transport insurance	3 545	3 245	3 070	2 911	4 815	2 732	2 187	2 340
Freight insurance	31 107	33 819	36 319	39 175	41 305	43 059	30 091	34 733
Fire and other property damage insurance	224 336	232 328	243 389	248 174	250 765	258 294	174 853	191 502
Pecuniary loss insurance	34 967	35 133	33 690	36 271	38 699	41 003	36 874	38 337
General liability insurance	183 263	191 562	204 069	208 722	211 362	218 298	144 286	160 208
Accident and health	550 291	566 173	646 938	714 394	761 509	799 804	803 339	852 838
***of which:** Health*	..	..	..	..	..	..	..	..
Other non-life insurance	3 179	3 505	3 780	3 728	3 921	4 493	3 716	3 720
Treaty reinsurance	..	..	0	0	0	..	..	..
Total non-life insurance	1 360 207	1 408 312	1 551 144	1 647 272	1 735 184	1 826 883	1 492 630	1 593 177
1.2 Gross claims payments								
Life								
Domestic undertakings	356 040	369 618	357 201	376 240	396 611	416 664	436 219	461 577
Foreign controlled undertakings	66 275	66 267	69 748	68 967	79 082	86 000	92 293	89 797
Foreign companies (branches)	0	0	0	0	0	0	0	0
All undertakings	356 040	369 618	357 201	376 240	396 611	416 664	436 219	461 577
Non-life								
Domestic undertakings	920 214	917 856	980 750	1 077 317	1 145 423	1 228 757	1 055 839	1 112 688
Foreign controlled undertakings	80 801	84 201	76 540	79 309	84 878	95 499	71 727	70 810
Foreign companies (branches)	723	234	240	359	504	609	649	661
All undertakings	920 937	918 090	980 990	1 077 676	1 145 927	1 229 366	1 056 488	1 113 349
Composite, all undertakings	..	..	..	..	..	..	..	..
Total								
Domestic undertakings	1 276 254	1 287 474	1 337 951	1 453 557	1 542 034	1 645 421	1 492 058	1 574 265
Foreign controlled undertakings	147 076	150 468	146 288	148 276	163 960	181 499	164 020	160 607
Foreign companies (branches)	723	234	240	359	504	609	649	661
All undertakings	1 276 977	1 287 708	1 338 191	1 453 916	1 542 538	1 646 030	1 492 707	1 574 926
1.3 Commissions								
Life								
Domestic undertakings	..	..	53 082	56 784	67 963	59 387	..	71 982
Foreign controlled undertakings	..	..	11 165	10 339	10 639	10 700	..	9 946
Foreign companies (branches)	..	..	0	0	0	0	..	0
All undertakings	..	..	53 082	56 784	67 963	59 387	..	71 982
Non-life								
Domestic undertakings	..	..	..	..	..	..	..	..
Foreign controlled undertakings	..	..	..	..	..	..	..	..
Foreign companies (branches)	..	..	..	..	..	..	..	..
All undertakings	..	..	..	..	..	..	..	..
Composite, all undertakings	..	..	..	..	..	..	..	..
Total								
Domestic undertakings	..	..	53 082	56 784	67 963	59 387	..	71 982
Foreign controlled undertakings	..	..	11 165	10 339	10 639	10 700	..	9 946
Foreign companies (branches)	..	..	0	0	0	0	..	0
All undertakings	..	..	53 082	56 784	67 963	59 387	..	71 982

UNITED STATES

Table 1. Selected aggregates *(cont.)*

Million USD

	2012	2013	2014	2015	2016	2017	2018	2019
1.4 Gross operating expenses								
Life								
Domestic undertakings	67 534	65 424	67 225	68 488	69 722	75 161	75 904	78 079
Foreign controlled undertakings	9 962	9 814	10 285	9 952	11 175	11 838	12 374	10 951
Foreign companies (branches)	0	0	0	0	..	..	0	0
All undertakings	67 534	65 424	67 225	68 488	69 722	75 161	75 904	78 079
Non-life								
Domestic undertakings	250 270	261 844	281 766	298 911	308 839	310 003	343 131	339 686
Foreign controlled undertakings	22 153	23 185	23 274	23 035	26 711	26 891	31 608	30 224
Foreign companies (branches)	312	165	194	410	354	360	300	146
All undertakings	250 582	262 009	281 960	299 321	309 193	310 363	343 431	339 832
Composite, all undertakings	..	..	..	..	..	..	..	..
Total								
Domestic undertakings	317 804	327 268	348 991	367 399	378 561	385 164	419 035	417 765
Foreign controlled undertakings	32 115	32 999	33 559	32 987	37 886	38 729	43 982	41 175
Foreign companies (branches)	312	165	194	410	354	360	300	146
All undertakings	318 116	327 433	349 185	367 809	378 915	385 524	419 335	417 911
1.5 Insurance business written abroad by branches, gross premiums								
Life								
Branches and agencies	..	..	..	..	..	..	..	..
Subsidaries	..	..	..	..	..	..	..	..
Total	..	..	..	..	..	..	..	..
Non-life								
Branches and agencies	..	..	..	..	..	..	..	..
Subsidaries	..	..	..	..	..	..	..	..
Total	..	..	..	..	..	..	..	..
Composite total	..	..	..	..	..	..	..	..
Total								
Branches and agencies	..	..	..	..	..	..	..	..
Subsidaries	..	..	..	..	..	..	..	..
Total	..	..	..	..	..	..	..	..

.. Not available

Note: Detailed metadata at: *http://metalinks.oecd.org/ins/20210324/4e49.*

Source: *OECD Insurance Statistics (database)*

UNITED STATES

Table 2. Number of companies and employees

	2012	2013	2014	2015	2016	2017	2018	2019
2.1 Number of companies								
Life								
Domestic undertakings	904	995	1 031	1 030	738	735	715	728
Foreign controlled undertakings	162	156	158	158	168	157	157	149
Foreign companies (branches)	..	..	..	..	..	..	0	0
All undertakings	904	995	1 031	1 030	738	735	715	728
Non-life								
Domestic undertakings	3 428	3 425	3 404	3 185	3 205	3 419	3 430	3 471
Foreign controlled undertakings	407	403	404	390	418	405	399	388
Foreign companies (branches)	9	11	9	13	19	13	14	15
All undertakings	3 437	3 436	3 413	3 198	3 224	3 432	3 444	3 486
Composite, all undertakings	**0**	**0**	**0**	**0**	**0**	..	..	..
Reinsurance								
Domestic undertakings	250	247	234	354	221	228	235	228
Foreign controlled undertakings	62	65	64	76	52	44	48	48
Foreign companies (branches)	1	1	1	4	2	1	1	2
All undertakings	251	248	235	358	223	229	283	230
Total								
Domestic undertakings	4 582	4 667	4 669	4 569	4 164	4 382	4 380	4 427
Foreign controlled undertakings	631	624	626	624	638	606	604	585
Foreign companies (branches)	10	12	10	17	21	14	15	17
All undertakings	4 592	4 679	4 679	4 586	4 185	4 396	4 442	4 444
2.2 Number of employees								
Insurance undertakings	..	..	..	..	..	..	..	..
Intermediaries	..	..	..	..	..	..	..	..
Total	..	..	..	..	..	..	..	..

.. Not available

Note: Detailed metadata at: *http://metalinks.oecd.org/ins/20210324/4e49*.

Source: *OECD Insurance Statistics (database)*

www.ingramcontent.com/pod-product-compliance
Lightning Source LLC
Chambersburg PA
CBHW061214240926
51846CB00006B/1225
9789264763395